权威·前沿·原创

皮书系列为
"十二五"国家重点图书出版规划项目

法律声明

"皮书系列"(含蓝皮书、绿皮书、黄皮书)之品牌由社会科学文献出版社最早使用并持续至今,现已被中国图书市场所熟知。"皮书系列"的LOGO( )与"经济蓝皮书""社会蓝皮书"均已在中华人民共和国国家工商行政管理总局商标局登记注册。"皮书系列"图书的注册商标专用权及封面设计、版式设计的著作权均为社会科学文献出版社所有。未经社会科学文献出版社书面授权许可,任何使用与"皮书系列"图书注册商标、封面设计、版式设计相同或者近似的文字、图形或其组合的行为均系侵权行为。

经作者授权,本书的专有出版权及信息网络传播权为社会科学文献出版社享有。未经社会科学文献出版社书面授权许可,任何就本书内容的复制、发行或以数字形式进行网络传播的行为均系侵权行为。

社会科学文献出版社将通过法律途径追究上述侵权行为的法律责任,维护自身合法权益。

欢迎社会各界人士对侵犯社会科学文献出版社上述权利的侵权行为进行举报。电话:010-59367121,电子邮箱:fawubu@ssap.cn。

社会科学文献出版社

城市生活质量蓝皮书

BLUE BOOK OF
QUALITY OF LIFE IN CITIES

中国城市生活质量报告 (2015)

REPORT ON THE QUALITY OF LIFE IN CHINESE CITIES
(2015)

人心向上　经济承压

主　　编/张连城　张　平　杨春学　郎丽华
副 主 编/赵家章　张自然

社会科学文献出版社
SOCIAL SCIENCES ACADEMIC PRESS (CHINA)

图书在版编目(CIP)数据

中国城市生活质量报告.2015，人心向上 经济承压/张连城等主编.—北京：社会科学文献出版社，2015.7
（城市生活质量蓝皮书）
ISBN 978-7-5097-7721-3

Ⅰ.①中… Ⅱ.①张… Ⅲ.①城市-生活质量-指数-研究报告-中国-2015 Ⅳ.①D669.3

中国版本图书馆CIP数据核字（2015）第135203号

城市生活质量蓝皮书
中国城市生活质量报告（2015）
——人心向上 经济承压

| 主　　编 / 张连城　张　平　杨春学　郎丽华 |
| 副 主 编 / 赵家章　张自然 |
| 英文翻译 / 王宏彧　刘　敏 |

出 版 人 / 谢寿光
项目统筹 / 恽　薇　王楠楠
责任编辑 / 王楠楠　于　飞

| 出　　　版 / 社会科学文献出版社·经济与管理出版分社（010）59367226
地址：北京市北三环中路甲29号院华龙大厦　邮编：100029
网址：http://www.ssap.com.cn |
| 发　　　行 / 市场营销中心（010）59367081　59367090
读者服务中心（010）59367028 |
| 印　　　装 / 北京季蜂印刷有限公司 |
| 规　　　格 / 开　本：787mm×1092mm　1/16
印　张：23.25　字　数：268千字 |
| 版　　　次 / 2015年7月第1版　2015年7月第1次印刷 |
| 书　　　号 / ISBN 978-7-5097-7721-3 |
| 定　　　价 / 89.00元 |

皮书序列号 / B-2013-292

本书如有破损、缺页、装订错误，请与本社读者服务中心联系更换

▲ 版权所有 翻印必究

编委会名单

主　　编 张连城　张　平　杨春学　郎丽华
副 主 编 赵家章　张自然

执 笔 人 张连城　赵家章　张自然　王　银
　　　　　　赫宇彪　陈建先　杜雯翠

组织和策划本次调研的人员
　　　　　　张　平　张连城　杨春学　纪　宏　刘霞辉
　　　　　　郎丽华　徐　雪　王　诚　张晓晶　田新民
　　　　　　袁富华　张自然　赵家章　王　银　蔡　斌

中国经济实验研究院简介

改革开放以来，特别是社会主义市场经济体制建立以来，中国经济发展已经进入一个崭新的阶段。中国已经成为世界第二大经济体，人均国民收入已经达到中等收入国家的水平；同时，中国改革正在从"浅水区"进入"深水区"，改革所面临的形势将更为艰巨和复杂，中国改革必须从"摸着石头过河"的"实践试错"向着利用现代手段进行政策模拟和评估的"实验试错"转变。与此同时，从学科发展的角度看，经济学发展到今天，科学研究正在向协同研究和交叉学科研究的方向发展。这在客观上要求我国的高等院校、研究机构要打破学科界限、打破单位界限，整合一切可利用的资源，精诚合作，不断创新，才有可能应对中国社会所面临的新挑战。在这种背景下，经过长期调研、论证和精心准备，首都经济贸易大学与中国社会科学院经济研究所合作，共同成立了"中国经济实验研究院"。

早在2006年，首都经济贸易大学与中国社会科学院经济研究所就组建了"中国经济增长与周期研究中心"，并且联合香港经济导报社从2007年开始，成功举办了6届"中国经济增长与周期论坛"。目前，该论坛已经成为国内研究宏观经济的著名学者进行学术交流的重要平台。2010年，首都经济贸易大学与中国社会科学院经济研究所又组建了"中国城市生活质量研究中心"，经过对城市生活质量指数体系的深入研究和几个月的调研，在2011年举办的第五届"中国经济增长与周期论坛"上，首次发布了中国30个省会城市的生活质量指数，在国内引起了很大的反响，并引起了国际同行和世界银行等国际机构的关注。中国经济实验研究院就是在上述研究机构的基础上成立的。

目前，中国经济实验研究院设有"中国经济增长与周期研究中心""中国城市生活质量研究中心""数量经济研究中心""WTO研究中心"，并且设有经济运行与国际贸易实验室、经济预警实验室、经济数据处理与计算机仿真实验室和数字化调查中心。

中国经济实验研究院成立以后，在对原有机构和实验室进行整合的基础上，拟设如下机构：

1. 中国经济实验研究院专家委员会；
2. 中国经济增长与周期研究中心；
3. 中国城市生活质量研究中心；
4. 数量经济研究中心；
5. 博士后流动站；
6. 中国经济增长与周期论坛；
7. 北京经济转型发展研究中心；
8. 经济运行与经济预警实验室、计算机仿真实验室。

中国经济实验研究院成立以后，近期的主要任务如下。

第一，进一步深入开展中国经济增长与经济周期的研究，继续办好"中国经济增长与周期论坛"，并且将逐步实现国际化。

第二，进一步扩大生活质量指数研究的覆盖面，使其逐步从省会城市扩展到全国中等城市、从国内扩展到国际，同时实现指数发布的常态化。此外，生活质量只是经济增长质量的一部分内容，中国经济实验研究院将逐步把经济增长质量纳入自己的研究视野，争取获得一批高质量的科研成果。

第三，不断拓展经济实验研究的范围，开展经济改革实验、政策效应实验、经济增长压力实验等，为中国改革、政府机构及相关部门提供可量化的决策支持，并且努力服务社会。

第四，成立具有国际化特色的研究生指导团队，同时开展与国外大学的紧密合作，共同指导硕士和博士研究生，招收博士后，为首都经济贸易大学的人才队伍建设做出贡献。

第五，中国经济实验研究院目前与国外20多所高校有着紧密的合作关系，并将以此为基础，开展广泛的国际合作和国际学术交流，共同进行科学研究，协同创新，构造研究院的国际化特色。

中国经济实验研究院的宗旨是：推动经济实验研究，繁荣经济科学，为推进我国的经济体制改革、提高经济增长质量、促进经济发展服务。中国经济实验研究院的目标是：在未来，经过我们的不懈努力，争取把中国经济实验研究院建设成为这一领域的具有国际一流水平的高度开放的研究机构。

主要编撰者简介

张连城 首都经济贸易大学研究生毕业，2004年曾在美国新英格兰大学进修。现为首都经济贸易大学教授、博士生导师，中国经济实验研究院院长，校学位委员会副主任。在首都经济贸易大学（北京经济学院）任教30余载。1998~2002年担任首都经济贸易大学经济系副主任，2002~2012年担任首都经济贸易大学经济学院院长，并在2009~2011年兼任研究生部主任。大学任教期间，于1981~1985年先后兼任中国经济学团体联合会机关报《全国经济学团体通信》和《经济学周报》编辑部主任、记者部主任、研究发展部主任。1985~1987年在国家经济体制改革研究所兼任城市经济体制改革办公室副主任并从事研究工作。目前在多家学会兼任副会长、常务理事。

主要研究领域为：经济增长、经济周期与宏观经济政策。在该领域发表了近百篇学术论文和10余部专著、教材、译著，其中5项科研成果获教育部、北京市哲学社会科学优秀科研成果一、二等奖。由于自身的学术成就，2011年被国务院批准为享受政府特殊津贴的专家。1986年以来，曾主持多项社科基金课题，目前主持着国家社会科学基金重大项目"正确处理经济平稳较快发展、调整经济结构、管理通胀预期的关系研究"（12&ZD038），担任着我国经济理论界《现代外国经济学大系》丛书的主编工作，领导着国家级经济学特色专业、国家级经济学国际化人才培养实验区、国家级经济学核心课程教学团队的建设工作。

张　平　中国社会科学院经济研究所副所长、研究员，中国社会科学院研究生院教授、博士生导师。参与和主持了多项与世界银行、亚洲开发银行、世界劳工组织等开展国际合作的项目、社科基金重点课题和国家交办的课题。负责中国社会科学院重大课题"中国经济增长的前沿"、国家社会科学基金重大招标课题"我国经济结构战略性调整和增长方式转变"以及"加快经济结构调整与促进经济自主协调发展研究"等。1995年、2005年分别两次获孙冶方经济科学奖。出版专著若干本，在《经济研究》和其他核心刊物上发表或合作发表了几十篇论文，共计百余万字。

杨春学　1962年11月生于云南新平，彝族。1979~1986年就读于云南大学经济系，获学士和硕士（经济学）学位。1986~1992年执教于云南财经大学（原云南财贸学院），讲授西方经济学、发展经济学和国际金融。1992年考入中国社会科学院研究生院，1995年获博士学位。之后，一直在中国社会科学院经济研究所从事研究工作，并于1998年起在中国社会科学院研究生院讲授中级经济学课程。2001年9月~2002年9月在云南经济贸易委员会挂职，任主任助理。研究领域为：经济思想史、当代西方经济学说、某些现实经济问题的政治经济学。出版著作《经济人与社会秩序分析》，发表论文《利他主义经济学的追求》《和谐社会的政治经济学基础》等。

郎丽华　吉林通化人，经济学博士，教授，博士生导师，首都经济贸易大学经济学院院长、校学位委员会委员、经济学院学位委员会主任、学术委员会副主任、世界贸易组织研究中心副主任，兼任北京国际贸易学会副会长、中国服务贸易专家委员会副主任委员等职。研究领域为：国际贸易理论与政策、国际贸易战略、世界经济。长期从事国际经济与贸易的教学科研工作，为本科生、研究生、留学生讲授《国际经济学》《国际贸易理论与政策》等课程，是北京市精品课程《国际贸易》、国家级双语示范课《国际经济学》的主讲教师，国家级双语示范课《国际商务》的项目负责人,国家级经济学国际化人才培养实验区、北京市经济学国际化人才培养模式创新试验区主要负责人。1990年以来,先后在《人民日报》《经济研究》《世界经济》《管理世界》《经济学动态》《经济管理与研究》等报刊和杂志发表数十篇学术论文。主持并参与了北京市哲学社会科学规划项目、北京市教育委员会社会科学研究计划项目、国家社科基金重大项目等的研究工作。

摘 要

中国经济实验研究院城市生活质量研究中心 2015 年继续对全国 35 个城市居民的生活质量主观满意度进行电话调查，同时对 35 个城市居民的客观生活质量指数进行计算。本次生活质量调查历时两个多月，参与调研的人员超过 200 人，是课题组继 2011 年以来的第 5 次跟踪调查。课题组通过调查和测算得到了 35 个城市生活质量的主观满意度指数和客观指数。调查结果显示：35 个城市生活质量主观满意度指数继续小幅提高；客观指数在经济下行的背景下出现了小幅回落。本次专项调查结果显示：35 个城市房价上涨预期大幅度下降；居民最关注的影响生活质量的因素仍旧是空气质量，其次是食品安全、物价和交通状况；"互联网+"时代已经到来，居民认为互联网对人们生活的影响主要表现在沟通联系方面，其次为购物、服务便利和金融理财。本次调查给我们的启示是：在新常态背景下，我国经济增速放缓，尽管 35 个城市生活质量客观指数有所降低，但生活质量主观满意度却有所提高。这说明普通民众对未来发展充满信心，中央政府在稳增长、惠民生等方面的政策措施更有针对性，并收到了实效。但是，生活成本较高、空气质量堪忧、食品安全问题频出、生活节奏加快等问题依然是城市居民生活质量进一步提高的阻力。

关键词：城市生活质量　主观满意度指数　客观指数　房价预期　互联网+

目 录

B Ⅰ 总报告

B.1　2015年城市生活质量调查 …………………………………… 001
　　一　引言 ……………………………………………………… 001
　　二　主要结论 ………………………………………………… 002
　　三　框架安排 ………………………………………………… 004
B.2　城市生活质量研究最新进展 ………………………………… 006
　　一　生活质量的概念 ………………………………………… 006
　　二　国内外生活质量研究现状 ……………………………… 008
　　三　生活质量的影响因素 …………………………………… 013
　　四　欧盟的"生活质量指数" ……………………………… 018

B Ⅱ 观测篇

B.3　对2015年城市生活质量调查的说明 ………………………… 022
B.4　2015年中国35个城市生活质量指数 ………………………… 025
B.5　中国35个城市生活质量的细分指数 ………………………… 035

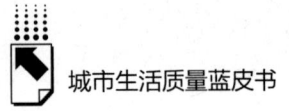

B Ⅲ 专项调查篇

B.6 房价预期调查 …………………………………………… 128
B.7 居民最关注因素调查 ……………………………………… 134
B.8 互联网对生活质量影响的调查 …………………………… 138

B Ⅳ 结论篇

B.9 结论和启示 ………………………………………………… 142

参考文献…………………………………………………………… 166

总 报 告

B.1
2015年城市生活质量调查

一 引言

中国经济实验研究院城市生活质量研究中心从2011年开始对全国35个城市的生活质量进行调查，课题组通过主观问卷调查得到了35个城市生活质量主观满意度指数，通过分析和计算客观统计数据得到了35个城市的客观生活质量指数，即社会经济数据指数。截止到2015年4月，课题组对城市生活质量的调查已经连续进行了5年。目前，我国正处于经济增长速度换挡期、结构调整阵痛期和前期刺激政策消化期的"三期叠加"阶段，经济步入了新常态。在这一阶段，持续关注人们的生活质量具有十分重要的现实意义。一方面，提高居民的生活质量有助于社会稳定，而社会稳定是经济增长、经济转型和经济体制改革的重要基础；另一方面，经济增长、经济转型和经济体制

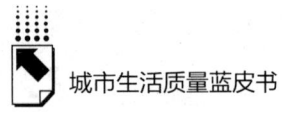

改革的终极目标是提高人民的生活质量,两者是内在统一的,居民生活质量提高的过程同时也是经济增长和发展的过程。

城市生活质量的主观满意度指数是通过随机电话调查得到的,通过随机尾号调查方法,得到有效随机样本22939个。整体主观指数的标准误差从2014年的0.15缩小到2015年的0.139,这使得本次调查的可靠性进一步增强。根据电话调查所获得的数据,通过统计分析得出描述城市生活质量的5个主观满意度分指数(生活水平满意度指数、生活成本满意度指数、人力资本满意度指数、社会保障满意度指数、生活感受满意度指数)。在房价预期调查和居民最关注因素调查的基础上,2015年新增了关于互联网的调查,这对于深入了解互联网发展对城市居民生活质量的影响具有重要意义。

城市生活质量的客观指数即社会经济数据指数,是根据国家权威机构发布的35个城市的社会经济数据计算出来的,从而保证了该指数的客观性和权威性,同时,我们在设计上保持了与主观指数的一致性,即客观指数包括生活水平客观指数、生活成本客观指数、人力资本客观指数、社会保障客观指数、生活感受客观指数,5个客观社会经济数据分指数涵盖了20个社会经济数据指标,基本上反映了我国现阶段城市居民生活质量的各个方面。

二　主要结论

根据调查结果,2015年,35个城市生活质量主观满意度指数平均值有所提高,从2014年的51.57上升到55.38,处于满意区间,但根据我们对主观满意度调查结果的答案赋值,其整体上仍旧处于偏低水平。2015年,35个城市的主观满意度指数均超过50,比2014年增加了4个城市。城市生活质量主观满意度指数的5个分指数平均值情况如下:人力资本满意度指数为61.73,社会保障满意度指数为60.47,

生活水平满意度指数为60.07,生活感受满意度指数为55.66,生活成本满意度指数为38.94。与2014年相比,5个分指数加权平均值均有所上升,其中,人力资本满意度指数、社会保障满意度指数、生活水平满意度指数上升幅度较大。

生活质量主观满意度指数的区域特征明显,东部城市高于中西部城市。排名前10位的城市为:杭州市(1)、厦门市(2)、宁波市(3)、海口市(4)、昆明市(5)、合肥市(6)、南京市(7)、长春市(8)、哈尔滨市(9)、上海市(10)。排名后10位的城市是:西安市(26)、呼和浩特市(27)、北京市(28)、乌鲁木齐市(29)、天津市(30)、深圳市(31)、银川市(32)、贵阳市(33)、太原市(34)、兰州市(35)。

2015年计算出的生活质量客观指数即社会经济数据指数显示,东部城市仍旧高于中西部城市,但同时部分城市存在主客观指数的反差。2015年,35个城市的客观社会经济数据指数平均值为55.84,比2014年的57.87有所降低。得分在50以上的城市有31个,比2014年减少了3个。5个客观分指数的平均值情况如下:生活水平客观指数为59.83,人力资本客观指数为57.34,生活感受客观指数为56.17,社会保障客观指数为51.26,生活成本客观指数为54.58。与2014年相比,生活水平和社会保障客观指数有所下降,人力资本、生活感受和生活成本客观指数略微有所上升。客观总指数排名前10位的城市是:北京市(1)、南京市(2)、西安市(3)、杭州市(4)、广州市(5)、上海市(6)、深圳市(7)、昆明市(8)、武汉市(9)、长沙市(10)。排名后10位的城市是:太原市(26)、福州市(27)、哈尔滨市(28)、海口市(29)、天津市(30)、兰州市(31)、南宁市(32)、西宁市(33)、郑州市(34)、重庆市(35)。

2015年专项调查结果显示,2015年,35个城市中,32个城市的受访者把空气质量视为影响生活质量的最重要因素,3个城市的受访者把食品安全作为影响生活质量的最重要因素。2014年，共有17个城市把空气质量视为最重要因素，2015年调查增加了15个城市，由此看出人们对空气质量关注的程度进一步大幅提高。调查结果显示，受访者认为影响生活质量的最重要因素分别是空气质量（39.12%）、食品安全（28.77%）、物价（21.17%）、交通状况（10.94%）。整体上看，居民认为空气质量是影响生活质量最为重要的因素。房价预期的专项调查显示：预期房价指数平均值为43.86，不仅低于2014年的平均值60.78，并且35个城市的房价预期指数均低于房价上涨和下跌的临界点（得分为50），这表明35个城市的居民对房价的预期有了改变，即预期未来房价将呈现下跌趋势。

在新常态背景下，我国经济增速放缓，尽管35个城市的生活质量客观指数有所降低，但生活质量主观满意度指数却有所提升。这说明普通民众对未来发展充满信心，中央政府在稳增长、惠民生等方面的政策措施更有针对性，并获得了实效。但是，生活成本较高、空气质量堪忧、食品安全问题频出、生活节奏加快等问题依然是生活质量进一步提高的阻力。

三 框架安排

本书的第二篇报告是城市生活质量研究的最新进展。从生活质量的概念以及国内外研究现状的角度，对生活质量的相关研究进行重新回顾；并进一步从4个方面（经济、社会文化、政治、人口）分析了生活质量的影响因素；最后，对欧盟近期公布的"8+1"生活质量指标体系进行了介绍。

第三篇报告是对2015年城市生活质量调查的说明。主要内容包括主观数据调查的技术说明、客观数据指标的设计、客观数据的来源。

第四篇报告详细介绍了2015年中国35个城市生活质量指数，包括对主观满意度指数和客观指数的排序和说明。为了便于分析各城市生活质量的动态变化，本报告将各个城市生活质量总指数的评分和排序逐个列出，并与前4次调查获取的指数进行比较。同时，我们分别给出了2012~2014年主客观指数的直方图，以及35个城市主客观指数的柱形图。

第五篇报告介绍了2015年中国35个城市生活质量的细分指数。分别列出了35个城市生活质量的细分指数及排序情况，并给出了35个城市生活质量一级指标的雷达图；同时给出了城市生活质量细分指数的直方图和柱状图，以便对城市生活质量指数进行动态比较。

第六、七、八篇报告分别是针对3项专项调查的说明，即房价预期调查、居民最关注因素调查以及新增的互联网对生活质量的影响调查。

第九篇报告介绍了本次调查的主要结论、启示以及政策建议。

B.2
城市生活质量研究最新进展

工业化革命以来，随着科学技术的发展，人类不断增强改造自然的能力，创造了巨大的物质财富，现代文明也随之产生。进入20世纪以来，随着科学技术的迅猛发展，人类不断扩大自己的实践活动范围，进一步增强了创造财富的能力，使得物质文明和精神文明得到了快速发展。然而，人类在取得巨大成就的同时，也面临着气候变暖、环境恶化、资源枯竭、收入差距扩大等全球性问题。在一些国家里，虽然经济发展迅速，但人民的生活质量却没有得到相应的提高，幸福感没有增强。马克思认为，人类发展的最终目标是实现人的自由全面发展。而这些问题的出现显然与人类社会发展的终极目标相悖。因此，如何在经济增长和物质生活条件得到改善的同时，让人们的生活质量得到相应提高，幸福感上升，是当今世界普遍面临的重大课题。因此，研究如何在经济增长过程中促进人民生活质量和幸福感提高，具有十分重要的意义。

一 生活质量的概念

生活质量是个多维度的概念，拥有广泛的内涵。学术界对于生活质量的概念莫衷一是，并没有统一公认的规定。不同学科对生活质量内涵的理解和侧重点各有不同。医学和心理学从微观个体的角度来研究生活质量。在医学和心理学的有关文献中，生活质量通常被称为"与健康相关的生活质量"（Health-related Quality of Life），即健康质量。研究内容主要是根据对患者心理、生理和社会功能三大方面的评估,分析其所接受的医疗保健服务水平。其他学科更多关注的是居民生活质量,它综合反映了一个国家或地区居民生存和发展的状况。世界卫生组织将生活质量的内涵概括为4个方面:居民的物质水平、生理功能状态、社会功能状态和心理健康状态。

随着经济的发展和社会的进步,居民的物质生活水平和精神生活水平达到了一定高度,人们对生活质量的追求也越来越高,对生活质量的认识也不断深化。尽管如此,人们对生活质量的概念仍有着不同的理解。

许多美国学者往往偏重于从主观和微观方面理解生活质量。Campbell等(1976)提出了生活质量的定义,他们提出"生活质量是生活幸福的总体感受"。Galbaith在《丰裕社会》一书里提出"生活质量是人们在生活舒适、便利程度以及精神上得到的乐趣和享受"。林南(1985)把生活质量定义为"人们对生活各个方面的总体感受"。从某种意义上说,主观上的生活质量概念与幸福感概念是基本一致的。当人们的生活质量较高时,幸福感也会增强;反之亦然。

厉以宁和罗斯托是从客观方面理解生活质量的代表性经济学家。厉以宁认为生活质量包括自然层面和社会层面两个部分。自然层面包括环境的美化、优化和净化等,社会层面包括社会文化、教育、医疗卫生、社会风俗和秩序等。Rostow(1971)提出了相似的定义。冯立天(1992)认为"生活质量是生活条件的综合反映,是指一定经济发展阶段上人口生活条件的综合状态"。风笑天和易松国(2000)认为,"生活质量是对一个社会中人们总体生活水平的综合描述,同时也是衡量一个社会整体发展水平的重要指标"。

我们认为,生活质量的概念复杂且丰富,既包括主观和客观的因素,也涉及宏观和微观层面。从主观的角度来看,生活质量是指人们对现实生活的满意程度,是一种心理上的主观感受,这种感受既涉及微观层面,如对个人收入水平、生活成本、受教育状况的感受等,同时也涉及宏观层面,如对收入分配是否公平合理、城市安全或社会治安状况、社会保障制度优劣的感受等。人们对生活质量的主观感受毕竟源于客观存在。因此,要全面评价人们生活质量的高低,还必须考虑各种客观因素对人们生活质量的影响,这同样包括宏观和微观两个层面的内容。例如,人们的可支配收入水平、人均可支配收入的增长速度、通货膨胀率、社会保障水平、医疗保险状况、就业率或失业率、生活便利状况、生态环境等,都在客观上决定着人们生活质量的高低。

因此,我们认为,生活质量概念应该是指一个国家或地区人们生活水平的总体状态,反映了一个社会整体发展的水平。它涉及自然、政治、经济、社会、文化和宗教等各个领域。高水平的生活质量应该包括:①优美舒适的自然环境和居住环境;②较高的物质生活水平、可支配收入水平和相对平等的收入分配状况,也包括较少的贫困人群、较低的社会失业率,以及较高的生活便利程度;③丰富的精神生活、充裕的休闲时间和较为普及的文化消费;④稳定的政治和社会环境、良好的社会秩序和安全感;⑤完善的社会保障制度;⑥完善的医疗系统和教育系统以及较高的服务水平;⑦舒缓的生活节奏;⑧人们对未来经济、社会发展及个人发展的良好预期;等等。当然,对生活质量内涵的认识不是一成不变的,而是随着人类社会的发展而不断发展的。

二 国内外生活质量研究现状

国外对生活质量的研究起步较早,是随着经济增长和人们对生活质量认知的演变而不断发展的,是经济增长和社会文明进步的产物。20世纪初,以庇古为代表的福利经济学家提出了福利概念,并逐步形成了以效用、生产者剩余、消费者剩余等理论为基础,以帕累托效应理论为判断标准的理论体系。这个时候的研究侧重于经济福利研究，尚未提升至生活质量层面的研究。换句话说，以庇古为代表的福利经济学家重在物质生产方面的研究，而没有考虑到人们的精神生活和幸福感等主观因素。

1927年，W.Ogburn教授开始关注美国社会动向问题，出版了以《近期美国社会动向》为代表的诸多成果。这些研究逐渐发展为两大主流：生活质量的研究和社会指标的研究[①]。随着经济的不断发展，人们的基本需求得到了满足，生活条件进一步改善。与此同时，以美国为首的西方国家出现了一系列社会和生态问题，诸如收入差距、资源过度开发、环境污染、生态环境恶化等，影响了人们的生存状态。人们逐渐发现物质生活改善只是人类追求的一部分，精神文化生活也是非常重要的内容。生活质量意识被唤醒了，追求生活质量成为现实生活中的迫切需求。在此背景下，生活质量研究也逐渐兴起，并迅速引起各界的关注，相关著作也相继问世。Veroff和Field（1957）对美国人的精神健康和幸福感进行了抽样调查。经济学家Galbaith（1958）提出了生活质量的概念，并把生活质量定义为人们从生活舒适、便利程度中得到的精神满足或享受。他认为，社会整体价值不仅包括经济价值的实现，也包括文化价值的实现。社会追求的目标应该是生活质量的提高，它是一个经济价值和文化价值的综合体。在提出生活质量概念的基础上，他进一步认为应该用"生活质量"来重新评估经济增长与社会福利。Samuelson（1970）也认为，现代经济学不能仅仅重视数量而忽略生活质量。这个观点得到了经济学家Tobin和Nordhaus的认同。

Rostow在1971年出版了《政治和成长阶段》，为生活质量理论研究做出了巨大贡献。他把经济发展划分6个阶段：传统社会阶段→

---

① 易松国：《国外城市居民生活质量概述》，《深圳大学学报》1998年第1期。

起步准备阶段→起步阶段→成熟阶段→大众化高度消费阶段→追求生活质量阶段。他认为社会发展的终极目标是人们有非常高的生活质量水平。经济增长和社会进步的衡量标准应该是生活质量的改善程度，而非有形产品的数量。Goulet（1971）认为生活质量可分为3个层次：生存、尊严和自由。自由是生活质量的最高形式。

随着生活质量研究的深入，不同学科的学者分别从不同角度研究生活质量。社会学家Campbell（1976）认为生活质量是指"生活幸福的总体感觉"，生活质量是人们对现实生活的主观感受。Milbrath认为生活质量依赖于自然环境，没有良好的自然环境，生活质量也不能得到保证。

我国对生活质量的研究起步较晚，始于20世纪80年代改革开放之后。生活质量概念从国外引进到国内，受到了国内学者的关注。早期的研究侧重于对居民生活质量的评估和调研。1985年和1987年天津社会科学院社会学所和上海社会科学院社会学所分别对我国的天津和上海两个城市的居民生活质量做过调查，评估了两个城市的居民生活质量和满意度。1986年著名经济学家厉以宁教授提出了自己的生活质量理论。

近年来，国内对该领域的研究发展非常迅速。我们在中国知网数据库里以"生活质量"和"幸福感"为关键字搜集了相关文献，并对其进行了统计，统计结果见表1。从发表的文献数量来看，我国生活质量研究可分为4个阶段：第一阶段是1980~1989年萌芽阶段。在该时期，该领域的文献较少，10年间共发表论文26篇，年均2.6篇。第二阶段是1990~1997年起步阶段。在这个阶段，生活质量的研究发展较快。在这8年里我国共发表了404篇论文，年均发表50.5篇。第三阶段是1998~2004年发展阶段，在该阶段，每年的研究论文都超过百篇。这7年里的论文总数为1817篇，年均近260篇，约是上一阶段的5倍。2005年起至今是快速发展的第四阶段。随着人们对生活质量重视程度的提高，学术界也发表了大量的研究文献。最近10年的论文总数达到24290篇，年均发表2429篇。不仅如此，文献也涉及各个领域，包括经济学、社会学、医学、心理学等。

表1 国内有关生活质量的文献统计

单位：篇，%

年 份	生活质量	幸福感	合 计	百分比
1980	1	0	1	0.00
1981	1	0	1	0.00
1982	0	0	0	0.00
1983	2	0	2	0.01
1984	1	0	1	0.00
1985	3	0	3	0.01
1986	2	0	2	0.01
1987	1	0	1	0.00
1988	6	0	6	0.02
1989	9	0	9	0.03
1990	18	0	18	0.07
1991	18	1	19	0.07
1992	24	1	25	0.09
1993	32	1	33	0.12
1994	51	0	51	0.19
1995	72	1	73	0.28
1996	86	3	89	0.34
1997	91	5	96	0.36
1998	121	6	127	0.48
1999	146	5	151	0.57
2000	192	9	201	0.76
2001	246	6	252	0.95
2002	322	26	348	1.31
2003	488	56	544	2.05
2004	128	66	194	0.73

续表

年　份	生活质量	幸福感	合　计	百分比
2005	868	150	1018	3.84
2006	1112	250	1362	5.13
2007	1052	530	1582	5.96
2008	1151	526	1677	6.32
2009	1271	727	1998	7.53
2010	1512	825	2337	8.81
2011	1678	1550	3228	12.16
2012	1901	1514	3415	12.87
2013	2169	1507	3676	13.85
2014	2549	1448	3997	15.06
总　计	17324	9213	26537	100.00

从学科分布来看，在所有的有关生活质量的文献中，医学方面的论文共有15405篇，占了绝大部分。经济学方面的论文排名第二，共有1220篇论文。政治学方面的论文排名第三，共有751篇论文。而人口学对生活质量的研究相对较少。图1是我们对生活质量文献的学科统计。

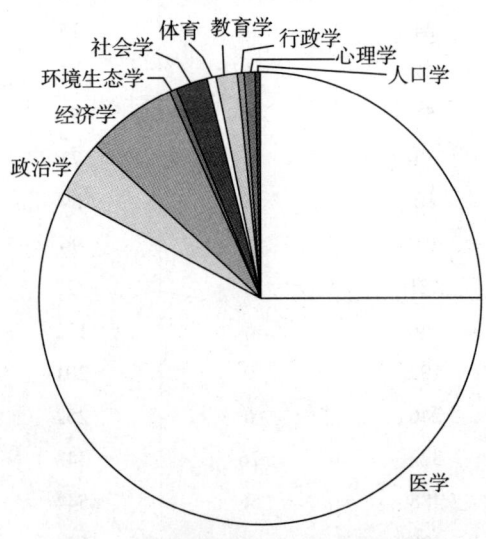

图1　生活质量文献的学科统计

总而言之，对生活质量的研究是经济发展到一定阶段的必然产物。当经济增长到一定程度以后，物质水平提高了，基本生存需求得到了满足，人们便开始关注经济增长过程中产生的负面影响，如资源枯竭、环境污染和贫富差距扩大等。这些问题影响了人们的客观生活质量和心理感受。为了满足现实需要，学术界在生活质量研究领域快速发展，并形成了各种理论体系。这些理论体系是人类不断探索自然和改造自然的宝贵财富。

三 生活质量的影响因素

影响生活质量的因素不仅有客观因素，也有主观因素。鉴于这种理解，我们认为影响生活质量的因素涉及经济、社会文化、政治、人口等诸多方面。

（一）经济因素

收入水平是影响生活质量最重要的经济因素。Diener 和 Biswas（2002）研究了财富和幸福感之间的关系，结论表明，富裕国家的人比贫穷国家的人拥有更高的幸福感。在同一国家内，富裕的人幸福感指数也优于贫穷的人。微观经济学把效用看作是收入、闲暇时间、个人因素和工作参数的函数，记为 $U=U(y, h, i, j)$，其中 U 代表个人效用水平，效用水平值越高，说明幸福感越强，生活质量水平越高；y 表示居民的绝对收入水平，与效用呈正相关关系；h 为闲暇时间；i、j 分别表示个人因素和工作参数。如果 h、i、j 不变，绝对收入 y 越大，总体效用水平 U 也就越高。

然而，人们发现，绝对收入水平和生活质量的变化趋势并不总是一致的。经济增长和绝对收入增加只是提高了客观生活质量，却不一定能够提高主观生活质量。Easterlin（1974）认为，假如把所有人的收入同比例增加，幸福感可能会保持不变。Kubiszewski 等（2013）的研究发现，虽然当前经济总量是 1950 年的 4 倍，但人们的实际福利水平却呈现倒 U 特征，即 1950~1978 年逐步上升，1978 年达到峰值，1978 年后开始下降。他们的研究还得出了一个惊人的结论，即在人均国内生产总值大于 7000 美元以后，福利水平就基本难以提高了。显然，相对于绝对收入水平，相对收入水平对生活质量的影响似乎更大。1960 年相对福利学说认为相对收入对于个人幸福更具有意义。效用不仅是绝对收入的函数，更是相对收入或者参考收入的函数，记为 $U=U(y, y', h, i, j)$。其中，y' 是指相对收入或者参考收入。对于个人而言，如果绝对收入增加了，而相对收入不变或下降，那么总体效用水平也会相应提高。如果绝对收入增加了，而相对收入或参考收入也增加，那么两者可能互相抵消，总体效用水平可能不会改变。

相对福利学说告诉我们，人们的生活质量和幸福感是受收入水平和收入差距共同影响的。Wilkinson 和 Picot 在《不平等的痛苦：收入差距如何导致社会问题》里指出，物质生活水平对人们幸福感的边际贡献是递减的。降低社会不平等程度有利于改善人们总体生活质量水平。王彤和苏征社（2002）指出，在社会不平等加剧和收入差距过大的情况下，收入较低的人们没有办法享受到经济增长的成果，心理容易失衡，不满、愤怒和反社会情绪高涨，萌发仇富心理。这种"社会迁怒"是由不平等和收入差距过大造成的，不仅影响了个人生活质量水平，而且对整个社会生活质量也有显著的影响。

（二）社会文化因素

居民生活质量在不同的社会文化环境中存在着差异。在中国传统文化里，社会价值得到重视，个人意志需要与集体意志和国家意志保持和谐一致，个人行为要与群体行为相协调，个人观点和感受不受到鼓励。相反，在西方文化中个人价值得到重视，个人行为和自我价值得到鼓励。因此，不同社会文化背景下，中西方生活质量和幸福感也是不同的。随着社会变迁和社会融合，人们所处的社会文化环境不断变化，也影响了人们对生活幸福的感受。

一是社会变迁影响人们的主观生活质量。改革开放以来，社会文化环境发生了很大变化，集中体现为思想观念蜕变、社会家庭问题日益突出和社会变革加剧等。这些社会文化变迁不仅影响了人们的客观生活质量水平，也对不同人在世界观、人生观、价值观等方面的个体心理产生巨大冲击，影响了主观生活质量状态。对于一些个体而言，他们能够随着社会变迁不断调整自己的心态，生活乐观积极，面对新生事物主动应对，主观生活质量也会随着社会变迁而不断提高的；而对于另一些人，他们不愿意接受新生事物，坚持传统价值观念内形成的心理和行为模式，在面对社会变迁所带来的外部压力时，这些人常常会不习惯，惊慌失措，产生不安和焦虑情绪，他们的主观生活质量也很难得到改善。

二是社会文化融合程度对生活质量的影响。文化融合过程是不同文化相互配合和适应的过程。对于个人来说，能否调整自己的观念和行为以适应不同的文化环境，对其主观生活质量有着重大的影响。如果个人能融入不同的社会文化环境，接受和适应不同的价值观念，在新的环境中重新塑造自己在社会当中的位置，找到文化认同感，那么他的生活质量也较高。相反，如果不能融入新的社会文化环境，不能接受甚至排斥新文化价值观念，缺乏社会文化认同感，对新的文化保持距离感，那么他的幸福感也会降低，生活质量水平难以提高。

三是不同文化情况下个人生活质量存在差异性。Kennon 和 Tim

(2001)研究发现,不同社会文化背景中个人拥有不同的生活幸福感、社会取向、世界观、价值观。当个人的行为符合社会文化常规模式时,个人生活满意度和幸福感就会提高。Oishi、Diener和Lucas(2003)认为,当个人的行为是朝着自己的目标努力时,个体就会感受到幸福感。Marks等(1996)却认为个体幸福感存在差异的首要因素并不是文化,而是个体对所处文化的看法和认同。不同国家的文化存在差异,人们的生活方式和价值观各有不同,客观条件也截然不同,人们的生活质量也高低不一。

(三)政治因素

从现有文献来看,政治民主也影响了人们的生活质量水平。西方学者对两者关系进行了相关研究,得出了正相关的结论,即相对民主和发达的国家拥有较高的生活质量水平,而相对不民主和落后的国家在各个生活质量评价指标上都劣于民主和发达的国家。Moon和Dixon(1985)收集了116个国家的横截面数据,实证分析了两者之间的关系,结论表明民主确实提高了客观生活质量水平。Moon(1991)采取了更为精准的数据,得出了相似的结论。London和Williams(1990)收集了1965~1970年的国家数据,拓展了Moon和Dixon(1985)的研究,得到了两者是正相关关系的结论,政治民主显著提高了生活质量水平。Wickrama和Mulford(1996)利用欠发达国家的样本数据,得到了相似的结论。Frey和Roumi(1999)利用更为广泛的样本数据,这些样本数据不仅包含了发达国家的数据,也包含了欠发达国家的数据,年份分别为1970年、1980年和1990年。在控制了国家发展水平、政府干预程度、人口压力等因素后,研究结果显示,在1970年、1980年和1990年,政治民主和生活质量之间均存在正相关关系,政治民主程度越高,居民生活质量水平也越高。

以上文献均发现，政治民主和生活质量存在正相关关系。在其他因素不变的情况下，一个国家的政治民主制度越完善，居民生活质量水平也越高。那么，政治民主如何影响生活质量水平？传导路径是什么？在政治民主促进生活质量提高的机制方面，西方学术界虽然有着不同的观点，但仍存在4种广为接受的机制。它们分别是政治参与机制、竞争选举机制、自由媒介机制和反对党机制。

（四）人口因素

影响生活质量的人口因素较多，性别、年龄、就业状态、受教育程度等都影响个体的生活质量水平，进而影响整个社会的生活质量水平。

一是生活质量的性别差异性。由于男性和女性在不同社会中承担的角色和所处的生活地位各有不同，其生活质量存在差异。相对于男性，女性往往更加敏感，情感水平的积极性也高于男性。Fujita（1991）研究发现，如果女性满意自己现在的生活，那么她们的幸福感比男性更加强烈。然而，郑雪等（2001）发现，随着经济的发展，中国女性面临着与男性相似的生活和工作压力，生活质量的性别差异也变得不是很明显。

二是年龄不同导致生活质量的差异。随着年龄的增加，人们的社会认知、人生阅历、思维方式、情感控制、兴趣爱好等方面都会发生变化，从而导致对生活质量的感受也会发生明显的变化。Diener和Eunkook（1997）研究发现，20岁是个人情感和幸福感较高的时期，而随着年龄增加，个人情感和幸福感下降。严标宾等（2003）发现，年轻人比老年人有着更强烈的生活热情，理想更加丰富，而老年人比年轻人对社会有着更深刻的认识，思维方式更加成熟，所以老年人和年轻人的生活质量也不尽相同。

三是就业与失业状态所引起的生活质量差异。一个人的社会工作机会越多，上升渠道越通畅，个人的生活质量水平往往越高。就业是个人获取客观生活资料的主要来源。一个拥有理想工作的人，个人价值得到充分体现，社会认同感较高，生活幸福感受较强，生活质量水平也较高。相反，对于一个非自愿失业的个体而言，其个人价值无法得到体现，社会认同感缺失，其对生活失去信心，基本生活需求甚至无法得到保证，容易产生负面情绪，进而影响其生活质量水平。

四是受教育程度也是影响生活质量的重要因素。受教育程度是反映一个国家或地区人口质量的重要指标。对于个人而言，受教育程度不同，生活质量水平也会存在差异。在相同的物质和收入水平下，相对于受教育程度高的人而言，受教育程度低的人由于对生活的期望值较低，主观生活质量比较高。但是，受教育程度高的人有着较强的能力，工作机会和晋升机会较多，更容易得到社会的认同，更受人关注和尊重，生活质量水平也较高。相反，受教育程度低的人能力较差，自信心较为缺乏，易于产生自卑心理，随之而来的可能是负面甚至是反社会情绪，从而降低其生活质量水平。

五是健康状况。正如 Edwards 和 Mark（1973）所指出的那样：健康是幸福感（生活质量）的较佳预测指标，特别是在年龄、社会地位等其他变量不变时，更是如此。

四 欧盟的"生活质量指数"

生活质量（Quality of Life）是一个非常宽泛的概念，包含一系列不同维度（我们认为各种元素或者因素组成一个实体，它可以通过一组子维度和许多与其相关的指标来衡量）。它包括客观因素（如对物质资源的要求、健康、工作状态、生活条件和其他）

及对它们做出反应的主观因素。后者主要取决于市民的偏好和需求。用一个可比较的方式衡量不同人群和国家的生活质量是一项复杂的课题，出于研究目的，一个包含许多相关维度的体系是必要的。

欧洲一体化建设的一个主要目标是追求可持续的经济和社会进步。《马斯特里赫特条约》把这一目标概括为"改善和提高成员国的生活质量和生活条件"。"欧洲生活质量指标体系"是欧盟近年来逐渐完善的重要成果，它的不断完善为学术界监测和分析欧盟各成员国福利和生活质量的发展提供了重要的参考依据。

有些研究简单地用GDP这个指标来衡量生活质量，这其实是不全面的。GDP是最常见的衡量一个国家或地区在指定时间内的经济活动的指标，许多决策和政策制定者都将它作为标准尺度，为其决策或建议提供依据。它包括一个经济体生产的所有最终商品和服务，并提供了一个快照式的大致印象。GDP在市场生产的衡量上非常有用。尽管它并不能作为指示社会进步的标准，但它的确被认为与居民福祉有密切联系。

为了弥补用GDP度量生活质量的不足，2014年上半年欧盟统计局发布了新的"生活质量指数"（Quality of Life Indicators），该生活质量指数涵盖"8+1"项指标，构成了一个立体衡量维度。其中"8"包括：物质生活条件（Material living conditions）、生产活动（Productive or main activity）、健康（Health）、教育（Education）、休闲和社会互动（Leisure and social interactions）、经济和生活安全（Economic and physical safety）、政府治理和基本权利（Governance and basic rights）、自然和生活环境（Natural and living environment），"1"指的是整体生活感受（Overall experience of life）。表2是欧盟的"8+1"生活质量指数框架。

表2 欧盟"8+1"生活质量指数框架

物质生活条件（Material living conditions）	①收入 ②消费 ③物质条件（住房）	收入是一个重要的指标，因为它能够影响大多数框架内的其他指标。消费包括的指标有人均家庭消费、总人均消费以及其他来自家庭预算调查的指标。物质条件（住房）为这些以货币为基础的方法提供重要的补充信息
生产活动（Productive or main activity）	①可获得的工作数量 ②可获得的工作质量	公民每天的生活都进行大量活动，最突出的是他们的工作。工作机会的数量和质量主要从工作时间、平衡工作和非工作生活、就业的安全和伦理几个方面考虑，这是一些在欧洲常使用的衡量这方面生活质量的指标
健康（Health）	①预期寿命 ②婴儿死亡率 ③健康生活年数 ④医疗保健的权利 ⑤健康的自我评价	健康是公民生活质量的一个重要组成部分。不佳的健康状况会影响社会的总体进步。生理或心理问题对主观幸福感也有一个非常有害的影响。健康状况主要用客观健康结果指标测量，但也有主观指标
教育（Education）	①人口的受教育程度 ②早期毕业生的数量 ③自我评价和评估技能 ④参与终身学习	在以知识为基础的经济体中，教育在公民的生活中起着举足轻重的作用，是决定他们进步的非常重要的因素。教育程度可以决定一个人的工作。有限的个人技能和能力通常被排除在大部分工作之外，有时甚至会错过在社会中实现价值目标的机会
休闲和社会互动（Leisure and social interactions）	①与其他人一起运动或参加文化活动的频率 ②为不同类型的组织做志愿者的频率	用该指标衡量个人的福祉时，不应低估网络和社会关系的力量，因为它们直接影响生活满意度。此外，在此维度下应纳入可能得到的社会支持和社会交往的频率指标
经济和生活安全（Economic and physical safety）	每个国家杀人犯的数量	公民生活的安全性是一个重要的方面。能够提前计划和克服任何突然恶化的经济状况和更广泛的环境变化对人们的生活质量有着重要影响。对于后者，财富指标应该被使用，但目前此项指标在所有欧洲国家没有可比数据。因此，可将在面对意想不到的费用时有无欠款作为替代变量

续表

政府治理和基本权利（Governance and basic rights）	①居民对公共和政治生活的参与 ②公民对机构的信任程度 ③公民对公共服务的满意程度 ④工资差距	与公共辩论和影响公共政策制定的权利是体现生活质量的一个重要方面。此外，为公民提供正确的立法保障是民主社会的一个基本方面
自然和生活环境（Natural and living environment）	①主观（个人的感受） ②客观（空气污染指数）	在过去的几十年里环境保护在欧洲的议程中已经具有非常高的地位。绝大多数的欧洲公民认为保护环境是重要的。暴露在空气、水和噪音污染中会直接影响人们的健康和社会经济的繁荣。环境指标在综合评估生活质量上是非常重要的，包括主观（个人的看法）和客观（空气污染指数）等指标
整体生活感受（Overall experience of life）	①生活满意度 ②影响 ③获得幸福的方法	影响包括一个人的感情或情绪状态，可以从正负两个方面，同时参考特定时间点进行测量

观 测 篇

B.3 对2015年城市生活质量调查的说明

为了保证调查结果的连续性和可比性，2015年，我们在调查方法、指标体系设置以及样本的选取方面基本延续了前三年的做法，同时在局部做了细微的调整和完善。

一 对本次调查的整体说明

对于样本的选择，我们保持了连续性，仍旧是30个省会城市和5个计划单列市，总计35个城市。主观满意度指数的调查依旧采取电脑辅助电话调查的方法（CATI），对固定电话号码的抽取仍旧采用分层二阶段随机抽样的方法，使调查在城市空间分布上保持广泛性，同时保证了样本抽取的随机性。我们同时对移动电话用户和固定电话用户进行调查，且均采用相同的抽样方法。2015年的调查历时两个多月，总共拨打了395537个电话，共产生有效随机样本22939个，其中固话12669个，手机10270个。此次调查的可靠性进一步增强，整体主观指数的标准误差缩小到0.139。客观指标延续了2014年的获取方法，具体可参考《中国城市生活质量报告（2014）》。

二 主客观指标体系的构建和专项调查

根据我们的理解和中国的实际情况，2011年，中国经济实验研究院创建了中国城市生活质量指数体系，即QLICC体系。这个体系包括两个部分：主观满意度指数体系和客观指数（社会经济数据指数）体系。2015年，主观满意度指标体系和客观指标体系的构建延续了2012年以来的做法（见表1和表2）。

表1 中国城市生活质量主观满意度指标体系

满意度指数（主观指数）	主观问题	答案赋值				
		100	75	50	25	0
生活水平满意度指数	收入现状（50%）	很满意	满意	一般	不满意	很不满意
	收入预期（50%）	很乐观	乐观	一般	不乐观	很不乐观
生活成本满意度指数	生活成本	很低	低	一般	高	很高
人力资本满意度指数	人力资本	很满意	满意	一般	不满意	很不满意
社会保障满意度指数	医疗和养老保障（50%）	很满意	满意	一般	不满意	很不满意
	城市安全状况（50%）	很满意	满意	一般	不满意	很不满意
生活感受满意度指数	生活节奏（50%）	很慢	慢	一般	快	很快
	生活便利（50%）	很便利	便利	一般	不便利	很不便利

表 2 中国城市生活质量客观指标体系

社会经济数据指数（客观指数）	一级指标	二级指标	对城市生活质量的影响
生活水平客观指数	收入水平	消费率（消费/收入）	+
		人均财富（包含人均储蓄和人均住房财富）	+
		人均可支配收入	+
	生活改善指数	人均消费增长	+
		人均财富增长	+
		人均可支配收入增长	+
生活成本客观指数	生活成本指数	房屋销售价格指数	−
		通货膨胀率	−
		房价收入比	−
人力资本客观指数	人力资本指数	教育提供指数（包含万人学校数和万人教师数）	+
		教育文化娱乐消费支出比	+
社会保障客观指数	社会保障指数	社保覆盖率	+
		基本医疗保险覆盖率	+
		失业保险覆盖率	+
生活感受客观指数	生活便利指数	交通提供能力（包含人均铺装道路面积、万人拥有公共电汽车数量、万人出租车数量）	+
		万人影剧院数	+
		医疗提供能力（包含万人床位数、万人医院数、万人拥有医生数）	+
	生态环境指数	人均绿地面积	+
		空气质量	+
	收入差距感受指数	基尼系数	−

注：表内"+"为正影响，"−"为负影响。

此外，在2015年主观满意度的电话调查中，除了继续对城市住房价格预期和城市居民最关注因素的调查外，新增了互联网消费对生活质量影响的专项调查，试图了解互联网消费对城市居民生活质量的影响。专项调查的结果仍旧不纳入QLICC体系，但通过这3项专项调查，可以进一步了解居民对生活成本以及生活感受的满意度。

B.4
2015年中国35个城市生活质量指数

一 2015年城市生活质量主观满意度指数

2015年，中国35个城市生活质量主观满意度指数的调查结果及排序情况见表1。

表1 中国35个城市生活质量主观满意度指数

城 市	2015年			2014年		2013年		2012年	
	得分	排序	上升位次	得分	排序	得分	排序	得分	排序
杭州市	57.58	1	3	52.83	4	52.05	10	54.04	2
厦门市	57.57	2	3	52.82	5	53.00	3	52.30	9
宁波市	57.24	3	5	52.63	8	52.17	7	52.51	7
海口市	57.09	4	12	51.83	16	51.80	11	50.05	23
昆明市	57.03	5	29	49.63	34	48.73	33	48.72	32
合肥市	56.85	6	6	51.94	12	52.34	5	53.20	5
南京市	56.70	7	13	51.43	20	51.70	12	50.75	16
长春市	56.60	8	-6	52.88	2	52.34	4	54.51	1
哈尔滨市	56.59	9	13	51.05	22	49.79	29	48.78	31
上海市	55.74	10	1	51.94	11	50.53	20	50.24	20
济南市	55.73	11	-2	52.57	9	53.68	1	53.78	4
大连市	55.49	12	14	50.61	26	50.10	26	50.37	18
成都市	55.46	13	-3	52.14	10	51.40	13	52.13	12
南昌市	55.41	14	7	51.31	21	50.35	23	48.41	33

续表

城 市	2015年			2014年		2013年		2012年	
	得分	排序	上升位次	得分	排序	得分	排序	得分	排序
沈阳市	55.40	15	-12	52.85	3	51.25	16	49.73	26
武汉市	55.34	16	12	50.45	28	49.07	32	49.95	24
重庆市	55.26	17	-10	52.69	7	51.01	19	52.28	11
南宁市	55.24	18	14	50.00	32	49.81	28	49.60	27
青岛市	55.18	19	-18	53.06	1	53.05	2	52.31	8
郑州市	55.03	20	10	50.25	30	51.28	15	50.76	15
广州市	55.00	21	10	50.05	31	49.21	31	49.74	25
石家庄市	54.95	22	-4	51.75	18	52.17	8	53.86	3
福州市	54.92	23	-9	51.90	14	52.06	9	52.60	6
长沙市	54.89	24	5	50.37	29	50.15	25	50.29	19
西宁市	54.72	25	-12	51.94	13	52.21	6	51.57	14
西安市	54.65	26	1	50.58	27	51.16	17	50.40	17
呼和浩特市	54.64	27	-2	50.62	25	50.37	22	50.14	22
北京市	54.49	28	-11	51.78	17	50.16	24	49.47	28
乌鲁木齐市	54.48	29	-5	50.76	24	50.38	21	50.23	21
天津市	54.22	30	-24	52.81	6	51.35	14	52.07	13
深圳市	54.06	31	4	49.51	35	48.68	34	49.16	30
银川市	53.81	32	-17	51.90	15	51.07	18	52.29	10
贵阳市	53.77	33	0	49.94	33	49.58	30	47.33	35
太原市	53.32	34	-11	50.90	23	49.9	27	49.38	29
兰州市	53.30	35	-16	51.50	19	48.57	35	47.95	34
平均值		55.38			51.57		50.87		50.88

表1显示，2015年，全国35个城市生活质量主观满意度指数加权平均值为55.38，与前面几次调查的平均值相比有了一定幅度的提

高，保持在满意区间内。但由于满意区间的答案赋值为 50~75，因此仍处于基本满意的水平。35 个城市生活质量满意度指数得分全部超过50。尽管仍旧没有得分超过 60 的城市，但是最高得分比 2014 年有所提高，排名第 1 的杭州市得分为 57.58，高于 2014 年排名第 1 的青岛市的得分。整体上看，城市生活质量满意度指数自 2012 年以来稳中上升。图 1 的直方图很好地描述了城市生活质量主观满意度指数的变化趋势。

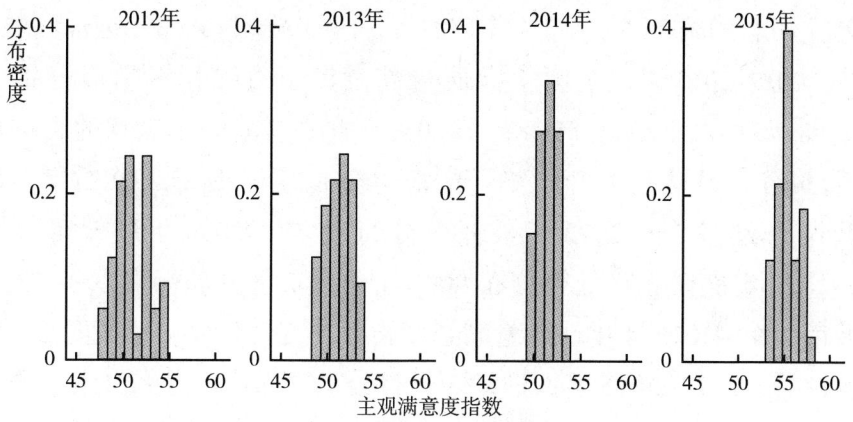

图1　2012~2015 年主观满意度指数

调查显示，生活质量主观满意度指数排名前 10 位的城市为：杭州市（1）、厦门市（2）、宁波市（3）、海口市（4）、昆明市（5）、合肥市（6）、南京市（7）、长春市（8）、哈尔滨市（9）、上海市（10）。其中，2012 年以来连续 4 年排名前 10 位的城市有杭州市、厦门市、宁波市、长春市；2012 年以来首次进入前 10 名的城市有海口市、昆明市、南京市、哈尔滨市；2015 年被挤出前 10 名的城市有济南市、成都市、沈阳市、重庆市、青岛市。

排名后 10 位的城市分别是：西安市（26）、呼和浩特市（27）、北京市（28）、乌鲁木齐市（29）、天津市（30）、深圳市（31）、银川市（32）、贵阳市（33）、太原市（34）、兰州市（35）。深圳市、贵阳市已经连续4年排名后10位；4年以来首次落入后10名的城市有乌鲁木齐市、天津市、银川市。2012~2015年，北京市的生活质量满意度排名分别为28、24、17、28。昆明市在2014年排名后10位，在2015年一跃进入前10名。大连市、武汉市、南宁市、郑州市、广州市、长沙市也都进入了排名12~24的行列。

从地区分布来看，生活质量满意度指数排名前10位的城市中，有6个东部城市、3个中部城市、1个西部城市；生活质量满意度指数排名后10位的城市中，有3个东部城市、1个中部城市、6个西部城市。

2012~2015年，全国生活质量满意度指数加权平均值分别为50.88、50.87、51.57、55.38，于2013年越过满意与不满意的临界点后，4年中总体呈上升趋势。最低得分也逐渐提高，2012年，最低得分为47.33，2013年最低得分为48.57，2014年最低得分为49.51，本次调查最低得分在50以上。图2的柱状图显示了35个城市2012~2015年生活质量满意度指数的变动情况。根据图2，分城市看，2012~2015年，连续3年得分上升的城市有海口市、哈尔滨市、上海市、南昌市、沈阳市、南宁市、青岛市、呼和浩特市、北京市、乌鲁木齐市、贵阳市、太原市、兰州市、昆明市14个城市，占三分之一强。

与2014年相比，排名上升幅度较大的城市有：昆明市（29）、大连市（14）、南宁市（14）、南京市（13）、哈尔滨市（13）、海口市（12）、武汉市（12）、郑州市（10）、广州市（10）；排名下降比较明显的城市有：天津市（-24）、青岛市（-18）、银川市（-17）、兰州市（-16）、沈阳市（-12）、西宁市（-12）、北京市（-11）、太原市（-11）、重庆市（-10）[①]。

[①] 括号中的数据是城市排名上升或下降的位次。

2015年中国35个城市生活质量指数

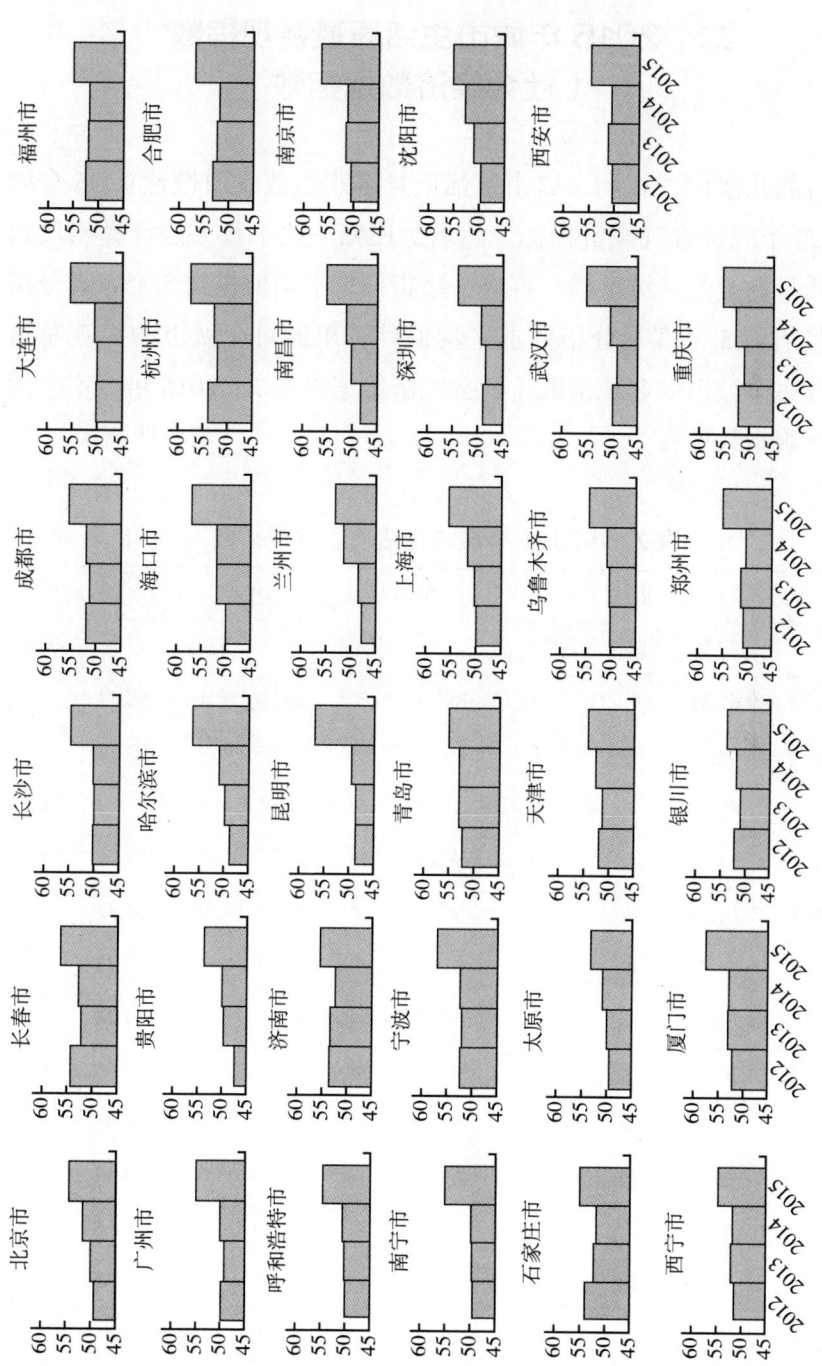

图 2 2012~2015 年 35 个城市主观满意度指数(纵轴为得分)

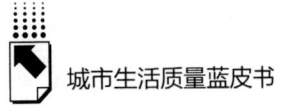
城市生活质量蓝皮书

二 2015年城市生活质量客观指数 （社会经济数据指数）

与前几次调查相同，城市生活质量客观指数是通过计算35个城市的20个二级客观经济指标，然后运用归一化平权方法计算出反映生活质量的8个一级指标，再将一级指标求平均值得到5个客观分指数，最后将5个客观分指数求平均值计算出的每个城市的客观总指数，即每个城市的客观指数（社会经济数据指数）。2015年城市生活质量客观指数见表2。

表2 中国35个城市生活质量客观指数

城 市	2015年			2014年		2013年		2012年	
	得分	排序	上升位次	得分	排序	得分	排序	得分	排序
北京市	67.41	1	0	68.78	1	69.80	1	68.72	1
南京市	63.37	2	1	65.52	3	66.65	3	62.38	5
西安市	62.39	3	2	61.61	5	64.65	4	61.59	6
杭州市	61.70	4	9	59.49	13	59.54	12	59.09	8
广州市	61.08	5	-3	66.39	2	66.85	2	64.87	2
上海市	59.95	6	1	61.30	7	61.78	8	62.72	4
深圳市	59.87	7	-3	63.25	4	63.93	5	64.24	3
昆明市	59.69	8	2	60.61	10	58.05	15	54.08	14
武汉市	58.87	9	3	60.33	12	58.93	13	56.61	10
长沙市	58.48	10	4	59.15	14	58.36	14	53.53	16
呼和浩特市	58.16	11	-2	60.99	9	62.22	7	59.55	7
沈阳市	57.22	12	-1	60.41	11	59.99	10	56.59	11
银川市	57.19	13	4	56.77	17	57.68	16	52.45	18

续表

城　市	2015年			2014年		2013年		2012年	
	得分	排序	上升位次	得分	排序	得分	排序	得分	排序
贵阳市	56.92	14	4	56.46	18	52.45	29	50.98	25
宁波市	55.70	15	−7	61.11	8	61.47	9	55.21	12
长春市	55.22	16	−1	57.63	15	59.64	11	52.29	19
青岛市	55.03	17	4	55.87	21	54.76	25	54.05	15
大连市	54.38	18	1	56.15	19	55.64	20	52.00	21
厦门市	54.32	19	−13	61.58	6	61.89	7	58.86	9
石家庄市	54.00	20	5	54.44	25	54.78	24	50.49	28
乌鲁木齐市	53.53	21	5	54.42	26	54.59	26	49.73	32
成都市	53.35	22	1	54.89	23	55.96	19	51.15	24
南昌市	52.88	23	9	51.29	32	53.03	27	49.03	34
济南市	52.72	24	−4	56.10	20	56.84	17	53.22	17
合肥市	52.69	25	−9	56.83	16	56.73	18	50.92	26
太原市	52.15	26	5	51.62	31	55.45	21	52.15	20
福州市	51.55	27	0	53.96	27	52.66	28	51.37	22
哈尔滨市	51.45	28	0	53.80	28	51.86	30	50.44	29
海口市	51.28	29	0	53.72	29	51.50	31	51.17	23
天津市	51.25	30	−8	55.48	22	55.42	22	54.30	13
兰州市	51.22	31	−7	54.79	24	55.22	23	50.08	31
南宁市	49.79	32	−2	52.93	30	50.00	33	50.69	27
西宁市	49.08	33	1	50.15	34	49.29	34	45.21	35
郑州市	48.68	34	1	48.39	35	50.54	32	50.26	30
重庆市	47.93	35	−2	51.04	33	47.83	35	49.40	33
平均值		55.84			57.87		57.75		54.56

从表2可以看出，2015年，全国35个监测城市生活质量客观指数综合值的均值为55.84。从动态的角度观察，平均值在2013年较2012年有较大幅度的上升，2014年保持相对稳定，2015年首次小幅回落，生活质量客观指数下降了2.03，但仍旧保持在满意区间。

中国35个城市生活质量客观指数的计算结果显示，生活质量客观指数排名前10位的城市为：北京市（1）、南京市（2）、西安市（3）、杭州市（4）、广州市（5）、上海市（6）、深圳市（7）、昆明市（8）、武汉市（9）、长沙市（10）。排名第1的北京市2015年得分为67.41，仍没有超过70。2012年以来长沙市首次进入前10名，呼和浩特市首次被挤出前10名，但变化不大，排名第11位。

城市生活质量客观指数排名后10位的城市是：太原市（26）、福州市（27）、哈尔滨市（28）、海口市（29）、天津市（30）、兰州市（31）、南宁市（32）、西宁市（33）、郑州市（34）、重庆市（35）。天津市自2012年以来首次落入后10名，兰州市自2013年以来首次落入后10名。另外，中国35个城市生活质量客观指数得分2014年只有郑州市低于50，2015年除郑州市得分继续低于50外，又增加了南宁市、西宁市和重庆市，得分最低的是重庆市（47.93）。2012年以来，在35个城市中，重庆市始终处于后3名的位置。根据QLICC体系的答案赋值标准，生活质量客观指数得分低于临界点50就意味着进入了不满意区间，即从客观指标的计算来看，这4个城市的生活质量是令人不满意的。

从地区分布来看，城市生活质量客观指数排名前10位的城市中，东部城市、中部城市以及西部城市的比例为6:2:2。城市居民生活质量客观指数排名后10位的城市中，东部城市、中部城市以及西部城市的比例为3:3:4。这表明生活质量在地域分布上有明显的差异。可以看出，东部城市的生活质量客观数据普遍高于中西部城市。图3的直方图展现了2012~2015年城市生活质量客观指数的变化趋势。

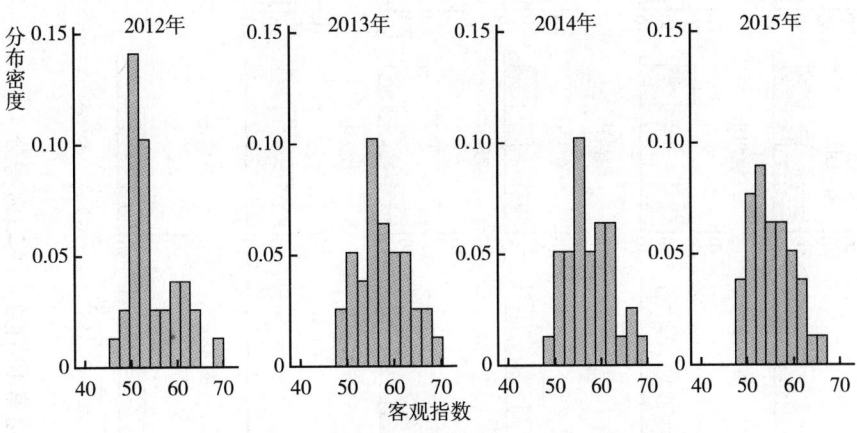

图3　2012~2015年城市生活质量客观指数

图4中的柱状图描述了35个城市2012~2015年生活质量客观指数的变化情况。根据图4，分城市看，在35个城市中，2013~2015年生活质量客观指数连续2年呈现持续小幅下降的城市有北京市、南京市、广州市、上海市、深圳市、呼和浩特市、宁波市、长春市、厦门市、石家庄市、乌鲁木齐市、成都市、济南市、兰州市，占三分之一强。值得注意的是，在经济持续下行的背景下，贵阳市生活质量客观指数保持了3年的连续增长，杭州市4年来稳中有升。

从排名顺序的变化看，杭州市与和南昌市位次上升最明显，杭州市从2014年的第13名上升到2015年的第4名，上升9位；南昌市从2014年的第32名上升到2015年的第23名，同样上升9位。厦门市下降最为明显，由2014年的第6名下降到2015年的第19名，下降了13位。排名下降比较明显的城市还有：合肥市（-9）、天津市（-8）、宁波市（-7）、兰州市（-7）。

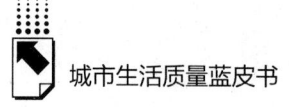

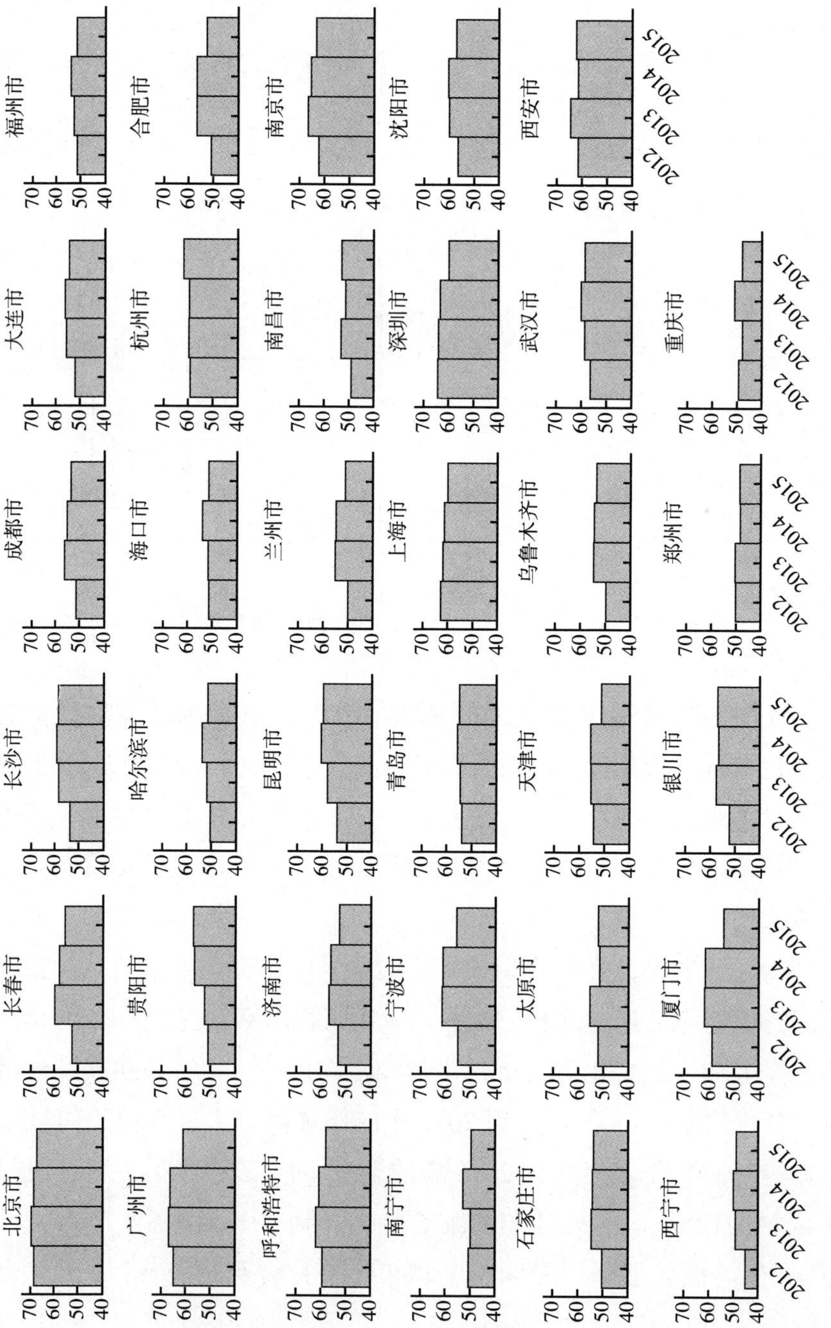

图 4 2012~2015 年 35 个城市生活质量客观指数（纵轴为得分）

B.5
中国35个城市生活质量的细分指数

35个城市生活质量主观满意度指数和客观指数（社会经济数据指数）的得分高低及排序情况，均可以从各自的细分指数中得到解释[1]。本报告将把描述城市生活质量的主观满意度指数和客观指数的各个细分指数进行对比分析。

一 生活水平指数

生活水平指数包括生活水平的主观满意度指数和客观指数（社会经济数据指数）。前者是根据电话调查并结合答案赋值得到的，包括对收入现状和收入预期的调查及其对调查结果的答案赋值；后者是由35个城市的社会经济指标，包括收入水平、生活改善指数两个一级指标及其所属的6个二级指标计算得出的，不存在任何主观色彩。

（一）生活水平满意度指数

表1列出了2012~2015年35个城市生活水平满意度指数和排序情况。

---

[1] 与前面几次调查一样，支撑35个城市生活质量总指数的细分指数包括生活水平指数、生活成本指数、人力资本指数、社会保障指数和生活感受指数。每个细分指数都包括主观满意度指数和客观指数（社会经济数据指数）。

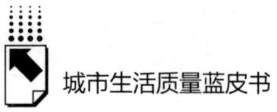

表1 中国35个城市生活水平满意度指数

城　市	2015年			2014年		2013年		2012年	
	得分	排序	上升位次	得分	排序	得分	排序	得分	排序
宁波市	63.16	1	11	54.58	12	54.62	6	52.77	8
海口市	62.78	2	2	56.03	4	56.46	1	54.75	3
昆明市	62.28	3	20	52.91	23	52.84	17	52.32	11
合肥市	62.27	4	13	53.99	17	54.14	9	55.76	2
厦门市	62.26	5	0	55.78	5	55.69	3	52.18	13
杭州市	62.04	6	4	54.97	10	54.10	10	56.49	1
长春市	61.64	7	0	55.32	7	53.07	16	53.74	5
哈尔滨市	61.31	8	19	52.27	27	49.86	33	48.89	30
广州市	61.09	9	16	52.77	25	52.32	20	50.97	21
青岛市	60.97	10	-4	55.37	6	55.81	2	52.59	10
南京市	60.65	11	15	52.69	26	52.34	19	49.23	29
北京市	60.43	12	-11	58.68	1	52.19	22	50.37	23
深圳市	60.41	13	7	53.49	20	51.65	26	52.08	14
长沙市	60.31	14	-1	54.53	13	53.44	14	50.29	25
乌鲁木齐市	60.29	15	-4	54.90	11	54.10	11	50.99	20
银川市	60.29	16	13	52.16	29	51.10	29	49.74	27
济南市	60.27	17	-1	54.28	16	54.29	8	51.43	17
上海市	60.16	18	-15	56.60	3	52.59	18	51.65	15
武汉市	60.07	19	3	53.25	22	50.39	31	49.95	26
西宁市	60.04	20	10	51.99	30	55.00	4	52.31	12
南昌市	60.00	21	0	53.48	21	52.18	23	48.27	32
成都市	59.91	22	-14	55.02	8	53.30	15	51.39	18
福州市	59.76	23	-8	54.40	15	54.64	5	53.76	4
大连市	59.74	24	0	52.84	24	50.28	32	50.69	22
太原市	59.25	25	7	51.84	32	50.42	30	48.27	33
郑州市	59.08	26	9	50.98	35	48.00	35	52.86	7
重庆市	59.00	27	-25	56.63	2	52.11	24	52.64	9
西安市	58.94	28	0	52.26	28	53.88	12	48.79	31
沈阳市	58.89	29	-11	53.65	18	51.54	27	46.95	34
南宁市	58.58	30	1	51.89	31	51.48	28	51.47	16
石家庄市	58.46	31	2	51.69	33	51.79	25	53.38	6
呼和浩特市	58.14	32	-18	54.43	14	54.31	7	50.36	24

续表

城市	2015年			2014年		2013年		2012年	
	得分	排序	上升位次	得分	排序	得分	排序	得分	排序
兰州市	58.04	33	1	51.42	34	49.72	34	46.88	35
天津市	57.89	34	−25	54.98	9	52.24	21	51.27	19
贵阳市	57.58	35	−16	53.61	19	53.74	13	49.40	28
平均值	60.07			54.32		52.51		51.28	

表1显示，2015年，全国35个城市的生活水平满意度指数加权平均值为60.07，从这几年的调查结果来看，呈逐年上升的趋势，虽然超过了60，但仍位于满意区间，距离对收入现状和收入预期很满意或很乐观区间（76~100）还有很大距离。35个城市生活水平满意度指数均超过满意与不满意区间的临界点（50），且有21个城市的得分超过60，所有城市的得分都比上一年有了较大幅度的提高，排名第1的是宁波市，得分为63.16，高于2014年得分最高的北京市。整体上看，城市生活水平满意度指数逐年稳步上升。图1的直方图很好地展现了这一上升趋势。

调查显示，生活水平满意度指数排名前10位的城市为：宁波市（1）、海口市（2）、昆明市（3）、合肥市（4）、厦门市（5）、杭州市（6）、长春市（7）、哈尔滨市（8）、广州市（9）、青岛市（10）。

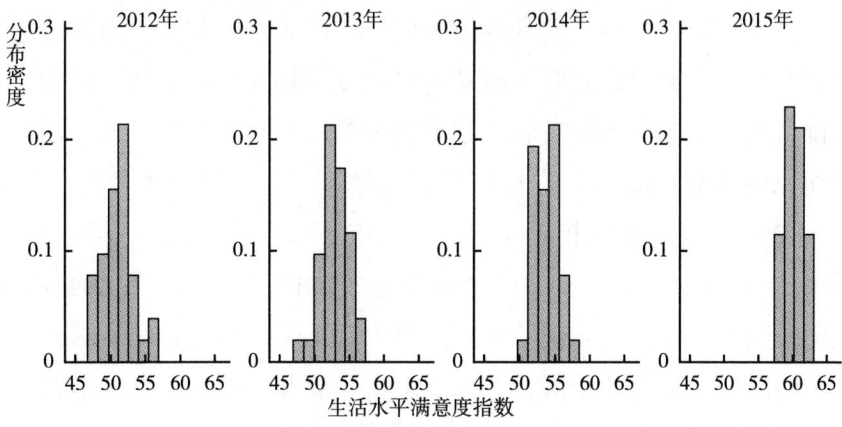

图1　2012~2015年生活水平满意度指数

排名后10位的城市分别是：郑州市（26）、重庆市（27）、西安市（28）、沈阳市（29）、南宁市（30）、石家庄市（31）、呼和浩特市（32）、兰州市（33）、天津市（34）、贵阳市（35）。

从地区来看，城市生活水平满意度指数排名前10位的城市中，有6个东部城市、3个中部城市、1个西部城市；排名后10位的城市中，有3个东部城市、1个中部城市、6个西部城市。

2012~2015年，全国35个城市生活水平满意度指数加权平均值分别为51.28、52.51、54.32、60.07，4年都在满意区间内，且满意度总体呈上升趋势，最低分也逐年增加。2012年，得分最低的城市为兰州，得分为46.88；2013年，得分最低的城市为郑州，得分为48；2014年，郑州依然得分最低，得分为50.98；而2015年得分最低的城市是贵阳，得分为57.58。图2的柱状图描述了35个城市2012~2015年城市生活水平满意度指数的变化情况。分城市看，连续3年得分均上升的城市有昆明市、厦门市、哈尔滨市、广州市、南京市、北京市、长沙市、乌鲁木齐市、银川市、上海市、武汉市、南昌市、成都市、太原市、沈阳市、南宁市、呼和浩特市、兰州市、天津市19个城市，占所有调查城市的54.3%。

排名上升比较明显的城市有：昆明市（20）、哈尔滨市（19）、广州市（16）、南京市（15）、合肥市（13）、银川市（13）、宁波市（11）、西宁市（10）。上升的原因因城市而异：哈尔滨、南京、银川排名上升是因为居民对收入现状的满意度大幅上升；宁波、昆明、合肥排名上升是因为居民对收入预期的乐观度大幅上升；广州、西宁两方面原因皆有。排名下降比较明显的城市有：天津市（-25）、重庆市（-25）、呼和浩特市（-18）、贵阳市（-16）、上海市（-15）、成都市（-14）、北京市（-11）、沈阳市（-11）。下降原因因城而异，沈阳是因为居民对收入现状的满意度大幅下降；贵阳是因为居民对收入预期的乐观度大幅下降；北京、上海、成都、重庆、呼和浩特、天津两方面原因皆有。

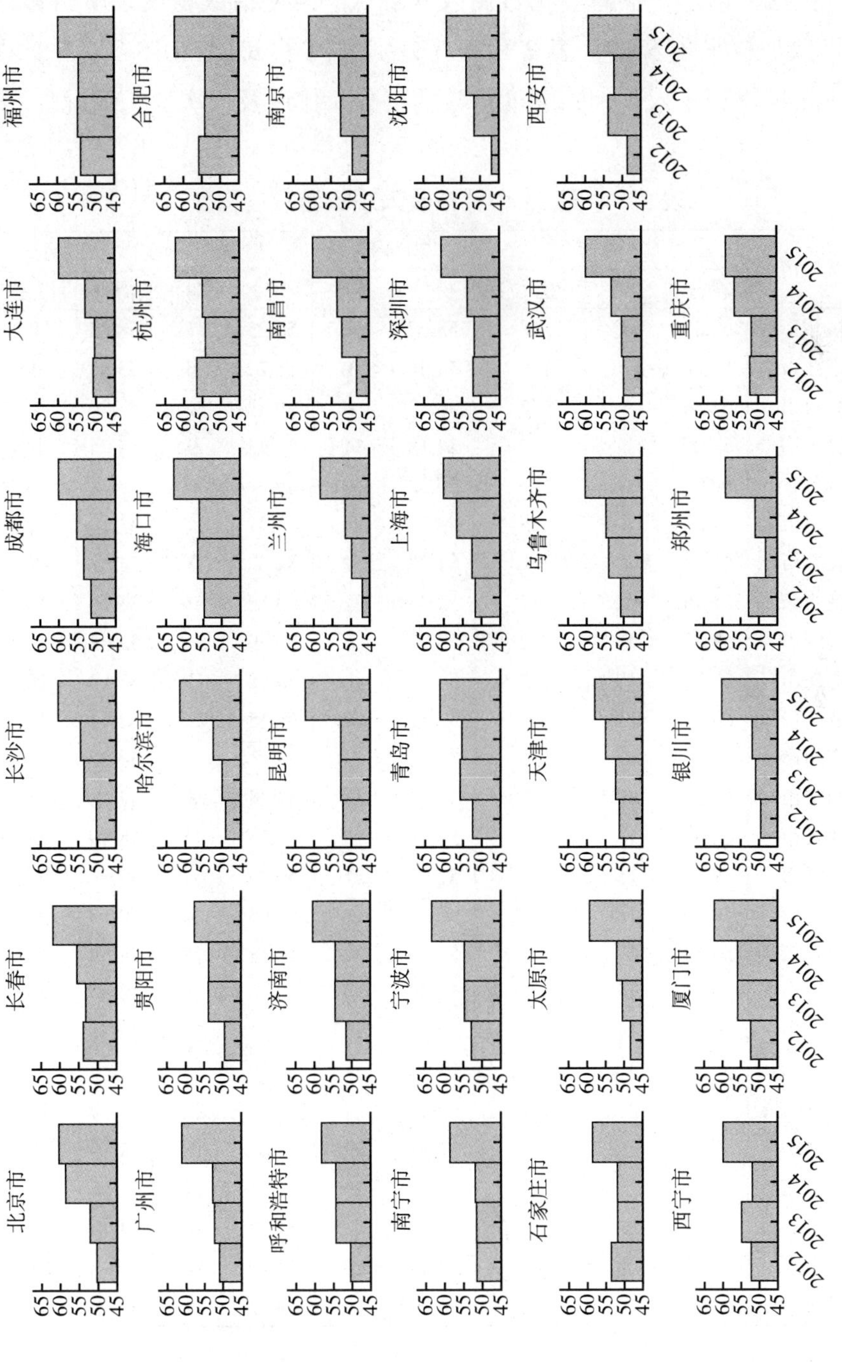

中国35个城市生活质量的细分指数

图 2 2012~2015 年 35 个城市生活水平满意度指数（纵轴为得分）

上述生活水平满意度指数由收入现状满意度指数和收入预期满意度指数加权平均获得，表2和表3分别列出了2012~2015年35个城市收入现状和收入预期满意度指数的得分、排序及位次变化情况。

表2　中国35个城市收入现状满意度指数

城　市	2015年			2014年		2013年		2012年	
	得分	排序	上升位次	得分	排序	得分	排序	得分	排序
杭州市	63.38	1	3	55.67	4	56.25	5	58.25	1
宁波市	63.28	2	8	54.58	10	55.21	6	53.65	6
海口市	62.86	3	−2	56.83	1	56.87	1	57.50	2
合肥市	62.09	4	7	54.15	11	54.42	9	55.04	3
哈尔滨市	62.09	5	25	50.52	30	49.33	32	47.78	33
银川市	61.65	6	28	49.28	34	51.37	26	53.13	11
长春市	61.49	7	5	54.12	12	54.52	7	54.01	5
昆明市	61.05	8	14	52.05	22	53.17	16	51.76	16
厦门市	60.83	9	−2	54.92	7	56.39	3	52.03	15
青岛市	60.77	10	−2	54.85	8	56.58	2	53.18	10
济南市	60.72	11	8	52.52	19	54.15	11	52.11	14
广州市	60.65	12	13	51.20	25	52.94	17	50.57	21
西宁市	60.57	13	5	52.72	18	54.44	8	52.78	13
西安市	60.07	14	15	50.73	29	53.25	15	48.30	28
武汉市	59.80	15	6	52.17	21	50.39	31	49.68	25
北京市	59.80	16	−14	56.56	2	51.65	24	50.10	22
南昌市	59.68	17	7	51.49	24	51.18	28	48.58	26
大连市	59.68	18	5	51.86	23	50.46	30	49.69	24
太原市	59.55	19	9	50.78	28	48.32	35	48.51	27
上海市	59.54	20	−14	55.33	6	52.60	19	51.43	17
深圳市	59.37	21	6	50.98	27	51.12	29	51.39	18
长沙市	59.37	22	−5	52.83	17	52.62	18	48.10	30
郑州市	59.08	23	10	49.44	33	48.42	34	53.10	12
乌鲁木齐市	59.08	24	−21	55.92	3	54.38	10	53.29	9
南京市	59.01	25	−5	52.46	20	53.42	14	48.08	31
成都市	58.99	26	−12	53.39	14	53.82	12	50.88	19

续表

城 市	2015年			2014年		2013年		2012年	
	得分	排序	上升位次	得分	排序	得分	排序	得分	排序
福州市	58.90	27	-11	53.00	16	56.39	4	54.19	4
重庆市	58.57	28	-23	55.58	5	51.38	25	53.45	7
南宁市	58.45	29	2	50.05	31	51.20	27	50.00	23
沈阳市	58.12	30	-17	53.40	13	51.75	23	46.57	34
天津市	57.34	31	-22	54.67	9	52.15	20	50.79	20
石家庄市	57.22	32	0	49.95	32	51.85	22	53.43	8
呼和浩特市	56.89	33	-18	53.13	15	53.80	13	48.21	29
贵阳市	56.33	34	-8	51.17	26	51.98	21	47.86	32
兰州市	56.12	35	0	49.03	35	48.87	33	44.60	35
平均值	59.65			52.92		52.54		51.52	

表2显示，2015年，全国35个城市的收入现状满意度指数加权平均值为59.65，与前几年的调查结果相比呈逐年上升的趋势，仍位于满意区间。35个城市收入现状满意度得分均超过50，且有14个城市的得分超过60，所有城市得分都比上一年有了较大幅度的提高，排名第1的是杭州市，得分为63.38，高于2014年得分最高的海口市。整体上看，城市收入现状满意度指数逐年稳步上升。图3的直方图展现了这一上升趋势。

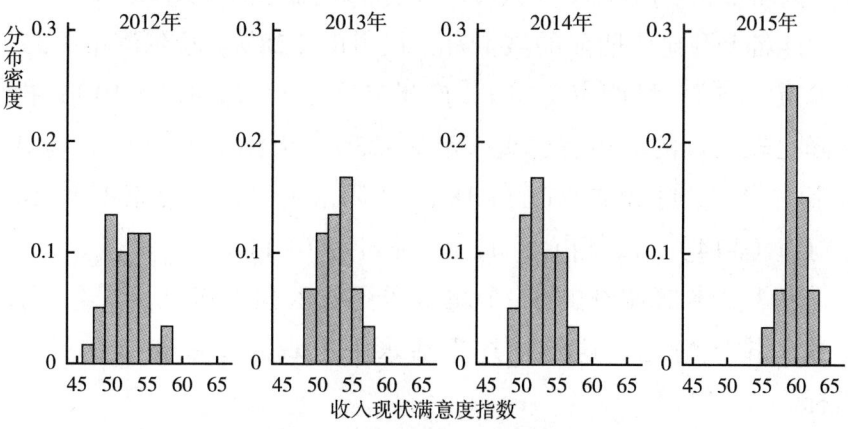

图3　2012~2015年收入现状满意度指数

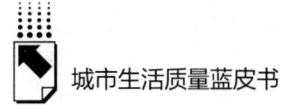

调查显示，城市收入现状满意度指数排名前10位的城市为：杭州市（1）、宁波市（2）、海口市（3）、合肥市（4）、哈尔滨市（5）、银川市（6）、长春市（7）、昆明市（8）、厦门市（9）、青岛市（10）。排名后10位的城市分别是：成都市（26）、福州市（27）、重庆市（28）、南宁市（29）、沈阳市（30）、天津市（31）、石家庄市（32）、呼和浩特市（33）、贵阳市（34）、兰州市（35）。

从地区来看，城市收入现状满意度指数排名前10位的城市中，有5个东部城市、3个中部城市、2个西部城市；排名后10位的城市中，有4个东部城市、6个西部城市，没有中部城市。

从动态变化看，2012~2015年，全国35个城市收入现状满意度指数加权平均值分别为51.52、52.54、52.92、59.65，4年都在满意区间内，且满意度总体上呈上升趋势。最低分也逐年增加；2012年，最低得分为44.60；2013年，最低得分为48.32；2014年，最低得分为49.03；本次调查最低得分为56.12。图4的柱状图直观地展示了2012~2015年35个城市收入现状满意度指数的变化情况。分城市看，连续3年得分均上升的城市有哈尔滨市、武汉市、北京市、南昌市、大连市、上海市、长沙市、乌鲁木齐市、沈阳市、天津市、兰州市11个城市，占全部调查城市的31.4%。

排名上升比较明显的城市有：银川市（28）、哈尔滨市（25）、西安市（15）、昆明市（14）、广州市（13）、郑州市（10）；排名下降比较明显的城市有：重庆市（-23）、天津市（-22）、乌鲁木齐市（-21）、呼和浩特市（-18）、沈阳市（-17）、北京市（-14）、上海市（-14）、成都市（-12）、福州市（-11）。

表3是本次调查的35个城市居民收入预期满意度（乐观度）指数和排序情况，这是描述生活水平主观满意度指数的另一个指标。

中国 35 个城市生活质量的细分指数

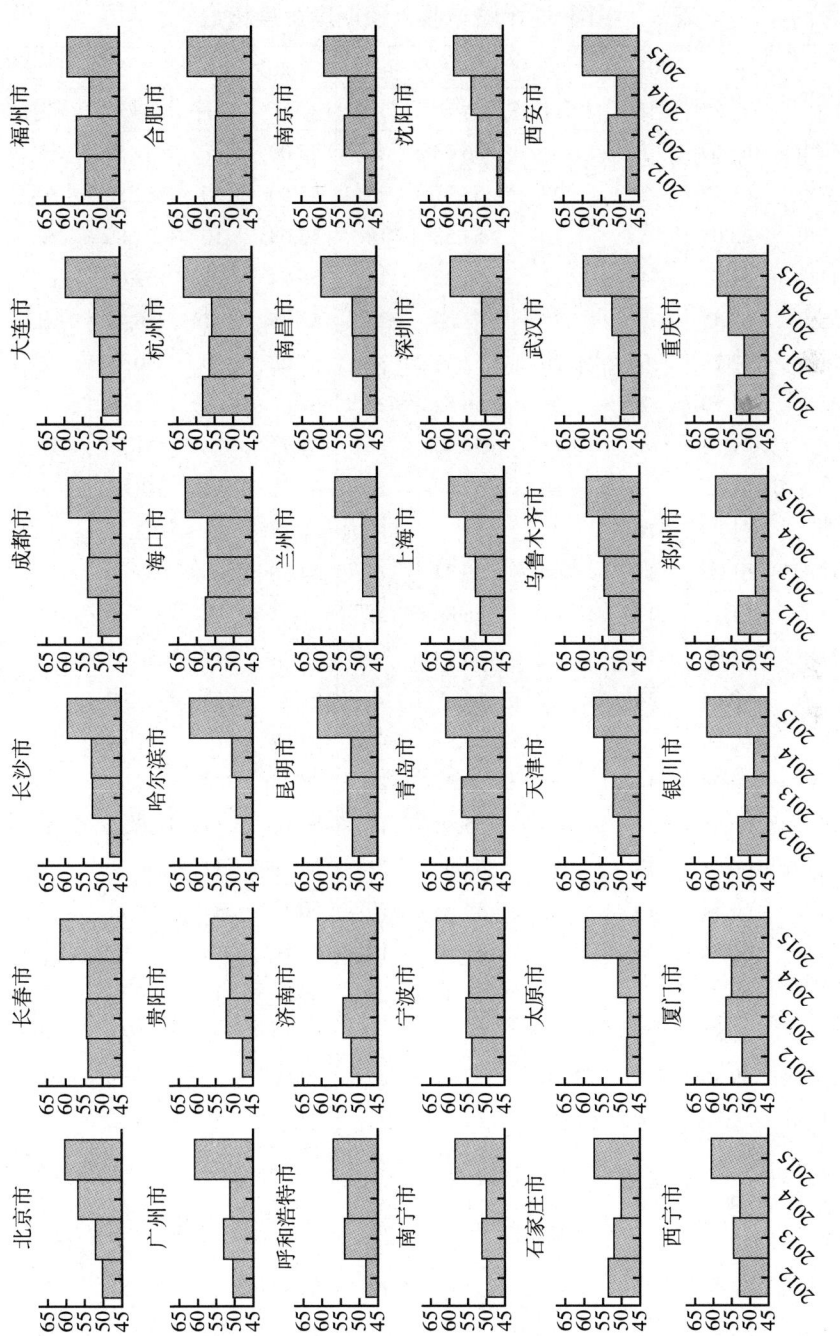

图 4 2012~2015 年 35 个城市收入现状满意度指数（纵轴为得分）

表 3　中国 35 个城市收入预期满意度指数

城　市	2015 年			2014 年		2013 年		2012 年	
	得分	排序	上升位次	得分	排序	得分	排序	得分	排序
厦门市	63.69	1	4	56.63	5	55.00	5	52.33	12
昆明市	63.52	2	27	53.77	29	52.50	20	52.88	7
宁波市	63.03	3	15	54.58	18	54.03	10	51.89	16
海口市	62.70	4	12	55.22	16	56.04	1	52.00	14
合肥市	62.45	5	20	53.83	25	53.85	11	56.47	1
南京市	62.28	6	26	52.91	32	51.26	29	50.38	26
长春市	61.80	7	-1	56.52	6	51.62	27	53.48	3
广州市	61.53	8	11	54.34	19	51.71	26	51.38	22
乌鲁木齐市	61.51	9	15	53.87	24	53.81	12	48.68	31
深圳市	61.46	10	0	55.99	10	52.18	22	52.78	8
长沙市	61.25	11	-4	56.23	7	54.26	9	52.49	11
青岛市	61.17	12	-1	55.89	11	55.04	4	52.00	13
北京市	61.05	13	-12	60.79	1	52.74	17	50.63	25
成都市	60.84	14	-10	56.65	4	52.78	16	51.90	15
上海市	60.79	15	-13	57.87	2	52.57	18	51.88	17
杭州市	60.69	16	5	54.27	21	51.94	23	54.72	2
福州市	60.61	17	-5	55.80	12	52.90	14	53.32	5
哈尔滨市	60.53	18	4	54.03	22	50.39	32	50.00	28
武汉市	60.34	19	1	54.33	20	50.39	33	50.21	27
南昌市	60.31	20	-6	55.46	14	53.18	13	47.97	33
兰州市	59.97	21	6	53.80	27	50.56	31	49.15	30
济南市	59.82	22	-13	56.04	9	54.43	8	50.75	24
大连市	59.80	23	3	53.81	26	50.09	34	51.69	21
石家庄市	59.70	24	7	53.43	31	51.74	25	53.33	4
沈阳市	59.67	25	-2	53.90	23	51.33	28	47.34	34
西宁市	59.51	26	9	51.27	35	55.56	2	51.85	18
重庆市	59.43	27	-24	57.67	3	52.84	15	51.82	19
呼和浩特市	59.40	28	-15	55.73	13	54.82	6	52.50	10
郑州市	59.08	29	5	52.51	34	47.58	35	52.62	9

续表

城 市	2015年			2014年		2013年		2012年	
	得分	排序	上升位次	得分	排序	得分	排序	得分	排序
太原市	58.95	30	3	52.90	33	52.51	19	48.02	32
银川市	58.93	31	-14	55.05	17	50.82	30	46.35	35
贵阳市	58.83	32	-24	56.05	8	55.51	3	50.95	23
南宁市	58.70	33	-3	53.72	30	51.76	24	52.93	6
天津市	58.45	34	-19	55.29	15	52.34	21	51.75	20
西安市	57.81	35	-7	53.79	28	54.50	7	49.27	29
平均值	60.50			55.50		52.48		51.36	

表3显示，2015年，全国35个城市的收入预期满意度指数加权平均值为60.50，与前几年的调查结果相比呈现逐年上升的趋势，仍位于满意区间。35个城市的收入预期满意度得分均超过50，且有20个城市的得分超过60，所有城市的得分都比上一年有所上升，排名第1的是厦门市，得分为63.69，高于2014年得分最高的北京市。整体上看，城市收入预期满意度指数逐年稳步上升。图5的直方图展现了这一上升趋势。

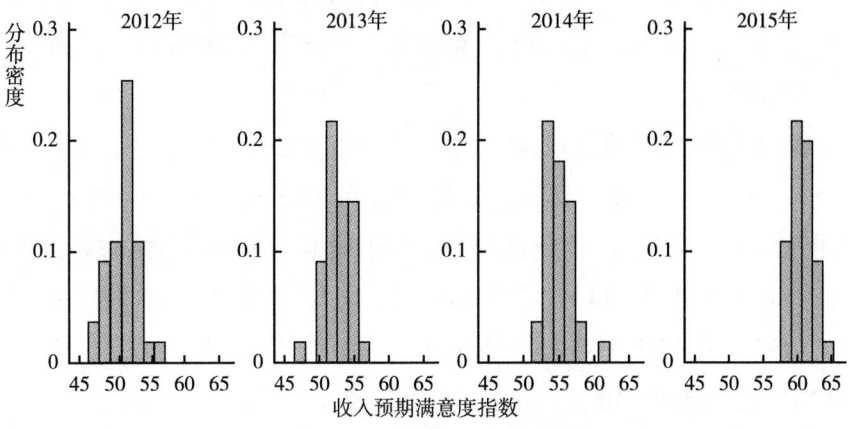

图5 2012~2015年收入预期满意度指数

调查显示，收入预期满意度指数排名前10位的城市为：厦门市（1）、昆明市（2）、宁波市（3）、海口市（4）、合肥市（5）、南京市（6）、长春市（7）、广州市（8）、乌鲁木齐市（9）、深圳市（10）。排名后10位的城市分别是：西宁市（26）、重庆市（27）、呼和浩特市（28）、郑州市（29）、太原市（30）、银川市（31）、贵阳市（32）、南宁市（33）、天津市（34）、西安市（35）。

从地区来看，城市收入预期满意度指数排名前10位的城市中，有6个东部城市、2个中部城市、2个西部城市；排名后10位的城市中，有1个东部城市、2个中部城市、7个西部城市。

从动态变化看，2012~2015年，全国35个城市收入预期满意度指数加权平均值分别为51.36、52.48、55.50、60.50，4年都在满意区间内，且满意度总体上呈上升趋势。最低分也逐渐增加；2012年，最低得分为46.35；2013年，最低得分为47.58；2014年，最低得分为51.27；本次调查最低得分为57.81。图6的柱状图给出了2012~2015年35个城市的收入预期满意度指数。根据图6，分城市看，连续3年得分均上升的城市有厦门市、宁波市、南京市、广州市、乌鲁木齐市、长沙市、青岛市、北京市、成都市、上海市、哈尔滨市、武汉市、南昌市、兰州市、济南市、沈阳市、重庆市、呼和浩特市、太原市、银川市、贵阳市、天津市22个城市，占所调查城市的62.9%。

排名上升比较明显的城市有：昆明市（27）、南京市（26）、合肥市（20）、宁波市（15）、乌鲁木齐市（15）、海口市（12）、广州市（11），并且这7个城市都名列前10位；排名下降比较明显的城市有：重庆市（-24）、贵阳市（-24）、天津市（-19）、呼和浩特市（-15）、银川市（-14）、上海市（-13）、济南市（-13）、北京市（-12）、成都市（-10）。

中国 35 个城市生活质量的细分指数

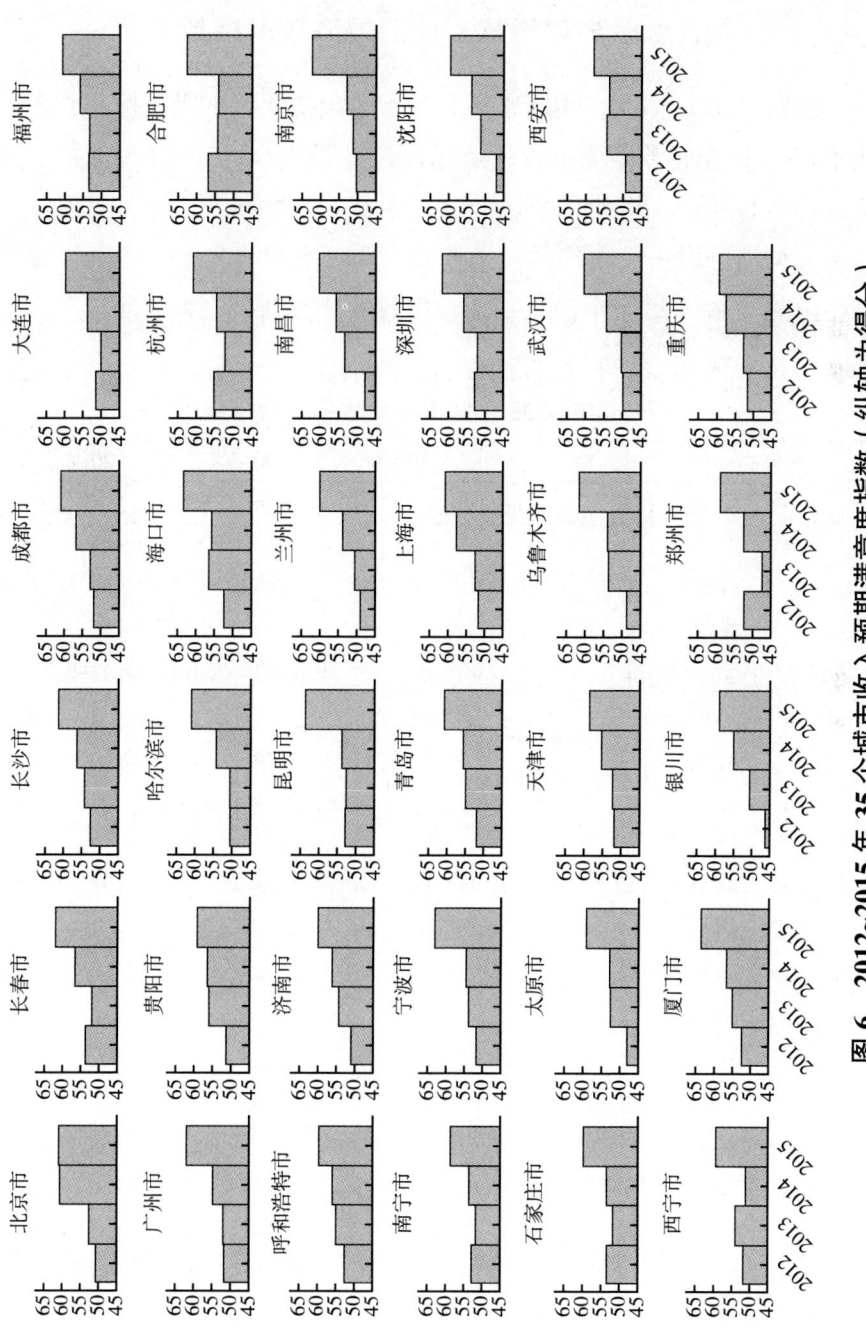

图 6 2012~2015 年 35 个城市收入预期满意度指数（纵轴为得分）

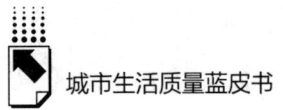

（二）生活水平客观指数（社会经济数据指数）

根据 QLICC 体系，生活水平客观指数包括两个一级指标和 6 个二级指标，生活水平客观指数就是通过计算 35 个城市的收入水平、生活改善指数两个一级指标所属的消费率、人均财富、人均可支配收入以及人均消费增长、人均财富增长、人均可支配收入增长 6 个二级指标得出的。35 个城市生活水平客观指数的计算结果如表 4 所示。

表 4　中国 35 个城市生活水平客观指数

城　市	2015 年			2014 年		2013 年		2012 年	
	得分	排序	上升位次	得分	排序	得分	排序	得分	排序
北京市	80.00	1	0	80.00	1	77.84	5	80.03	1
上海市	79.02	2	0	79.45	2	73.93	6	77.84	2
杭州市	76.42	3	7	72.60	10	73.83	7	76.79	3
长沙市	70.09	4	1	76.15	5	60.91	20	50.97	24
南京市	69.77	5	−1	77.90	4	80.00	1	66.33	6
成都市	62.62	6	7	71.21	13	72.13	10	58.80	11
西安市	62.55	7	13	64.90	20	78.59	4	56.07	15
宁波市	62.08	8	−1	75.54	7	72.47	8	68.70	5
青岛市	61.36	9	10	65.47	19	56.06	28	64.76	8
广州市	60.71	10	−4	75.76	6	70.24	11	72.14	4
贵阳市	60.58	11	15	62.79	26	49.09	32	47.86	27
厦门市	60.56	12	−9	79.43	3	79.22	2	52.40	23
武汉市	59.72	13	−1	71.82	12	60.51	22	50.81	25
深圳市	59.30	14	−6	75.18	8	78.91	3	64.78	7
乌鲁木齐市	59.11	15	9	63.78	24	58.61	26	47.54	28
南昌市	58.46	16	18	52.77	34	60.59	21	46.60	31
福州市	57.98	17	−2	67.16	15	61.51	17	60.75	9
长春市	57.86	18	−2	66.77	16	63.27	16	53.67	20
银川市	57.45	19	14	54.12	33	60.00	24	45.55	33

续表

城 市	2015年			2014年		2013年		2012年	
	得分	排序	上升位次	得分	排序	得分	排序	得分	排序
大连市	57.17	20	2	64.56	22	61.23	19	47.14	29
郑州市	56.44	21	11	57.00	32	61.40	18	56.11	14
合肥市	55.80	22	-13	74.09	9	67.04	14	55.75	17
天津市	55.56	23	-9	68.39	14	60.42	23	57.02	13
海口市	55.30	24	-1	64.21	23	69.40	12	59.80	10
济南市	55.16	25	-14	71.92	11	72.27	9	57.43	12
石家庄市	53.79	26	1	60.53	27	58.80	25	53.09	21
西宁市	53.61	27	1	59.10	28	54.92	30	40.00	35
昆明市	53.32	28	3	57.07	31	55.27	29	40.76	34
呼和浩特市	52.83	29	-11	65.87	18	68.67	13	55.87	16
沈阳市	52.73	30	-13	66.32	17	57.82	27	48.84	26
哈尔滨市	50.58	31	-6	63.60	25	49.04	33	55.47	18
兰州市	50.15	32	-11	64.84	21	65.59	15	46.30	32
南宁市	45.35	33	-4	59.04	29	41.04	34	52.98	22
重庆市	44.60	34	-4	58.86	30	40.00	35	53.90	19
太原市	40.00	35	0	40.00	35	52.32	31	46.87	30
平均值		59.83			68.06		56.28		59.83

从表4可以看出，2015年，全国35个城市的城市生活水平客观指数加权平均值为59.83，与前几年调查的结果相比，2015年的平均值与2012年持平，高于2013年，低于2014年。35个城市生活水平最低得分为40，最高得分为80，且有32个城市的得分超过50；与2014年相同，排名第1的依然是北京市。整体上看，城市生活水平客观指数近几年有升有降，上下波动。图7的直方图很好地展现了这种波动趋势。

表4显示，城市生活水平客观指数排名前10位的城市为：北京市（1）、上海市（2）、杭州市（3）、长沙市（4）、南京市（5）、成都市（6）、西安市（7）、宁波市（8）、青岛市（9）、广州市（10）。

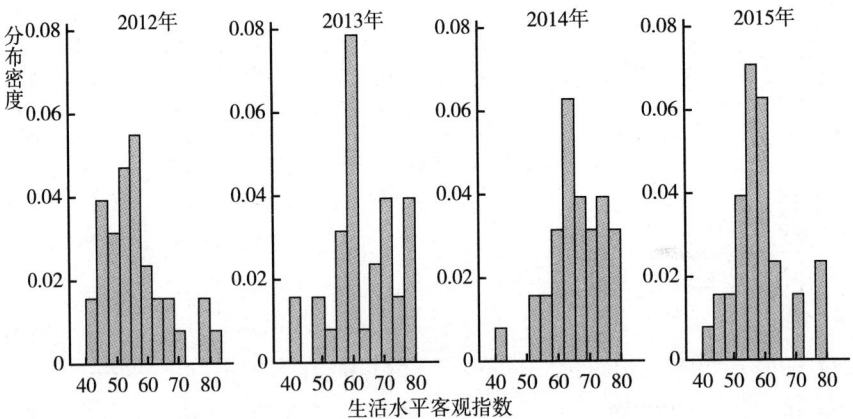

图7 2012~2015年生活水平客观指数

其中，北京市、上海市、杭州市、南京市、宁波市5个城市已经连续4年排名前10位。排名后10位的城市分别是：石家庄市（26）、西宁市（27）、昆明市（28）、呼和浩特市（29）、沈阳市（30）、哈尔滨市（31）、兰州市（32）、南宁市（33）、重庆市（34）、太原市（35）。西宁市、昆明市、太原市已经连续4年排名后10位。其中，南宁市、重庆市连续3年排名后10位。从地区来看，城市生活水平客观指数排名前10位的城市中，有7个东部城市、1个中部城市、2个西部城市；排名后10位的城市中，有2个东部城市、2个中部城市、6个西部城市。

从动态变化看，2012~2015年，全国35个城市生活水平客观指数加权平均值分别为59.83、56.28、68.06、59.83，总体上呈波动趋势。图8的柱状图描述了2012~2015年35个城市生活水平客观指数的变动情况。分城市看，所有城市的生活水平客观指数都呈现出一种波动状态，没有连续3年上升或者下降的城市。排名上升比较明显的城市有：南昌市（18）、贵阳市（15）、银川市（14）、西安市（13）、郑州市（11）、青岛市（10）；排名下降比较明显的城市有：济南市（-14）、合肥市（-13）、沈阳市（-13）、呼和浩特市（-11）、兰州市（-11）。

中国 35 个城市生活质量的细分指数

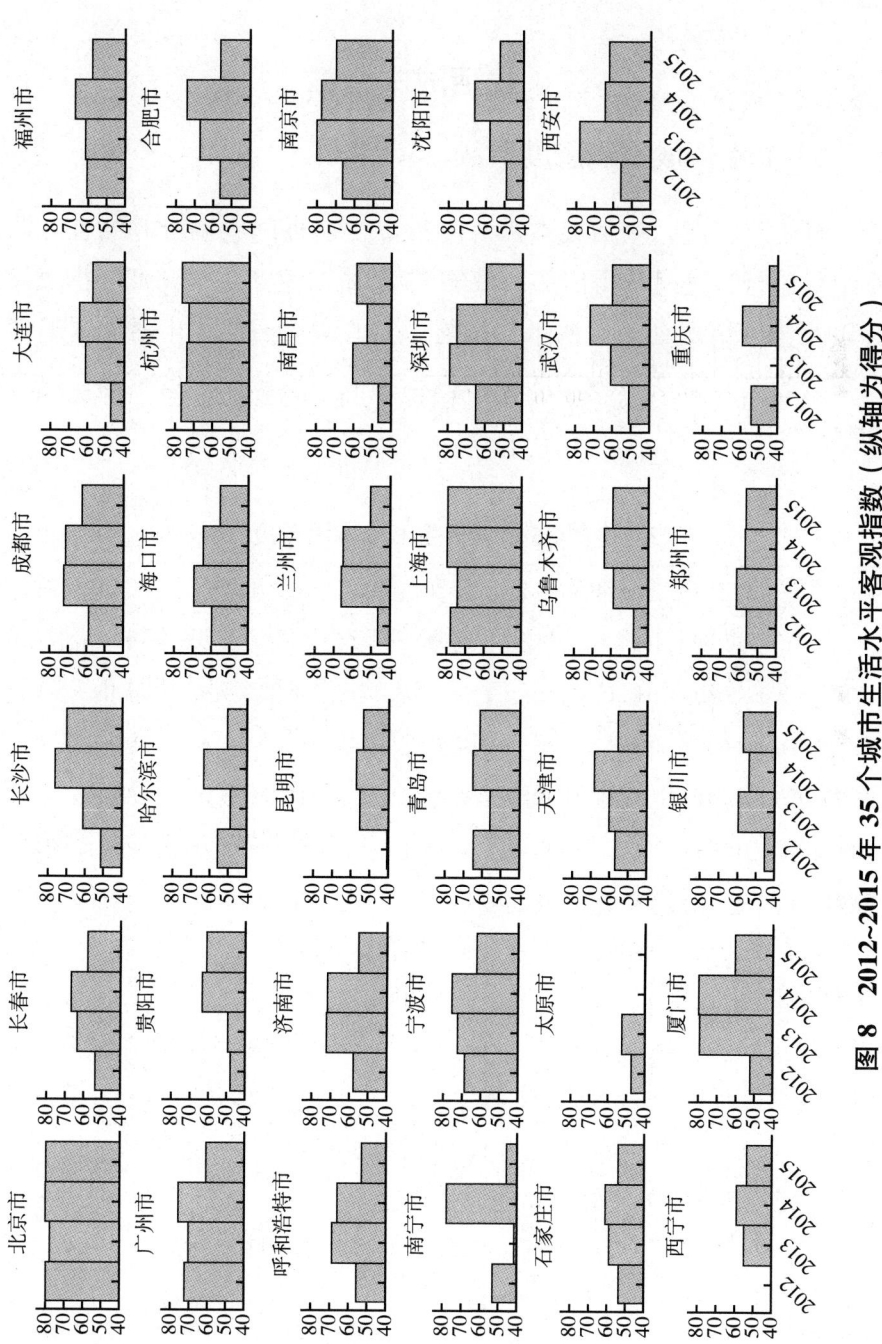

图 8　2012~2015 年 35 个城市生活水平客观指数（纵轴为得分）

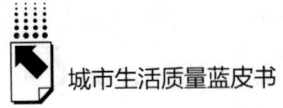

二 生活成本指数

（一）生活成本满意度指数

与往年相同，生活成本满意度指数是通过问卷调查并结合对调查结果进行答案赋值得出的。中国35个城市生活成本满意度指数得分以及排序情况如表5所示。与前3年的调查一样，生活成本满意度指数越高，说明该城市的生活成本越低，居民满意度越高；反之亦然。

表5　中国35个城市生活成本满意度指数

城　市	2015年			2014年		2013年		2012年	
	得分	排序	上升位次	得分	排序	得分	排序	得分	排序
长春市	43.86	1	4	34.89	5	36.02	4	34.36	3
合肥市	43.82	2	1	35.02	3	34.40	6	35.43	1
厦门市	43.34	3	19	31.25	22	32.36	16	28.49	15
昆明市	42.97	4	12	31.82	16	30.00	22	28.04	18
南京市	42.50	5	16	31.55	21	30.10	21	27.95	19
海口市	42.28	6	29	28.25	35	33.96	8	26.00	29
哈尔滨市	42.21	7	4	32.33	11	32.06	17	28.38	17
杭州市	42.19	8	12	31.58	20	29.10	24	28.42	16
宁波市	41.49	9	4	32.21	13	29.03	25	26.62	27
济南市	41.33	10	−8	35.72	2	36.16	3	35.39	2
沈阳市	40.45	11	−10	37.48	1	36.31	2	31.73	7
石家庄市	40.26	12	−8	34.92	4	39.13	1	34.27	4
南宁市	40.15	13	5	31.72	18	33.45	10	27.16	24

续表

城市	2015年			2014年		2013年		2012年	
	得分	排序	上升位次	得分	排序	得分	排序	得分	排序
大连市	40.06	14	16	29.70	30	27.04	32	25.15	33
南昌市	39.68	15	−8	33.87	7	33.18	12	28.66	14
郑州市	39.66	16	1	31.75	17	35.03	5	31.67	8
长沙市	38.93	17	9	30.49	26	31.08	19	27.63	21
福州市	38.87	18	1	31.70	19	33.65	9	31.21	9
重庆市	38.76	19	−7	32.27	12	32.94	14	30.98	10
西安市	38.19	20	−11	32.98	9	33.03	13	31.92	6
上海市	37.96	21	11	28.58	32	25.59	35	25.45	31
成都市	37.93	22	−8	32.12	14	32.41	15	30.92	12
武汉市	37.81	23	−13	32.44	10	31.96	18	30.57	13
天津市	37.77	24	−18	34.82	6	33.32	11	32.62	5
乌鲁木齐市	37.10	25	6	29.23	31	28.53	28	24.67	34
深圳市	37.03	26	8	28.42	34	26.56	33	25.30	32
青岛市	36.80	27	−3	30.75	24	28.78	27	27.12	25
兰州市	36.79	28	−13	31.84	15	27.82	30	26.70	26
银川市	36.56	29	−1	30.29	28	27.47	31	27.60	22
呼和浩特市	36.15	30	−7	30.99	23	30.85	20	26.43	28
贵阳市	35.71	31	−2	30.19	29	29.38	23	25.71	30
广州市	35.58	32	−5	30.39	27	28.46	29	27.79	20
西宁市	35.48	33	−8	30.62	25	28.89	26	27.31	23
太原市	35.32	34	−26	33.04	8	34.22	7	30.94	11
北京市	33.76	35	−2	28.53	33	26.13	34	23.06	35
平均值	38.94			31.81		31.22		28.91	

表5显示，2015年，全国35个城市生活成本满意度指数加权平均值为38.94，与前面几次调查的平均值比较有了较大幅度的提高，说明35个城市居民对生活成本的满意度有所提高，但仍然处于不满意区间（得分在50以下）。35个城市生活成本满意度得分全部超过30，其中得分在40以上的城市有14个，均高于前3年得分最高分。整体上来看，城市生活成本满意度指数在2015年明显上升，各分数段均匀分布，图9的直方图很好地描述了上述变化趋势。

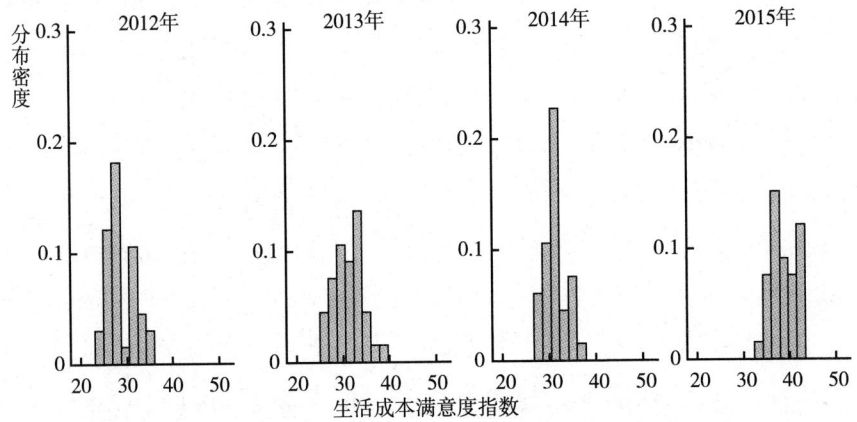

图9　2012~2015年生活成本满意度指数

调查显示，生活成本满意度指数排名前10位的城市为：长春市（1）、合肥市（2）、厦门市（3）、昆明市（4）、南京市（5）、海口市（6）、哈尔滨市（7）、杭州市（8）、宁波市（9）、济南市（10）。其中，长春市、合肥市、济南市已经连续4年排名前10位。排名后10位的城市分别是：深圳市（26）、青岛市（27）、兰州市（28）、银川市（29）、呼和浩特市（30）、贵阳市（31）、广州市（32）、西宁市（33）、太原市（34）、北京市（35）。其中，深圳市和北京市已经连续4年排名后10位，广州市和银川市已经连续3年排名后10位。

从地区分布来看，生活成本满意度指数排名前10位的城市中，有6个东部城市、3个中部城市、1个西部城市；生活成本满意度指数排名后10位的城市中，有4个东部城市、1个中部城市、5个西部城市。

从动态变化看，2012~2015年，全国生活成本满意度指数加权平均值分别为28.91，31.22，31.81，38.94，已经连续3年上升，2015年上升幅度尤为明显，表明人们对生活成本的满意度在不断提高。2012~2015年，生活成本满意度指数的最低得分在逐步提高：2012年，最低得分为23.06；2013年，最低得分为25.59；2014年，最低得分为28.25；2015年，最低得分为33.76。

图10的柱状图描述了2012~2015年35个城市生活成本满意度指数的变化情况。分城市看，连续3年得分上升的有昆明市、南京市、哈尔滨市、杭州市、宁波市、沈阳市、大连市、南昌市、上海市、武汉市、天津市、乌鲁木齐市、深圳市、青岛市、兰州市、呼和浩特市、贵阳市、广州市、西宁市、北京市20个城市。

排名上升比较明显的城市有：海口市（29）、厦门市（19）、南京市（16）、大连市（16）、昆明市（12）、杭州市（12）、上海市（11）；排名下降比较明显的城市有：太原市（-26）、天津市（-18）、武汉市（-13）、兰州市（-13）、西安市（-11）、沈阳市（-10）。

（二）生活成本客观指数（社会经济数据指数）

根据QLICC体系，城市生活成本客观指数是通过计算每个城市的房屋销售价格指数、通货膨胀率、房价收入比3个二级指标得出的。中国35个城市生活成本客观指数及其排序情况如表6所示。

城市生活质量蓝皮书

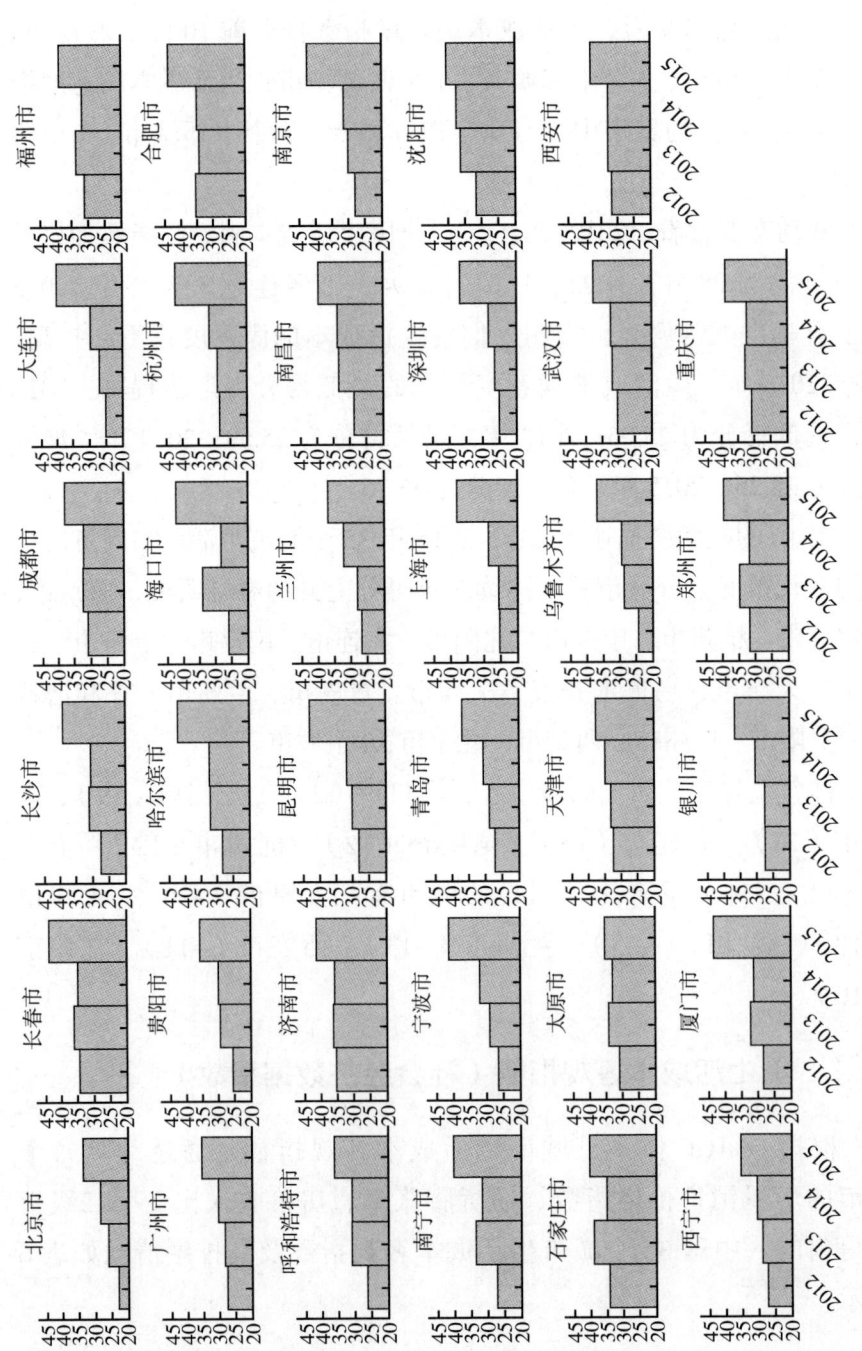

图10 2012~2015年35个城市生活成本满意度指数（纵轴为得分）

中国35个城市生活质量的细分指数

表6 中国35个城市生活成本客观指数

城 市	2015年			2014年		2013年		2012年	
	得分	排序	上升位次	得分	排序	得分	排序	得分	排序
昆明市	80.00	1	0	80.00	1	80.00	1	74.00	2
长沙市	72.10	2	1	68.58	3	71.79	3	69.57	3
西安市	71.13	3	1	63.89	4	65.27	6	61.38	9
呼和浩特市	69.49	4	-2	72.25	2	77.96	2	79.97	1
银川市	61.74	5	2	60.96	7	65.18	7	59.38	14
石家庄市	61.45	6	-1	62.30	5	66.75	4	64.74	4
南昌市	61.35	7	1	59.61	8	64.81	8	63.36	5
西宁市	60.30	8	-2	61.08	6	66.05	5	60.51	10
青岛市	60.11	9	2	58.38	11	63.40	10	62.34	8
武汉市	59.73	10	2	57.75	12	62.61	13	59.68	13
沈阳市	59.19	11	4	56.66	15	62.89	12	60.11	11
济南市	58.94	12	-3	59.29	9	64.59	9	59.19	16
重庆市	58.35	13	-3	58.89	10	63.36	11	63.34	6
成都市	57.21	14	2	55.97	16	61.68	15	60.06	12
贵阳市	56.32	15	-1	56.67	14	61.67	16	58.21	17
郑州市	55.75	16	-3	56.88	13	62.30	14	63.02	7
大连市	55.35	17	7	52.44	24	57.15	24	56.00	18
兰州市	55.20	18	-1	55.50	17	59.93	19	52.63	22
乌鲁木齐市	54.76	19	4	52.94	23	58.33	22	46.58	29
南宁市	54.44	20	-2	54.83	18	60.61	18	54.24	19
长春市	53.84	21	-2	54.10	19	59.57	20	53.58	20
哈尔滨市	53.71	22	-1	53.87	21	58.67	21	52.46	23
合肥市	52.21	23	-3	53.89	20	58.17	23	51.49	26
南京市	50.60	24	2	50.28	26	55.70	25	52.18	24
福州市	50.26	25	3	49.00	28	55.43	26	51.01	27
厦门市	49.57	26	-4	53.86	22	60.70	17	59.22	15
杭州市	48.89	27	5	44.41	32	48.73	32	42.50	33
天津市	48.50	28	-3	51.02	25	54.63	28	51.83	25
广州市	48.16	29	2	46.32	31	53.15	30	53.24	21
宁波市	47.78	30	-3	49.75	27	55.19	27	46.16	30
太原市	47.17	31	-1	46.66	30	53.84	29	46.09	31

057

续表

城市	2015年			2014年		2013年		2012年	
	得分	排序	上升位次	得分	排序	得分	排序	得分	排序
海口市	46.31	32	-3	47.74	29	40.00	35	39.97	35
上海市	45.57	33	0	43.59	33	50.00	31	44.50	32
北京市	42.99	34	1	40.00	35	45.17	34	40.80	34
深圳市	40.00	35	-1	40.87	34	45.82	33	50.14	28
平均值	54.58			53.84		58.67		56.10	

表6显示，2015年，全国35个城市生活成本客观指数加权平均值为54.58，与2014年的平均值相比略有提高，仍旧保持在满意区间。35个城市生活成本客观指数的得分均超过40，最高得分和上两年均保持一致，得分为80。整体上看，城市生活成本客观指数基本保持稳定，但略有下降。图11的直方图描述了这一变化趋势。

调查显示，生活成本客观指数排名前10位的城市为：昆明市（1）、长沙市（2）、西安市（3）、呼和浩特市（4）、银川市（5）、石家庄市（6）、南昌市（7）、西宁市（8）、青岛市（9）、武汉市（10）。昆明市已经连续3年排名第1，并且得分一直稳定在80。昆

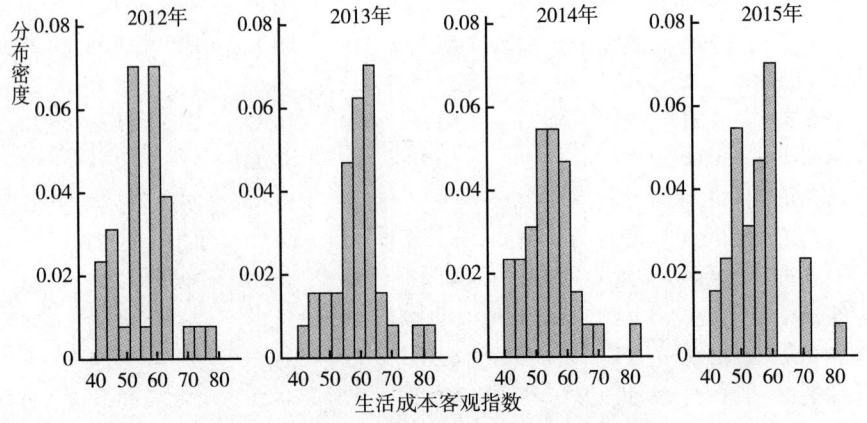

图11 2012~2015年生活成本客观指数

明、长沙、西安、呼和浩特、石家庄、南昌、西宁7个城市已经连续4年排名前10位。排名后10位的城市分别是：厦门市（26）、杭州市（27）、天津市（28）、广州市（29）、宁波市（30）、太原市（31）、海口市（32）、上海市（33）、北京市（34）、深圳市（35）。在2015年排名后10位的城市中，除天津市和厦门市外，其余8个城市已经连续4年排名后10位，说明这些城市在35个城市中的生活成本一直是相对较高的。厦门市2015年首次落入后10位，天津市在4年中有两年排名后10位，另有两年排名后11位。福州市在2012~2014年连续3年排名后10位后，于2015年首次脱离后10位的阵营，排名倒数11位。

从地区分布来看，生活成本客观指数排名前10位的城市中，有2个东部城市、3个中部城市、5个西部城市；生活成本客观指数排名后10位的城市中，有9个东部城市、1个中部城市，没有西部城市。这表明东部城市的生活成本绝对高于西部城市。

从动态变化看，2012~2015年，全国生活成本客观指数加权平均值分别为56.10、58.67、53.84、54.58，2014年得分下降明显，2015年有小幅上涨。最低得分基本没有变化：2012年，最低得分为39.97；2013年、2014年、2015年的最低得分均为40。

图12的柱状图描述了2012~2015年35个城市生活成本客观指数的变化情况。分城市看，连续3年分值下降即生活成本上升的城市有呼和浩特市、郑州市、深圳市。2013~2015年连续2年分值下降即生活成本上升的城市有呼和浩特市、石家庄市、西宁市、济南市、重庆市、贵阳市、郑州市、兰州市、南宁市、长春市、哈尔滨市、合肥市、厦门市、天津市、宁波市、深圳市16个城市。从排名顺序来看，排名变动情况不大，其中排名上升比较明显的城市有：大连市（7）、杭州市（5），昆明市和上海市排名没有变化。排名下降的城市的变动幅度均不大，下降幅度最大的厦门市也仅仅下降了4位。

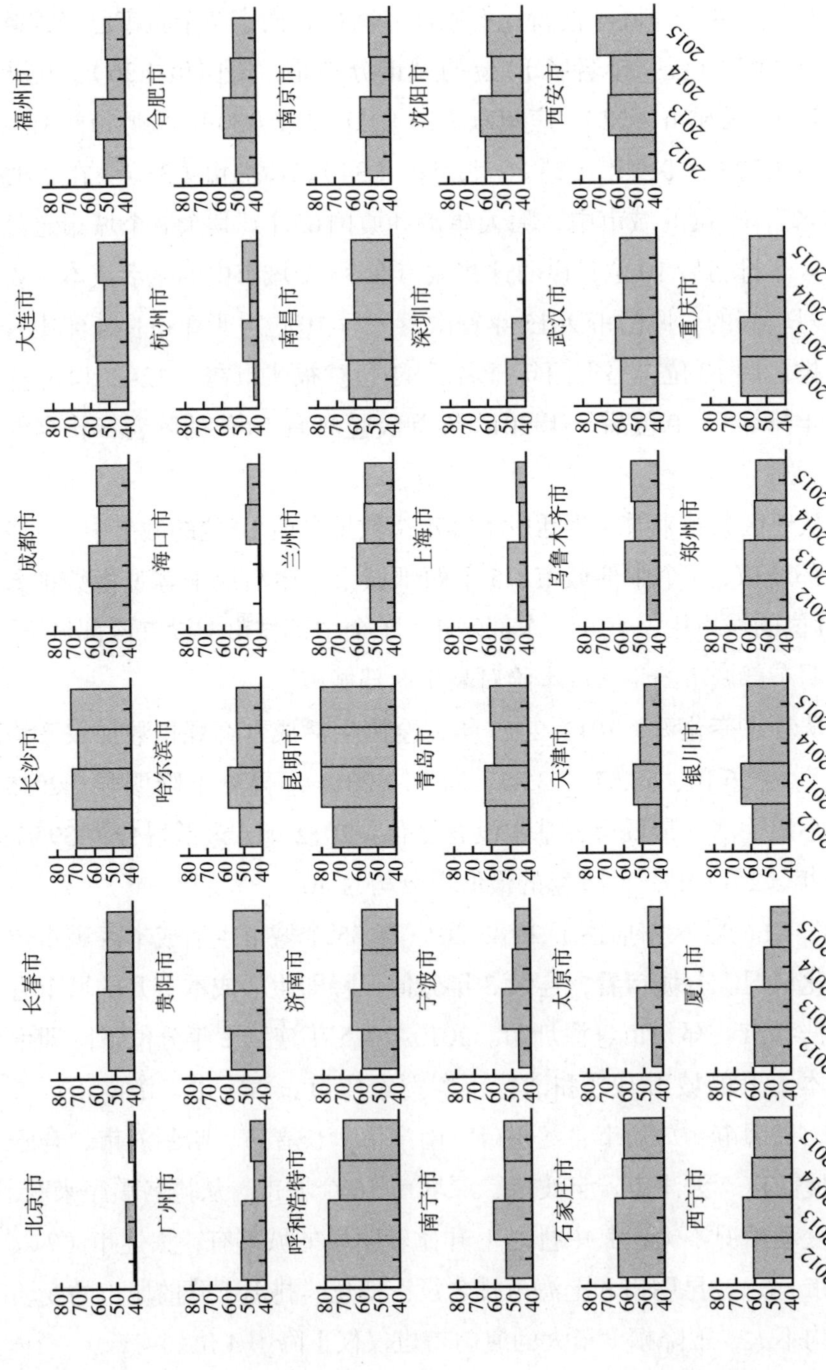

图 12 2012~2015 年 35 个城市生活成本客观指数（纵轴为得分）

三 人力资本指数

（一）人力资本满意度指数

人力资本满意度指数是通过问卷调查并结合对调查结果进行答案赋值得出的。2015年35个城市人力资本满意度指数的调查结果如表7所示。

表7 中国35个城市人力资本满意度指数

城 市	2015年			2014年		2013年		2012年	
	得分	排序	上升位次	得分	排序	得分	排序	得分	排序
厦门市	65.60	1	11	59.75	12	59.03	18	59.01	19
宁波市	64.32	2	6	60.24	8	60.14	9	64.19	1
杭州市	63.43	3	3	60.57	6	59.24	16	62.38	6
海口市	63.37	4	−1	61.69	3	59.11	17	58.00	27
广州市	63.03	5	18	57.71	23	57.59	28	59.43	14
合肥市	62.90	6	14	58.50	20	61.37	6	59.71	13
西宁市	62.48	7	−3	61.59	4	60.09	10	58.80	21
上海市	62.44	8	−3	61.26	5	60.35	8	58.79	22
武汉市	62.43	9	17	57.67	26	57.09	31	58.09	26
北京市	62.36	10	−3	60.47	7	59.68	11	59.33	16
沈阳市	62.36	11	0	59.78	11	57.79	26	57.61	28
南京市	62.27	12	9	58.10	21	59.29	15	59.36	15
哈尔滨市	62.10	13	9	58.01	22	57.23	29	56.76	30
青岛市	61.91	14	−13	61.84	1	62.61	1	62.62	5
成都市	61.86	15	12	57.66	27	58.17	25	59.14	18
重庆市	61.70	16	−3	59.56	13	57.74	27	58.83	20
长春市	61.58	17	−3	59.48	14	58.90	19	63.37	2
南宁市	61.52	18	7	57.69	25	58.73	21	58.18	25
西安市	61.46	19	12	57.29	31	56.65	33	56.19	31
济南市	61.39	20	−4	58.98	16	61.99	2	62.20	7
郑州市	61.29	21	7	57.51	28	61.54	5	58.45	24
大连市	61.20	22	7	57.45	29	61.67	4	59.20	17
昆明市	61.19	23	12	56.15	35	54.33	34	55.45	34

续表

城 市	2015年			2014年		2013年		2012年	
	得分	排序	上升位次	得分	排序	得分	排序	得分	排序
天津市	61.10	24	−15	60.20	9	59.30	14	61.27	9
福州市	61.02	25	−15	60.13	10	59.60	13	62.72	4
石家庄市	60.99	26	−9	58.67	17	58.86	20	63.31	3
乌鲁木齐市	60.80	27	−9	58.54	18	61.86	3	61.18	10
南昌市	60.78	28	−9	58.51	19	58.45	23	56.10	32
呼和浩特市	60.63	29	1	57.29	30	60.96	7	61.07	11
深圳市	60.54	30	4	56.75	34	57.03	32	57.34	29
长沙市	59.76	31	1	57.26	32	58.20	24	60.38	12
贵阳市	59.50	32	1	56.98	33	59.60	12	55.48	33
兰州市	59.09	33	−31	61.74	2	57.20	30	58.52	23
银川市	58.63	34	−19	59.13	15	58.52	22	61.98	8
太原市	58.34	35	−11	57.70	24	53.49	35	55.20	35
平均值			61.73		58.98		58.89		59.42

根据调查结果，2015年，全国35个城市的人力资本满意度指数加权平均值为61.73，4年来首次超过60，较前3年有一定程度的提高，但依然处于满意区间内。35个城市中有30个城市得分超过60。尽管没有得分超过70的城市，但最高分较2014年有所提高，排名第1的是厦门市，得分为65.60。总体上看，城市居民人力资本满意度指数在2013年后开始稳步上升。图13的直方图描述了这一变化趋势。

35个城市居民人力资本满意度指数调查结果显示，城市居民人力资本满意度指数排名前10位的城市为：厦门市（1）、宁波市（2）、杭州市（3）、海口市（4）、广州市（5）、合肥市（6）、西宁市（7）、上海市（8）、武汉市（9）、北京市（10）。宁波市连续4年、西宁市和上海市连续3年排名在前10位。排名处在后10位的城市是：石家庄市（26）、乌鲁木齐市（27）、南昌市（28）、呼和浩特市（29）、深圳市（30）、长沙市（31）、贵阳市（32）、兰州市（33）、银川市（34）、太原市（35）。深圳市已经连续4年排名在后10位城市行列。

中国 35 个城市生活质量的细分指数

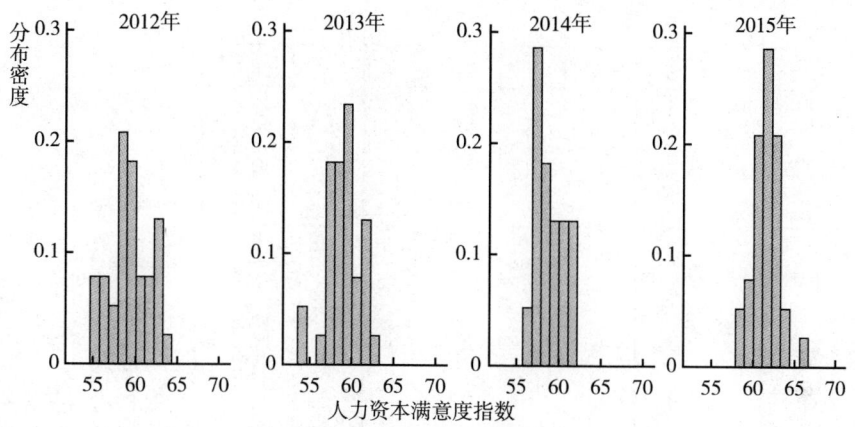

图 13　2012~2015 年人力资本满意度指数

按地区分布分析，城市居民人力资本满意度指数排名前 10 位的城市中，东部城市、中部城市、西部城市的比例为 7∶2∶1。城市居民人力资本满意度指数排名后 10 位的城市中，东部城市、中部城市、西部城市的比例为 2∶3∶5。根据以上结果，我们认为，城市居民人力资本满意度的地区差异较大。

按时间趋势分析，2012~2015 年，全国城市居民人力资本满意度指数加权平均值分别为 59.42、58.89、58.98、61.73。图 14 描述了 2012~2015 年 35 个城市人力资本满意度指数的变化情况。分城市看，北京市、哈尔滨市、海口市、南昌市、上海市、西宁市、厦门市、沈阳市、西安市 9 个城市在这一个指标上保持了连续 3 年的增长；青岛市在这个指标上连续 3 年得分下降；其余城市 2012~2015 年得分不稳定。从排名的变化看，广州市上升位次最明显，从 2014 年后段位的第 23 名上升到 2015 年的第 5 名，上升了 18 位。上升明显的城市还有：武汉市（17）、合肥市（14）、成都市（12）、西安市（12）、昆明市（12）、厦门市（11）；兰州市下降最为明显，直接由 2014 年的第 2 名下降到 2015 年的第 33 名，下降了 31 位。排名下降比较明显的城市还有：银川市（-19）、天津市（-15）、福州市（-15）、青岛市（-13）、太原市（-11）。

063

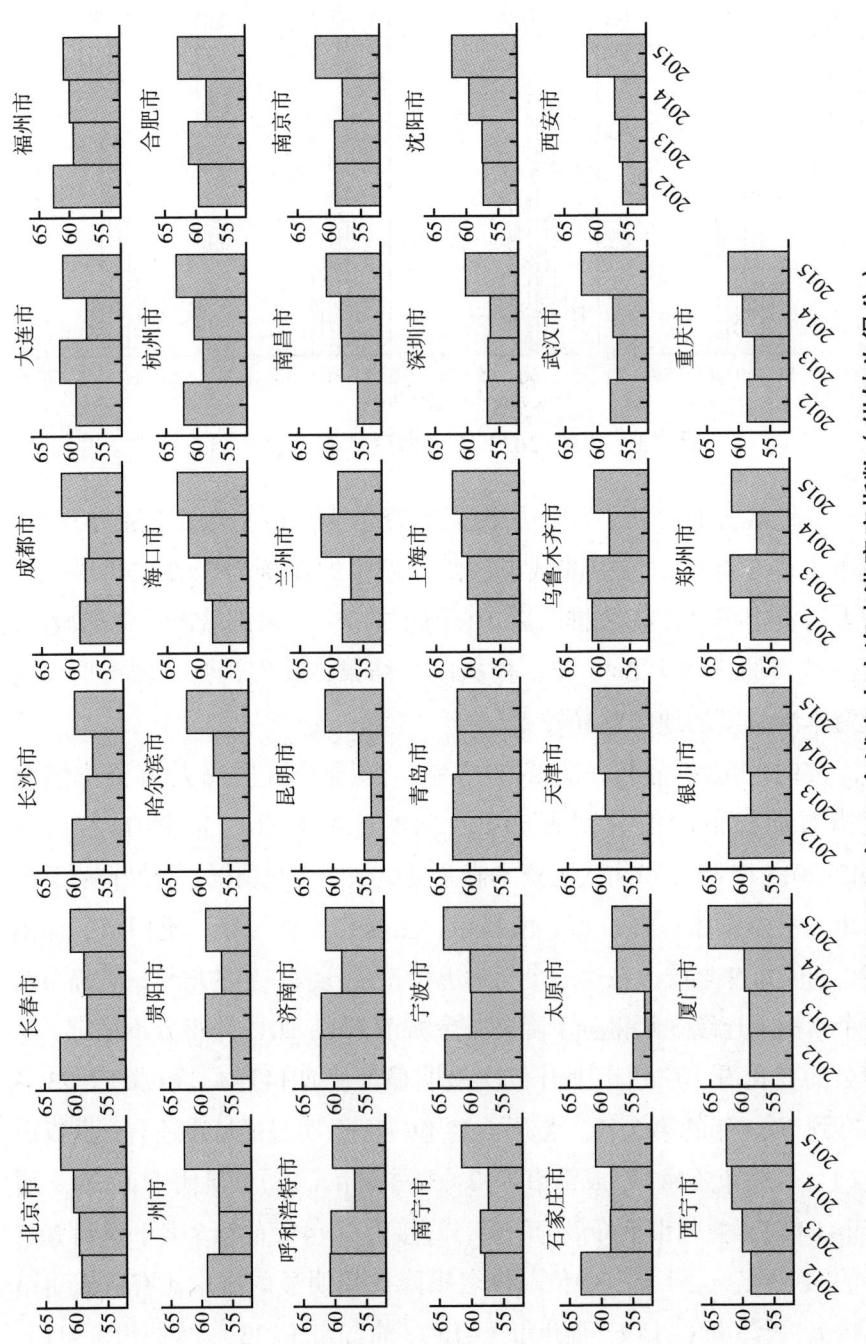

图14 2012~2015年35个城市人力资本满意度指数(纵轴为得分)

（二）人力资本客观指数（社会经济数据指数）

根据 QLICC 体系，城市人力资本客观指数是通过计算每个城市的教育提供指数、教育文化娱乐消费支出比两个二级指标得出的。2015 年 35 个城市人力资本客观指数的计算结果如表 8 所示。

表 8　中国 35 个城市人力资本客观指数

城　　市	2015 年			2014 年		2013 年		2012 年	
	得分	排序	上升位次	得分	排序	得分	排序	得分	排序
南京市	80.00	1	0	80.00	1	79.73	2	79.52	2
贵阳市	71.66	2	2	67.62	4	61.65	9	62.79	7
广州市	71.29	3	−1	78.68	2	80.00	1	80.01	1
西安市	70.29	4	−1	70.94	3	72.94	3	79.42	3
北京市	67.89	5	0	67.51	5	68.76	4	70.96	4
武汉市	67.81	6	1	63.45	7	60.89	10	58.52	13
太原市	64.28	7	−1	63.84	6	64.68	6	69.05	5
上海市	62.68	8	0	62.25	8	63.03	7	66.15	6
昆明市	61.64	9	1	59.92	10	56.19	17	57.20	17
长春市	61.19	10	−1	61.22	9	61.79	8	54.72	21
石家庄市	59.99	11	4	57.15	15	55.22	19	47.11	33
呼和浩特市	58.65	12	1	57.59	13	58.83	13	61.75	8
银川市	58.23	13	1	57.17	14	56.57	15	57.57	16
杭州市	58.16	14	7	55.18	21	52.89	23	53.38	24
长沙市	57.50	15	−3	57.92	12	66.65	5	58.80	11
合肥市	57.15	16	−5	58.70	11	60.28	11	59.72	10
南宁市	56.49	17	−1	56.98	16	58.27	14	60.93	9
大连市	55.84	18	4	53.98	22	52.62	24	52.09	27
济南市	55.51	19	0	55.33	19	55.28	18	57.66	15
福州市	55.01	20	−2	56.40	18	56.38	16	51.09	28
沈阳市	54.56	21	−1	55.32	20	54.67	20	55.90	20
宁波市	54.15	22	−5	56.55	17	59.09	12	58.62	12
哈尔滨市	52.53	23	0	52.17	23	52.90	22	52.83	25
天津市	52.24	24	0	51.76	24	51.63	27	56.58	18
深圳市	52.08	25	3	50.48	28	49.79	28	54.43	22
南昌市	52.06	26	0	51.40	26	51.88	25	48.30	30
兰州市	50.44	27	−2	51.73	25	53.68	21	54.33	23

续表

城市	2015年			2014年		2013年		2012年	
	得分	排序	上升位次	得分	排序	得分	排序	得分	排序
成都市	49.95	28	-1	50.77	27	51.79	26	50.62	29
乌鲁木齐市	49.26	29	0	49.40	29	49.17	29	56.49	19
青岛市	48.10	30	1	47.37	31	46.32	33	45.56	34
郑州市	48.03	31	-1	47.47	30	48.02	31	47.50	32
海口市	47.14	32	0	46.59	32	46.39	32	58.08	14
重庆市	45.26	33	0	46.15	33	48.03	30	48.28	31
厦门市	41.32	34	0	42.54	34	43.09	34	52.32	26
西宁市	40.00	35	0	40.00	35	40.00	35	39.99	35
平均值	57.34			57.33		57.78		57.66	

根据计算结果，2015年，全国35个城市的人力资本客观指数加权平均值为57.34，与前3年的平均值基本持平，处于满意区间内。在35个城市中，有27个城市人力资本客观指数得分超过50，处于满意区间，但是有8个城市的分值低于50，处于不满意区间。排名第1的是南京市，得分为80，已经进入很满意区间（得分为76~100）。总体上看，城市人力资本客观指数波动幅度不大。图15描述了上述变化趋势。

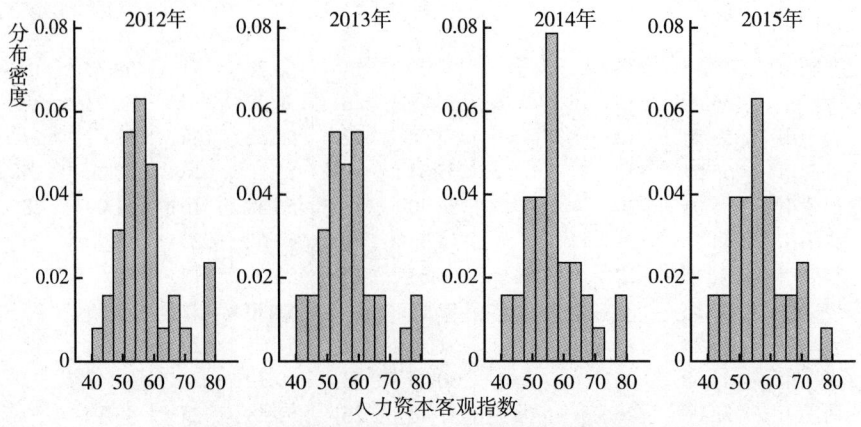

图15 2012~2015年人力资本客观指数

35个城市人力资本客观指数计算结果显示，城市人力资本客观指数排名前10位的城市为：南京市（1）、贵阳市（2）、广州市（3）、西安市（4）、北京市（5）、武汉市（6）、太原市（7）、上海市（8）、昆明市（9）、长春市（10）。在排名前10位的城市中，南京、贵阳、广州、西安、北京、太原、上海7个城市已经连续4年排在前10名的行列中；武汉和长春两个城市连续3年排在前10名的行列中。排名处在后10位的城市是：南昌市（26）、兰州市（27）、成都市（28）、乌鲁木齐市（29）、青岛市（30）、郑州市（31）、海口市（32）、重庆市（33）、厦门市（34）、西宁市（35）。其中，西宁、厦门、重庆、郑州、青岛5个城市已经连续4年排在后10名城市的行列中；海口和乌鲁木齐两个城市连续3年排在后10名城市的行列中。

按地区分布分析，城市人力资本客观指数排名前10位的城市中，东部城市、中部城市、西部城市的比例为4∶3∶3。城市人力资本客观指数排名后10位的城市中，东部城市、中部城市、西部城市的比例为3∶2∶5。排名前10位的城市中，人力资本客观指数在地域分布上差异不大。排名后10位的城市中，人力资本客观指数在地域分布上的差异较大，其中西部城市占比较大，达到50%。

2012~2015年，35个城市人力资本客观指数加权平均值分别为57.66、57.78、57.33、57.34，不同年份间差异较小，处于基本持平的状态。分城市看，观察图16的柱状图，大连市、青岛市、石家庄市、武汉市4个城市在这一指标上保持了连续3年的增长；南宁市、兰州市、厦门市、西安市、重庆市5个城市在这一指标上连续3年下降；其余城市2012~2015年的分值上下波动。从排名的变化看，杭州市上升位次最明显，从2014年的第21名上升到2015年的第14名，上升了7位。上升较为明显的城市还有石家庄市（4）、大连市（4）、深圳市（3）；合肥市和宁波市排名下降最为明显，但也只是分别下降了5位。排名下降比较明显的城市还有长沙市（-3）。

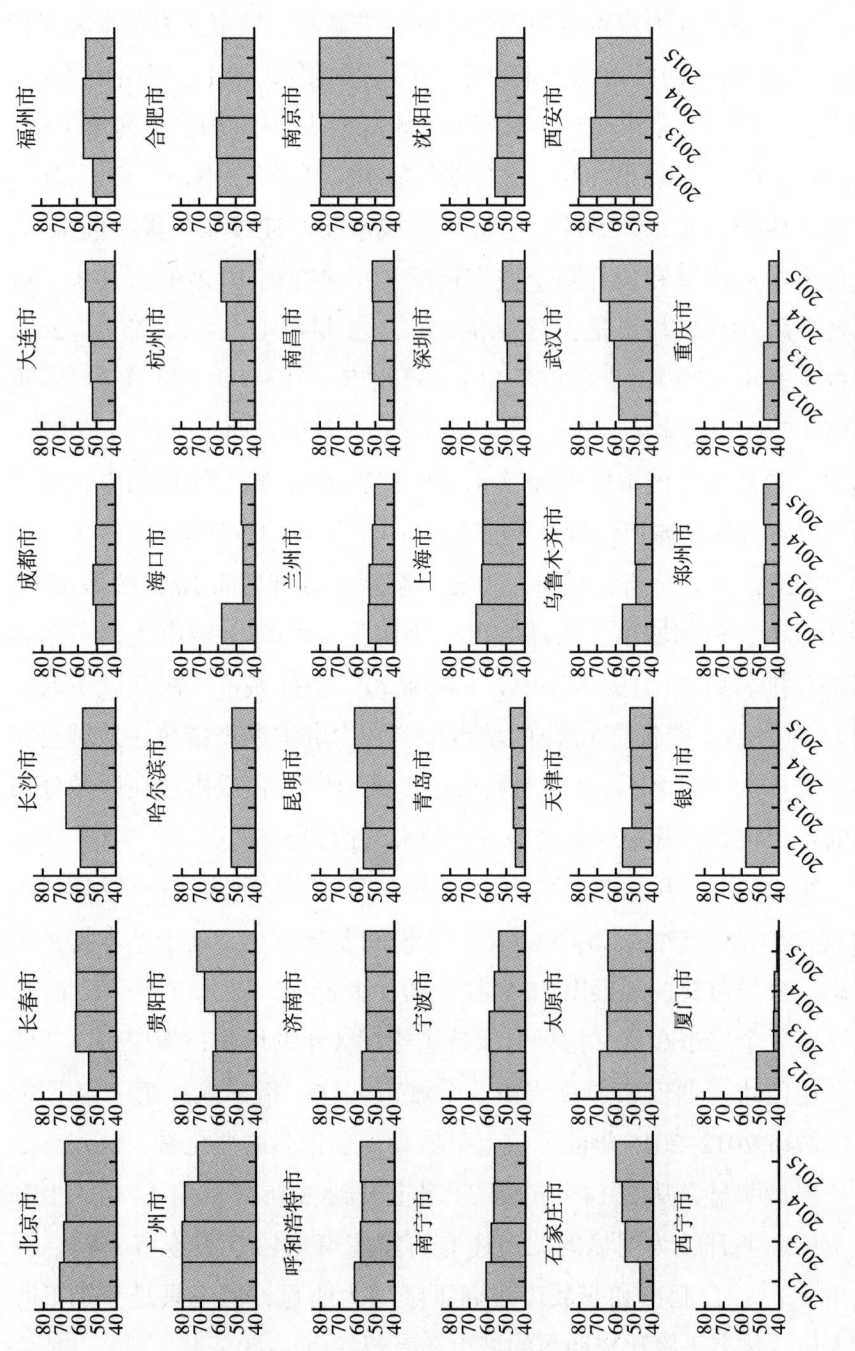

图 16 2012~2015 年 35 个城市人力资本客观指数(纵轴为得分)

四 社会保障指数

(一) 社会保障满意度指数

根据QLICC体系,社会保障满意度指数是医疗和养老保障满意度指数、城市安全状况满意度指数的加权平均值,和往年一样,也是通过问卷调查并对调查结果进行答案赋值得到的。35个城市社会保障满意度指数和排序情况如表9所示。

表9 中国35个城市居民社会保障满意度指数

城 市	2015年			2014年		2013年		2012年	
	得分	排序	上升位次	得分	排序	得分	排序	得分	排序
杭州市	62.60	1	0	61.17	1	60.76	3	64.68	1
上海市	61.94	2	5	59.44	7	58.04	10	58.71	18
北京市	61.57	3	11	58.85	14	58.94	9	61.27	12
宁波市	61.44	4	0	60.61	4	60.52	4	63.65	2
西宁市	61.38	5	11	57.97	16	59.31	7	62.04	9
济南市	61.34	6	3	59.13	9	59.82	6	62.65	6
武汉市	61.28	7	25	55.39	32	52.64	32	56.83	26
昆明市	61.06	8	27	51.88	35	54.09	30	54.65	34
青岛市	61.04	9	-6	60.80	3	61.87	1	62.26	7
厦门市	60.95	10	-8	61.03	2	61.25	2	62.79	4
海口市	60.95	11	0	59.06	11	53.86	31	55.75	32
南昌市	60.94	12	15	56.08	27	54.09	28	55.18	33
成都市	60.81	13	4	57.90	17	57.05	14	61.33	11
长沙市	60.77	14	20	54.23	34	54.09	29	56.14	31

续表

城市	2015年			2014年		2013年		2012年	
	得分	排序	上升位次	得分	排序	得分	排序	得分	排序
贵阳市	60.76	15	15	55.83	30	51.98	35	52.26	35
重庆市	60.73	16	−8	59.14	8	55.61	24	62.78	5
广州市	60.54	17	16	55.03	33	54.70	27	56.81	27
大连市	60.49	18	−5	58.91	13	57.18	13	61.73	10
南京市	60.47	19	−9	59.07	10	59.22	8	59.17	17
哈尔滨市	60.29	20	−2	57.83	18	55.86	21	56.27	30
呼和浩特市	60.28	21	3	56.55	24	52.63	33	60.18	14
南宁市	59.84	22	9	55.61	31	52.43	34	56.33	29
长春市	59.64	23	−18	60.47	5	57.59	12	62.83	3
福州市	59.60	24	−9	58.45	15	56.23	20	58.60	20
沈阳市	59.60	25	−4	57.26	21	56.40	18	57.04	25
郑州市	59.55	26	0	56.47	26	55.74	22	56.67	28
乌鲁木齐市	59.50	27	1	56.00	28	56.57	17	58.06	22
石家庄市	59.38	28	−6	57.05	22	56.64	15	61.24	13
天津市	59.36	29	−17	58.92	12	55.14	25	58.57	21
西安市	59.16	30	−1	55.84	29	56.27	19	59.65	16
太原市	59.16	31	−8	57.03	23	56.63	16	58.66	19
合肥市	59.11	32	−13	57.48	19	57.71	11	59.80	15
深圳市	59.06	33	−8	56.48	25	55.11	26	57.04	24
兰州市	59.01	34	−14	57.26	20	55.65	23	57.67	23
银川市	58.89	35	−29	59.74	6	60.03	5	62.24	8
平均值	60.47			57.87		56.64		59.19	

中国 35 个城市生活质量的细分指数

表 9 显示，全国 35 个城市居民社会保障满意度指数的加权平均值为 60.47，与前几年相比有了较大幅度的提高，仍旧保持在满意区间。35 个城市中有 21 个城市社会保障满意度指数得分超过 60，而 2014 年只有 5 个城市。值得注意的是，2015 年排名第 1 的杭州市在 2014 年和 2012 年的排名也是第 1，2013 年排名第 3。这表明杭州市的医疗和养老保障满意度指数以及城市安全状况满意度指数相当稳定。虽然杭州市的医疗和养老保障满意度指数排名不太靠前，但是它的城市安全状况满意度指数排名第 1，从而决定了它的社会保障满意度指数排名第 1。整体来说，由于医疗和养老保障满意度指数以及城市安全状况满意度指数继续稳步上升，城市社会保障满意度指数继续稳步上升。图 17 的直方图展示了这一上升趋势。

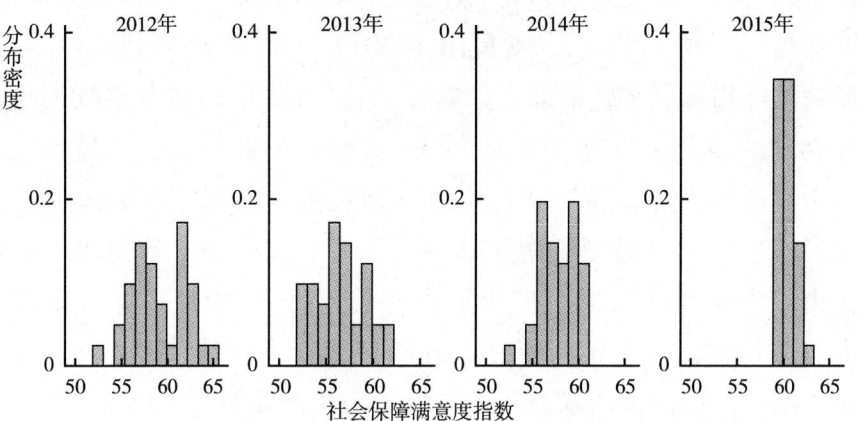

图 17　2012~2015 年社会保障满意度指数

调查显示，2015 年社会保障满意度（主观）指数排名前 10 位的城市为：杭州市（1）、上海市（2）、北京市（3）、宁波市（4）、西宁市（5）、济南市（6）、武汉市（7）、昆明市（8）、青岛市（9）、厦门市（10）。值得注意的是，杭州、宁波、济南、青岛、厦门 5 个城市已经连续 4 年、上海连续 3 年位于前 10 名城市的行列。排名后

10位的城市分别是：郑州市（26）、乌鲁木齐市（27）、石家庄市（28）、天津市（29）、西安市（30）、太原市（31）、合肥市（32）、深圳市（33）、兰州市（34）、银川市（35）。

从地区来看，社会保障满意度指数排名前10位的城市中，有7个东部城市、1个中部城市、2个西部城市；社会保障满意度指数排名后10位的城市中有3个东部城市、3个中部城市、4个西部城市。

从动态变化的角度来看，2012~2015年，35个城市社会保障满意度指数加权平均值分别为59.19、56.64、57.87、60.47，虽然社会保障满意度指数在2013年和2014年降低了不少，但在2015年又有所提高，呈先下降后上升的趋势。2012~2015年，社会保障满意度指数最低分分别为52.26、51.98、51.88、58.89，也呈现一种先下降后上升的趋势。图18展示了2012~2015年35个城市社会保障满意度指数的变化情况。分城市来看，2013~2015年连续两年得分上升的城市有杭州市、上海市、宁波市、武汉市、海口市、南昌市、成都市、长沙市、贵阳市、重庆市、广州市、大连市、哈尔滨市、呼和浩特市、南宁市、福州市、沈阳市、郑州市、石家庄市、天津市、太原市、深圳市、兰州市23个城市，占调查城市总数的65.7%。排名明显上升的城市有：昆明市（27）、武汉市（25）、长沙市（20）、南昌市（15）、贵阳市（15）、北京市（11）、西宁市（11）；排名显著下降的城市有：银川市（-29）、长春市（-18）、天津市（-17）、兰州市（-14）、合肥市（-13）5个城市。

社会保障满意度指数是由医疗和养老保障满意度指数和城市安全状况满意度指数构成的。两个细分指数的调查结果分别由表10和表11所示。

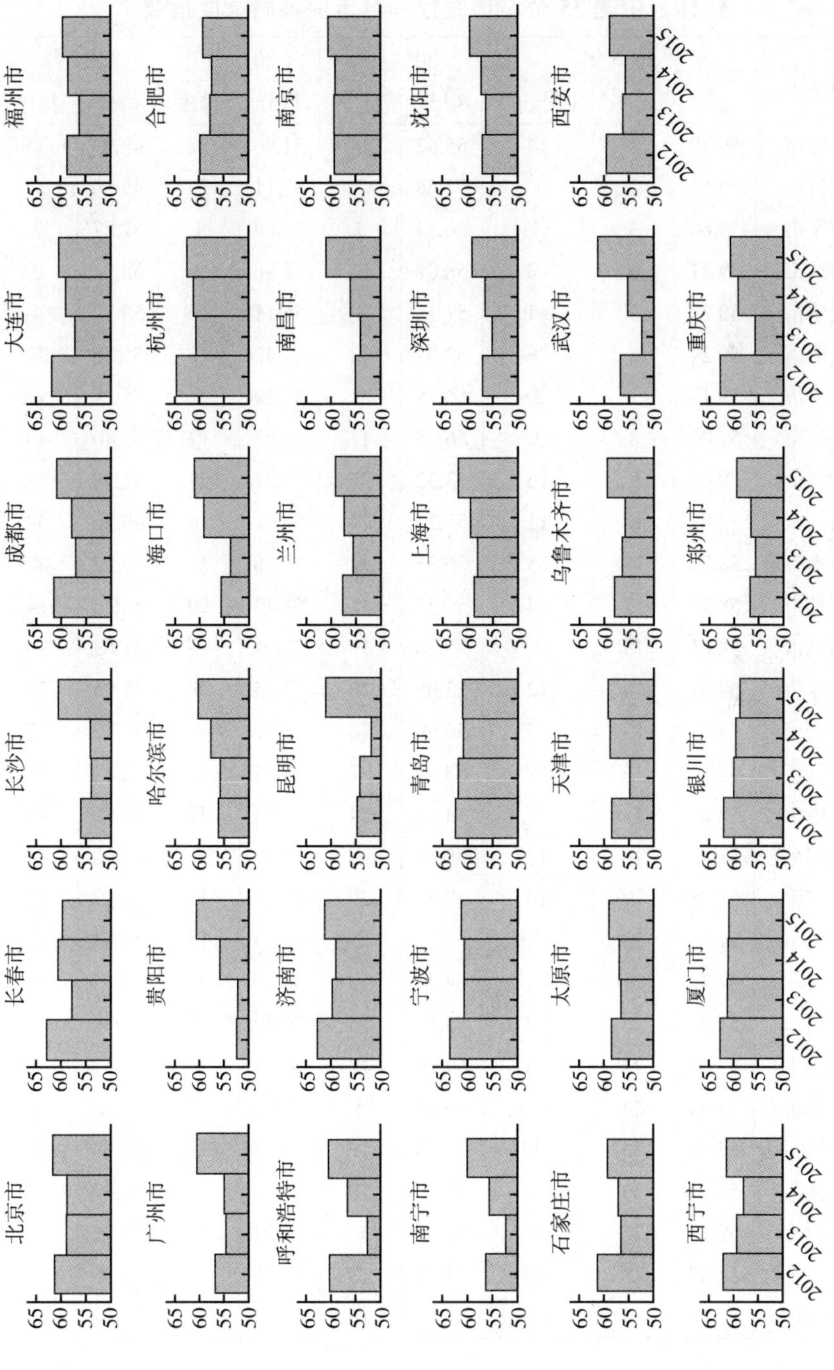

中国 35 个城市生活质量的细分指数

图 18　2012~2015 年 35 个城市社会保障满意度指数（纵轴为得分）

表10　中国35个城市医疗和养老保障满意度指数

城　市	2015年			2014年		2013年		2012年	
	得分	排序	上升位次	得分	排序	得分	排序	得分	排序
上海市	59.79	1	13	55.62	14	51.96	32	48.93	35
海口市	59.65	2	1	57.68	3	53.11	25	49.50	34
西宁市	59.60	3	4	56.34	7	61.67	1	57.87	3
宁波市	59.31	4	−3	58.02	1	58.96	2	58.24	2
杭州市	59.23	5	−1	57.14	4	56.11	10	58.37	1
昆明市	59.21	6	26	52.62	32	54.42	18	51.76	27
北京市	59.17	7	2	56.15	9	57.29	5	55.71	12
厦门市	59.05	8	3	56.06	11	55.83	12	56.40	10
广州市	59.01	9	16	53.32	25	52.37	29	51.38	29
南京市	58.83	10	13	53.73	23	54.61	16	49.74	32
乌鲁木齐市	58.76	11	−5	56.37	6	56.36	9	57.57	4
成都市	58.70	12	−4	56.23	8	54.40	20	55.26	14
南昌市	58.61	13	3	55.36	16	55.64	13	51.63	28
长沙市	58.51	14	12	53.05	26	52.45	28	52.05	25
青岛市	58.51	15	−5	56.09	10	58.19	4	53.42	17
武汉市	58.33	16	11	53.01	27	50.45	35	52.52	20
济南市	58.09	17	7	53.44	24	54.24	22	51.96	26
沈阳市	57.88	18	17	52.15	35	54.37	21	50.00	31
南宁市	57.85	19	10	52.85	29	52.11	31	52.47	21
重庆市	57.84	20	−18	57.75	2	54.79	15	53.74	15
石家庄市	57.78	21	−2	54.79	19	56.39	8	56.55	9
银川市	57.75	22	−7	55.53	15	56.59	7	55.73	11
贵阳市	57.60	23	−6	54.94	17	56.64	6	53.57	16
长春市	57.44	24	−19	56.73	5	52.90	26	57.22	6
呼和浩特市	57.34	25	−13	55.73	12	54.53	17	57.50	5
大连市	57.22	26	4	52.75	30	52.13	30	53.37	18
深圳市	57.13	27	7	52.58	34	51.23	34	52.98	19
福州市	57.07	28	−15	55.73	13	53.75	24	51.30	30
兰州市	56.98	29	−11	54.89	18	58.33	3	52.27	23

续表

城市	2015年			2014年		2013年		2012年	
	得分	排序	上升位次	得分	排序	得分	排序	得分	排序
合肥市	56.89	30	−9	53.79	21	54.42	19	55.58	13
哈尔滨市	56.85	31	2	52.58	33	52.47	27	49.52	33
天津市	56.19	32	−12	54.33	20	51.64	33	52.06	24
西安市	56.15	33	−5	52.90	28	55.96	11	57.04	8
郑州市	56.13	34	−3	52.73	31	54.82	14	52.38	22
太原市	55.72	35	−13	53.74	22	54.05	23	57.18	7
平均值	58.04			54.80		54.34		53.61	

表10表明，全国35个城市医疗和养老保障满意度指数的加权平均值为58.04，与前几年相比，分值有了较大幅度的提高，仍旧保持在满意区间。2015年，35个城市的医疗和养老保障满意度指数得分全部超过55，而2014年只有16个城市，得分超过55的城市数量有了大幅的提高。整体上看，城市医疗和养老保障满意度指数处于持续稳定上升的态势。图19的直方图很好地描述了上述变化趋势。

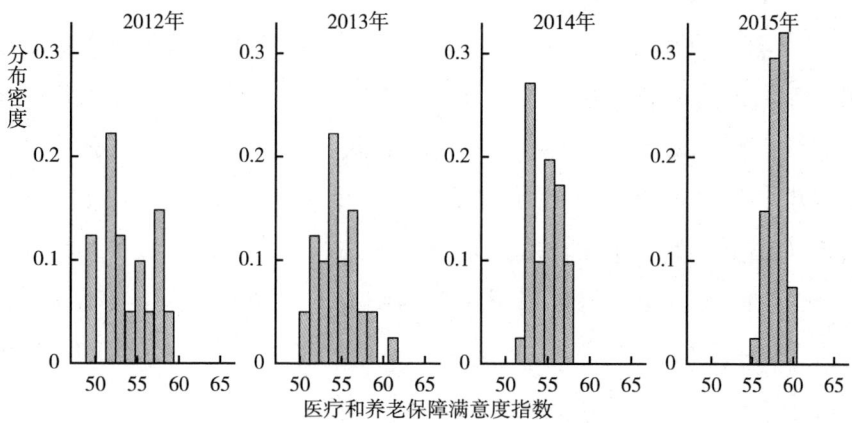

图19　2012~2015年医疗和养老保障满意度指数

调查显示，城市医疗和养老保障满意度指数排名前10位的城市为：上海市（1）、海口市（2）、西宁市（3）、宁波市（4）、杭州市（5）、昆明市（6）、北京市（7）、厦门市（8）、广州市（9）、南京市（10）。西宁、宁波、杭州3个城市已经连续4年位于前10名城市的行列；北京连续3年位于前10名城市的行列。城市医疗和养老保障满意度指数排名后10位的城市为：大连市（26）、深圳市（27）、福州市（28）、兰州市（29）、合肥市（30）、哈尔滨市（31）、天津市（32）、西安市（33）、郑州市（34）、太原市（35）。哈尔滨市已经连续4年位于后10名城市的行列，大连和深圳两个城市连续3年位于后10名城市的行列。

从地区分布来看，城市医疗和养老保障满意度指数排名前10位的城市中，有8个东部城市、2个西部城市；城市医疗和养老保障满意度指数排名后10位的城市中，有4个东部城市、4个中部城市、2个西部城市。

从动态变化的角度看，2012~2015年，35个城市医疗和养老保障满意度指数加权平均值分别为53.61、54.34、54.80、58.04，总体呈上升趋势。最低分也逐渐提高，2012年，最低得分为48.93，2013年最低得分为50.45，2014年，最低得分为52.15，2015年，最低得分为55.72。图20的柱状图描述了2012~2015年35个城市医疗和养老保障满意度指数的变化情况。分城市看，2012~2015年，连续3年得分上升的城市有上海市、海口市、广州市、长沙市、重庆市、福州市、哈尔滨市。排名显著上升的城市是：昆明市（26）、沈阳市（17）、广州市（16）、南京市（13）、上海市（13）、长沙市（12）、武汉市（11）、南宁市（10）；排名下降较为明显的城市有：长春市（-19）、重庆市（-18）、福州市（-15）、呼和浩特市（-13）、太原市（-13）、天津市（-12）、兰州市（-11）。

中国 35 个城市生活质量的细分指数

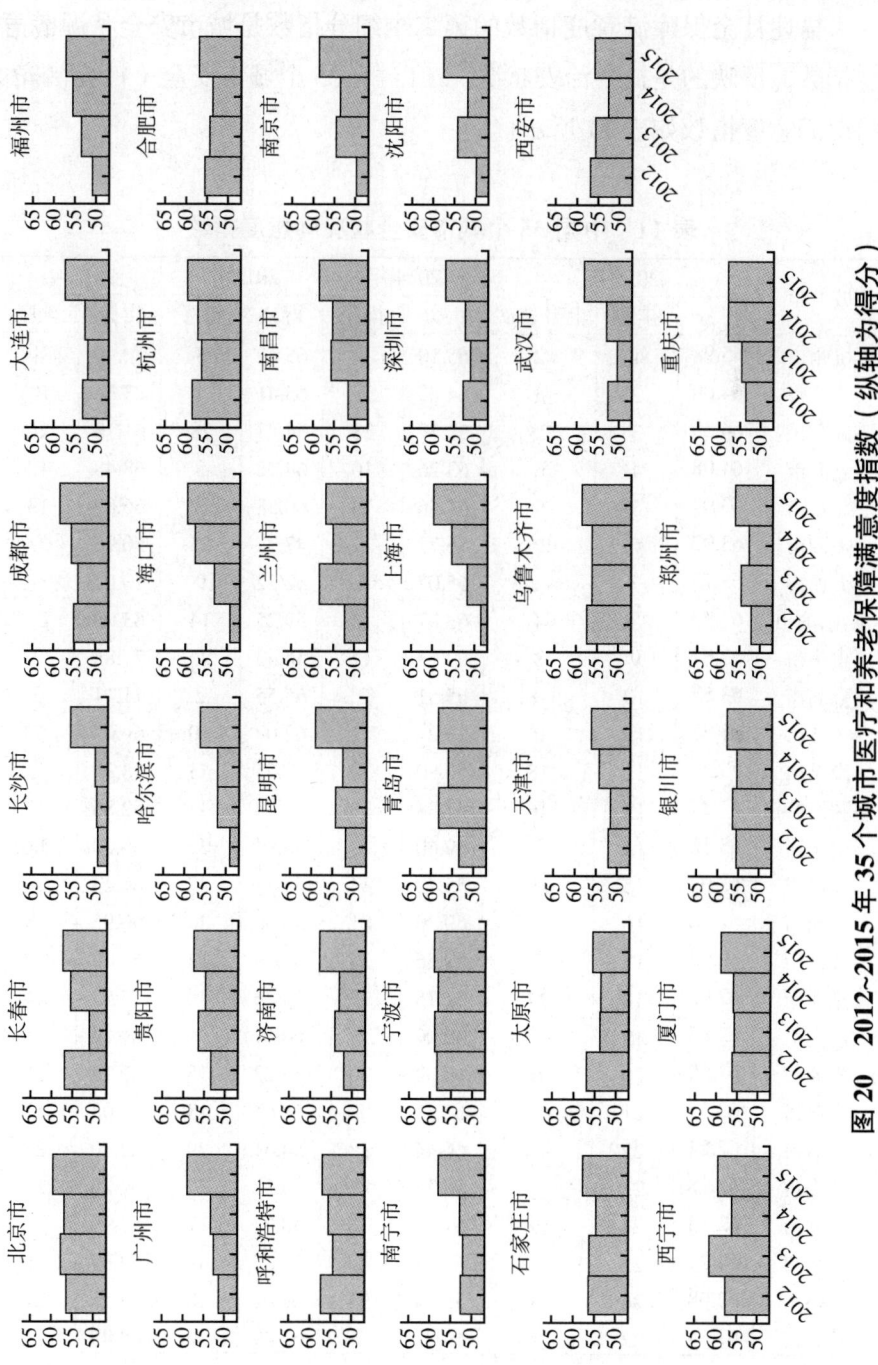

图 20　2012~2015 年 35 个城市医疗和养老保障满意度指数（纵轴为得分）

描述社会保障满意度指数的第二个细分指数是城市安全状况满意度指数，反映的是社会治安状况。2015年，35个城市安全（社会治安）状况满意度指数如表11所示。

表11 中国35个城市安全状况满意度指数

城 市	2015年			2014年		2013年		2012年	
	得分	排序	上升位次	得分	排序	得分	排序	得分	排序
杭州市	65.98	1	2	65.20	3	65.42	3	70.99	4
济南市	64.60	2	3	64.82	5	65.41	4	73.34	1
武汉市	64.23	3	25	57.77	28	54.83	28	61.13	26
上海市	64.08	4	6	63.26	10	64.12	5	68.48	10
北京市	63.97	5	9	61.56	14	60.58	12	66.82	13
贵阳市	63.92	6	26	56.73	32	47.32	35	50.95	35
大连市	63.75	7	−3	65.07	4	62.22	9	70.09	5
哈尔滨市	63.73	8	4	63.07	12	59.25	14	63.03	21
重庆市	63.62	9	8	60.53	17	56.43	26	71.83	2
青岛市	63.57	10	−8	65.51	2	65.55	2	71.11	3
宁波市	63.57	11	0	63.21	11	62.08	10	69.05	7
南昌市	63.28	12	18	56.80	30	52.55	33	58.74	32
呼和浩特市	63.21	13	16	57.38	29	50.73	34	62.86	22
西宁市	63.16	14	9	59.60	23	56.94	21	66.20	14
长沙市	63.02	15	19	55.42	34	55.73	27	60.23	29
郑州市	62.96	16	5	60.20	21	56.66	24	60.95	28
成都市	62.92	17	7	59.56	24	59.69	13	67.40	12
昆明市	62.92	18	17	51.15	35	53.75	30	57.53	34
厦门市	62.85	19	−18	66.00	1	66.67	1	69.19	6
太原市	62.60	20	0	60.32	20	59.22	15	60.15	31
天津市	62.54	21	−12	63.51	9	58.64	18	65.08	17
海口市	62.24	22	−4	60.44	18	54.61	29	62.00	25
西安市	62.18	23	3	58.78	26	56.58	25	62.26	23
福州市	62.13	24	−8	61.17	16	58.71	17	65.90	16
南京市	62.11	25	−19	64.41	6	63.83	6	68.59	9
广州市	62.08	26	5	56.74	31	57.02	20	62.25	24
长春市	61.84	27	−20	64.22	7	62.29	8	68.45	11

续表

城市	2015年			2014年		2013年		2012年	
	得分	排序	上升位次	得分	排序	得分	排序	得分	排序
南宁市	61.83	28	-1	58.37	27	52.75	32	60.19	30
合肥市	61.33	29	-14	61.18	15	61.00	11	64.03	19
沈阳市	61.32	30	-17	62.37	13	58.43	19	64.09	18
兰州市	61.03	31	-9	59.63	22	52.97	31	63.07	20
深圳市	60.98	32	-13	60.39	19	58.98	16	61.11	27
石家庄市	60.97	33	-8	59.32	25	56.89	22	65.93	15
乌鲁木齐市	60.25	34	-1	55.63	33	56.78	23	58.55	33
银川市	60.04	35	-27	63.94	8	63.46	7	68.75	8
平均值	62.90			60.45		58.93		64.58	

根据调查结果，2015年全国35个城市安全状况满意度指数加权平均值为62.90，高于2013年和2014年的水平，略低于2012年的分值，处在满意区间内。35个城市的安全状况满意度指数得分都超过了60，而2014年得分超过60的城市为21个，2013年只有12个。这表明，2013年以来，社会治安状况有了明显的好转。尽管如此，2015年的分值依然低于2012年。这表明，在维持社会治安保障城市安全方面，我们还需要做出更大的努力。图21的直方图直观地描述了上述变动趋势。

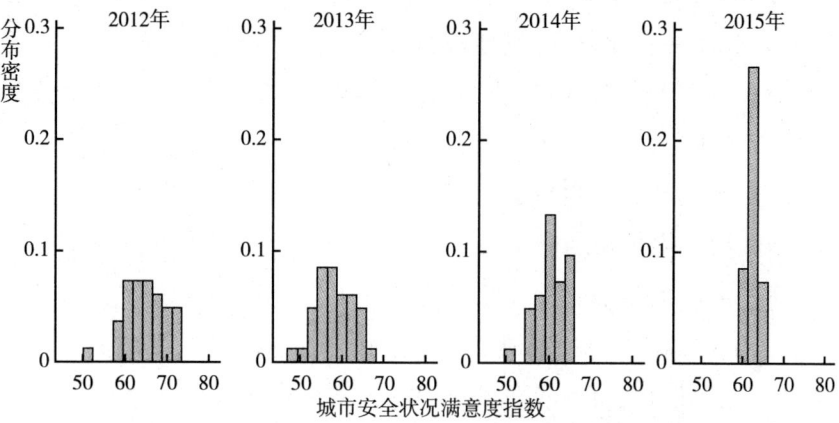

图21 2012~2015年城市安全状况满意度指数

调查显示，城市安全状况满意度指数排名前10位的城市为：杭州市（1）、济南市（2）、武汉市（3）、上海市（4）、北京市（5）、贵阳市（6）、大连市（7）、哈尔滨市（8）、重庆市（9）、青岛市（10）。其中，杭州市、济南市、上海市、大连市、青岛市已经连续4年位于前10名城市的行列。排名后10位的城市分别是：广州市（26）、长春市（27）、南宁市（28）、合肥市（29）、沈阳市（30）、兰州市（31）、深圳市（32）、石家庄市（33）、乌鲁木齐市（34）、银川市（35）。其中，只有南宁市连续4年排在后10名城市的行列中。

从地区分布来看，城市安全状况满意度指数排名前10位的城市中，有8个东部城市、1个中部城市、1个西部城市；城市安全状况满意度指数排名后10位的城市中，有4个东部城市、2个中部城市、4个西部城市。

从动态变化看，2012~2015年，全国城市安全状况满意度指数加权平均值分别为64.58、58.93、60.45、62.90，4年间，2013年分值明显下降，之后的两年呈上升趋势，即社会治安状况明显好转。2012年，得分最低的城市为贵阳市（50.95），2013年最低得分城市为贵阳市（47.32），2014年最低得分城市为昆明市（51.15），2015年，最低得分城市为银川市（60.04），最低得分呈现一种先下降后上升的趋势。图22的柱状图直观地展现了2012~2015年35个城市安全状况（即社会治安状况）满意度指数。分城市看，由于2013年普遍得分较低，因此没有连续3年得分上升的城市。城市安全状况满意度指数连续两年上升的城市有武汉市、北京市、贵阳市、哈尔滨市、重庆市、宁波市、南昌市、呼和浩特市、西宁市、郑州市、太原市、海口市、西安市、福州市、南宁市、合肥市、兰州市、深圳市、石家庄市19个城市。城市安全状况满意度指数排名显著上升的城市有：贵阳市（26）、武汉市（25）、长沙市（19）、南昌市（18）、昆明市（17）、呼和浩特市（16）；排名显著下降的城市有：银川市（-27）、长春

中国 35 个城市生活质量的细分指数

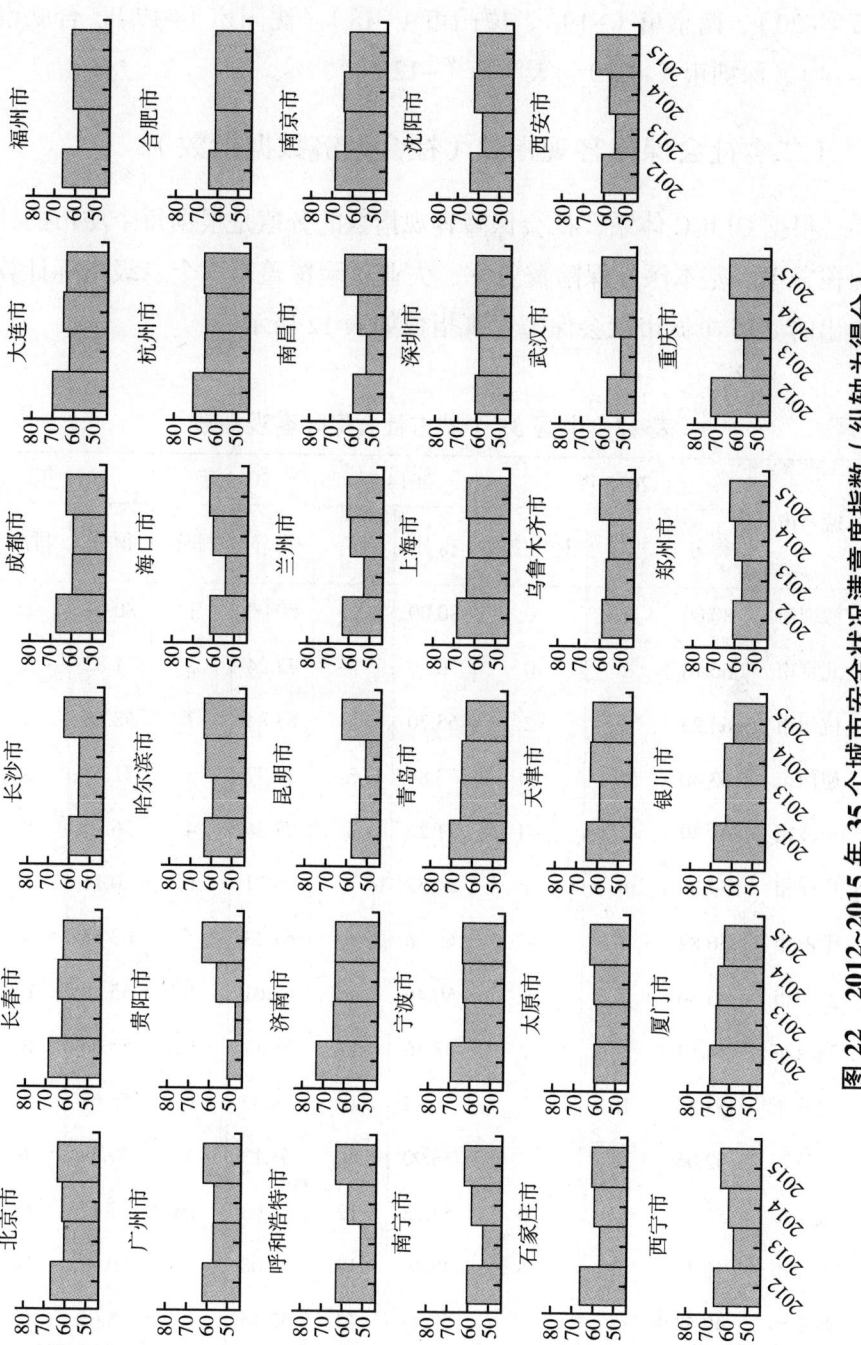

图 22　2012~2015 年 35 个城市安全状况满意度指数（纵轴为得分）

市（-20）、南京市（-19）、厦门市（-18）、沈阳市（-17）、合肥市（-14）、深圳市（-13）、天津市（-12）。

（二）社会保障客观指数（社会经济数据指数）

根据QLICC体系，社会保障客观指数的分值是根据每个城市的社保覆盖率、基本医疗保险覆盖率、失业保险覆盖率3个二级指标计算得出的。35个城市社会保障客观指数如表12所示。

表12 中国35个城市社会保障客观指数

城　市	2015年			2014年		2013年		2012年	
	得分	排序	上升位次	得分	排序	得分	排序	得分	排序
深圳市	80.00	1	0	80.00	1	80.00	1	80.01	1
北京市	66.18	2	0	76.39	2	77.24	2	71.82	2
杭州市	64.23	3	2	65.70	5	63.84	7	58.36	7
厦门市	63.40	4	-1	73.85	3	74.37	3	71.43	3
宁波市	61.39	5	-1	71.22	4	72.36	4	56.19	8
广州市	57.36	6	1	64.52	7	66.71	6	60.11	5
上海市	56.82	7	-1	65.66	6	67.23	5	68.68	4
沈阳市	55.30	8	0	60.46	8	62.01	9	55.20	12
南京市	54.14	9	2	58.56	11	58.11	12	55.65	10
大连市	53.26	10	0	58.85	10	59.82	11	55.67	9
天津市	52.06	11	-2	58.90	9	63.13	8	59.89	6
银川市	50.42	12	0	53.28	12	51.93	16	47.15	18
太原市	50.23	13	6	49.40	19	49.08	19	50.61	14
西安市	49.57	14	-1	52.48	13	52.15	15	55.62	11

续表

城　市	2015年			2014年		2013年		2012年	
	得分	排序	上升位次	得分	排序	得分	排序	得分	排序
成都市	48.60	15	0	51.14	15	50.84	17	45.00	22
乌鲁木齐市	48.14	16	-2	51.79	14	52.63	13	51.44	13
青岛市	47.16	17	0	50.50	17	52.34	14	48.63	16
呼和浩特市	47.01	18	2	46.75	20	46.91	21	45.68	21
长春市	46.95	19	-1	50.17	18	59.84	10	48.23	17
济南市	46.94	20	1	46.71	21	47.36	20	46.08	20
武汉市	46.69	21	-5	50.71	16	50.48	18	49.51	15
贵阳市	45.70	22	2	45.22	24	44.95	25	44.14	24
长沙市	45.20	23	0	45.92	23	45.97	23	43.07	27
重庆市	44.82	24	1	44.97	25	44.57	26	41.48	32
南宁市	44.61	25	-3	46.04	22	46.09	22	40.85	34
福州市	43.76	26	1	44.79	27	44.06	27	42.17	31
兰州市	43.54	27	-1	44.91	26	45.14	24	46.35	19
合肥市	43.49	28	2	44.14	30	43.72	29	44.71	23
郑州市	43.19	29	5	40.61	34	40.98	34	42.99	28
石家庄市	42.89	30	2	41.80	32	41.77	31	40.86	33
昆明市	42.77	31	-2	44.52	29	41.21	33	42.85	29
海口市	42.55	32	-4	44.72	28	43.91	28	42.54	30
南昌市	41.59	33	-2	42.87	31	43.05	30	43.46	25
哈尔滨市	41.04	34	-1	41.58	33	41.73	32	43.21	26
西宁市	40.00	35	0	40.00	35	40.00	35	39.98	35
平均值		51.26		54.66		55.26		50.85	

根据调查结果，2015 年，全国 35 个城市社会保障客观指数加权平均值为 51.26，与前面几次调查的平均值相比有了较大幅度的降低。35 个城市中有 22 个城市的社会保障客观指数得分低于 50，而 2014 年只有 17 个城市的社会保障客观指数得分低于 50。值得注意的是，深圳市在 2012~2015 年 4 年中排名均为第 1，并且得分都在 80 以上，进入了"很满意"的区间（得分为 76~100）。整体上看，城市社会保障客观指数在 2013 年短暂上升后便呈现下降趋势。图 23 直观地展现了 2012~2015 年社会保障客观指数的变动情况。

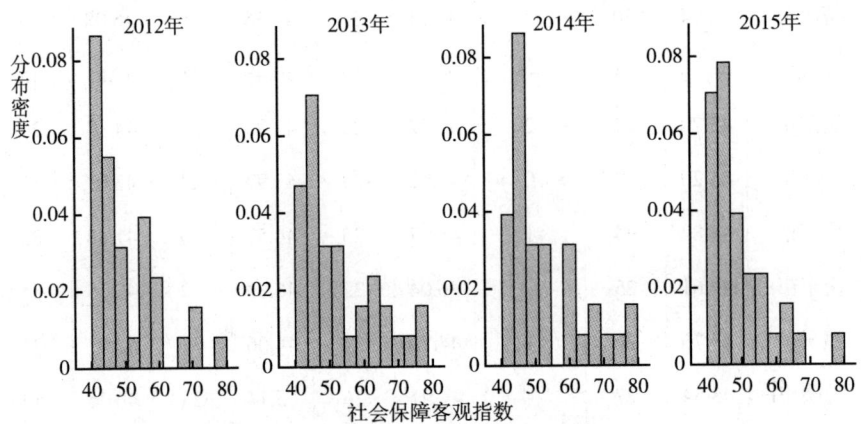

图 23　2012~2015 年社会保障客观指数

本次调查显示，城市社会保障客观指数排名前 10 位的城市为：深圳市（1）、北京市（2）、杭州市（3）、厦门市（4）、宁波市（5）、广州市（6）、上海市（7）、沈阳市（8）、南京市（9）、大连市（10）。其中，深圳、北京、杭州、厦门、宁波、广州、上海 7 个城市已经连续 4 年排在前 10 名城市的行列中，2015 年排第 8 名的沈阳市也已经连续 3 年排在前 10 名城市的行列中。城市社会保障客观指数排名后 10 位的城市分别是：福州市（26）、兰州市（27）、合肥市（28）、郑州市（29）、石家庄市（30）、昆明市（31）、海口市（32）、南昌市（33）、哈尔滨市（34）、西宁市（35）。其中，福州、郑州、石家庄、昆明、海口、南昌、哈尔滨、西宁8个城市已经连续4年排在后10名城市的行列中；合肥和南昌两个城市连续3年排在后10名城市的行列中；西宁则连续4年垫底。此外，值得注意的是，社会保障客观指数得分最高为80，最低为40，相差一倍。

从地区分布来看，城市社会保障客观指数排名前10位的城市都是东部城市。城市社会保障客观指数排名后10位的城市中，有3个东部城市、3个中部城市、4个西部城市。

从动态变化看，2012~2015年，全国城市社会保障客观指数加权平均值分别为50.85、55.26、54.66、51.26，4年的分值呈现先上升后下降的趋势。2012年最低得分为39.98，2013年最低得分为40，2014年最低得分为40，2015年最低得分为40。图24直观地展现了2012~2015年35个城市社会保障客观指数的动态变化情况。分城市看，分值连续3年上升的只有贵阳和石家庄两个城市。2015年，排名明显上升的有太原市（6）、郑州市（5）；排名明显下降的是武汉市（-5）、海口市（-4）。总体说来，排名没有太大变化。

五 生活感受指数

（一）生活感受满意度指数

根据QLICC体系，生活感受满意度指数是通过问卷调查由生活节奏满意度指数和生活便利满意度指数加权平均得到的。2015年35个城市生活感受满意度指数的调查结果如表13所示。

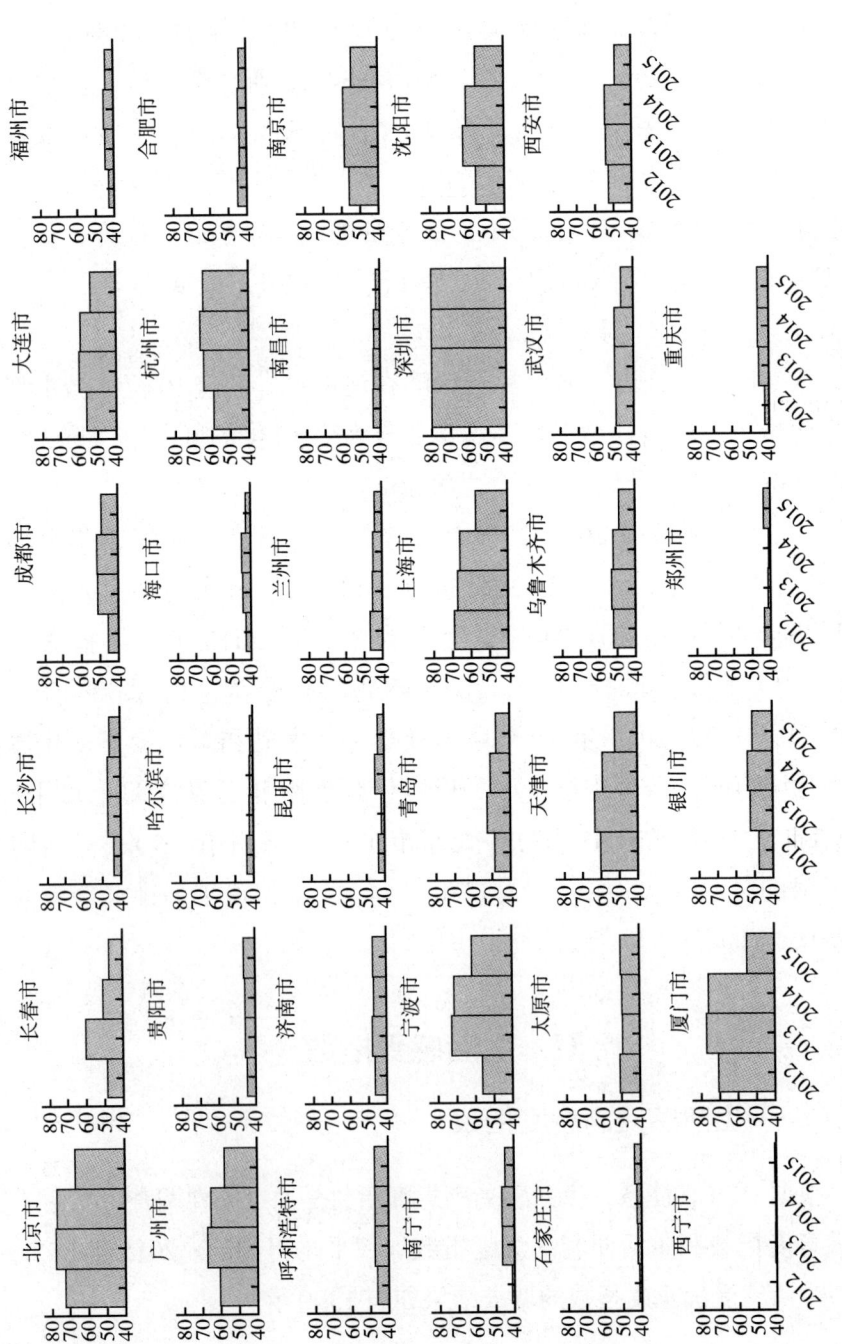

图 24 2012~2015 年 35 个城市社会保障客观指数（纵轴为得分）

中国35个城市生活质量的细分指数

表13 中国35个城市生活感受满意度指数

城　市	2015年			2014年		2013年		2012年	
	得分	排序	上升位次	得分	排序	得分	排序	得分	排序
呼和浩特市	57.98	1	29	53.82	30	53.07	29	52.68	34
杭州市	57.65	2	7	55.85	9	57.05	4	58.25	3
昆明市	57.63	3	9	55.37	12	52.40	34	53.13	33
南京市	57.60	4	6	55.75	10	57.54	3	58.08	5
哈尔滨市	57.04	5	13	54.83	18	53.95	23	53.62	31
成都市	56.78	6	-4	58.01	2	56.06	15	57.86	6
长春市	56.25	7	19	54.26	26	56.14	11	58.22	4
上海市	56.22	8	21	53.84	29	56.10	13	56.58	14
合肥市	56.17	9	12	54.70	21	54.09	22	55.31	21
南宁市	56.11	10	23	53.09	33	52.96	32	54.86	23
重庆市	56.10	11	-3	55.85	8	56.66	7	56.18	16
海口市	56.09	12	16	54.14	28	55.63	17	55.75	17
大连市	55.97	13	14	54.17	27	54.35	20	55.06	22
宁波市	55.79	14	-3	55.49	11	56.56	8	55.34	19
厦门市	55.74	15	-9	56.30	6	56.67	6	59.01	2
沈阳市	55.72	16	-9	56.08	7	54.21	21	55.33	20
石家庄市	55.66	17	-12	56.43	5	54.43	19	57.11	9
南昌市	55.66	18	4	54.61	22	53.84	26	53.86	27
郑州市	55.59	19	4	54.55	23	56.09	14	54.17	25
西安市	55.48	20	4	54.51	24	55.96	16	55.46	18
福州市	55.36	21	-2	54.82	19	56.20	10	56.72	12
贵阳市	55.28	22	10	53.12	32	53.18	28	53.81	29

087

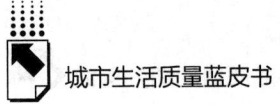

续表

城市	2015年			2014年		2013年		2012年	
	得分	排序	上升位次	得分	排序	得分	排序	得分	排序
青岛市	55.17	23	-19	56.54	4	56.20	9	56.96	11
武汉市	55.11	24	7	53.48	31	53.29	27	54.31	24
天津市	54.95	25	-9	55.13	16	56.75	5	56.63	13
广州市	54.76	26	-1	54.36	25	52.99	31	53.67	30
长沙市	54.69	27	-14	55.33	13	53.94	24	57.02	10
乌鲁木齐市	54.69	28	-13	55.14	15	50.85	35	56.25	15
银川市	54.65	29	-28	58.17	1	58.24	1	59.90	1
太原市	54.52	30	-13	54.91	17	54.75	18	53.84	28
北京市	54.35	31	4	52.39	35	53.87	25	53.30	32
济南市	54.32	32	-12	54.76	20	56.13	12	57.23	8
西宁市	54.20	33	-30	57.52	3	57.76	2	57.41	7
兰州市	53.59	34	-20	55.27	14	52.47	33	50.00	35
深圳市	53.26	35	-1	52.40	34	53.07	30	54.02	26
平均值	55.66			54.88		55.07		55.63	

从表13可以看出，2015年全国35个城市生活感受满意度指数均值为55.66，略高于上两年的分值，与2012年基本持平，4年的分值比较稳定，均处于满意区间，并且城市间的差距并不明显，2015年得分最高的是呼和浩特市，得分只有57.98，得分最低的是深圳市，得分为53.26，两者相差不大。相比过去3年，最高分数呈略微下降的态势，这或许是随着经济增长，人们对生活感受提出了更高要求的

中国 35 个城市生活质量的细分指数

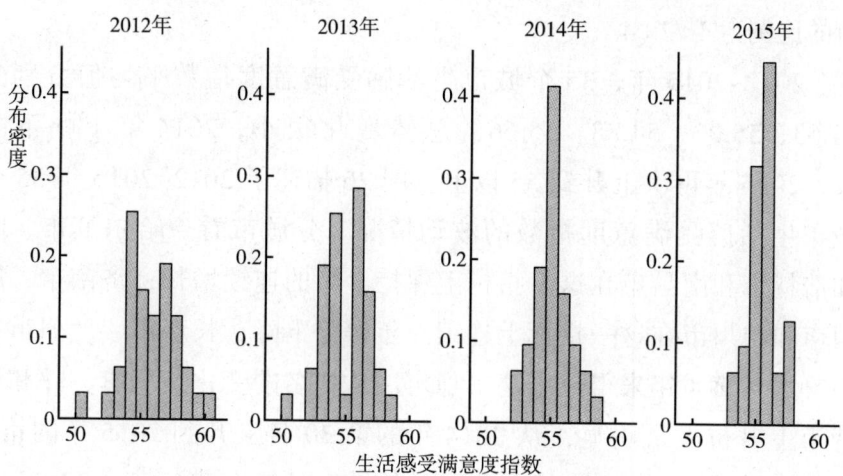

图 25 2012~2015 年生活感受满意度指数

缘故。但 2015 年的最低分相比之前 3 年有明显的上升。图 25 展现了 2012~2015 年城市生活感受满意度指数的情况。

2015 年，35 个城市生活感受满意度指数调查结果显示，生活感受满意度指数排名前 10 位的城市为：呼和浩特市（1）、杭州市（2）、昆明市（3）、南京市（4）、哈尔滨市（5）、成都市（6）、长春市（7）、上海市（8）、合肥市（9）、南宁市（10）。其中，杭州市和南京市已经连续 4 年排在前 10 名城市的行列中。排名处在后 10 位的城市是：广州市（26）、长沙市（27）、乌鲁木齐市（28）、银川市（29）、太原市（30）、北京市（31）、济南市（32）、西宁市（33）、兰州市（34）、深圳市（35）。其中，深圳市已经连续 4 年排在后 10 名城市的行列中；在 2012~2015 年的 4 年中，北京市和广州市均有 3 年位于排名后 10 位城市的行列，且均有 1 年排倒数 11 名。

按地区分布分析，城市生活感受满意度指数排名前 10 位的城市中，东部城市、中部城市、西部城市的比例为 3∶3∶4。城市生活感受满意度指数排名后 10 位的城市中，东部城市、中部城市、西部城市的比例为4:2:4。

2012~2015年，35个城市生活感受满意度指数平均值分别为55.63、55.07、54.88、55.66，总体变化很小，2014年小幅下降后，2015年再次上升到55以上。图26描述了2012~2015年35个城市生活感受满意度指数的波动情况。分城市看，哈尔滨市、呼和浩特市和南昌市在这一指标上保持3年的连续增长；济南市、厦门市和银川市在这一指标上连续3年得分下降；长春市、兰州市和乌鲁木齐市4年来得分震荡不稳定。从排名的变化情况看，呼和浩特市上升位次最明显，从2014年的第30名上升到2015年的第1名，上升了29位。排名上升明显的城市还有：南宁市（23）、上海市（21）、长春市（19）、海口市（16）、大连市（14）、哈尔滨市（13）、合肥市（12）、贵阳市（10）、昆明市（9）。在排名下降的城市中，西宁市下降最为明显，直接由2014年的第3名下降到2015年的33名，下降了30位。排名下降比较明显的城市还有：银川市（-28）、兰州市（-20）、青岛市（-19）、长沙市（-14）、乌鲁木齐市（-13）、太原市（-13）、石家庄市（-12）、济南市（-12）；此外，厦门市、沈阳市、天津市的排名均下降了9位。从上述数据看，2014~2015年，城市生活感受满意度指数不仅波动幅度大，而且发生波动的城市比较多。

生活感受满意度指数是由生活节奏满意度指数和生活便利满意度指数两个细分指数构成的，根据QLICC体系的规定，对上述两个细分指数分别取以50%的权重。因此，城市生活感受满意度指数的变化可以由两个细分指数的变化予以说明。下面将分别介绍这两个细分指数。

根据2015年的调查结果，中国35个城市的居民生活节奏满意度指数及其与往年指数的对比情况如表14所示。

中国 35 个城市生活质量的细分指数

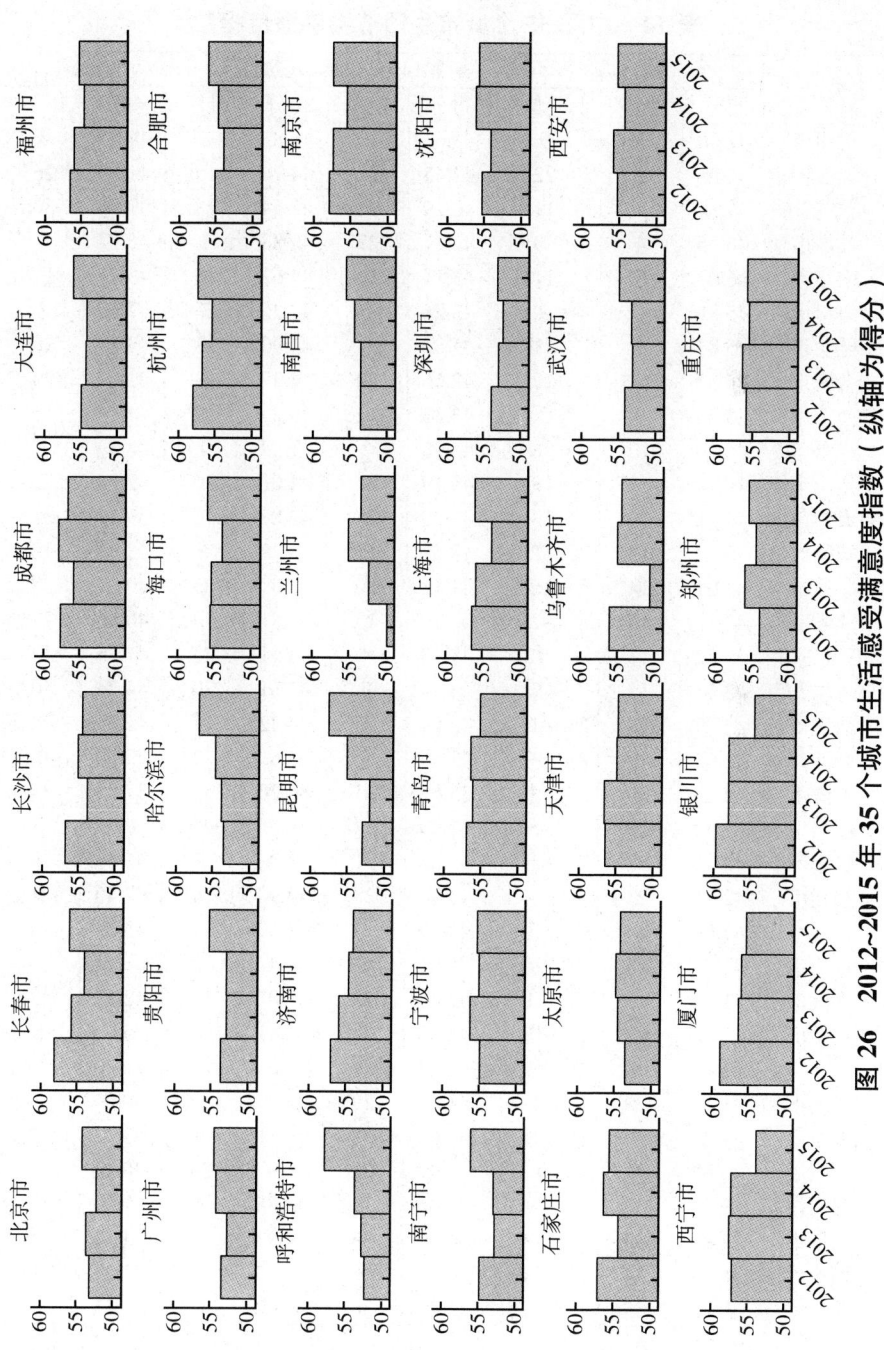

图 26 2012~2015 年 35 个城市生活感受满意度指数（纵轴为得分）

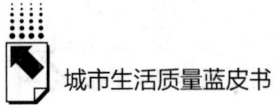

表14 中国35个城市生活节奏满意度指数

城市	2015年			2014年		2013年		2012年	
	得分	排序	上升位次	得分	排序	得分	排序	得分	排序
杭州市	47.06	1	9	43.63	10	45.83	8	44.93	8
呼和浩特市	46.96	2	22	42.45	24	44.74	15	41.43	26
哈尔滨市	46.88	3	11	43.29	14	42.54	28	39.96	30
长春市	46.35	4	23	42.17	27	49.88	1	45.72	5
南京市	46.07	5	11	43.11	16	44.62	16	43.21	17
海口市	45.89	6	9	43.24	15	47.25	3	47.50	3
昆明市	45.83	7	−1	45.32	6	44.90	13	43.27	16
合肥市	45.67	8	12	42.66	20	44.27	18	42.27	23
南宁市	45.40	9	3	43.38	12	44.23	19	44.44	11
成都市	45.10	10	−8	45.98	2	47.22	4	48.39	2
重庆市	44.15	11	15	42.19	26	44.01	20	42.34	22
大连市	44.12	12	13	42.20	25	42.87	26	39.57	31
郑州市	43.63	13	−2	43.57	11	46.27	6	42.98	18
宁波市	43.61	14	16	41.17	30	42.99	25	40.54	28
沈阳市	43.56	15	−2	43.29	13	41.81	29	40.86	27
石家庄市	43.52	16	−12	45.48	4	43.11	23	44.35	12
乌鲁木齐市	43.23	17	−10	44.54	7	41.81	30	44.74	10
西安市	42.79	18	−1	42.84	17	44.32	17	42.23	24
南昌市	42.63	19	−10	43.66	9	43.62	22	43.90	13
上海市	42.43	20	13	35.69	33	38.20	33	37.05	34
厦门市	42.42	21	−3	42.80	18	43.06	24	44.77	9
贵阳市	42.31	22	−1	42.65	21	45.90	7	45.48	7
福州市	42.27	23	5	41.90	28	44.90	14	42.49	21
武汉市	42.09	24	−5	42.80	19	43.69	21	43.49	14
兰州市	41.99	25	−20	45.44	5	46.47	5	41.48	25
济南市	41.97	26	−3	42.45	23	45.02	11	42.92	19
长沙市	41.85	27	−19	44.02	8	42.81	27	45.61	6
天津市	41.70	28	3	39.93	31	44.95	12	42.70	20
青岛市	41.25	29	0	41.69	29	39.22	32	40.09	29
太原市	41.21	30	−8	42.63	22	45.11	9	43.32	15
广州市	40.83	31	1	39.07	32	36.67	34	38.12	32
银川市	39.88	32	−31	47.36	1	45.05	10	50.00	1
深圳市	38.84	33	2	34.90	35	34.93	35	35.81	35
西宁市	38.83	34	−31	45.83	3	47.95	2	47.22	4
北京市	38.72	35	−1	35.41	34	39.32	31	37.11	33
平均值	43.12			41.90		42.97		42.87	

从表 14 可以看出，2015 年城市居民生活节奏满意度指数的均值为 43.12。与过去几年相比没有明显的变化，并且分值较低，一直处于对生活节奏不满意的区间。城市间分值差距较大，得分最高的是杭州市，得分为 47.06，得分最低的是北京市，得分为 38.72 分。相比过去三年，最高分数呈稳中下滑状态。综合来看，全国 35 个城市生活节奏满意度相对较差，这可能是生活节奏普遍加快所致。图 27 描述了 2012~2015 年生活节奏满意度指数的变动情况。

表 14 中 35 个城市居民生活节奏满意度指数调查结果显示，生活节奏满意度指数排名前 10 位的城市为：杭州市（1）、呼和浩特市（2）、哈尔滨市（3）、长春市（4）、南京市（5）、海口市（6）、昆明市（7）、合肥市（8）、南宁市（9）、成都市（10）。其中，只有成都市连续 4 年处于排名前 10 位的城市行列中。排名处在后 10 位的城市是：济南市（26）、长沙市（27）、天津市（28）、青岛市（29）、太原市（30）、广州市（31）、银川市（32）、深圳市（33）、西宁市（34）、北京市（35）。其中，北京市、深圳市、广州市、青岛市已经连续 4 年位于排名后 10 位的城市行列中；银川市和西宁市 2012~2014 年曾连续 3 年处于排名前 10 位的城市行列中，且于 2015 年首次落入排名后 10 位的城市行列中。

按地区分布分析，城市生活节奏满意度指数排名前 10 位的城市中，东部城市、中部城市、西部城市的比例为 4∶2∶4。城市生活节奏满意度指数排名后 10 位的城市中，东部城市、中部城市、西部城市的比例为 6∶2∶2。中部地区的城市居民对生活节奏相对比较满意，东部地区部分城市的居民感觉生活节奏偏快，特别是北京、上海、广州、深圳四大城市。

2012~2015 年，35 个城市生活节奏满意度指数平均值分别为 42.87、42.97、41.90、43.12，总体变化很小，2014 年分值小幅下降后，2015 年略有上升。图 28 给出了 2012~2015 年 35 个城市生活节奏

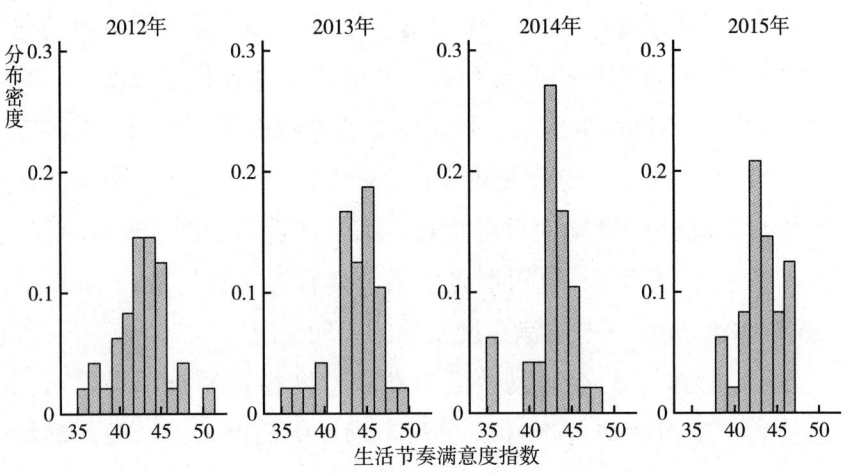

图 27　2012~2015 年生活节奏满意度指数

满意度指数的变动情况。分城市看，哈尔滨市、昆明市和沈阳市在这个指标上保持了连续 3 年的增长；成都市和厦门市在这个指标上连续 3 年得分下降；长春市和呼和浩特市 4 年得分震荡不稳定；南昌市和南宁市 4 年得分比较平稳。从排名的变化看，长春市的上升位次最明显，2015 年上升了 23 位，排名第 4。上升明显的城市还有：呼和浩特（22）、宁波市（16）、重庆市（15）、大连市（13）、上海市（13）、合肥市（12）、哈尔滨市（11）、南京市（11），杭州市和海口市均上升了 9 位；在排名下降的城市中，银川市和西宁市下降最为明显，均下降了 31 位。排名下降比较明显的城市还有：兰州市市（-20）、长沙市（-19）、石家庄市（-12）、乌鲁木齐市（-10）、南昌市（-10）。

描述生活感受满意度指数变化的除了生活节奏满意度指数外，还有生活便利满意度指数。2015 年 35 个城市生活便利满意度指数如表 15 所示。

中国 35 个城市生活质量的细分指数

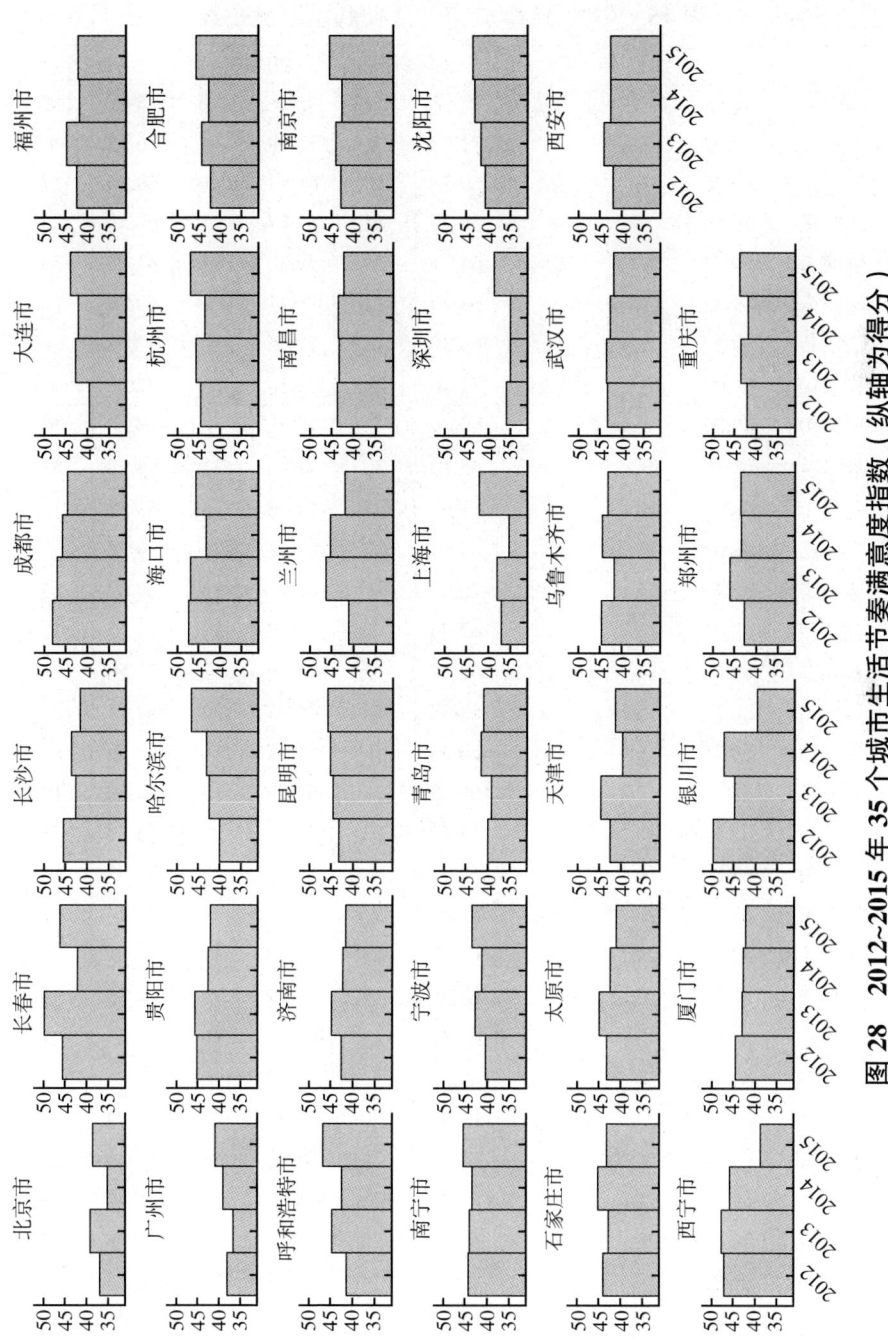

图 28 2012~2015 年 35 个城市生活节奏满意度指数（纵轴为得分）

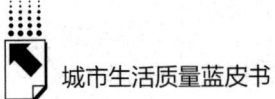

表15 中国35个城市生活便利满意度指数

城 市	2015年			2014年		2013年		2012年	
	得分	排序	上升位次	得分	排序	得分	排序	得分	排序
上海市	70.02	1	0	71.98	1	73.99	1	76.12	1
北京市	69.98	2	8	69.38	10	68.42	11	69.50	17
西宁市	69.56	3	8	69.20	11	67.57	14	67.59	23
昆明市	69.44	4	25	65.41	29	59.90	33	62.98	33
银川市	69.42	5	7	68.99	12	71.43	3	69.79	16
南京市	69.13	6	8	68.39	14	70.46	5	72.95	4
青岛市	69.09	7	−5	71.40	2	73.18	2	73.82	2
厦门市	69.05	8	−1	69.79	7	70.28	6	73.26	3
呼和浩特市	68.99	9	21	65.19	30	61.40	31	63.93	31
南昌市	68.69	10	17	65.57	27	64.06	25	63.82	32
广州市	68.68	11	−3	69.65	8	69.31	9	69.23	18
成都市	68.46	12	−8	70.03	4	64.90	23	67.32	24
福州市	68.44	13	3	67.74	16	67.49	15	70.95	8
杭州市	68.25	14	1	68.07	15	68.26	12	71.58	6
贵阳市	68.24	15	19	63.58	34	60.45	32	62.14	34
天津市	68.21	16	−13	70.33	3	68.55	10	70.56	10
西安市	68.18	17	7	66.18	24	67.59	13	68.69	19
武汉市	68.14	18	15	64.17	33	62.89	28	65.13	28
重庆市	68.06	19	−10	69.51	9	69.31	8	70.01	13
宁波市	67.97	20	−14	69.81	6	70.14	7	70.14	12
沈阳市	67.87	21	−8	68.86	13	66.60	17	69.80	15
太原市	67.83	22	−4	67.19	18	64.39	24	64.36	29
大连市	67.83	23	2	66.13	25	65.83	19	70.55	11
石家庄市	67.80	24	−7	67.37	17	65.75	20	69.86	14
深圳市	67.68	25	−20	69.89	5	71.21	4	72.22	5
郑州市	67.54	26	2	65.54	28	65.91	18	65.36	26
长沙市	67.54	27	−6	66.64	21	65.07	22	68.42	20
哈尔滨市	67.20	28	−6	66.37	22	65.36	21	67.28	25
南宁市	66.82	29	6	62.81	35	61.69	30	65.28	27
合肥市	66.68	30	−10	66.74	20	63.91	27	68.35	21

续表

城市	2015年			2014年		2013年		2012年	
	得分	排序	上升位次	得分	排序	得分	排序	得分	排序
济南市	66.67	31	−12	67.07	19	67.25	16	71.54	7
海口市	66.29	32	0	65.04	32	64.01	26	64.00	30
长春市	66.16	33	−10	66.35	23	62.39	29	70.72	9
乌鲁木齐市	66.16	34	−8	65.74	26	59.89	34	67.76	22
兰州市	65.18	35	−4	65.09	31	58.48	35	58.52	35
平均值	68.20			67.66		67.18		68.39	

根据调查结果，2015年城市生活便利满意度指数均值为68.20，略高于2013年和2014年，略低于2012年，但仍处在对生活便利程度满意的区间。相比过去3年，最高分数持续小幅度下滑，但值得注意的是，最低得分有所提高，2015年比2012年提高近12%。综合来说，中国35个城市的居民对生活便利程度普遍感到满意。图29展现了2012~2015年生活便利满意度指数的变动情况。

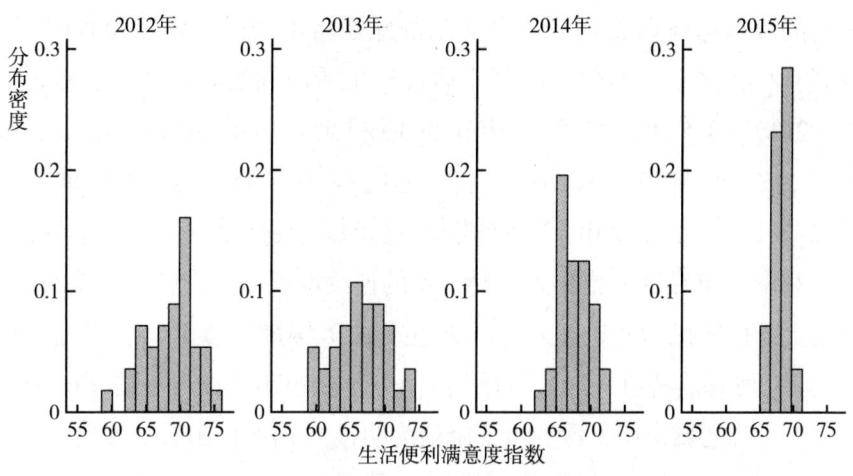

图29 2012~2015年生活便利满意度指数

在表15中，35个城市生活便利满意度指数调查结果显示，生活便利满意度指数排名前10位的城市为：上海市（1）、北京市（2）、西宁市（3）、昆明市（4）、银川市（5）、南京市（6）、青岛市（7）、厦门市（8）、呼和浩特市（9）、南昌市（10）。其中，上海市、青岛市、厦门市已经连续4年位于前10名的城市行列，更值得注意的是，上海市已经连续4年排名第1，并且曾经在2012年得分76.12，进入到"很满意"区间（得分为76~100）。排名处在后10位的城市是：郑州市（26）、长沙市（27）、哈尔滨市（28）、南宁市（29）、合肥市（30）、济南市（31）、海口市（32）、长春市（33）、乌鲁木齐市（34）、兰州市（35）。其中，南宁市、海口市、兰州市已经连续4年、乌鲁木齐市连续3年位于后10名的城市行列，并且兰州市在4年中已经有过3次垫底，即排名第35位。

按地区分布分析，城市生活便利满意度指数排名前10位的城市中，东部城市、中部城市、西部城市的比例为5:1:4。城市生活便利满意度指数排名后10位的城市中，东部城市、中部城市、西部城市的比例为2:5:3。分析认为，东部地区交通基础设施比较完善，配套的交通运输设施量大，因此东部地区城市居民对生活便利的评价较高，相比之下，西部地区城市居民对生活便利的满意度评价较低。

2012~2015年，35个城市生活便利满意度指数平均值分别为68.39、67.18、67.66、68.20，总体变化很小。图30直观地展现了2012~2015年35个城市生活便利满意度指数的变化情况。分城市看，海口市和南昌市在这一指标上保持3年的连续增长。从排名的变化看，昆明市上升位次最为明显，上升了25位，2015年排名第4。上升明显的城市还有：呼和浩特市（21）、贵阳市（19）、南昌市（17）、武汉市（15）。在排名下降的城市中，深圳市下降最为明显，下降了20位，2015年排名第25。排名下降比较明显的城市还有：宁波市（-14）、天津市（-13）、济南市（-12）、重庆市（-10）、合肥市（-10）、长春市（-10）。

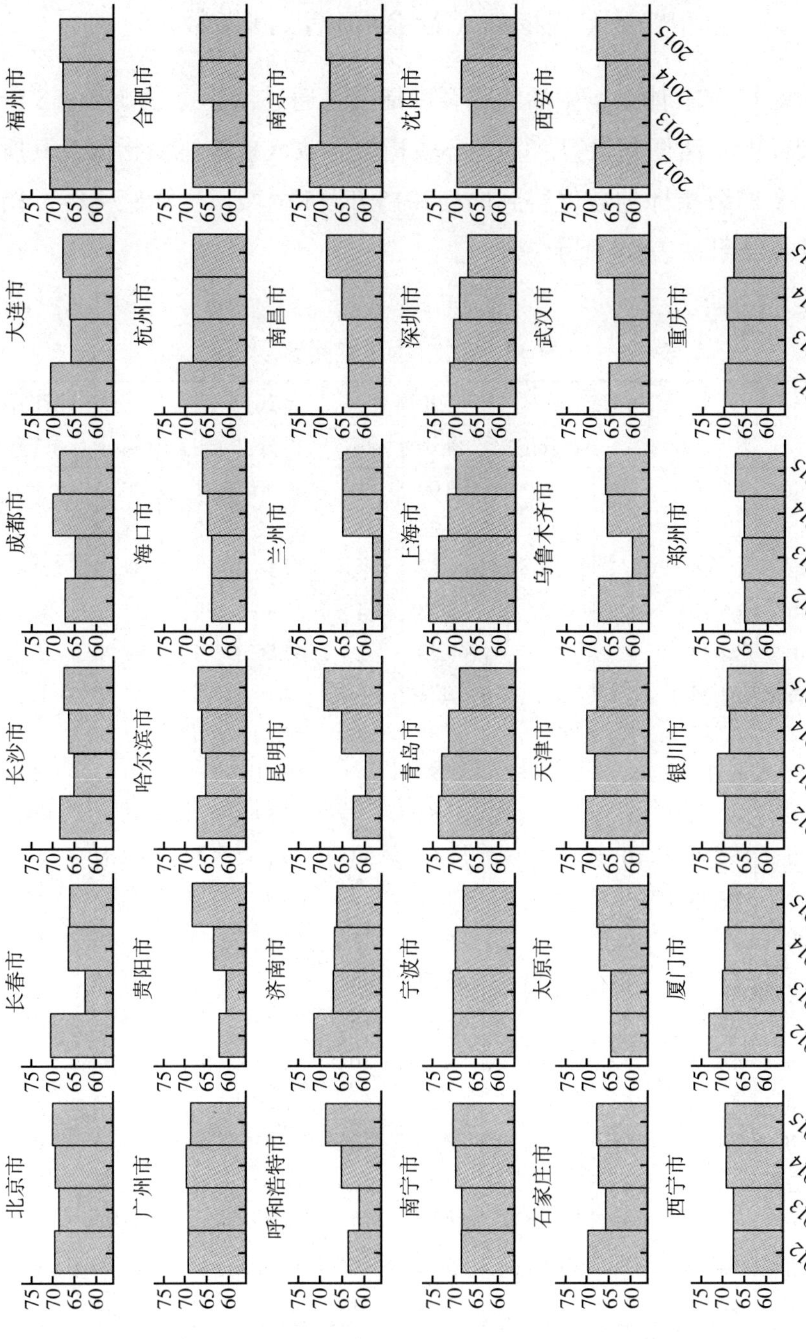

中国 35 个城市生活质量的细分指数

图 30 2012~2015 年 35 个城市生活便利满意度指数（纵轴为得分）

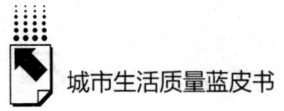

（二）生活感受客观指数（社会经济数据指数）

根据 QLICC 体系，生活感受客观指数是通过计算每个城市的 3 个一级指标即生活便利指数、生态环境指数、收入差距感受指数及其所属的 6 个二级指标的数值得到的。2015 年 35 个城市生活感受客观指数的计算结果如表 16 所示。

表 16　中国 35 个城市生活感受客观指数

城　市	2015 年			2014 年		2013 年		2012 年	
	得分	排序	上升位次	得分	排序	得分	排序	得分	排序
北京市	80.00	1	0	80.00	1	80.00	1	80.01	1
深圳市	67.95	2	0	69.71	2	65.12	2	71.86	2
广州市	67.86	3	0	66.66	3	64.16	3	58.88	7
海口市	65.12	4	0	65.35	4	57.80	9	55.45	12
沈阳市	64.32	5	0	63.28	5	62.56	4	62.90	5
呼和浩特市	62.84	6	0	62.51	6	58.74	7	54.50	13
南京市	62.35	7	1	60.84	8	59.70	6	58.24	8
杭州市	60.82	8	1	59.56	9	58.41	8	64.43	4
昆明市	60.70	9	-2	61.54	7	57.57	10	55.61	10
武汉市	60.39	10	3	57.93	13	60.15	5	64.52	3
哈尔滨市	59.39	11	3	57.77	14	56.98	12	48.25	20
太原市	59.08	12	-1	58.23	11	57.34	11	48.10	21
西安市	58.43	13	5	55.87	18	54.32	17	55.46	11
青岛市	58.42	14	1	57.63	15	55.68	13	48.97	19
银川市	58.14	15	-5	58.31	10	54.74	14	52.58	14
兰州市	56.78	16	0	56.98	16	51.76	21	50.77	17
厦门市	56.77	17	-5	58.20	12	52.07	20	58.95	6
乌鲁木齐市	56.39	18	2	54.22	20	54.20	18	46.58	23
长春市	56.28	19	-2	55.92	17	53.70	15	51.25	16
上海市	55.67	20	-1	55.57	19	54.71	15	56.45	9
合肥市	54.81	21	0	53.30	21	54.46	16	42.91	31

续表

城市	2015年			2014年		2013年		2012年	
	得分	排序	上升位次	得分	排序	得分	排序	得分	排序
宁波市	53.10	22	0	52.51	22	48.24	23	46.35	24
石家庄市	51.87	23	3	50.43	26	51.39	22	46.63	22
西宁市	51.52	24	1	50.56	25	45.51	28	45.60	27
南昌市	50.93	25	3	49.82	28	44.81	30	43.40	30
福州市	50.76	26	−3	52.46	23	45.93	27	51.84	15
贵阳市	50.34	27	0	49.98	27	44.89	29	41.91	32
大连市	50.29	28	−4	50.90	24	47.37	24	49.07	18
成都市	48.35	29	5	45.34	34	43.35	33	41.30	34
南宁市	48.05	30	−1	47.77	29	43.97	32	44.47	29
天津市	47.91	31	−1	47.34	30	47.28	25	46.20	25
长沙市	47.48	32	0	47.20	32	46.47	26	45.23	28
济南市	47.07	33	−2	47.26	31	44.71	31	45.72	26
重庆市	46.61	34	−1	46.34	33	43.18	34	40.02	35
郑州市	40.00	35	0	40.00	35	40.00	35	41.65	33
平均值	56.17			55.57		53.67		51.89	

表16显示，2015年35个城市生活感受客观指数的均值为56.17，略高于2014年，处于满意区间。最高得分仍然是北京市（80.00）。35个城市居民生活感受指数最低的城市仍为郑州市（40.00），最低值也未发生变化。整体来看，35个城市间最高分值和最低分值相差悬殊，从二级指标来看，城市间交通提供能力、万人影剧院数、医疗提供能力、人均绿地面积、空气质量、基尼系数等方面存在较大差距。图31的直方图展现了2012~2014年生活感受客观指数的变动情况。

35个城市生活感受客观指数调查结果显示，生活感受客观指数得分排名前10位的城市为：北京市（1）、深圳市（2）、广州市（3）、海口市（4）、沈阳市（5）、呼和浩特市（6）、南京市（7）、杭州市（8）、昆明市（9）、武汉市（10）。前6位的排名与上年相比保持不变。

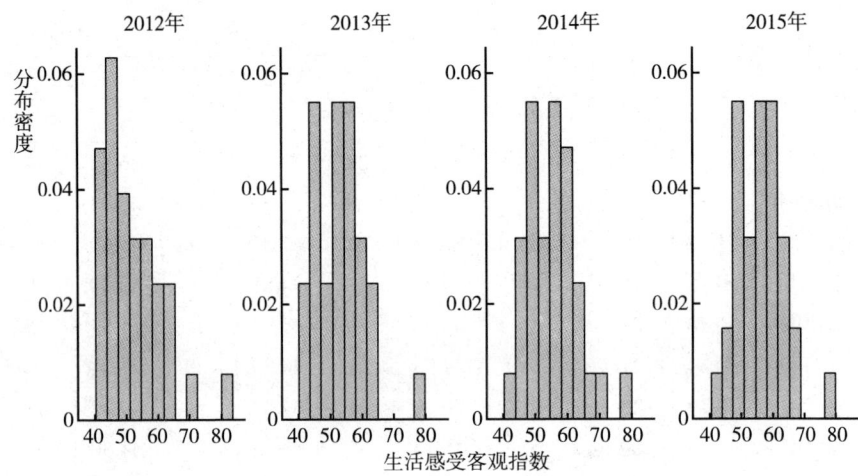

图31　2012~2014年生活感受客观指数

北京、深圳、广州、沈阳、南京、杭州、昆明7个城市已经连续4年保持在前10名城市的行列，海口和呼和浩特两个城市也已经连续3年保持在前10名城市的行列。北京市已经连续4年排名第1，并且得分均在80分或80分以上。排名处在后10位的城市是：福州市（26）、贵阳市（27）、大连市（28）、成都市（29）、南宁市（30）、天津市（31）、长沙市（32）、济南市（33）、重庆市（34）、郑州市（35）。其中，贵阳、成都、南宁、长沙、济南、重庆、郑州7个城市已经连续4年位于排名后10位城市的行列；郑州市已经连续3年垫底，即排在第35位。

按地区分布分析，生活感受客观指数排名前10位的城市中，东部城市、中部城市、西部城市的比例为7∶1∶2；排名后10位的城市中，东部城市、中部城市、西部城市的比例为4∶2∶4。分析表明，地域对生活感受客观指数具有明显的影响，东部地区在排名中处于相对靠前的位置。

2012~2015年，35个城市生活感受客观指数总体平均值分别为51.89、53.67、55.57、56.17，连续3年小幅上升。图32的柱状图直

中国35个城市生活质量的细分指数

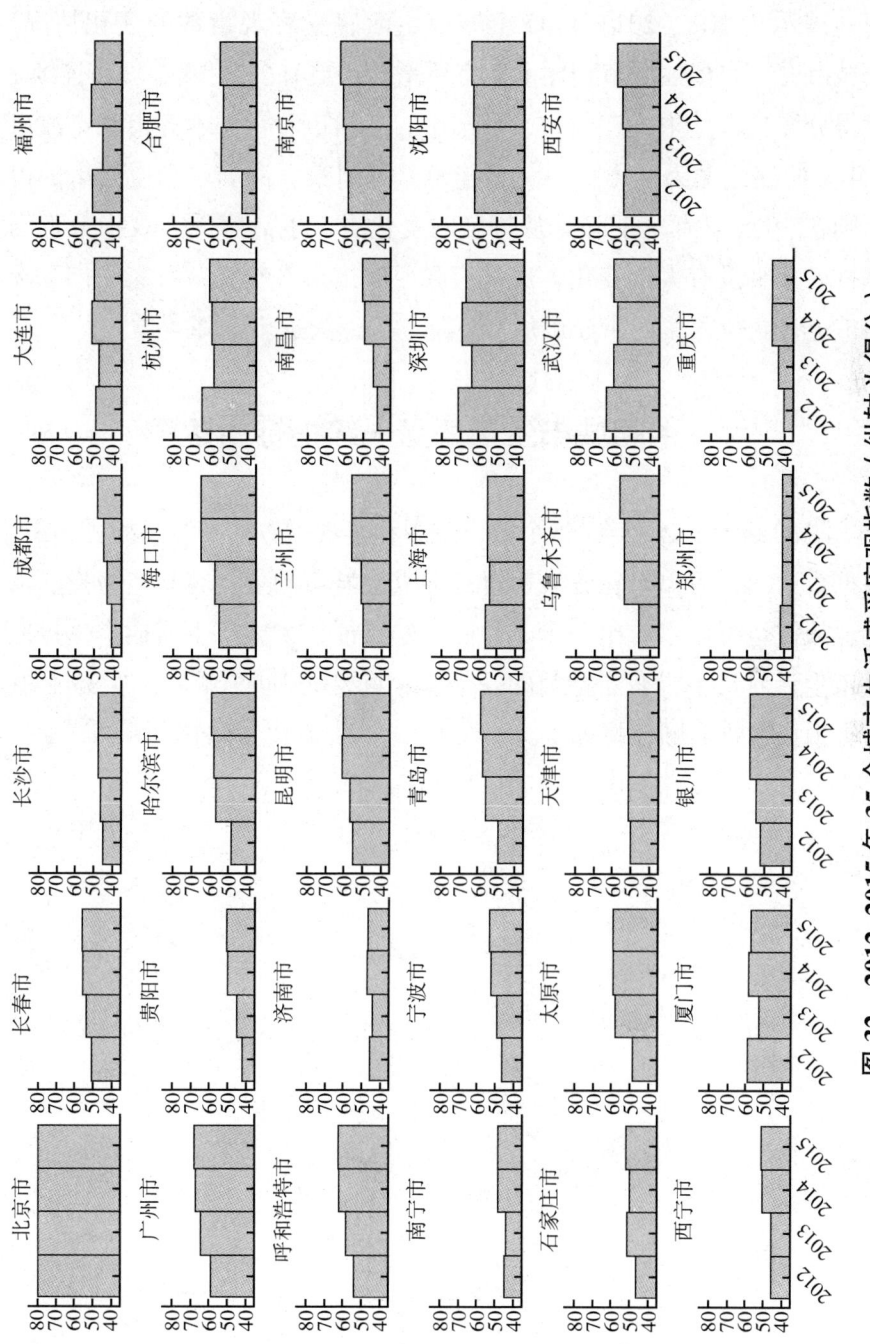

图32 2012~2015年35个城市生活感受客观指数（纵轴为得分）

观地展示了2012~2015年35个城市生活感受客观指数的变化情况。分城市看,大多数城市相比上年有所增长,更有多达14个城市连续3年得分增长,其中,广州市、贵阳市、南昌市、乌鲁木齐市和宁波市4年来的变化尤为突出。但是大连市、福州市、深圳市和厦门市的得分则在2015年有所下降。从排名的变化看,生活感受客观指数近两年排名几乎没有大的变化,成都市和西安市上升5位,石家庄市和南昌市上升3位;厦门市和银川市下降5位,大连市下降4位。

六 中国城市生活质量一级指标雷达图

图33给出了2015年35个城市主观和客观指数的一级指标雷达图。根据雷达图,可以对比各城市自身和其他城市的主、客观一级指标情况。从雷达图可以看出一个非常明显的特征,大城市生活成本是拉低城市生活质量主、客观指数的一个非常重要的因素(图33按35个城市客观指数排名顺序排列)。

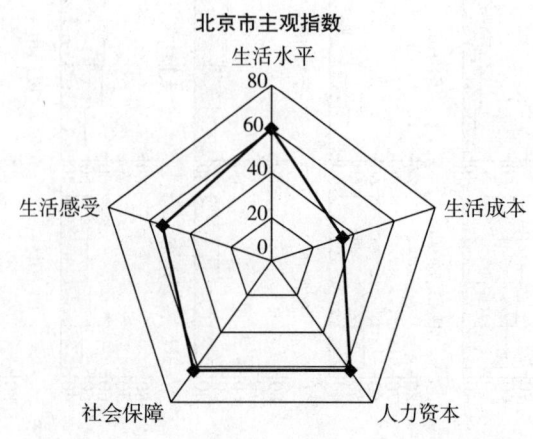

中国35个城市生活质量的细分指数

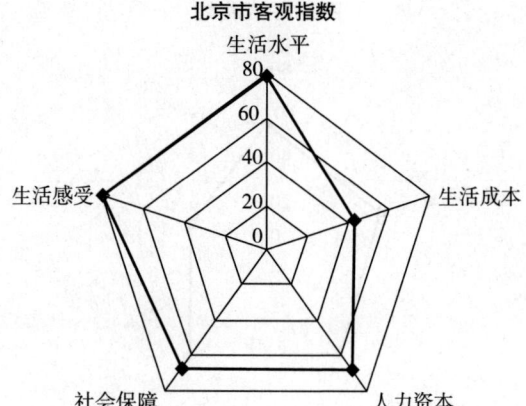

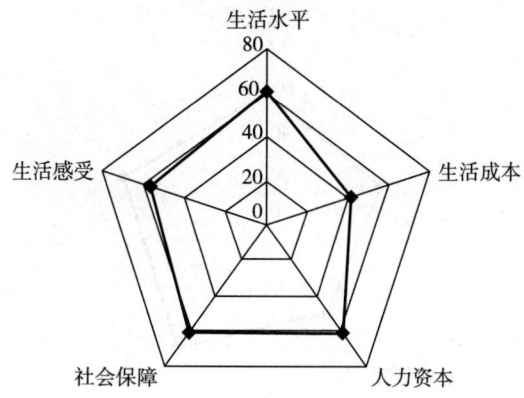

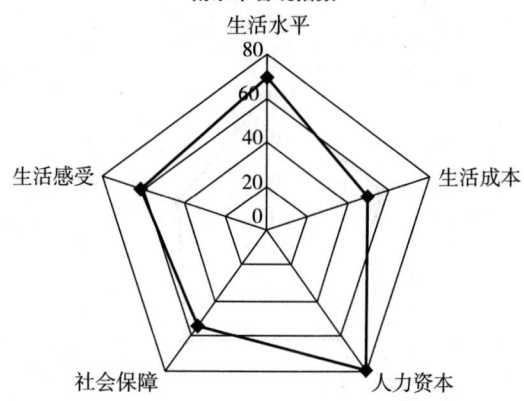

105

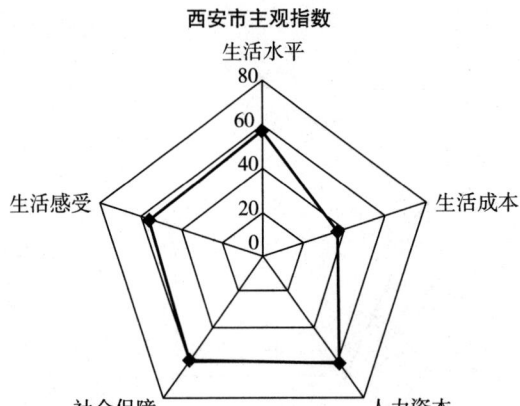

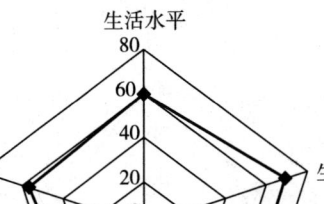

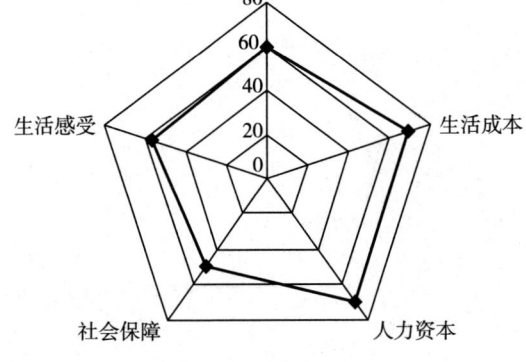

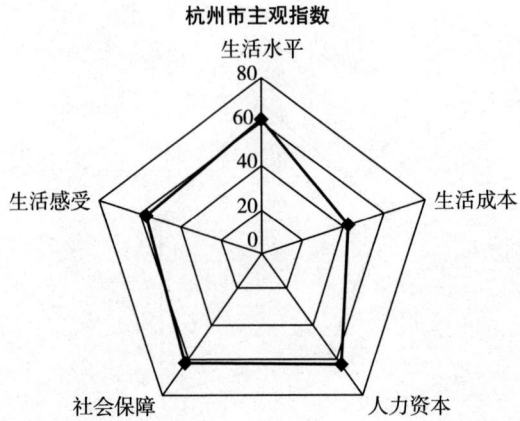

中国35个城市生活质量的细分指数

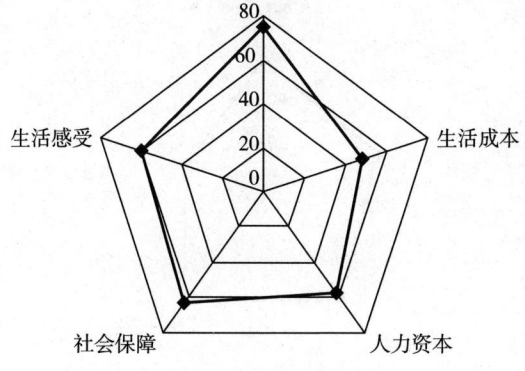

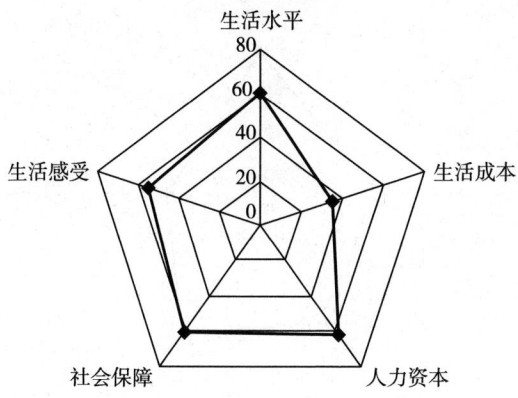

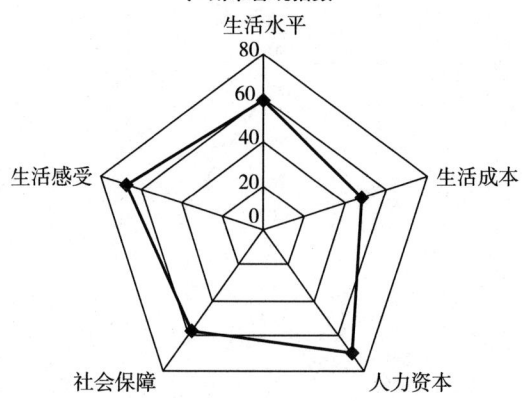

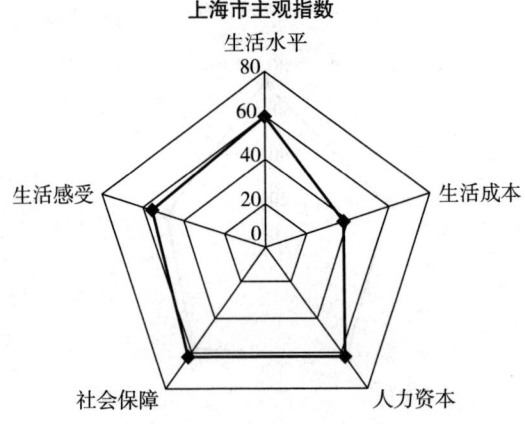

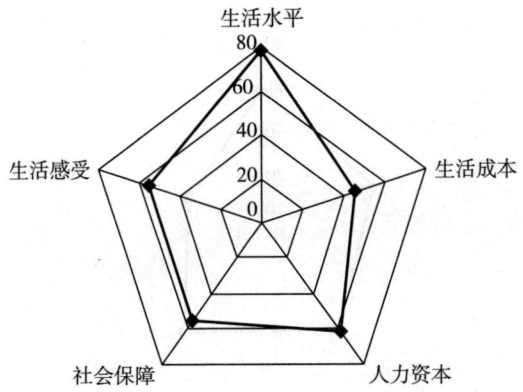

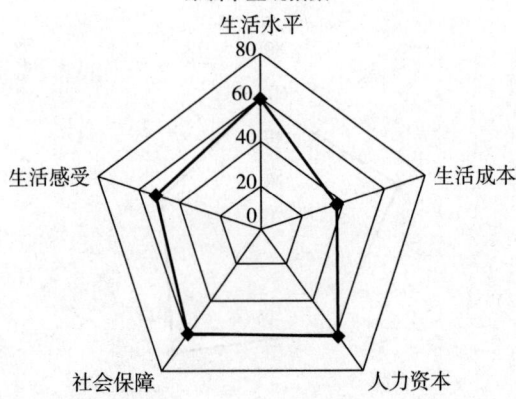

中国 35 个城市生活质量的细分指数

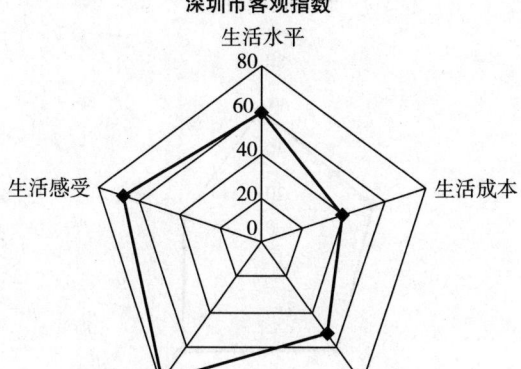

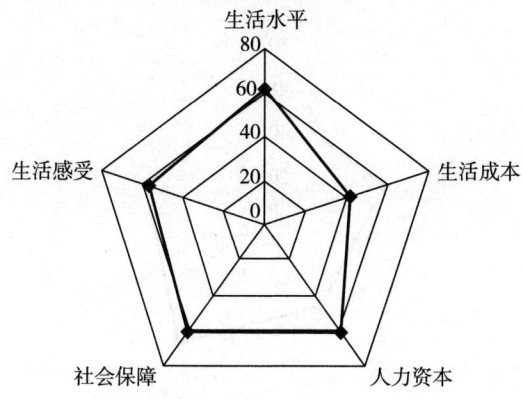

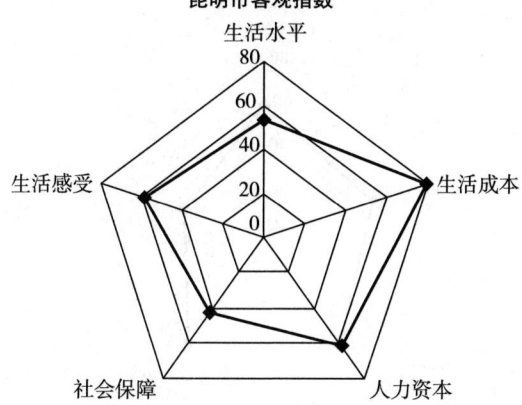

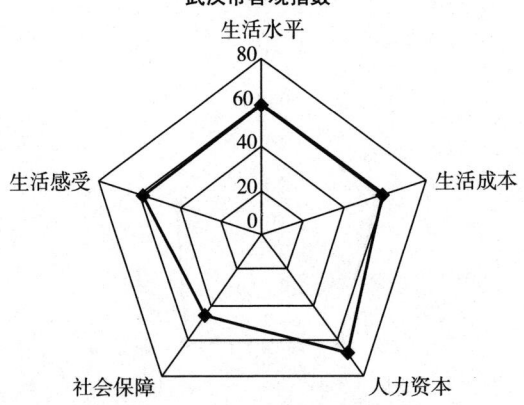

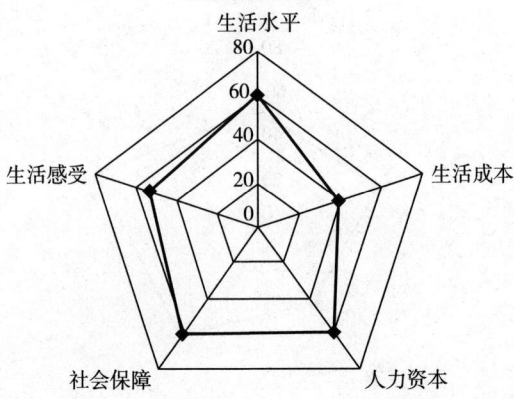

中国 35 个城市生活质量的细分指数

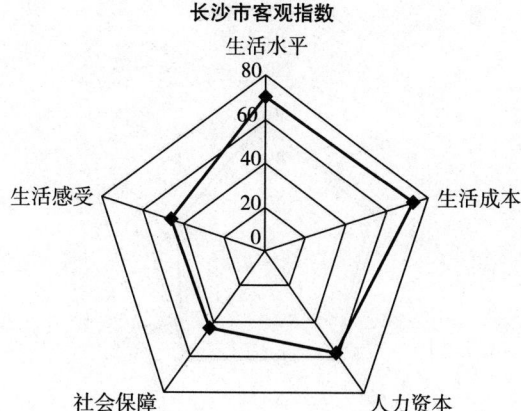

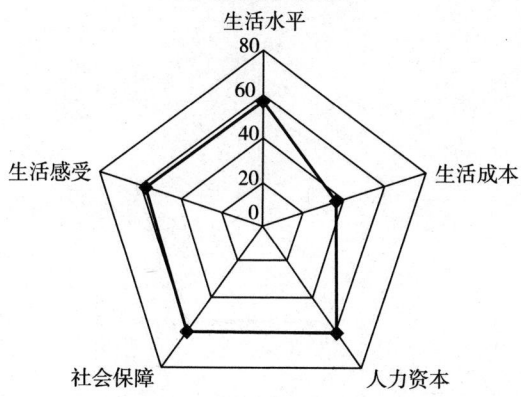

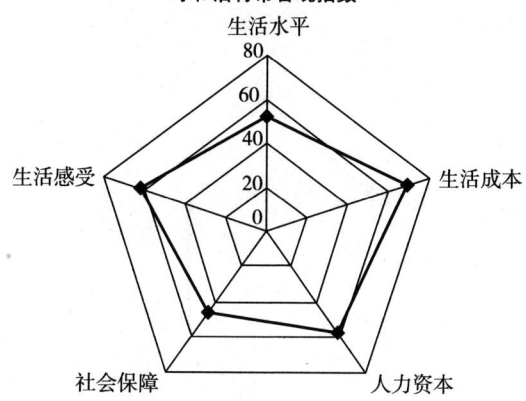

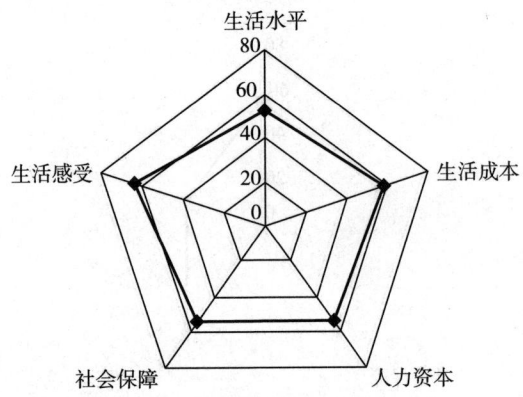

沈阳市主观指数

沈阳市客观指数

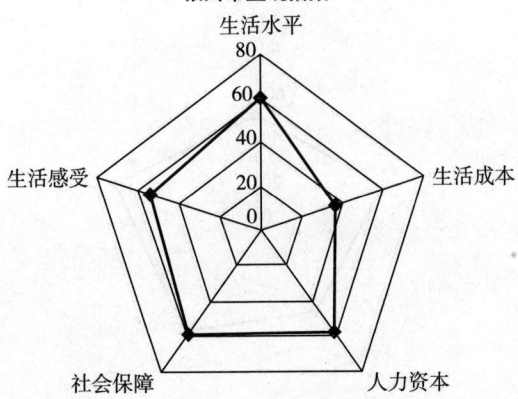

银川市主观指数

中国 35 个城市生活质量的细分指数

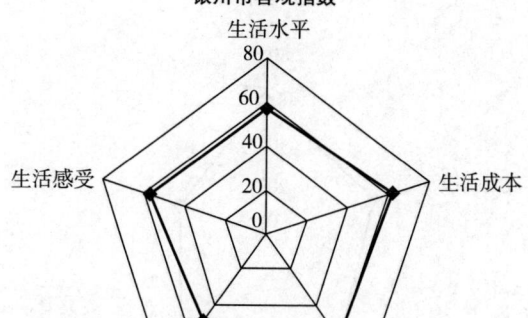

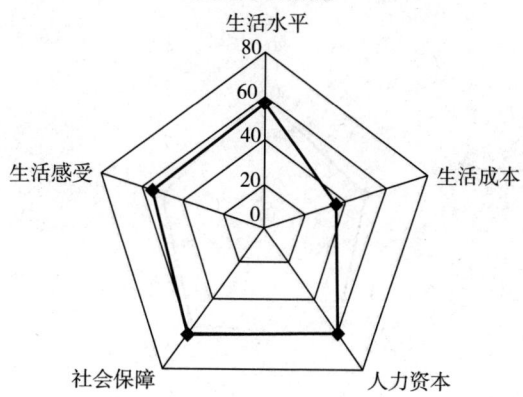

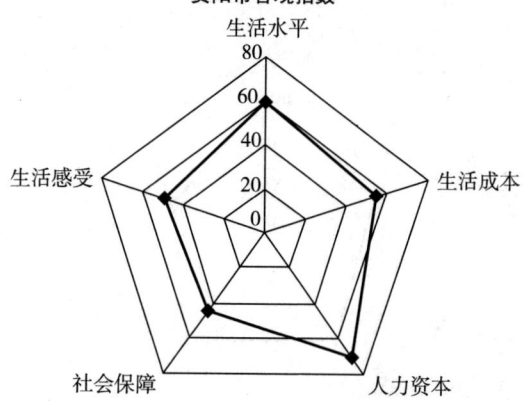

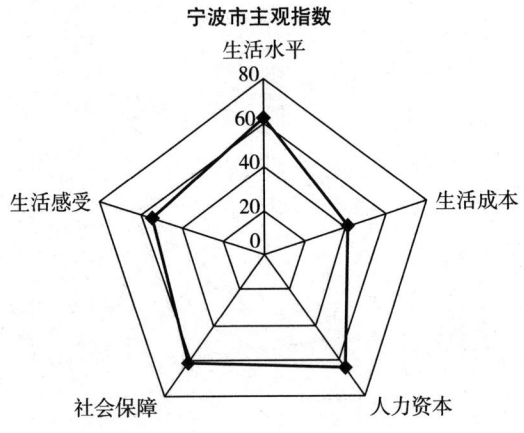

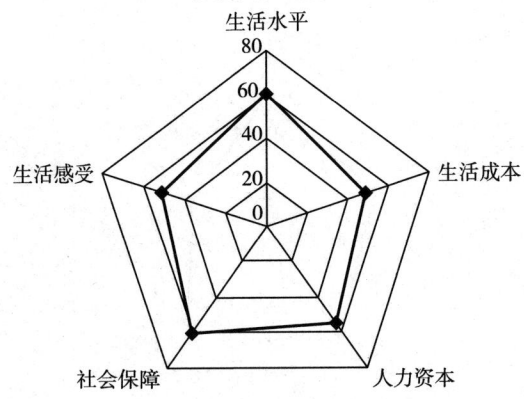

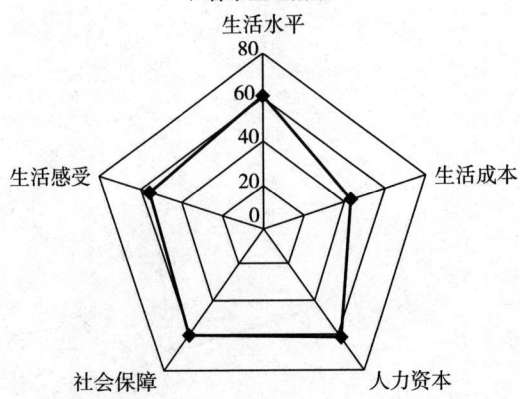

中国 35 个城市生活质量的细分指数

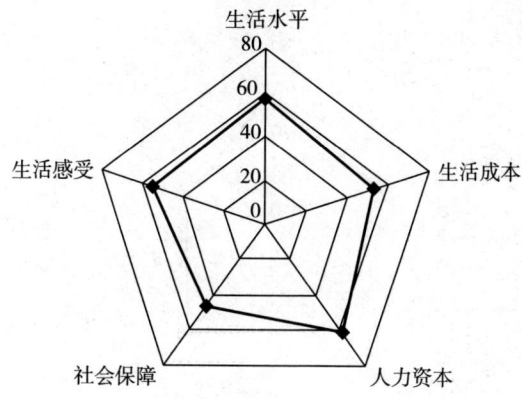

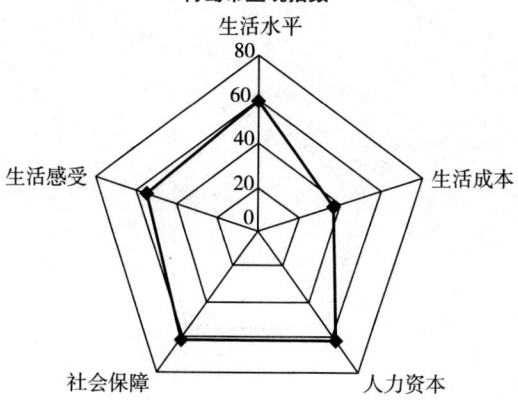

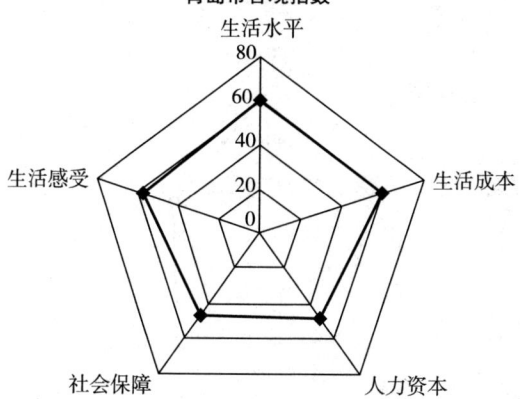

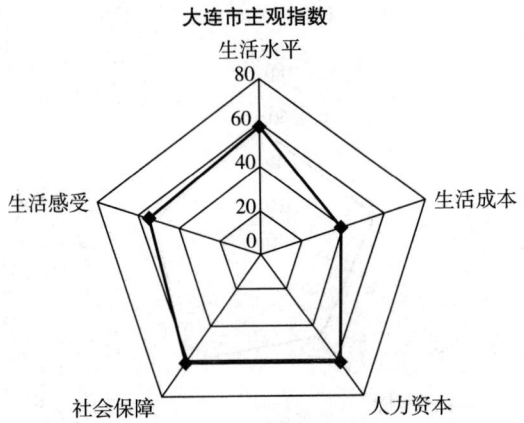

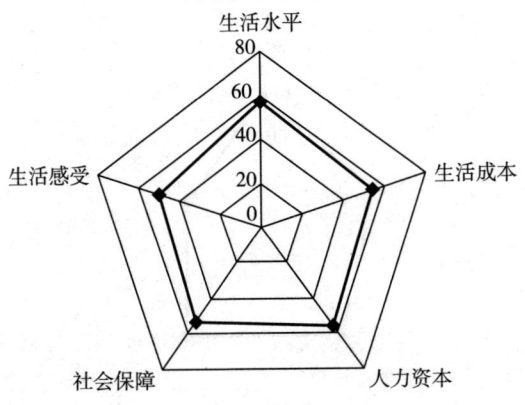

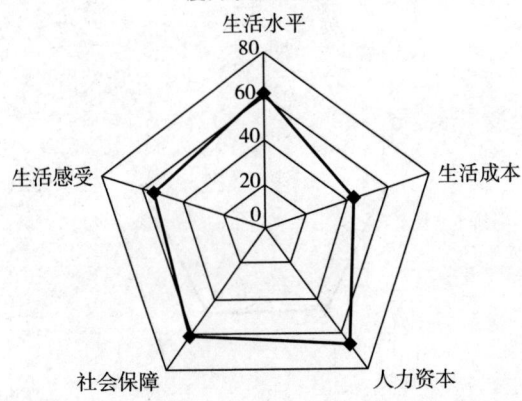

中国35个城市生活质量的细分指数

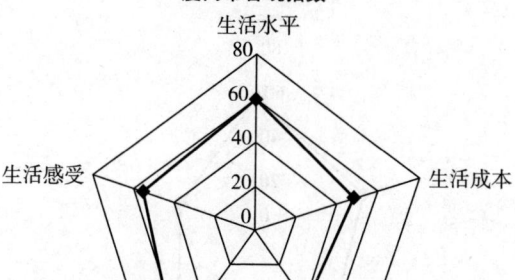

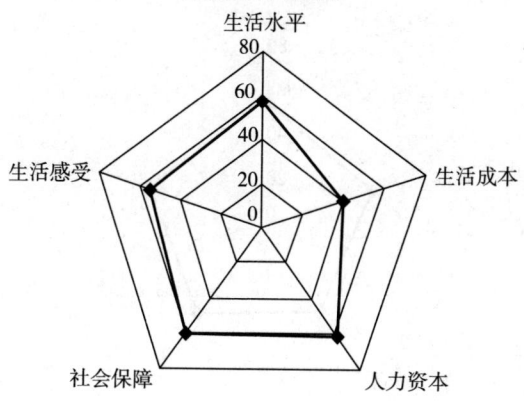

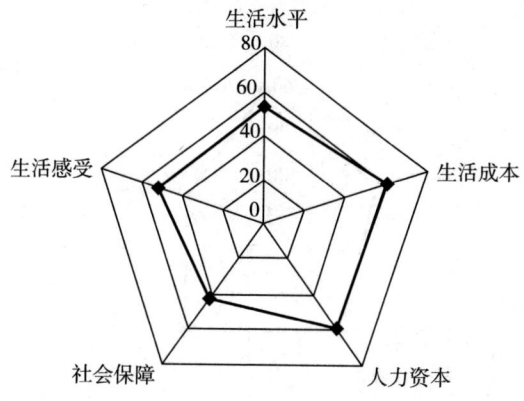

117

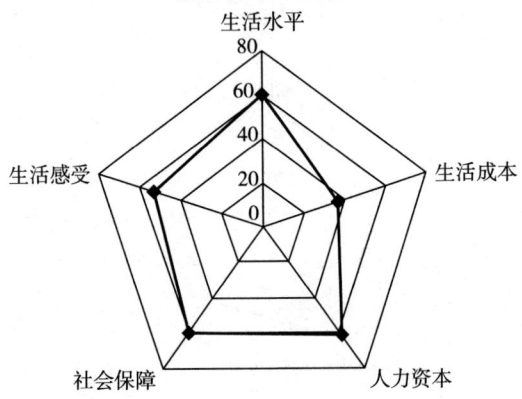

乌鲁木齐市主观指数

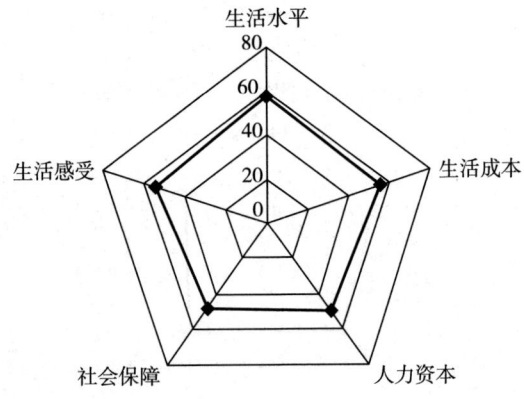

乌鲁木齐市客观指数

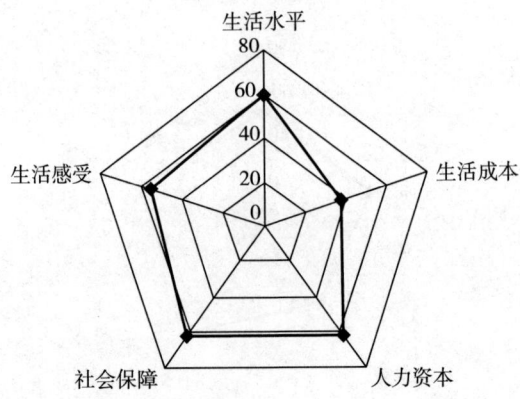

成都市主观指数

中国 35 个城市生活质量的细分指数

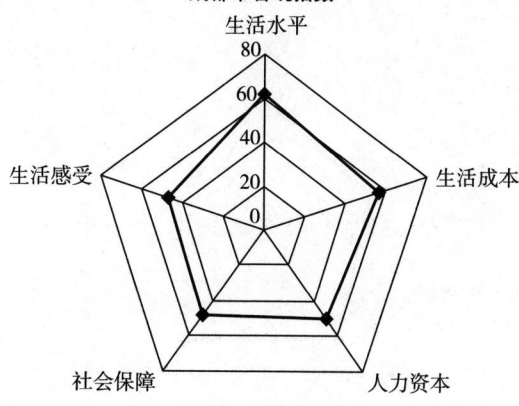

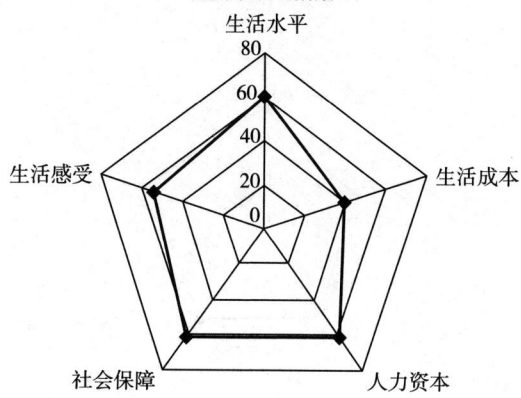

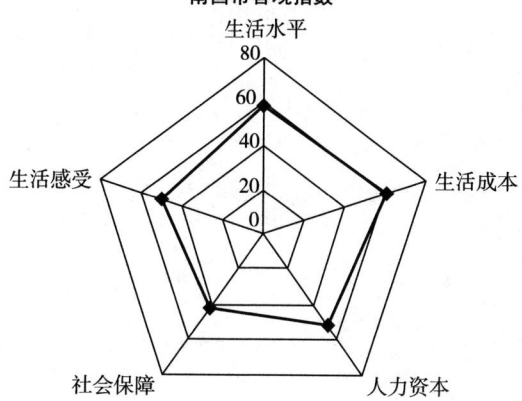

济南市主观指数

济南市客观指数

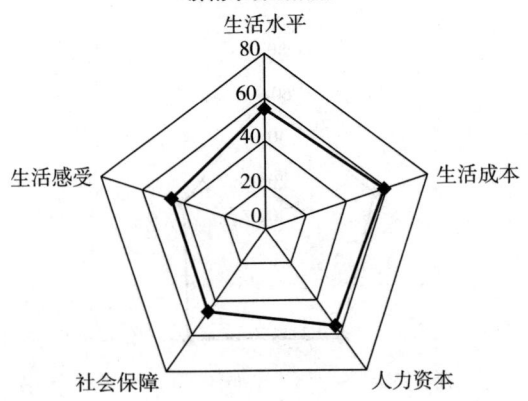

合肥市主观指数

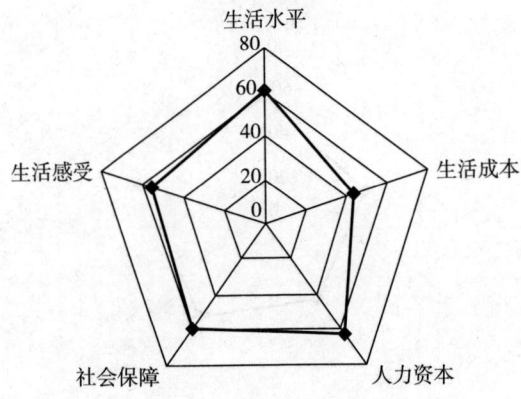

中国 35 个城市生活质量的细分指数

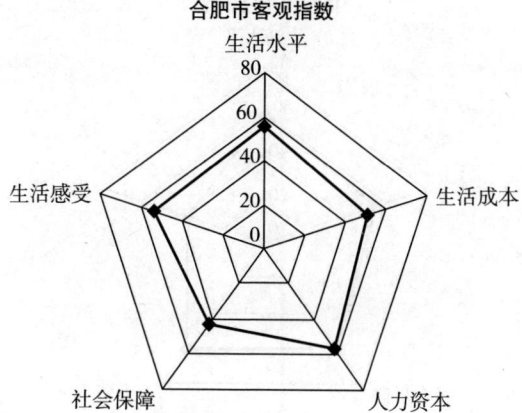

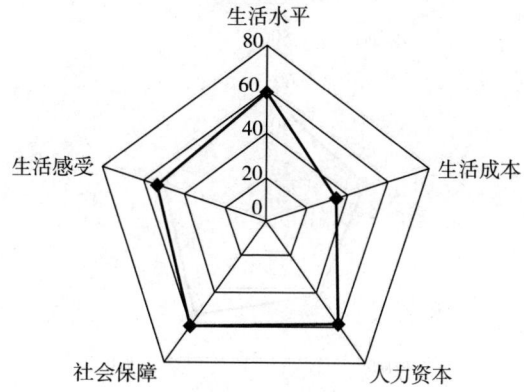

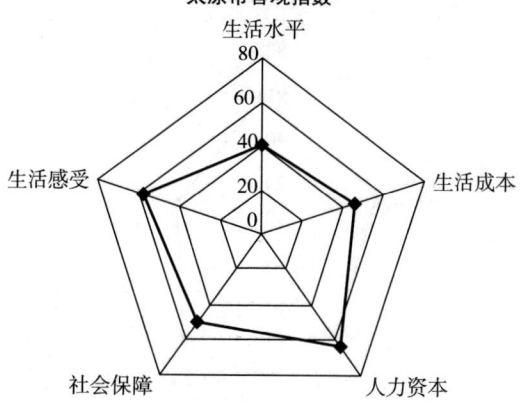

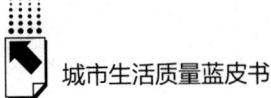

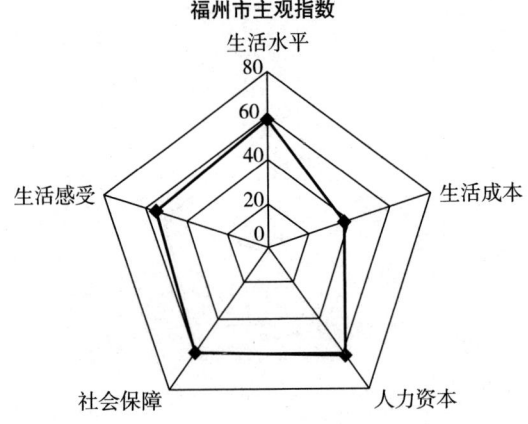

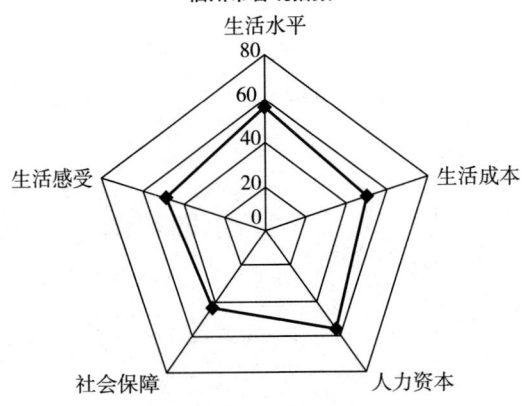

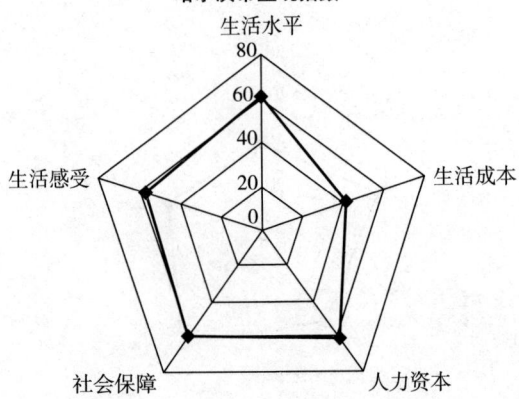

中国35个城市生活质量的细分指数

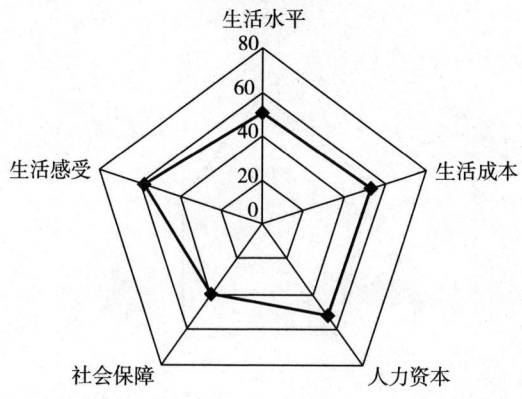

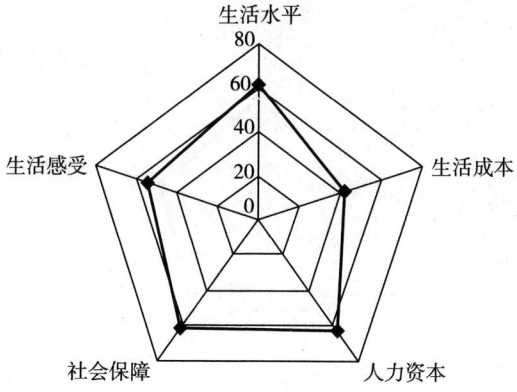

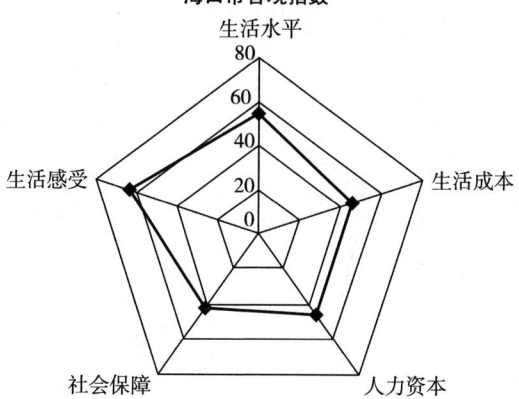

天津市主观指数

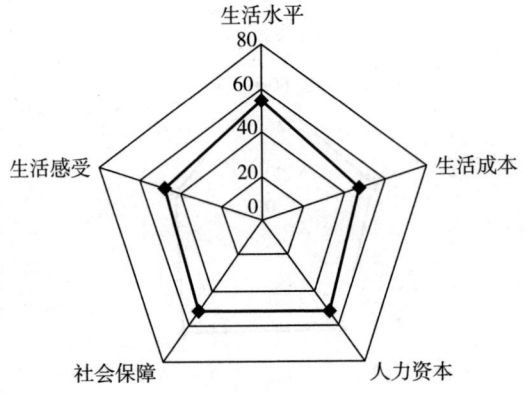

天津市客观指数

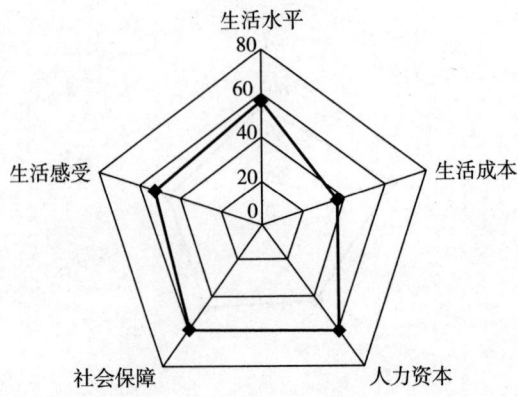

兰州市主观指数

中国 35 个城市生活质量的细分指数

兰州市客观指数

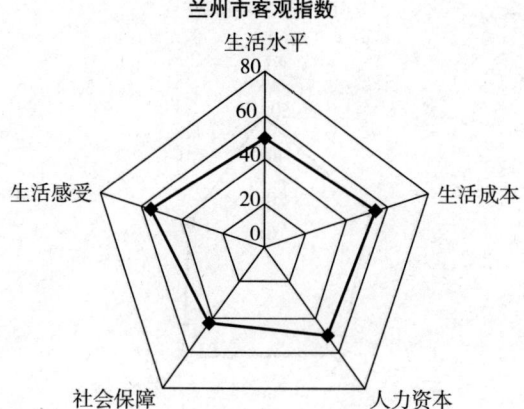

南宁市主观指数

南宁市客观指数

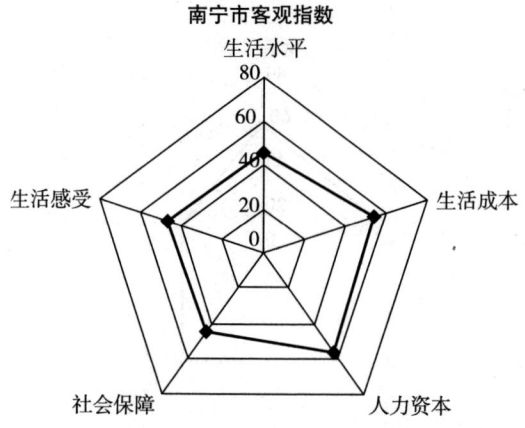

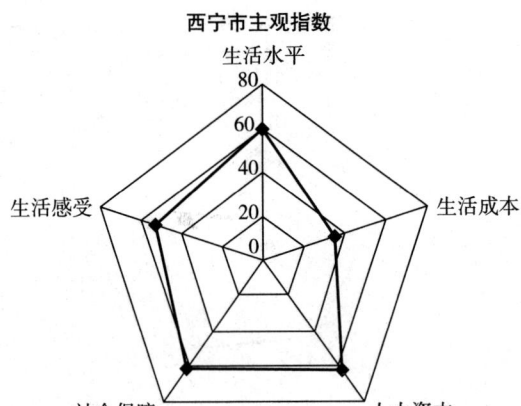

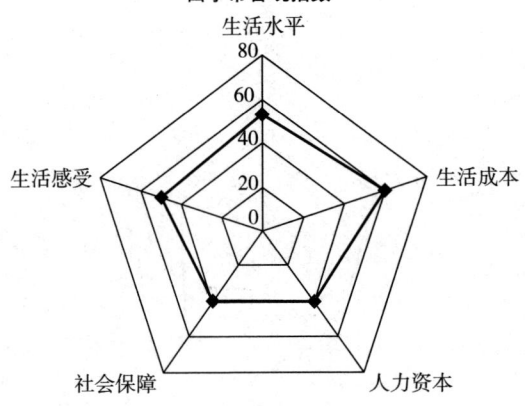

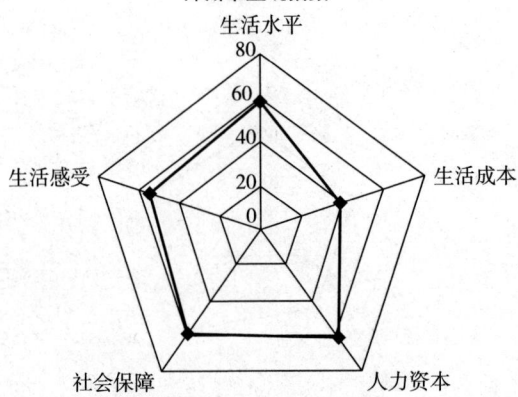

中国35个城市生活质量的细分指数

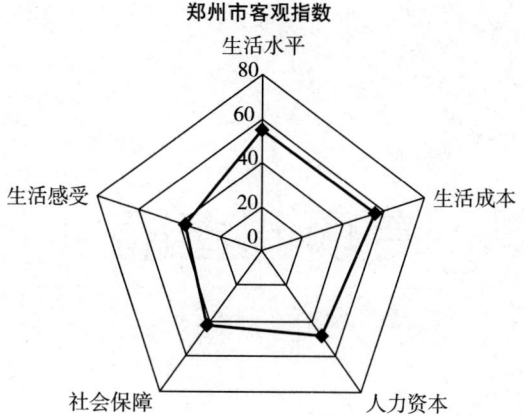

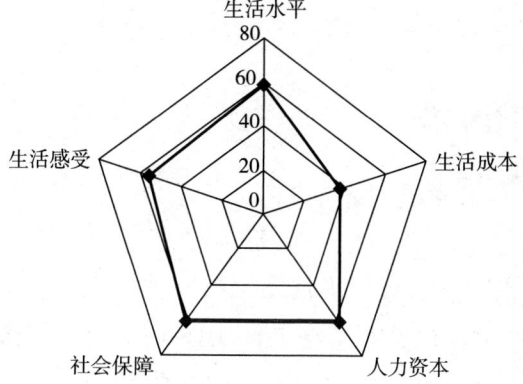

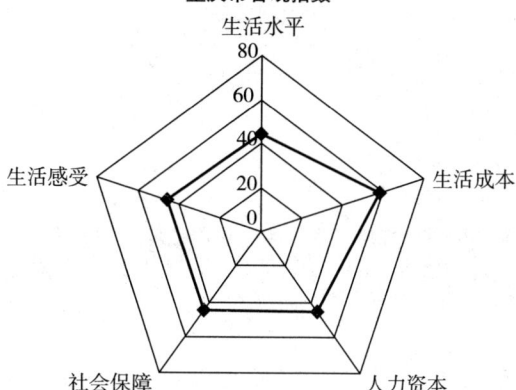

图33 中国35个城市生活质量一级指标

专项调查篇

B.6
房价预期调查

2015年,我们继续对房价预期进行专项调查[①]。35个城市房价预期指数如表1所示。根据调查结果,2015年房价预期指数的加权平均值为43.86,进入下跌区间,远低于2014年的60.78,自2013年以来持续降低。

[①] 我们对该问题的设计如下:您认为您所居住城市的房价今后(1~2年)是涨还是跌?①大涨;②涨;③一般;④跌;⑤大跌。答案和赋值分别是:①大涨(100);②涨(75);③一般(50);④跌(25);⑤大跌(0)。

表1 35个城市房价预期指数[①]

城 市	2015年			2014年		2013年		2012年	
	得分	排序	上升位次	得分	排名	得分	排序	得分	排序
合肥市	46.70	1	0	64.68	1	66.07	6	53.42	25
杭州市	46.40	2	29	58.05	31	62.85	29	47.17	34
南京市	45.83	3	6	61.98	9	65.92	10	54.36	22
宁波市	45.76	4	31	56.74	35	62.15	31	50.68	31
长春市	45.43	5	23	59.07	28	63.70	22	51.20	30
哈尔滨市	45.33	6	24	58.63	30	60.99	35	50.39	32
银川市	45.24	7	9	61.54	16	65.93	9	55.21	17
大连市	45.18	8	26	56.83	34	62.13	32	54.91	19
长沙市	44.97	9	14	60.16	23	63.39	25	51.90	29
石家庄市	44.62	10	7	61.49	17	65.19	15	54.13	23
福州市	44.44	11	10	60.61	21	64.45	20	52.75	27
重庆市	44.41	12	15	59.22	27	64.46	19	55.84	12
青岛市	44.39	13	2	61.63	15	64.57	17	46.82	35
西宁市	44.31	14	6	61.05	20	68.33	2	63.89	2
南宁市	44.24	15	-13	64.02	2	63.66	23	58.80	6
成都市	44.24	16	-6	61.80	10	63.06	27	54.53	20
贵阳市	44.05	17	-3	61.73	14	62.99	28	60.48	3
厦门市	43.98	18	-15	64.02	3	65.14	16	59.59	5
昆明市	43.98	19	5	60.02	24	65.38	14	55.77	13
沈阳市	43.89	20	6	59.33	26	62.43	30	56.35	10
上海市	43.66	21	-16	62.53	5	65.97	7	53.35	26
呼和浩特市	43.64	22	10	57.81	32	61.26	34	56.07	11
西安市	43.61	23	-1	60.36	22	63.64	24	55.10	18
南昌市	43.45	24	-5	61.13	19	66.73	4	55.28	14
兰州市	43.45	25	4	58.85	29	63.98	21	59.94	4

① 房价预期指数越高,说明该城市居民预期房价上涨的幅度越大或下降预期趋弱;越低,说明该城市居民预期房价上涨的幅度越小或下降预期趋强。房价预期上涨或下降的临界点分值是50。

续表

城市	2015年			2014年		2013年		2012年	
	得分	排序	上升位次	得分	排名	得分	排序	得分	排序
天津市	43.42	26	-1	59.49	25	63.18	26	53.65	24
广州市	43.04	27	-21	62.28	6	68.64	1	58.55	7
乌鲁木齐市	42.71	28	5	57.04	33	67.37	3	55.26	15
郑州市	42.67	29	-17	61.77	12	66.60	5	55.24	16
海口市	42.55	30	-17	61.75	13	61.26	33	64.00	1
济南市	41.97	31	-13	61.46	18	65.68	12	50.00	33
武汉市	41.74	32	-21	61.77	11	65.40	13	54.41	21
北京市	41.43	33	-25	62.08	8	65.71	11	52.04	28
太原市	41.03	34	-27	62.22	7	64.53	18	57.18	8
深圳市	40.15	35	-31	62.92	4	65.96	8	56.55	9
平均值	43.86			60.78		64.65		54.99	

从表1不难看出，本次调查中，35个城市房价预期指数全部低于50，这意味着与往年不同，2015年所有城市居民对未来房价的预期都是下跌。2012年，35个城市房价预期指数的平均值为54.99，得分低于50（即预期房价下跌）的城市只有杭州和青岛两个城市，其余33个城市的居民对未来房价全部看涨；2013年，35个城市房价预期指数的平均值为64.65，在调查的35个城市中，房价预期指数全部超过了60，说明所有城市的居民都预期房价将会上升；2014年的平均值为60.78，没有得分低于50的城市，其中24个城市的房价预期指数超过60，表明35个城市的居民均预期房价继续上涨；2015年则出现了逆转，平均值为43.86，没有一个城市的居民预期未来房价将会上涨。图1描述了2012~2015年35个城市房价预期指数的变动情况。

在本次调查的35个城市中，排名前10位的城市是：合肥市（1）、杭州市（2）、南京市（3）、宁波市（4）、长春市（5）、哈尔滨市（6）、银川市（7）、大连市（8）、长沙市（9）、石家庄市（10）。这

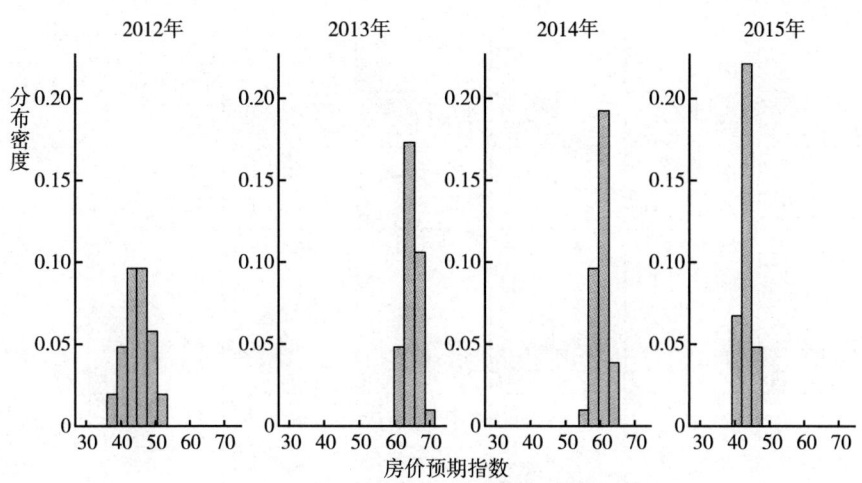

图 1 2012~2015 年房价预期指数

意味着上述 10 个城市虽然都预期房价将会下跌,但预期下跌的幅度相对较小或下跌预期趋弱。值得注意的是,合肥市和南京市已经连续 3 年排在前 10 名,并且合肥市已经连续两年排名第 1,这表明 2014 年合肥市居民对房价看涨的幅度相对最大,2015 年对房价看跌的幅度相对最小。在表 1 中,排名后 10 位的城市是:天津市(26)、广州市(27)、乌鲁木齐市(28)、郑州市(29)、海口市(30)、济南市(31)、武汉市(32)、北京市(33)、太原市(34)、深圳市(35)。这意味着上述 10 个城市预期未来房价下跌的幅度相对较大或下跌预期趋强。但需要说明的是,35 个城市间的分值相差不大,最高为 46.70,最低为 40.15。这说明对房价下跌预期趋强或趋弱的差距不大。

从动态角度看,与 2014 年相比,35 个城市房价预期指数排序上升位次较多的城市有:宁波市(31)、杭州市(29)、大连市(26)、哈尔滨市(24)、长春市(23)。排序下降位次较多的城市有深圳市(-31)、太原市(-27)、北京市(-25)、广州市(-21)、武汉市(-21)、郑州市(-17)、海口市(-17)。图 2 的柱状图展现了 2012~2015 年 35 个城市房价预期指数的变动情况。

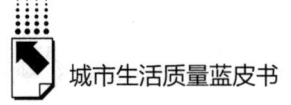

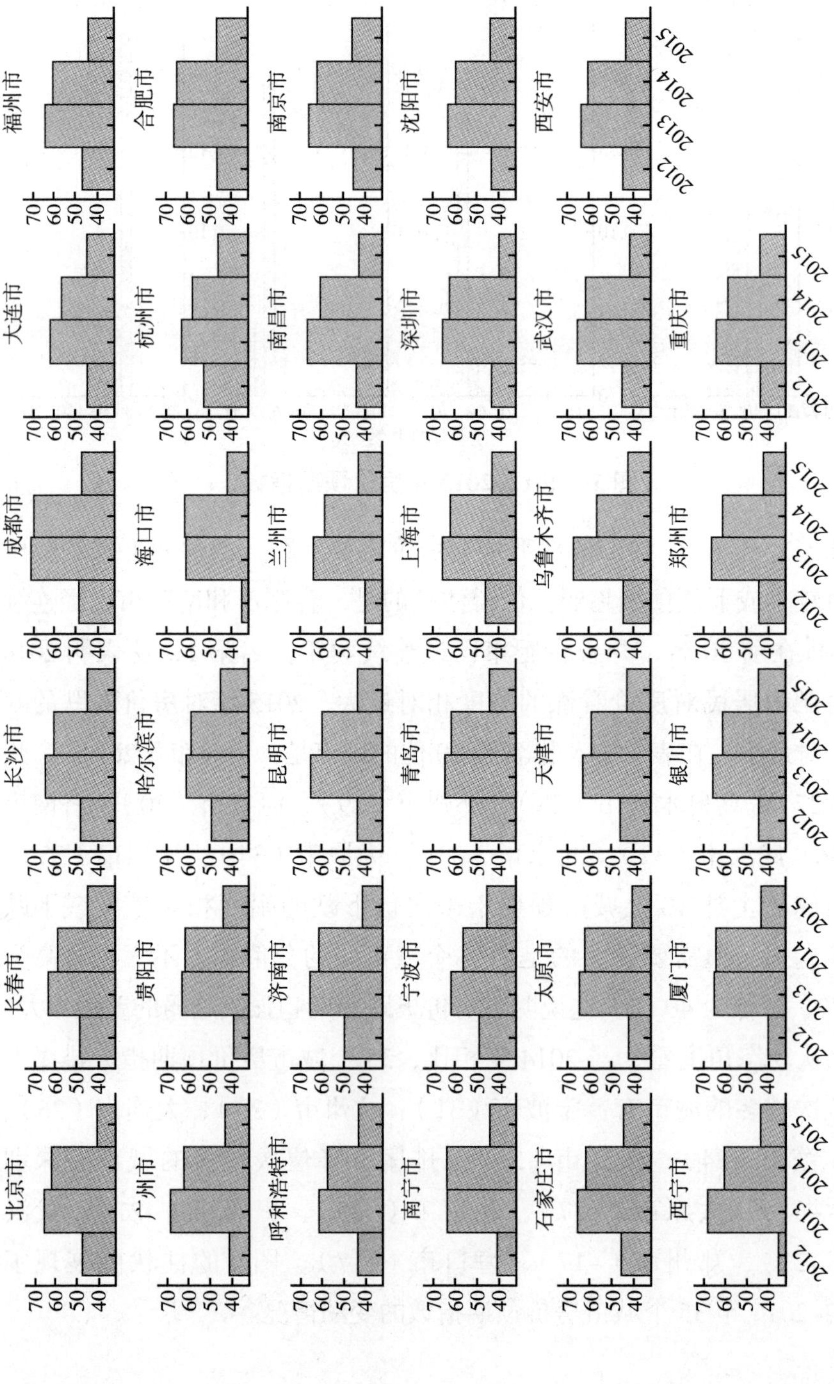

图 2 2012~2015 年 35 个城市房价预期指数（纵轴为得分）

预期包括适应性预期和理性预期。如果人们的预期不存在系统性偏差或错误，并应用了所有可能获得的信息，就是理性预期（Rational Expectations）；如果人们根据过去的行为形成他们的预期，就是适应性预期（Adaptive Expectations）。一般来说，理性预期只存在于经济学的理论假设中。在现实生活中，许多不可预知的因素，如政府对房地产市场的行政干预、政策冲击等，都可能使人们最初的预期出现偏差，因此，居民对房价的预期大多属于适应性预期。在没有外部因素冲击的情况下，如果多数人预期房价将会下跌，人们就会减少对房产的购买，从而导致实际房价下跌；反之亦然。假如未来一两年内房价果真如35个城市居民所预期的那样普遍出现下跌，那么将对未来城市居民的生活成本产生巨大影响，对城市居民生活质量的提高具有重要意义。

B.7 居民最关注因素调查

2014年，我们新增了城市居民最关注因素的调查，根据调查结果，空气质量和食品安全两个因素是排在前两位的影响居民生活质量的重要因素。2015年我们继续对上述问题进行了电话调查[①]，表1是本次调查的结果。

表1 生活质量影响因素调查结果

单位：%

城市	食品安全	空气质量	物价	交通状况
石家庄市	25.51	44.78	18.99	10.72
北京市	25.66	43.19	19.27	11.88
郑州市	25.74	42.56	20.67	11.03
武汉市	27.34	42.38	19.73	10.55
天津市	29.25	41.63	19.93	9.20
沈阳市	27.49	40.96	21.59	9.96
银川市	30.17	40.78	21.23	7.82
南京市	30.45	39.85	20.68	9.02
上海市	25.85	39.78	22.30	12.07
杭州市	29.73	39.71	20.79	9.77
长沙市	29.01	39.64	23.06	8.29
长春市	30.54	38.49	22.58	8.39
济南市	28.65	38.38	24.32	8.65
太原市	29.15	38.31	23.73	8.81

① 我们对该问题的设计是：您认为以下哪项对您的生活质量影响最大？备选答案分别是：①食品安全；②空气质量；③物价；④交通状况。

续表

城市	食品安全	空气质量	物价	交通状况
大连市	35.19	38.23	19.49	7.09
南昌市	32.34	38.07	21.10	8.49
厦门市	29.12	37.93	21.07	11.88
乌鲁木齐市	30.43	37.46	21.74	10.37
重庆市	30.22	37.35	20.86	11.57
西安市	28.52	37.08	21.81	12.58
福州市	34.00	36.91	17.82	11.27
西宁市	30.86	36.57	22.29	10.29
呼和浩特市	28.57	36.43	19.29	15.71
合肥市	30.51	36.25	20.85	12.39
成都市	29.84	35.92	23.26	10.98
哈尔滨市	30.60	35.79	23.91	9.70
深圳市	29.00	35.79	22.35	12.87
广州市	30.04	35.37	23.28	11.31
青岛市	31.08	35.35	22.38	11.19
贵阳市	30.91	35.27	23.27	10.55
南宁市	30.74	34.18	22.60	12.48
宁波市	33.94	33.13	25.10	7.83
兰州市	32.49	32.81	24.29	10.41
昆明市	33.02	32.08	23.27	11.64
海口市	33.33	28.99	20.29	17.39
平均值*	28.77	39.12	21.17	10.94

注：* 该平均值是根据所有受访者中选择每个最关注因素的人数除以受访者总人数获得的。

调查结果显示，2015年，在35个城市中，除了宁波、昆明、海口3个城市的受访者把食品安全视为影响生活质量的最重要因素外，其余32个城市的受访者均把空气质量视为影响生活质量的最重要因素，比2014年多出了15个城市，2014年，只有17个城市的受访者把空气质量视为影响生活质量的最重要因素。可以看出人们对空气质量的关注程度大幅度提高。总体来看，受访者认为影响生活质量的最重要因素分别是空气质量（39.12%）、食品安全（28.77%）、物价（21.17%）、交通状况（10.94%）。值得注意的是，石家庄市、北京市、郑州市、武汉市、天津市、沈阳市、银川市对空气质量的关注度均超过了40%，即这些城市40%以上的受访者认为空气质量是影响生活质量的最重要因素。整体上看，35个城市的居民认为空气质量是影响生活质量最为重要的因素，选择该选项的居民占受访者的39.12%，但人们对食品安全和物价的关注度也很高，选择这两项的居民分别占受访者的28.77%和21.17%。

进一步分析表明，受访者对空气质量、食品安全、物价和交通状况的关注程度因性别、学历、工作状态、年龄的不同而有所不同。表2和表3给出了这一调查结果。

表2 不同性别、学历、工作状态的居民对4项因素的关注度

单位：%

影响因素	性别		学历		工作状态	
	男	女	大专及以上	大专以下	有工作	没有工作
食品安全	28.20	29.24	28.42	29.72	29.24	27.98
空气质量	37.48	40.50	40.08	36.48	38.48	40.21
物价	22.14	20.36	20.55	22.88	21.20	21.13
交通状况	12.18	9.90	10.95	10.91	11.09	10.69
合计	100.00	100.00	100.00	100.00	100.00	100.00

根据表2，2015年的调查结果与2014年的情况类似，无论男性和女性、受教育程度以及工作状态如何，居民较为关注的都是空气质量和食品安全。相比较而言，男性对物价和交通状况的关注度高于女

性，而女性对食品安全和空气质量的关注度高于男性。学历高的人群更为关注空气质量，学历高低对其他3项因素的关注度并没有显著的影响。有工作的人更为关注食品安全，没有工作的人更为关注空气质量，工作状态对交通状况和物价的关注度并没有显著的影响。

表3给出了不同年龄段居民对4项因素的关注度。调查表明，年龄段越高，居民对食品安全的关注度越高，60岁以上的人群对食品安全的关注度最高，年轻人对食品安全的关注度最低。在空气质量方面，20~40岁的人群对空气质量的关注度较高；41~60岁的人群次之；60岁以上的人群对空气质量的关注度相对较低。其中，31~40岁的人群对空气质量的关注度最高。在物价方面，年龄段越低，居民对物价的关注度越高。在交通状况方面，20~30岁的人群对交通状况的关注度最高；31~40岁的人群次之，41~50岁的人群排第3位，60岁以上的人群排第4位；51~60岁的人群对交通状况的关注度最低。

表3　不同年龄段居民对4项因素的关注度

单位：%

影响因素	20~30岁	31~40岁	41~50岁	51~60岁	60岁以上
食品安全	26.45	29.09	31.96	33.87	37.03
空气质量	39.29	39.85	38.40	38.58	35.90
物价	22.20	20.48	20.28	19.55	18.26
交通状况	12.06	10.59	9.36	8.00	8.82
合计	100.00	100.00	100.00	100.00	100.00

B.8 互联网对生活质量影响的调查

互联网现在已经成为现代城市居民生活中不可或缺的一部分。因此，本次调查新增了互联网对城市生活质量影响的调查。我们对该问题的设计是：您觉得互联网在哪方面对您的生活影响最大？答案分别是：①买东西（购物）；②沟通联系；③金融理财；④服务便利。表1是本次对35个城市的调查结果。

表1 互联网对生活质量的影响

单位：%

城 市	购物	沟通联系	金融理财	服务便利
长春市	30.54	46.88	7.53	15.05
宁波市	30.72	45.38	9.44	14.46
合肥市	31.72	45.02	9.06	14.20
哈尔滨市	31.61	44.82	10.20	13.38
昆明市	33.02	43.71	9.43	13.84
南京市	30.45	43.23	9.59	16.73
石家庄市	35.22	42.61	6.96	15.22
厦门市	34.87	42.53	8.43	14.18
南宁市	32.73	42.31	8.32	16.64
贵阳市	38.91	42.18	5.45	13.45
广州市	35.24	42.00	7.41	15.34
长沙市	35.50	41.62	6.85	16.04
成都市	37.60	41.21	7.49	13.70
杭州市	37.42	40.96	8.11	13.51
福州市	34.36	40.73	8.55	16.36
海口市	28.99	40.58	13.04	17.39

续表

城市	购物	沟通联系	金融理财	服务便利
济南市	34.59	40.27	8.11	17.03
银川市	34.64	40.22	7.26	17.88
北京市	35.22	40.02	8.46	16.30
上海市	34.74	39.70	9.33	16.22
重庆市	37.29	39.57	6.65	16.49
深圳市	35.36	39.32	7.78	17.54
郑州市	38.53	39.05	5.78	16.64
呼和浩特市	36.43	38.93	7.86	16.79
乌鲁木齐市	36.79	38.46	8.03	16.72
天津市	35.61	38.09	6.96	19.34
武汉市	38.87	38.09	6.64	16.41
沈阳市	36.35	37.64	7.38	18.63
南昌市	38.07	37.61	7.34	16.97
西安市	36.74	37.58	7.72	17.95
大连市	37.47	37.22	9.87	15.44
兰州市	39.75	36.59	6.94	16.72
青岛市	36.59	36.59	11.01	15.81
太原市	40.68	34.92	7.12	17.29
西宁市	42.86	33.14	8.57	15.43
平均值*	35.52	40.27	8.07	16.14

注：* 该平均值是根据所有受访者中选择每个影响因素的人数除以受访者总人数得到的。

表1显示，除了武汉、南昌、大连、兰州、太原、西宁6个城市的居民认为互联网在购物方面对生活的影响最大、青岛市居民认为在购物和沟通联系方面对生活具有同等程度的影响外，其余28个城市的居民都认为互联网在沟通联系方面对生活的影响最大。从调查样本35个城市的平均数据来看，就互联网对城市生活的影响方面而言，

40.27%的居民认为是沟通联系，35.52%的居民认为是购物，16.14%的居民认为是服务便利，8.07%的居民认为是金融理财。总的来说，这4个方面的影响主要从生活便利性的角度体现了互联网对城市居民生活质量的影响。随着互联网的不断发展，互联网将会全方位地改变人们的生活，上述比例还将发生变化。

进一步分析表明，互联网对生活的影响因性别、学历、工作状态、年龄的不同而有所不同。表2给出了按照背景资料统计的互联网对居民生活影响的情况。

表2 不同性别、学历、工作状态对互联网使用的影响

单位：%

影响因素	性别		学历		工作状态	
	男	女	大专及以上	大专以下	有工作	没有工作
购物	32.32	38.19	36.22	33.61	36.37	34.10
沟通联系	40.48	40.09	40.56	39.45	39.57	41.45
金融理财	9.81	6.61	8.07	8.05	9.05	6.41
服务便利	17.39	15.11	15.15	18.88	15.01	18.04
合计	100.00	100.00	100.00	100.00	100.00	100.00

表2的数据显示，女性使用互联网购物的比例要高于男性，男性使用互联网进行金融理财和便利服务的比例要高于女性，在沟通联系方面，性别差异微乎其微；高学历人群认为互联网在购物、沟通联系方面对生活的影响要高于低学历人群；在金融理财方面，高学历人群和低学历人群的认识区别不大，前者仅略高于后者0.02个百分点，可以忽略不计；低学历人群更多地认为互联网给他们提供了服务便利；有工作的人认为互联网在购物和金融理财方面对生活的影响较大，没有工作的人认为互联网在沟通联系和服务便利方面对生活的

影响较大。

按年龄段分析，表3给出的调查结果是：所有年龄段的人选择比例最高的均是互联网在沟通联系方面对生活的影响；在20~30岁、31~40岁、41~50岁、51~60岁年龄段的人群中排第二的是互联网在购物方面的影响，在60岁以上的人群中排第二的则是互联网在服务便利方面的影响，在购物方面的影响排在第三位；在金融理财方面，选择比例最高的是41~50岁年龄段的人，其次是31~40岁年龄段的人，排在第三位和第四位的分别是51~60岁年龄段和20~30岁年龄段的人，60岁以上的人群排在最后；在互联网对服务便利的影响方面，60岁以上的人群选择这一项的比例最高，之后依次是51~60岁年龄段、41~50岁年龄段、20~30岁年龄段的人群，31~40岁年龄段的人群排在末位。

表3 不同年龄段对互联网的使用情况

单位：%

影响因素	20~30岁	31~40岁	41~50岁	51~60岁	60岁以上
购物	37.01	35.92	34.07	30.24	27.08
沟通联系	40.75	40.50	39.39	40.52	35.79
金融理财	6.58	10.05	10.44	7.41	6.05
服务便利	15.66	13.53	16.10	21.82	31.08
合计	100.00	100.00	100.00	100.00	100.00

结 论 篇

B.9
结论和启示

本次城市生活质量调查是在2015年3月到4月完成的，耗时近两个月，近200人参与了本次调查。本次调查的结论和给我们的启示如下。

一 城市生活质量主观满意度指数继续上升，但客观指数有所下降

2015年的调查结果显示，城市生活质量主观满意度指数为55.38，比2014年的51.57有所提高，处于满意区间。2015年城市生活质量主观满意度指数的5个分指数加权平均值分别为：人力资本满意度指数61.73、社会保障满意度指数60.47、生活水平满意度指数60.07、生活感受满意度指数55.66、生活成本满意度指数38.94，与2014年相比，35个城市的5个分指数加权平均值均有所上升，其中，人力资本、社会保障、生活水平满意度指数提高的幅度较大。

结论和启示

城市生活质量客观指数为 55.84，比 2014 年的 57.87 有所降低。2015 年生活质量客观指数的 5 个细分指数加权平均值从高到低依次为：生活水平客观指数 59.83、人力资本客观指数 57.34、生活感受客观指数 56.17、生活成本客观指数 54.58、社会保障客观指数 51.26。与 2014 年相比，生活水平和社会保障客观指数平均值有所降低，生活水平客观指数降幅较大，其他 3 项分指数加权平均值有所提高。

表 1 给出了描述 2012~2015 年 35 个城市生活质量主观满意度指数和生活质量客观指数的 5 个细分指数，从中可以看出各项细分指数的变化趋势。

表 1　2012~2015 年主客观细分指数

		2015 年	2014 年	2013 年	2012 年
主观满意度指数	生活水平满意度指数	60.07	54.32	52.51	51.28
	生活成本满意度指数	38.94	31.81	31.22	28.91
	人力资本满意度指数	61.73	58.98	58.89	59.42
	社会保障满意度指数	60.47	57.87	56.64	59.19
	生活感受满意度指数	55.66	54.88	55.07	55.63
客观指数	生活水平客观指数	59.83	68.06	63.39	56.28
	生活成本客观指数	54.58	53.84	58.67	56.10
	人力资本客观指数	57.34	57.33	57.78	57.66
	社会保障客观指数	51.26	54.66	55.26	50.85
	生活感受客观指数	56.17	55.57	53.67	51.89

根据表 1 的数据，我们发现，生活水平满意度指数首次高于生活水平客观指数。在经济新常态下，受经济增速下滑的影响，城市居民生活水平受到一定程度的影响，客观指数有所降低，但生活水平主观满意度指数不降反升。从描述城市居民生活水平指数的两个细分指数

即收入现状满意度指数和收入预期满意度指数来看，35个城市的均值都有所提高。居民对收入现状满意度的提高，也许可以用生活成本下降来解释；居民对收入预期满意度的提高，有可能是多种因素作用的结果，但至少我们可以认为，人们对中国未来的经济发展依然充满信心，是收入预期满意度提高的最主要原因。

表1的数据还表明，与前面几次调查相比，虽然生活成本客观指数增幅不大，但主观满意度指数上升的幅度较大；人力资本满意度指数和人力资本客观指数保持着稳中有升的态势，并且人力资本满意度指数仍旧高于人力资本客观指数。社会保障满意度指数有所上升，而社会保障客观指数有所下降。生活感受满意度指数在连续几年下降后于2015年开始上升，并且超过了以往几年的分值，开始与生活感受客观指数的变动相一致。

二 生活成本有所下降，但仍旧是拉低生活质量的主要因素

表1显示，35个城市生活成本满意度指数平均值为38.94，比前4次调查的平均值有了较大幅度的上升，得分上升说明城市居民的生活成本有所降低，人们的满意度有所提高，这与生活成本客观指数的提高是一致的。截止到2015年4月，全国居民消费价格总水平（CPI）连续8个月处在低于2%的低通胀区间，也佐证了这一点。生活成本满意度指数的提高也体现在最关注因素的调查结果中：35个城市受访者对物价因素的关注程度比2014年有所降低，从2014年的23.18%下降到2015年的21.69%。尽管如此，生活成本满意度指数平均值仍没有超过50，表明居民对生活成本的满意度仍然处于不满意区间。

李克强总理在2014年提到，"改革就是最大限度调动老百姓的创造力、积极性，解放生产力。简政放权能够让百姓创业收入提高，

生活成本降低，这'一高一低'就是政府应该做的事，让老百姓的生活好起来"。这表明，在降低城市生活成本方面，还有很大空间，这有赖于各级政府的不懈努力，更有赖于推进简政放权的经济体制改革。

在城市生活质量主观满意度指数的5个分指数中，生活成本满意度指数是最低的，5个分指数中只有该指数没有超过50这一临界点。这一事实表明，大城市生活成本过高，是制约城市居民生活质量提高的重要因素。

三 城市生活质量东部高于中西部

最近4年调查得出的35个城市的主客观指数加权平均值按东、中、西部3个区域进行排列见表2。结果发现，2012~2015年，主客观指数及其细分指数呈现出明显的区域特征。从主观满意度指数来看，东部城市要高于中部城市，中部城市要高于西部城市，并且3个地区的主观满意度指数基本呈现出稳中有升的态势。从客观指数来看，东部城市要高于中西部城市，中西部城市没有明显差异。

表2 按区域分主观满意度指数和客观指数

指数	地区	2015年	2014年	2013年	2012年
主观满意度指数	东部	55.71	51.90	51.44	51.44
	中部	55.50	51.14	50.65	50.66
	西部	54.76	51.06	50.39	50.24
客观指数	东部	56.93	59.60	59.59	57.46
	中部	53.80	54.88	55.57	51.90
	西部	54.48	55.88	55.27	52.26

5个主观满意度细分指数也呈现出典型的区域特征（见表3）。2012~2015年，东部城市生活水平满意度指数高于中西部城市，中西部城市之间没有显著差异。中部城市生活成本满意度指数仍旧最高，东部城市高于西部城市[①]。人力资本和社会保障满意度指数的区域特征基本一致，东部城市略高，中西部城市间的差异并不是特别显著。然而，在生活感受满意度指数方面，区域间不存在显著差异，比较来看，西部地区较高，中部地区次之，东部地区的满意度最低。

表3 按区域分5个主观满意度细分指数

指数	地区	2015年	2014年	2013年	2012年
生活水平满意度指数	东部	60.56	54.55	53.28	51.91
	中部	60.49	53.21	51.44	51.00
	西部	59.37	53.38	52.87	50.57
生活成本满意度指数	东部	39.48	31.62	30.98	28.54
	中部	40.16	32.98	33.49	30.96
	西部	37.80	31.28	30.43	27.95
人力资本满意度指数	东部	62.33	59.60	59.58	60.42
	中部	61.15	58.08	58.28	58.51
	西部	60.81	58.51	58.53	58.62
社会保障满意度指数	东部	60.65	58.83	57.86	60.12
	中部	60.09	56.87	55.54	57.80
	西部	60.13	56.70	55.60	58.84
生活感受满意度指数	东部	55.54	54.90	55.48	56.19
	中部	55.63	54.59	54.51	55.04
	西部	55.68	55.44	54.51	55.23

① 《中国城市生活质量报告（2014）》一书对此进行了解释。

表4给出了描述生活质量客观指数的5个细分指数。2015年的调查结果与之前的调查结果基本保持一致。生活水平客观指数呈现出明显的东、中、西递减态势，表明生活水平东部最高，中部次之，西部最低。与生活水平客观指数相反，生活成本客观指数东部最低，其次是中部，西部最高，表明东部生活成本最高，西部最低，中部居于两者之间。从变化趋势上看，2015年3个地区的生活成本均呈下降趋势。在5个细分指数中，东部和中部地区在人力资本客观指数方面没有明显的差距，但东部和中部两个地区均高于西部地区；社会保障客观指数仍旧是东部地区遥遥领先于中西部地区，但东部城市得分从60分以上降低到55.47；生活感受客观指数仍然是东部地区高于中西部地区。

表4 按区域分5个客观细分指数

指数	地区	2015年	2014年	2013年	2012年
生活水平客观指数	东部	62.31	71.53	69.00	62.99
	中部	56.12	62.77	59.39	52.03
	西部	54.74	61.96	58.54	49.60
生活成本客观指数	东部	50.85	50.37	54.96	52.12
	中部	56.98	56.42	61.47	57.41
	西部	61.72	61.18	65.46	60.94
人力资本客观指数	东部	57.25	57.32	57.18	58.72
	中部	57.57	57.02	58.39	56.18
	西部	55.62	55.30	55.19	57.22
社会保障客观指数	东部	55.47	60.16	60.89	57.08
	中部	44.80	45.67	46.86	45.72
	西部	45.92	47.37	46.95	45.50
生活感受客观指数	东部	58.77	58.61	55.95	56.37
	中部	53.55	52.52	51.74	48.16
	西部	54.38	53.58	50.20	48.07

生活质量的区域特征表明，总体来看，我国城市生活质量还存在区域间的不平衡状态，这是东、中、西部地区经济发展不平衡的表现。因此，从各级政府的角度看，推进体制改革、简政放权，为发展中西部经济"松绑"，让市场机制充分发挥资源配置的决定作用，是未来几年的重要任务之一。同时，中西部地区要抓住机遇，借助"一带一路"国家战略谋求地区经济发展，通过发展经济进一步提高居民生活质量。此外，中央政府制定区域协调发展、城乡协调发展的战略，也是当务之急。

四 房价预期持续下降，房产居住属性强化

2015年"两会"召开前夕，光明网推出"2015两会'对焦点'——老百姓眼中的改革关键词"网络调查。调查结果显示，"住房问题"连续3年排在光明网两会关注度排行榜的前5名。住房问题早已成为民众较为关注的民生问题之一。自2003年"房改"以来，房价就成为社会各界人士关注的热点，有关房价的争论也日益激烈；同时，中国各大城市房价步入上升通道。近几年来，房价过高成为城市居民生活成本高企的关键因素，并通过挤压民众的消费支出大大影响了城市居民的生活质量，这也是我们持续关注该问题并调查的原因。然而，本次调查显示，上述情况或许将有所改观。根据此次调查结果，房价预期指数的全国加权平均值为43.86，低于50这一临界点，相比2014年的60.78大幅下降，也就是说，房价预期由上涨转为下跌。自2012年开展本项调查以来，这种情况还是首次出现。

观察实际经济数据，全国70个大中城市的房价变动也印证了民众的房价预期。根据国家统计局发布的70个大中城市住宅销售价格指数，2014年6月以后，住宅销售价格环比总体呈现下降趋势，同比略微上涨；2014年10月以后，同比也开始出现总体下降的态势。然

而，我们认为，房价经过最近一年的调整，随着2015年初房地产相关政策的放宽，尽管全国房地产行业总体还将处于去库存化的阶段，房价走势总体疲软，但各级城市的房地产价格变动会出现一些分化。

这一趋势在最新的统计数据中已经有所显现。例如，根据2015年3月国家统计局发布的数据，全国70个大中城市新建商品住宅价格环比下降的城市有50个，比上月减少16个；持平和上涨的城市分别有8个和12个，分别比上月增加6个和10个；二手住宅价格环比下降的城市有48个，比上月减少13个；持平和上涨的城市分别有10个和12个，分别比上月增加6个和7个。上涨的城市分别为北京、天津、石家庄、太原、南京、厦门、郑州、武汉、深圳、南宁、贵阳、徐州；持平的城市为上海、福州、海口、包头、锦州、安庆、岳阳、常德。一线城市新建商品住宅价格和二手住宅价格环比综合平均，分别由上月下降0.1%和持平转为本月上涨0.2%和上涨0.3%。二、三线城市新建商品住宅价格和二手住宅价格环比综合平均虽仍然下降，但降幅均比上月收窄。因此，总的来看，2015年下半年起，一线城市的商品住宅价格将呈现跌幅收窄、基本稳定或者温和上涨的态势。其原因在于，我国区域间发展的差异总体来看还比较显著，一线城市就业和发展机会多、公共服务水平（尤其是教育和医疗水平）先进、基础设施便利程度高都是吸引外来务工人员定居的关键因素。而二、三线城市乃至四线城市，由于住房总体库存较大，前期房价上涨幅度过大，且城市在公共服务等方面发展缓慢，住宅供求矛盾将持续突出，房价向下调整的空间仍然较大。

党的十八大报告指出，"要多谋民生之利，多解民生之忧，解决好人民最关心、最直接、最现实的利益问题，在学有所教、劳有所得、病有所医、老有所养、住有所居上持续取得新进展，努力让人民过上更好的生活"。然而，住有所居是上述民生问题得以解决、实现个人自由和全民发展的关键因素。随着中国工业化和城市化的持续推进，不仅现有的城市居民的住房需求不断上升，而且还会有大批的农村居民市民化，城市住房潜在需求仍将继续上升。因此，关于房地产未来的发展趋势，从房地产良性发展和居民生活质量提高的角度来讲，我国房地产市场必须由原来的"投机性"倾向调整为"居住属性"倾向。为此，我们提出以下几项政策建议。第一，推进房产税立法和实施。房产税对于挤压房价泡沫、减少空置率、打压房地产投机具有重要意义，同时可以提高中小户型的比重，这是房地产行业长期良性可持续发展的重要配套制度。第二，进一步扩大棚户区和城市危房改造规模，加大保障房建设力度。棚户区居民或者城市危房的居住者多数为老企业职工，他们为城市的发展做出过突出贡献，实施棚户区改造可以改善他们的居住条件，同时可以兼顾改善城市环境，提升城市居民整体的生活质量。另外，还需要扩大保障房建设力度，满足城市其他低收入群体或者外来务工人员的住房需求。第三，进一步实施区域化发展战略，促进区域间协调发展，缩小区域发展差距。区域间发展与城乡发展失衡是目前中国大城市尤其是一线城市房价过快上涨的重要原因。因此，为了实现全国房地产市场总体的稳定持续发展，需要实现区域之间、城乡之间协调发展。只有各地发展机会、公共服务以及基础设施水平呈现出相对协调一致的局面，人口过度向大城市迁徙集中的趋势才能得以减缓，大城市住房的供需矛盾才能得以缓解，从而实现房地产稳定发展。

五 积极推动公众参与，切实改善环境质量

没有环境保护的繁荣是推迟的灾难，不节约资源、保护环境，经济就会陷入"增长的极限"。改革开放以来，我国以9.8%的经济年均增速创造了"中国奇迹"，但同时也付出了巨大的环境代价。根据世界银行提供的数据，2010年我国创造了约4.9万亿美元的国内生产总值，

但每创造1万美元的GDP,要消耗20千克石油当量,远高于全球15千克石油当量的平均水平,全球排名第16位,属于能源消耗强度较高的国家之一。同时,每创造1万美元的GDP,中国要排放21.58吨的CO_2,也远高于全球7.43吨的平均水平,全球排名第5位,属于污染排放强度较高的国家之一。可见,我国过去几十年来的高速增长是以高消耗、高污染为代价的,经济发展质量并不乐观,对环境的破坏不容忽视。

随着工业化与城镇化进程的不断推进,城市既成为工业生产的集中地,又成为人们生活的聚集地,由工业化引起的工业污染与由城镇化带来的生活污染在短时间内集聚在城市范围内,尤其是一些特大城市和大城市。交通拥挤、空气污染、资源短缺、生态环境压力过大等"城市病"不断蔓延,环境质量一时间成为城市居民热议的话题。表5比较了本次调查的城市居民对空气质量的关注程度以及调查城市的空气质量。

表5 城市空气质量及其受关注程度

城市	PM2.5年平均浓度		空气质量受关注程度		PM2.5年平均浓度排名与空气质量受关注程度排名之差
	微克/立方米	排名	%	排名	
石家庄市	154	33	44.78	1	32
郑州市	108	31	42.56	3	28
北京市	89	26	43.19	2	24
武汉市	94	27	42.38	4	23
天津市	96	28	41.63	5	23
济南市	110	32	38.38	13	19
沈阳市	78	19	40.96	6	13
南京市	78	20	39.85	8	12
长沙市	83	23	39.64	11	12
西安市	105	30	37.08	19	11
太原市	81	21	38.31	14	7
乌鲁木齐市	88	24	37.46	17	7
长春市	73	18	38.49	12	6

续表

城市	PM2.5年平均浓度		空气质量受关注程度		PM2.5年平均浓度排名与空气质量受关注程度排名之差
	微克/立方米	排名	%	排名	
成都市	96	29	35.92	23	6
杭州市	70	15	39.71	10	5
合肥市	88	25	36.25	22	3
上海市	62	11	39.78	9	2
南昌市	69	14	38.07	15	−1
银川市	51	5	40.78	7	−2
重庆市	70	16	37.35	18	−2
西宁市	70	17	36.57	20	−3
哈尔滨市	81	22	35.79	25	−3
呼和浩特市	57	9	36.43	21	−12
厦门市	36	2	37.93	16	−14
青岛市	67	12	35.35	27	−15
兰州市	67	13	32.81	31	−18
南宁市	57	10	34.18	29	−19
广州市	53	6	35.37	26	−20
深圳市	40	3	35.79	24	−21
贵阳市	53	7	35.27	28	−21
宁波市	54	8	33.13	30	−22
昆明市	42	4	32.08	32	−28
海口市	27	1	28.99	33	−32

注：空气质量受关注程度（%）以该城市中将空气质量视为影响生活质量最重要因素的受访者比例来衡量。由于福州和大连PM2.5年平均浓度的数据缺失，这里不包括这两个城市的数据。PM2.5空气质量排名是按照PM2.5年平均浓度由低至高的顺序进行的，排名越靠前，说明空气质量越好。空气质量受关注程度排名是按照空气质量受关注程度由高至低的顺序进行的，排名越靠前，说明居民对空气质量的关注程度越高。PM2.5年平均浓度排名与空气质量受关注程度排名的差较大，表明该城市空气质量较差，且公众对空气质量的关注度较高；差较小，表明该城市空气质量较好，且公众对空气质量的关注度较低；差接近零，表明该城市空气质量较差而公众关注不足，抑或是该城市空气质量较好而公众仍密切关注。

资料来源：PM2.5年平均浓度的数据来自《中国统计年鉴（2014）》，空气质量受关注程度来自本次"城市居民最关注因素调查"。

结论和启示

表 5 显示，在 33 个城市中，空气质量较差的 10 个城市依次为：石家庄市（33）、济南市（32）、郑州市（31）、西安市（30）、成都市（29）、天津市（28）、武汉市（27）、北京市（26）、合肥市（25）、乌鲁木齐市（24），这些城市 PM2.5 年平均浓度均在 88 微克/立方米及以上。空气质量较好的 10 个城市依次为：海口市（1）、厦门市（2）、深圳市（3）、昆明市（4）、银川市（5）、广州市（6）、贵阳市（7）、宁波市（8）、呼和浩特市（9）、南宁市（10）。需要说明的是，我国 PM2.5 标准采用世卫组织设定的最宽限值，即 PM2.5 年平均浓度限值 35 微克/立方米，而在我国空气较好的 10 个城市中，除海口和厦门低于和接近这一标准外，其他城市都在 40 微克/立方米及以上。

有趣的是，我们发现并不是空气质量好的地方，城市居民就不关注空气质量；也并不是空气质量差的地方，城市居民就十分关注空气质量。由表 5 可以看出，这些城市可以划分为 3 类。

第一类城市的空气质量并不算太差甚至相对较好，但当地居民却十分关注空气质量。例如，银川市、厦门市、上海市、沈阳市、杭州市、南京市。这一方面反映了上述城市居民对环境的重视程度较高，另一方面也说明这些城市的居民对环境质量的诉求能够通过媒体、议案、诉讼等途径自下而上地得到表达。另外，上述城市大多是东部人均收入较高的城市，说明随着收入的增加，人们对环境质量的关注度在不断提高，在解决了温饱问题后，环境安全成为人们关注的焦点。

第二类城市的空气质量较差甚至很差，但相对来说当地居民却不那么关心空气质量，例如，成都市、西安市、合肥市、济南市、哈尔滨市、兰州市。之所以出现这种结果，原因可能有两个：一是这些地区的经济发展水平不高，人们更加关注温饱而非环保；二是这些地区在历史上也大多是环境质量不佳的中西部地区，从当地居民的角度看，人们对环境质量的诉求本身并不高。

第三类城市空气质量排名与空气质量受关注程度排名相反,即空气质量好的城市居民对环境质量的关注度较低,空气质量差的城市居民对环境质量的关注度较高。例如,海口市、昆明市、宁波市、贵阳市、深圳市、广州市、重庆市、石家庄市、郑州市、北京市、武汉市、天津市、长沙市。这类城市中既有环境质量较高,环境受关注程度较低的地区,如海口市、昆明市、宁波市、贵阳市、深圳市、广州市;也有环境质量较差,环境受关注程度较高的地区,如石家庄市、郑州市、北京市、武汉市、天津市。因此,并不是环境质量受关注程度越高就越好,一些城市的环境质量受关注程度较高,是因为其空气质量糟糕,而一些城市的环境质量受关注程度较低,则源于其良好的环境本底[①]。

可见,由于经济社会发展阶段的差异,不同地区环境质量与环境受关注程度并不完全一致。经济较为发达的东部地区,尽管其环境质量并不是太差,但人们对环境的关注度却很高,充分体现了人们对生活质量的更高诉求。经济较不发达的中西部地区,尽管环境质量较差,但人们对环境的关注度却并不很高,从某种程度上讲,他们更愿意用环保换温饱。

作为世界上最大的发展中国家,没有一个国家如我国这样,正在经历着规模如此大、范围如此广、速度如此快的工业化与城镇化进程,也没有一个国家面临如此复杂而严峻的环境问题。人类要发展,就不得不首先利用自然,这不可避免地会造成环境污染。问题的关键在于,当人类利用自然环境创造了更多财富时,我们不仅要自己享受这些成果,更要与自然一起分享工业化的果实,及时修复生态环境,积极转变发展方式,实现人与自然的和谐发展。改善环境质量并不是一朝一夕的事情,面对环境质量的不断恶化、环境突发事件的频繁爆发,我们既要有坚定的信念,又要有淡定的心态,通过有效的环境规

---

① 环境本底是指自然环境在未受污染的情况下,各种环境要素中化学元素或化学物质的基线含量。

制、创新的环境管理、先进的环保技术、完善的环境规划，促进城镇化与环境污染拐点早日到来。

六　完善食品安全监管体系，保障居民饮食健康

2014年，我们新增了城市居民最关注因素的调查，根据调查结果，空气质量和食品安全两个因素是排在前两位的影响居民生活质量的最重要因素。2015年的调查结果显示，在35个城市中，32个城市的受访者把空气质量视为影响生活质量的最重要因素，3个城市的受访者把食品安全作为影响生活质量的最重要因素。这3个城市分别是：昆明市、宁波市和海口市。根据《中国统计年鉴（2014）》的数据，海口的PM2.5浓度为27微克/立方米，按照PM2.5浓度由低到高（或空气质量由好到差），在35个城市中排名第1；昆明的PM2.5浓度为42微克/立方米，在35个城市中排名第4；宁波的PM2.5浓度为54微克/立方米，在35个城市中排名第8。当空气质量较好时，人们可能更为关注食品安全，这是可以理解的。在35个城市中，共有19个城市中选择食品安全的受访者的比例超过30%。在所有的受访者中，食品安全被认为是除空气质量外，影响生活质量的最重要因素。食品是人类生存和发展的最基本的物质基础，食品安全是关乎人类生命健康的基础保障。然而，自1998年山西假酒案发生以来，食品安全问题即成为人们追求健康生活过程中挥之不去的"阴影"。

纵观世界各国食品安全发展的历程可以发现，食品安全问题发展大致经历了4个阶段[①]：第一阶段是食物匮乏阶段，市场的主要目的是提供充足的食物，尽管生产经营卫生条件恶劣，但人们的温饱问题尚未解决，还不至于关注食品安全问题；第二阶段为食品工业化和农业工业化粗放发展阶段，伴随着食品生产技术的发展，各种食品添

---

① 朱明春、何植民、蒋宇芝：《食品安全发展的阶段性及我国的应对策略》，《中国行政管理》2013年第2期。

加剂、色素、香料大量盲目用于食品生产过程，与此同时，在农牧业中，农药、化肥以及各种激素被大量使用，在这一阶段，制假售假、制售低劣违规产品的食品犯罪行为日渐增多；第三阶段是食品产业发展规范化、法制化的阶段，各种食品添加剂、色素等化学原料在食品生产中的使用量被严格限制，相关质量体系标准、法律法规制度日渐完善；第四阶段是食物营养健康阶段，也就是欧、美、日等发达国家和地区当前所处的阶段，行业发展的目的在于协助人们建立科学合理的膳食结构。当前，中国食品安全发展总体上处于第二向第三阶段的过渡期，各种食品生产故意违法犯罪行为非常突出。表6列出了2014年的重大食品安全事件。

表6 2014年重大食品安全事件

事件	曝光时间
事件一："毒豆芽"事件	2014年4月
事件二：家乐福散装菜干二氧化硫超标	2014年5月
事件三：麦当劳福喜腐肉事件	2014年7月
事件四：三无产品"吸血鬼饮料"事件	2014年7月
事件五：汉丽轩"口水肉"事件	2014年7月
事件六：粪水臭豆腐事件	2014年8月
事件七：顶新"黑心油"	2014年9月
事件八：毒凉皮事件	2014年11月
事件九：昆明毒米线流入市场	2014年12月

资料来源：中国网，http://food.china.com.cn/node_7217894.htm。

不断发生的恶性食品安全事件表明，我国食品安全问题呈现以下特点[①]：第一，食品安全的风险源头越发隐蔽，"技术含量"越来越高，尤其是上海福喜事件，反映出潜在的食品安全问题甚至在一定程

---

① 鄂璠：《2014最受关注十大焦点问题：最忧虑食品安全》，http://news.xinhuanet.com/food/2014-12/07/c_127283184.htm。

度上已经超出目前的监管水平和检验检测能力;二是互联网食品交易市场不断发展,但网络监管能力未能同步发展,因此现实中出现了大量"三无"自制食品,网络食品安全问题日益突出;三是食品源头污染与末端安全问题交织并存,食品安全已不再仅仅是生产、流通、餐饮服务的问题,土壤、水以及空气污染已经对食品生产的源头——种植和养殖环节构成严重威胁。

对于不断出现的食品安全问题,现有的大多数研究认为,信息不对称以及政府监管缺失是食品质量安全问题出现的关键原因。因此,食品安全问题治理机制的核心在于解决信息不对称。而根据经济学的理论知识,解决信息不对称的手段主要有以下几种:一是实行市场准入制度;二是强制信息披露;三是加强政府监管与法律约束。

2009年中国出台的《食品安全法》,从食品安全管理的各个方面做出了详细的制度安排,对我国食品安全监管发挥了积极的作用。然而,最近几年来,不断发生的食品安全事件表明,《食品安全法》还存在明显的缺陷与漏洞。具体表现如下。一是食品安全监管部门的设计存在矛盾冲突,从而导致部门职能不清晰、相互之间缺乏协调,造成食品监管体系的碎片化,出现事实上的监管不到位。二是对占食品生产企业总数80%、占食品工业产值20%的小微企业缺乏监管。《食品安全法》中所规定的生产经营许可制度主要针对规模以上企业,而对食品生产和加工小作坊及食品摊贩仅仅做了原则性规定,具体管理办法则交由省级人大去制定。然而,在实际法律执行中,各省市或自治区对小作坊的立法并不积极,5年间进行立法的省份仅有8个,这成为食品安全监管中的一大漏洞[①]。三是惩罚力度不足和惩罚性赔偿缺失。按照我国当前的《食品安全法》,对违法企业的罚款上限是"10万元以下罚款"或者"货值金额10倍以下罚款",相比不法企业

---

① 《专家争议食品安全法硬伤:80%小企业仍处监管之外》,http://finance.chinanews.com/cj/2015/03-10/7114609.shtml。

的违法所得而言,这样的违法成本堪称低廉,从成本—收益的角度而言,企业会产生违规操作的冲动。另外,迄今为止,我国仍未建立惩罚性赔偿制度。惩罚性赔偿制度的作用在于:在这一制度下,制假售假的企业一旦被调查落实,企业所有者就有倾家荡产的可能,企业违法成本大大提升,可以有力地遏制食品企业违法犯罪的发生。惩罚性赔偿制度在世界许多国家的实施已经证明其具有非常好的预防作用。当然,值得庆幸的是,自2013年10月起,相关部门开始对《食品安全法》进行全面的修订,修订工作有望在2015年上半年完成。修订完毕之后,上述缺陷或许能够得到比较全面的改善。

除完善《食品安全法》之外,为了强化食品安全管理,我国政府还需要进一步推动以下两个机制的建立。一是信息披露机制。食品安全信息披露机制指的是政府将食品相关信息以适当的方式公布于众,让公众及时了解、认识并监督食品卫生安全。高效的信息披露机制是解决食品信息不对称的一剂良方[1]。二是食品安全追溯制度。食品安全追溯制度作为一种信息披露的政策工具,其目的就是对食品供应链条中各个环节的产品安全信息进行跟踪与追溯,通过上下游各个成员行为主体的信息共享和紧密合作,形成集成化供应链(Integrated Supply Chain),以弥补单一控制方法的不足,为供给链条内的各行为主体、消费者、行业机构及监管者提供有关产品安全的真实可靠的信息,为消费者提供知情权和选择权[2]。建立完善有效的食品安全追溯制度已经成为世界发达经济体加强食品安全管理的关键手段。

总之,在食品安全领域,由于信息不对称是一种客观存在,市场机制自身无法解决食品安全问题,保障食品安全的责任在于政府。

---

[1] 《罗云波:食品安全亟待建立高效的信息披露机制》,http://gb.cri.cn/42071/2013/06/17/6851s4150245.htm。
[2] 乔娟、韩杨、李秉龙:《中国实施食品安全追溯制度的重要性与限制因素分析》,《中国畜牧杂志》2007年第6期。

七 大力发展公共交通，治理城市交通恶疾

根据本次对城市居民最关注的影响生活质量的4个相关因素的调查，交通状况虽然位列第4，关注度低于空气质量和食品安全，但从35个调查城市样本的平均值来看，仍有10.94%的受访者认为交通状况是影响生活质量的最重要因素。根据我们的城市生活质量指标体系（QLICC），生活感受指数是衡量城市生活质量的重要组成部分，而交通状况则属于生活感受指数中衡量生活便利性的重要指标。因此，城市交通状况的好坏直接影响着城市居民生活质量的高低。

从影响城市居民生活质量的角度来讲，评价城市交通状况的指标可以分为3个部分：一是交通安全指标，具体又可分为反映交通事故次数的相对指标——10万人交通事故率和反映交通事故严重程度的指标——10万人死亡率；二是居民出行满意度，具体由居民平均通勤出行时耗、日均道路交通运行指数、拥堵持续时间、公交站点500米半径覆盖率等指标来反映；三是公众健康，具体指由交通空气污染、交通噪声污染以及由采用私人机动化方式出行引起的健康问题[①]。

从交通安全角度来看，根据国家统计局发布的《2014年国民经济和社会发展统计公报》，2014年全国道路交通事故万车死亡人数为2.22人，相比2013年下降5.1%；2014年末全国民用汽车保有量达到15447万辆，比上年末增长12.4%。经过换算可以得出，2014年的交通事故死亡人数约为34292人，比2013年死亡人数31604人增加了2688人，增长率为8.5%；相比2012年的死亡人数30222人，增加了4070人，增长率为13.5%；相比2011年的死亡人数29618人，增加了4674人，增长率为15.8%。由此可以看出，交通安全状况不容乐观。交通事故

---

① 杨超、魏艳艳：《考虑居民生活质量的城市交通可持续发展指标》，《同济大学学报》（自然科学版）2013年第10期。

上升的原因在于机动车保有量和机动车驾驶人数量不断增加，但驾龄较短的人数也在增加，交通安全意识与驾驶技术堪忧。

从居民出行满意程度来说，堵车已经成为目前中国大中城市居民出行的最大困扰。2014年4月，荷兰知名交通导航服务商TomTom发布了全球拥堵城市排名，在全球最拥堵的100个城市中，中国大陆有21个城市上榜；全球拥堵前30名的城市中，中国大陆有10个城市出现，分别为重庆市、天津市、北京市、广州市、成都市、上海市、石家庄市、福州市、沈阳市、杭州市，其中拥堵情况最严重的城市是重庆，平均拥堵指数为38%，全球排名第12。此外，天津列第14位（38%），北京列第15位（37%），广州列第17位，成都列第19位，上海列第24位①。交通拥堵带来的是居民出行时耗的增加。2015年3月，央视财经频道重磅首发《中国经济生活大调查》大数据，数据结果显示，全国上班族每10个人中就有一人单程出行时间超过两小时，上班往返时间超过4小时。拥堵的交通对城市居民的身心健康造成了一定的伤害。2011年由慈铭体检集团联合中国医师协会、中国医院协会、北京市健康保障协会共同发布的调查报告指出，因交通堵塞，80%的人在不同程度上受到了"交通心理烦躁症"的侵袭，对上班、出行出现害怕、厌恶和逆反情绪。交通拥堵时，人们会产生烦躁、抱怨情绪②，以致现在出现了数量可观的"路怒族"。

从公众健康情况来看，城市交通对人们的身体健康也造成了较为显著的影响。机动车尾气排放成为空气污染的重要来源。公开资料显示，汽车尾气排放已经成为城市PM2.5的重要来源（如图1所示）。而根据2012年联合国环境规划署公布的《全球环境展望报告5》，全

---

① 《全球最拥堵城市排行榜：北京位列15 上海第24名》，http://news.xinhuanet.com/city/2015-04/06/c_127660388.htm。
② 李洪：《有车一族：五大疾病让健康亮红灯》，《中国卫生产业》2011年第6期。

结论和启示

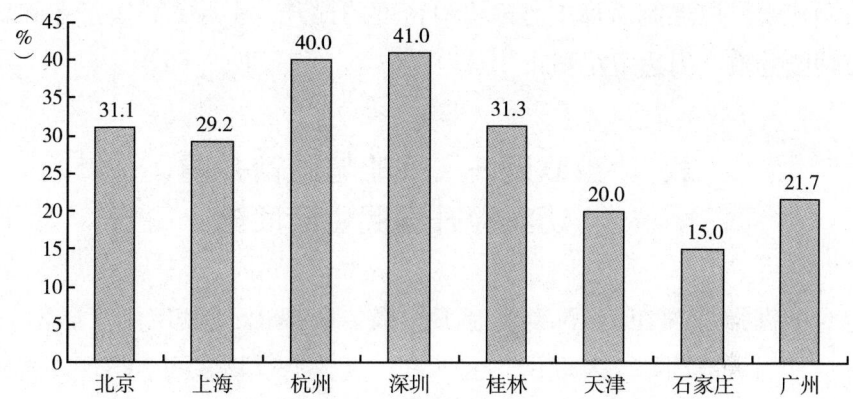

图1 部分城市 PM2.5 来源中汽车尾气排放占比
资料来源：笔者根据网络资料整理。

球每年有近 200 万的过早死亡病例与 PM2.5 颗粒物污染有关。除了空气污染外，城市交通还带来了噪声污染，我国尚无关于交通噪声污染对居民健康影响的相关研究报告。欧洲环境署 2014 年底公布了欧盟首份噪声评估报告，称超过 1.25 亿的欧洲人承受着超过法定指导水平的交通噪声污染，导致每年高达 1 万人过早死亡，交通噪声困扰着欧盟 28 个成员国近 2000 万的欧洲民众，影响了 800 多万名居民的睡眠[①]。

交通出行是人们生活中的一部分，从提升居民生活质量的角度出发，政府应该综合考虑交通安全、居民出行便利程度与公众健康之间的相互协调关系，制定科学有效的城市交通发展战略。从国际经验以及我国交通部的战略取向来看，大力发展公共交通是解决上述问题的最优途径。然而，公共交通能够解决目前城市交通问题的重要前提是合理控制城市规模以及实行面向交通的城市规划模式。从国际经验来看，一是推行混合用地模式，摒弃"雅典宪章"的功能分区观念，避免城市布局功能单一化；二是推进由中心城市与卫星城市相结合的城

---

① 《欧洲交通噪声每年致上万人过早死亡》，http://env.people.com.cn/n/2014/1229/c1010-26290849.html。

市圈建设，以遏制城市中心区人口密度的提升，引导人口、产业和城市功能分散至周边卫星城市①。

八 "互联网＋"战略与监管并重，切实提升居民生活质量

李克强总理在2015年政府工作报告中提出："制定'互联网＋'行动计划，推动移动互联网、云计算、大数据、物联网等与现代制造业结合，促进电子商务、工业互联网和互联网金融健康发展，引导互联网企业拓展国际市场。"② 所谓"互联网＋"，就是利用互联网平台，运用现代信息通信技术，把互联网平台与社会各个行业部门结合起来，通过生产、交易与消费方式的转变，推动行业变革升级。目前来看，"互联网＋"已经全面渗透至第三产业，形成了诸如互联网金融、互联网交通、互联网医疗、互联网教育等崭新的产业形态。展望未来，工业互联网和农业互联网业也会不断趋于完善。工业方面，"互联网＋"模式会逐渐由消费品工业向新材料、新能源以及装备制造等工业领域全面发展；农业方面，互联网将逐渐改变产品交易方式、消费方式乃至生产方式，推动农业产业升级③。也就是说，互联网不仅仅会改变人们的交流方式、消费方式、理财方式，甚至会完全改变人们的生产方式和生活方式。

就城市居民生活质量而言，互联网不仅仅会通过推动前述关于房地产、环境治理、交通状况以及食品安全的发展来影响人们的生活质

---

① 钱七虎：《城市交通拥堵和空气污染的治本之策》，《科技日报》2014年4月21日。
② 《（两会授权发布）政府工作报告》，http：//news.xinhuanet.com/politics/2015-03/16/c_1114659488_2.htm。
③ 《解读：李克强政府报告中的"互联网＋"是什么》，http：//www.ce.cn/cysc/ztpd/2015zt/9gz/bd/201504/01/t20150401_4997927.shtml。

结论和启示

量。而且互联网本身还可以从下述几个方面影响人们的生活质量。

第一,互联网的发展使人们的生活服务便利化程度显著提高。根据中国互联网络信息中心发布的《第35次中国互联网络发展状况统计报告》,截至2014年12月,我国网络购物用户规模达到3.61亿人,较2013年底增加了5953万人,增长率为19.7%;我国网民使用网络购物的比例从48.9%提高至55.7%,而且网购群体年龄跨度不断增大,网络购物出现普及化、全球化、移动化的发展趋势。网络购物可以让消费者更加深入全面地了解信息,使其具有更加广泛的商品选择空间,购物变得更加快捷高效。除了网购外,截至2014年12月,我国采用网络支付、购买互联网理财产品以及通过网络预订过机票、酒店、火车票或旅行度假产品的用户规模同比分别增长17.0%、18.6%和22.7%[①]。另外,还有更为重要的一点,互联网的发展使得人们彼此的沟通更加快捷、高效,沟通方式更加多元丰富。

第二,互联网的发展丰富了人们的文化生活与娱乐手段。随着网络信息技术的不断提升,网络资讯、网络游戏、网络文学、网络视频的内容不断丰富,人们只要利用一台电脑就可充分掌握世界每天发生的各种时事趣闻,使用各种游戏娱乐平台,阅读各种文学资料,观看各种网络视频,人们的文化生活与娱乐内容越来越充实。尤其是网络教育的发展,不仅丰富了人们的文化生活,而且使人们在家就可以通过网络分享世界名校的教育资源,有利于人力资本水平的提升,无论在主观上还是客观上,都有利于人力资本满意度的提高。

第三,互联网的发展可以在一定程度上降低人们的生活成本。首先,互联网可以给人们提供更充分的信息,以最小的时间成本做到"货比三家",以最小的支出成本完成自己的消费活动;其次,伴随互联网兴起的类似团购的营销模式,可以显著减少人们的消费开支;再

---

① 中国互联网络信息中心:《第35次中国互联网络发展状况统计报告》,http://www.cnnic.net.cn/hlwfzyj/hlwxzbg/。

次，互联网可以减少人们生活中的信息搜寻成本和交易成本；最后，互联网大幅提升了社会资源共享水平，可以充分发挥产业的规模效应，使人们获得更多的低价资源甚至免费资源。

第四，互联网发展对于提升人们的生活消费水平具有积极的推动作用。上述分析表明，互联网的发展增强了人们消费方式的便利性、消费内容的丰富性以及消费成本的低廉性，在一定程度上有助于提高人们的消费水平，进而提高生活质量。另外，互联网金融的发展，也为人们消费水平的提升提供了强劲的动力。金融发展是增加人们财产性收入、提高人们财富水平的重要途径。在传统金融模式下，受服务成本、信息不对称以及资金规模要求等因素的制约，金融资源更多地被20%的高端客户群体所拥有，广大中低端客户无法充分利用金融资源。然而随着互联网金融的发展，广大中低端人群的小额度、低风险、高流动性且相对较高收益的理财需求得到满足，在一定程度上可以增加普通居民的财产性收入，提高人们的消费水平[1]。

当然，互联网在为人们的生活带来诸多好处的同时，也给人们的生活造成了不少负面影响。随着互联网信息技术的日新月异，由于网络监管水平未能同步提高，"网络诈骗""消费陷阱""垃圾信息"等问题也在不断侵扰人们的生活，甚至打乱了人们正常的生活秩序。另外，人与人之间良好的人际互动是生活质量提升的重要途径。然而，早在2000年，斯坦福社会定量研究协会（SIQSS）发布的一份探究报告指出，互联网是一项"孤立技术"，它导致用户减少了与其他人的交流，并进而严重损害社区的社会结构甚至家庭关系[2]。最后，现实发展的种种迹象表明，互联网还对人们的身心健康造成了一定的负面影响，不利于人们生活水平的提高。显然，互联网的许多弊端是因疏于

---

[1] 孙立行：《互联网金融发展助推消费增长》，http://theory.gmw.cn/2014-07/23/content_12117617.htm。

[2] 《互联网为社会带来副作用》，http://news.chinabyte.com/108/1212608.shtml。

监管产生的，因此，要充分发挥互联网在提高人们生活质量方面的积极作用，加强对互联网的监管。

2015年城市生活质量调查表明，在我国经济新常态的背景下，由于经济增速放缓，35个城市生活质量客观指数虽然有所降低，但生活质量主观满意度却有所提升。这说明普通民众对中国经济的未来发展充满信心，中央政府在稳增长、调结构、惠民生等方面的政策措施更有针对性，并取得了一定实效。但是也应看到，生活成本偏高、空气质量不容乐观、食品安全问题频出等依然存在，仍是制约城市居民生活质量进一步提高的阻力。

参考文献

[1] 张连城等:《经济发展中的两个反差——中国 30 个城市生活质量调查报告》,《经济学动态》2011 年第 7 期。

[2] 张连城等:《生活质量:态势平稳,挑战严峻》,《经济学动态》2013 年第 8 期。

[3] 张连城等:《高生活成本拖累城市生活质量满意度提高——中国 35 个城市生活质量调查报告》,《经济学动态》2012 年第 7 期。

[4] 中国经济实验研究院:《中国城市生活质量报告(2012)》,社会科学文献出版社,2013。

[5] 中国经济实验研究院:《中国城市生活质量报告(2013)》,社会科学文献出版社,2014。

[6] 中国经济实验研究院:《中国城市生活质量报告(2014)》,社会科学文献出版社,2014。

Conclusions and Enlightenments

improving policies of the Central Government have become more specific and effective this year. At the same time, however, we still face challenges, such as the problems of living costs, air quality and food safety, which are hindering the further improvement of urban life quality.

end clients had no access to them. However, as internet banking develops, middle- or low-end clients find a way to make small-amount, low-risk, high-mobility and comparatively high-yield investments. This, to a certain extent, helps to increase the property incomes of common people and promote the level of consumption [1].

Of course, despite all the benefits, the Internet also brings troubles. As information technology upgrades, problems such as "internet frauds", "consumer traps" and "spam information" start to interfere with people's daily life, due to the lack of adequate supervision. Moreover, good interpersonal interaction is a major component of a quality life. However, as far back as 2000, the Stanford Institute for the Quantitative Study of Society (SIQSS) released a report and pointed out that the Internet is an "isolating technology" leading to the reduction of communications and resulting in damages to social structure or even family relations [2]. Finally, as is observed in real life, the Internet can also have negative impacts on people's physical and psychological health and drag down their quality of life. Obviously, the main cause of these problems is the lack of supervision. Thus, adequate supervision is needed in order to benefit fully from the Internet.

It can therefore be concluded that during the "new normal" phase, the economic growth in China has slowed down. Although the objective indexes of the 35 cities have somewhat dropped, the corresponding subjective indexes have improved. It means that our citizens are confident about the future development of China, and that the series of growth-stabilizing and life-

---

[1] Sun Lixing, *"Internet banking promotes consumption growth"*, http://theory.gmw.cn/2014-07/23/content_12117617.htm.

[2] *"Side-effects of the Internet on the society"*, http://news.chinabyte.com/108/1212608.shtml.

Conclusions and Enlightenments

to read all the news around the world, play all kinds of games, read different literatures and watch various videos. All this has enriched people's entertainment and cultural life. Most importantly, the development of on-line education has provided people with not only a better cultural life, but also educational resources of world-famous universities that one can access from home. It helps to improve the level of and the satisfaction with human capital both objectively and subjectively.

Third, development of the Internet can lower people's living costs to a certain extent. First of all, because the Internet provides sufficient information, buyers can then make comparisons with minimum time cost and purchase products at the lowest expense. Secondly, new marketing modes such as group-buying that spring up with the internet can cut living costs significantly. Thirdly, the Internet helps to reduce costs of transactions and information searching. Finally, the Internet has promoted the sharing of social resources and brought the economy of scale to full play. People can thus obtain many sources at lower costs or even for free.

Fourth, development of the Internet provides people with better living standards and higher consumption level. As is shown by the above analysis, development of the Internet has made consumption cheaper, more convenient and of more choices. Therefore, to a certain extent, it helps to raise people's level of consumption and improve their quality of life. On the other hand, the development of internet banking can also provide more funds for consumption. Financing is an important approach to increasing people's wealth and property incomes. Under traditional financial models, owing to factors such as service costs, information asymmetry and fund sizes, financial resources were mostly restricted to the 20% high-end clients, whereas the vast majority of middle- or low-management, but also their ways of life and production.

As far as residents' quality of life is concerned, influences of the Internet are not limited to the above-mentioned aspects such as real estates, environmental management, transportation and food safety. It can also have direct impacts on people's quality of life in the following aspects:

First, development of the Internet provides more convenient services. According to "the 35th Statistical Report on Internet Development in China" released by the China Internet Network Information Centre (CNNIC), by the end of December 2014, there had been 361 million on-line buyers in China – an increase of 59.53 million persons and 19.7% compared to that of 2013. Now the percentage of on-line buyers among internet users has risen from 48.9% to 55.7%. Besides, people of different age groups have now turned to on-line shopping. On-line shopping becomes more and more universalized, globalized and mobilized. It provides consumers with more comprehensive information and more extensive choices, thus making their shopping experience faster and more efficient. Moreover, by the end of December 2014, the users of E-Payment, internet financial products and on-line booking of air tickets, train tickets, hotels or tourism products have increased by 17.0%, 18.6% and 22.7% respectively compared with that of the same period last year [1]. More importantly, development of the Internet has enabled people to communicate quicker, more efficient and in more ways.

Second, development of the Internet provides more entertainments and enriches people's cultural life. As information technology upgrades, the internet is full of various internet information, on-line games, internet literature and network videos. With one computer, people are now able

---

[1] CNNIC, "the 35th Statistical Report on Internet Development in China," http://www.cnnic.net.cn/hlwfzyj/hlwxzbg/.

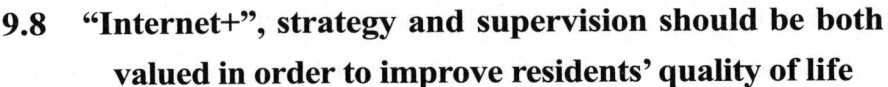

9.8 "Internet+", strategy and supervision should be both valued in order to improve residents' quality of life

In the 2015 Report on the Work of the Government, Premier Li Keqiang mentioned the need to "develop the 'Internet+' action plan to integrate the mobile Internet, cloud computing, big data, and the Internet of Things with modern manufacturing, to encourage the healthy development of e-commerce, industrial networks, and Internet banking, and to guide Internet-based companies to increase their presence in the international market."[1] The so-called "Internet+" is to push forward the reform and upgrade of the industries by making use of network platforms and modern information and communication technology, connecting network platforms with various industry sectors, and transforming the modes of production, trading and consumption. So far, "Internet+" has covered the entire tertiary industry in new industrial forms such as internet banking, internet-guided transportation, on-line medical service and on-line education. In the coming future, Internet will also be widely used in industry and agriculture. In the aspect of industry, "Internet+" will spread gradually from consumer good industry to other industries of new materials, new energy and equipment manufacturing, etc. And in the aspect of agriculture, the Internet will change the modes of product trading, consumption and production, and push forward the upgrading of the agriculture industry[2]. That is to say, the Internet will change not only people's ways of communication, consumption and wealth

---

[1] *"(Authorized by the Two Sessions) Report on the Work of the Government"*, http://news.xinhuanet.com/politics/2015-03/16/c_1114659488_2.htm.

[2] *"Interpretation: what is the 'Internet+' in Li Keqiang's Report on the Work of the Government"*, http://www.ce.cn/cysc/ztpd/2015zt/9gz/bd/201504/01/t20150401_4997927.shtml.

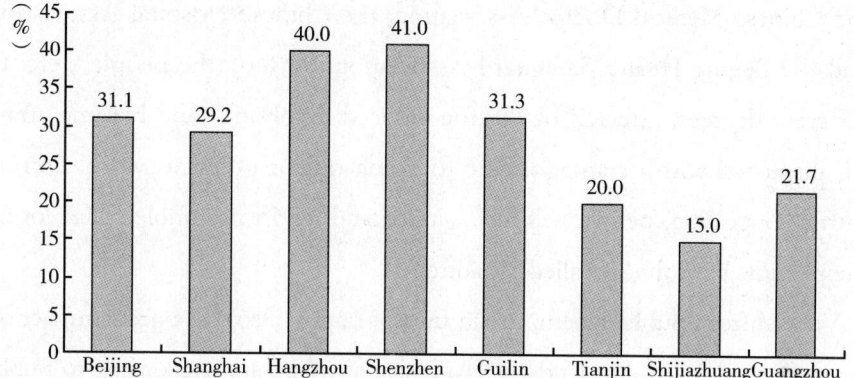

Graph 9.1: The Proportions of Automobile Exhaust Emission in PM2.5 Sources in Some Cities

Source: rearranged internet data.

the safety and convenience of transportation and public health, and work out scientific and effective strategies for the development of urban transportation. Viewed from international experiences and the strategic orientation of the Ministry of Transport, expanding public transport is the best solution to the above-mentioned problems. Nevertheless, the premise is that the scale of the cities should be limited, and that transportation should be included in city planning. According to international experiences, first, we had better abandon the idea of mono-functional sectorization in the "Athens Charter" and embrace the idea of comprehensive functions. Second, the construction of urban agglomerations (the combination of a central city and several satellite cities) should be promoted, in order to limit the population density of city centers and to spread people, businesses and urban functions into satellite cities [1].

---

[1] Qian Qihu, "A permanent cure for traffic congestion and air pollution in the cities", *Science and Technology Daily*, April 21, 2014.

the Chinese Medical Doctor Association, the Chinese Hospital Association and the Beijing Health Safeguard Association, 80% of the people were, to different degrees, affected by "traffic-induced dysphoria" and became afraid of, disgusted with or antagonistic to going out or going to work. During traffic congestion, people will feel agitated and tend to grumble [1]. A lot of people now have the so-called "road-rage".

Viewed from public health, urban transportation also has a great impact on people's physical health. End gas is a major air pollutant. According to public data, automobile exhaust has become a main PM2.5 source in the cities (as is shown in the following graph). And the GEO-5 published by the United Nations Environment Programme (UNEP) in 2012 reported that each year, there were around 2 million early deaths related to PM2.5 particulate pollution worldwide. Besides air pollution, urban transportation also brings noise pollution. So far, no research has been carried out in China on the influence of traffic noise pollution on residents' health. At the end of 2014, European Environment Agency (EEA) published the first noise assessment report of the EU. According to the report, over 125 million Europeans were harassed by traffic noise pollution beyond legal restrictions, resulting in the premature death of up to 10,000 persons each year. Traffic noises were bothering the 20 million Europeans in 28 EU members, and affected the sleep of over 8 million people [2].

Transportation is a natural part of people's daily life. For the improvement of residents' quality of life, the government should take into account both

---

[1] Li Hong, "Car owners: five common diseases are health danger signals", *China Health Industry*, 6 (2011).

[2] "*Traffic noises in Europe cause 10,000 early deaths each year*", http://env.people.com.cn/n/2014/1229/c1010-26290849.html.

34292 persons — 2688 persons more than that of 2013 (31604 persons), increasing by 8.5%. Compared to that of 2012 (30222 persons), the increase was 4070 persons and 13.5%. And compared to that of 2011 (29618 persons), the increase was 4674 persons and 15.8%. It is thus obvious that the situation of transportation safety is far from satisfactory. Rises in traffic accidents were caused by increases in not only vehicle parc and the number of vehicle drivers but also the ratio of less-experienced drivers, as well as lack of driving skills and the awareness of traffic safety.

Viewed from residents' satisfaction with transportation, traffic congestion has already become one of the biggest headaches for people living in large or medium-sized cities. In April 2014, a famous Dutch navigation service provider TomTom released a list of the most congested cities in the world. On the top 100 list, there were 21 Chinese cities. And on the top 30 list, there were 10 Chinese cities, namely Chongqing, Tianjin, Beijing, Guangzhou, Chengdu, Shanghai, Shijiazhuang, Fuzhou, Shenyang and Hangzhou. The problem of Chongqing was the worse, with an average congestion index of 38%, ranking No.12 worldwide. Besides, Tianjin ranked No.14 (38%), Beijing No.15 (37%), Guangzhou No.17, Chengdu No.19 and Shanghai No.24 [1]. Traffic congestion leads to the increase of travelling hours. In March 2015, CCTV-2 released the data of the "Investigation of Chinese Economic Life". As was shown by the data, 1 out of 10 commuters in China would spend over 2 hours one-way (or over 4 hours roundtrip) to work. Traffic congestion is harmful to the physical and psychological health of city dwellers. According to an investigation report published in 2011 by the Ciming Checkup Group with the help of

---

[1] *"The most congested cities in the world: Beijing ranks No.15 and Shanghai No.24"*, http://news.xinhuanet.com/city/2015-04/06/c_127660388.htm.

averages of the 35 surveyed city samples, although transportation seems not as important as air quality or food safety, 10.94% of the interviewees still choose it to be their primary concern. In the QLICC system, the living experience index is a major component in the measurement of urban quality of life, and transportation is an important indicator of the living convenience sub-index that supports the living experience index. Therefore, the quality of urban transportation has direct impact on the quality of residents' lives.

Viewed from the perspective of their effects on residents' QOL, indicators of urban transportation fall into three groups: the first is safety indicators, namely traffic accident rate per 100000 residents (a relative indicator reflecting the number of traffic accidents) and mortality rate per 100,000 residents (an indicator measuring the severity of traffic accidents). The second is satisfaction indicators, namely average commute hours, daily road traffic performance index, congestion time and bus stop coverage in a 500-meter radius. And the third is public health indicators, namely traffic air pollution, traffic noise pollution and health problems caused by using private vehicles [1].

Viewed from transportation safety, according to the Statistical Bulletin on National Economy and Social Development (2014) released by NBS, in 2014, the national road traffic accident death toll per 10000 vehicles was 2.22 persons, a 5.1% drop compared to that of 2013. And the national civilian vehicle parc by the end of 2014 was 15447, a 12.4% rise compared to that of last year. That is to say, the traffic accident death toll of 2014 was

---

[1] Yang Chao, Wei Yanyan, "Indexes of sustainable urban transport based on a consideration of residents' living quality," *Journal of Tongji University (Natural Science)*, 10 (2013).

time. An effective information disclosure system is the only solution to food information asymmetry[①]. The other is the food safety tracking system. As a policy instrument of information disclosure, the purpose of this system is to enable the tracking and tracing of product safety information throughout the links in the food supply chain, and to establish an integrated supply chain through information sharing and close cooperation among all the upstream or downstream behavioral agents, for the sake of better control. Thus, genuine and reliable information on product safety will be accessible to not only all the behavioral agents in the supply chain, but also consumers, industry bodies and supervisors, and consumers will be entitled to the rights to know and to choose[②]. Establishing an advance and effective food safety tracking system has been an important measure of food safety management taken in many developed countries.

In a word, as far as food safety is concerned, owing to the existence of information asymmetry and the fact that the market mechanism cannot solve its own food safety problem, the government should be mainly responsible for food safety management.

9.7 Public transport should be expanded to ease the nasty situation of urban transportation

According to the 2015 survey on primary concern, transportation has ranked No.4 among all the influential factors of QOL. Viewed from the

---

[①] "Luo Yunbo: *The need for food safety calls for an effective information disclosure system*", http://gb.cri.cn/42071/2013/06/17/6851s4150245.htm.

[②] Qiao Juan, Han Yang, Li Binglong, "An analysis on the importance and the limiting factors of establishing a food safety tracking system in China", *Chinese Journal of Animal Science*, 6 (2007).

Conclusions and Enlightenments

food manufacturers and contribute 20% of the total output value of the food industry. The production licensing system under the *Food Safety Law* mainly targets enterprises of a certain scale. As to individual workshops and street peddler, it merely provided a guideline and left the specific legislation to provincial congresses. In actuality however, the provinces or autonomous regions have been inactive on the matter, since in five years, only 8 provinces proceeded with it. This remains a big defect in food safety supervision[1].

Thirdly, there is no effective penalty or punitive damage. Under the *Food Safety Law*, the fine on an offender can be at most "CNY 100,000" or "worth 10 times the value of the commodities". Compared to their illegal gains, breaking the law costs very little. From the cost-benefit perspective, enterprises will be inclined to operate against regulations. Besides, there is still no punitive damage system in China so far. Under such a system, manufacturers and sellers of fake or shoddy products may become bankrupted once their offences are ascertained. At such a cost, it is unlikely for enterprises to break the law. The effectiveness of the punitive damage system has been proven by many other countries. Fortunately, since October 2013, the *Food Safety Law* has been under revision which may complete in the first half of 2015. Afterwards, the above-mentioned defects may disappear.

Besides the revision of the *Food Safety Law*, two systems should also be established with the support of the government for the better management of food safety. One is the information disclosure system in which the government releases food-related information in a proper manner, so that the public is able to understand and supervise food hygiene and safety in

---

[1] *"A dispute over the Achilles heel of the Food Safety Law: 80% of the small businesses remain unsupervised"*, http://finance.chinanews.com/cj/2015/03-10/7114609.shtml.

sources of food safety risks are now harder to detect, and the "technics" become more and more profound. The Shanghai Husi scandal indicates that latent food safety problems are, to an extent, even beyond the present ability of supervision and inspection. Second, as on-line food market develops, a lot of self-made illegal products appear. And due to the lack of on-line food supervision, food safety problems become increasingly severe on the internet. Third, pollution from the sources of food exists side by side with the safety problems at the end. Food safety is no longer an issue of production, distribution or catering services only, but a threat from the very beginning of food production (farming and breeding), owing to the pollution of soil, water and air.

On the issue of food safety, most studies agree that information asymmetry and the lack of governmental supervision are the primary causes of food safety problems. Therefore, the key to it lies in eliminating such information asymmetry. According to economic theories, it can be achieved by the following means: one, the market access system; two, mandatory information disclosure; and three, governmental supervision and legal restraints.

The *Food Safety Law* published in 2009 specified the details of food safety management, which has yielded positive results on food safety supervision. However, the emergence of food safety scandals in recent years shows that the *Food Safety Law* is after all flawed. To be specific, firstly, setup of food safety supervision departments is contradictory and confusing. Hence, the departments are not 100% clear of their own functions and find it hard to cooperate with each other. As a result, the food supervision system is fragmented and unable to perform its duty sometimes. Secondly, small or micro businesses are not well supervised, which make up 80% of all the

and legislation of the food industry when the usage of various chemicals such as food additives and coloring is strictly limited in food production. Meanwhile, relative quality systems and standards continue to improve, as well as laws and regulations. Stage four is nutrition and health - the stage where the developed countries such as US, Japan and European countries are. The purpose of the development of the food industry is to provide people with scientifically reasonable dietary patterns. At present, China's food safety development is going through the transition period between stage two and three when deliberate violations of food-related laws and regulations become noticeable. Major food safety scandals in 2014 are listed as follows:

Table 9.6 Major Food Safety Scandals in 2014

Scandal	Exposed in
① The "poisonous bean sprout" scandal	Apr 2014
② The Carrefour dried vegetables scandal for containing excessive SO_2	May 2014
③ McDonald's and the Husi expired meat scandal	Jul 2014
④ The illegal "vampire drink" scandal	Jul 2014
⑤ The Hanlixuan "recycled meat" scandal	Jul 2014
⑥ The liquid dung stinky tofu scandal	Aug 2014
⑦ The Ting Hsin "hogwash oil" scandal	Sep 2014
⑧ The poisonous cold rice noodle scandal for containing boron	Nov 2014
⑨ The Kunming carcinogenic rice noodle scandal	Dec 2014

Source: China.org.cn, http://food.china.com.cn/node_7217894.htm

Viewed from these frequently exposed severe food safety issues, the food safety problem of China has the following characteristics[1] : first, the

---

① E Fan: "*Top 10 hot issues of 2014: food safety is the primary concern*", http://news.xinhuanet.com/food/2014-12/07/c_127283184.htm.

(Kunming, Ningbo and Haikou) choose food safety. According to *China Statistical Yearbook 2014*, the PM2.5 density of Haikou is 27μg/m^3, ranking No.1 in the 35 cities. The PM2.5 density of Kunming is 42μg/m^3, ranking No.4. And the PM2.5 density of Ningbo is 54μg/m^3, ranking No.8. It is understandable that when air quality is good, people tend to pay more attention to food safety. In 19 out of the 35 cities, over 30% of the interviewees choose food safety as their primary concern. Among all the interviewees, food safety is considered the most influential factor next only to air quality. Food is the fundamental material basis of human existence and development, and food safety is the basic guarantee of our life and health. However, since the Shanxi adulterated wine scandal in 1998, food safety has become a lingering shadow hanging over people's head.

Viewed by the development history of food safety in different countries, the development of food safety usually goes through four stages[①] : Stage one is food shortage when the main purpose of the market is to provide enough food. Although the sanitary conditions of production and operation are abominable, people seldom pay attention to food safety, since the problem of food and clothing comes first. Stage two is the extensive development of food industrialization and agricultural industrialization when a great deal of food additives, coloring and flavors are used indiscriminately in food production as technology develops. At the same time, various pesticides, hormones and chemical fertilizers are also widely used in agricultural or livestock production. During this stage, food-related crimes, such as manufacturing or selling fake and shoddy products, are gradually noticed. Stage three is the standardization

---

① Zhu Mingchun, He Zhimin, Jiang Yuzhi, "The Periodic Characteristics of Food Security Development and Coping Strategies in China," *Chinese Public Administration*, 2 (2013).

Conclusions and Enlightenments

economy is less developed, although the environmental quality is bad, people do not pay much attention to it. To a certain extent, they would rather have better food and clothing than a better environment.

As the biggest developing country in the world, China is going through unprecedentedly intensive and extensive industrialization and urbanization, while facing extremely complicated and severe environmental problems. For the sake of development, human beings have to first make use of nature, resulting in inevitable environmental pollution. The point is that when we have accumulated enough wealth through exploring nature, we cannot keep all the benefits of industrialization to ourselves but share them with nature. We have to restore the ecological environment in time, transform the mode of economic development and work on the harmonious co-existence of human and nature. Environmental quality will not change overnight. As environmental quality deteriorates, and environmental emergencies occur frequently, we need both a firm belief and a calm mind. Through effective environmental regulations, innovative environmental management, advanced environmental technologies and sophisticated environmental planning, we endeavor to reach the turning point of urbanization and environmental pollution as soon as possible.

9.6 The food safety supervision system should be improved in order to provide residents with a healthy diet

In 2014, a new survey was added on residents' primary concern in which air quality and food safety were viewed as the most influential factors of residents' QOL. In the 2015 survey, interviewees in 32 out of the 35 cities choose air quality as their primary concern, while people in the rest 3 cities

than environmental protection, due to their restricted economic development; the other is that these cities are mostly in the central or the western region where environmental quality has been an existing problem in the past. Therefore, local residents have no appeal for better environmental quality.

In the third category, the rankings of their air quality are inversely proportional to the rankings of the amounts of attention paid. In other words, residents in cities with better air quality tend to pay less attention to environmental quality, while people in cities with worse air quality seem to pay more attention to it. Cities in the third category include: Haikou, Kunming, Ningbo, Guiyang, Shenzhen, Guangzhou, Chongqing, Shijiazhuang, Zhengzhou, Beijing, Wuhan, Tianjin and Changsha. Among them, there are cities with higher environmental quality and less amounts of attention, such as Haikou, Kunming, Ningbo, Guiyang, Shenzhen and Guangzhou. Besides, there are also cities with worse environmental quality and more amounts of attention, such as Shijiazhuang, Zhengzhou, Beijing, Wuhan and Tianjin. Therefore, the point is never the amount of attention paid to environmental quality, because high amounts of attention may have resulted from bad air quality, and low amounts of attention from excellent environmental background [1].

It is thus clear that owing to the difference in economic and social development stage, the environmental quality of different regions and the amounts of attention paid to it are not always consistent. In the eastern region where the economy is more advanced, although the environmental quality is not bad, people still pay much attention to it, because the local residents have a higher QOL pursuit. However, in central and western regions where the

---

[1] Environmental background refers to the baseline content of chemical elements or chemical substances contained in various environmental elements in an uncontaminated natural environment.

Conclusions and Enlightenments

As is shown in Table 9.5, among the 33 cities, cities ranked bottom 10 on the list of air quality are: Shijiazhuang (33), Jinan (32), Zhengzhou (31), Xi'an (30), Chengdu (29), Tianjin (28), Wuhan (27), Beijing (26), Hefei (25) and Urumqi (24), whose annual average PM2.5 densities are over $88\mu g/m^3$. And the top 10 cities on the list are: Haikou (1), Xiamen (2), Shenzhen (3), Kunming (4), Yinchuan (5), Guangzhou (6), Guiyang (7), Ningbo (8), Hohhot (9) and Nanning (10). It should be noted that the PM2.5 standard of China uses the maximum value set by the World Health Organization (WHO), namely the annual average PM2.5 density of $35\mu g/m^3$. And among the top 10 cities, except for Haikou and Xiamen whose values are lower or close to the standard, the densities of all the other cities are above $40\mu g/m^3$.

Interestingly, good air quality does not necessarily mean low public attention to air quality, and vice versa. As is shown in Table 9.5, the cities can fall into three categories:

In the first category, the air quality of the cities, such as Yinchuan, Xiamen, Shanghai, Shenyang, Hangzhou and Nanjing, is not bad or fairly good, but the residents still pay much attention. It shows that people in the above-mentioned cities are highly concerned for the environment, and that their appeal for better environmental quality can be expressed through different channels such as media, motions or lawsuits. Besides, most of these cities are in the eastern region with higher per capita income. It indicates that as income increases, people will pay more attention to environmental quality, after the problem of food and clothing is taken care of.

In the second category, the air quality of the cities, such as Chengdu, Xi'an, Hefei, Jinan, Harbin and Lanzhou, is not good or really bad, but the residents pay comparatively little attention to it. There may have been two reasons: one is that people in these cities are more concerned for food and clothing rather

Continued table

City	Annual average PM2.5 density		Amounts of attention paid to air quality		Difference between the PM2.5 annual average density and the ranking of the amounts of attention paid to air quality
	μg/m³	Ranking	%	Ranking	
Yinchuan	51	5	40.78	7	-2
Chongqing	70	16	37.35	18	-2
Xining	70	17	36.57	20	-3
Harbin	81	22	35.79	25	-3
Hohhot	57	9	36.43	21	-12
Xiamen	36	2	37.93	16	-14
Qingdao	67	12	35.35	27	-15
Lanzhou	67	13	32.81	31	-18
Nanning	57	10	34.18	29	-19
Guangzhou	53	6	35.37	26	-20
Shenzhen	40	3	35.79	24	-21
Guiyang	53	7	35.27	28	-21
Ningbo	54	8	33.13	30	-22
Kunming	42	4	32.08	32	-28
Haikou	27	1	28.99	33	-32

Note: the amount of attention paid to air quality (%) is the percentage of interviewees in a city who choose air quality as the most influential factor in their quality of life. Due to the lack of their annual average PM2.5 densities, Fuzhou and Dalian are not included in the table. PM2.5 rankings of air quality are in the order of annual average PM2.5 density from the lowest to the highest. The higher the ranking, the better the air quality. The rankings of the amounts of attention paid to air quality are in the order of the amounts of attention from the highest to the lowest. The higher the ranking, the more attention paid to air quality. The bigger the difference between the ranking of annual average PM2.5 density and the ranking of the amount of attention, the worse the air quality, and the more attention paid to air quality by the public. And the smaller the difference, the better the air quality, and the less attention paid. If the difference is close to 0, then the city either has poor air quality and low public attention, or good air quality and high public attention.

Source: the annual average PM2.5 densities come from *China Statistical Yearbook 2014*, while the amounts of attention paid to air quality come from the 2015 "survey on primary concern".

into not only industrial production centers but also highly populated places. Both industrial pollution caused by industrialization and domestic pollution caused by urbanization have concentrated in the cities within a short time, especially in some megacities and big cities. "City diseases" such as heavy traffic, air pollution, resource shortage and ecological pressure have kept spreading. And suddenly, environmental quality becomes a hot topic among city dwellers. In Table 9.5, comparison is made of the air quality and amounts of attention paid to it in different cities.

Table 9.5 Air Quality and Amounts of Attention in the Cities

City	Annual average PM2.5 density		Amounts of attention paid to air quality		Difference between the PM2.5 annual average density and the ranking of the amounts of attention paid to air quality
	$\mu g/m^3$	Ranking	%	Ranking	
Shijiazhuang	154	33	44.78	1	32
Zhengzhou	108	31	42.56	3	28
Beijing	89	26	43.19	2	24
Wuhan	94	27	42.38	4	23
Tianjin	96	28	41.63	5	23
Jinan	110	32	38.38	13	19
Shenyang	78	19	40.96	6	13
Nanjing	78	20	39.85	8	12
Changsha	83	23	39.64	11	12
Xi'an	105	30	37.08	19	11
Taiyuan	81	21	38.31	14	7
Urumqi	88	24	37.46	17	7
Changchun	73	18	38.49	12	6
Chengdu	96	29	35.92	23	6
Hangzhou	70	15	39.71	10	5
Hefei	88	25	36.25	22	3
Shanghai	62	11	39.78	9	2
Nanchang	69	14	38.07	15	-1

first-tier cities. Consequently, for the stability and sustainability of the real estate market, the development of different regions and between cities and the countryside must be coordinated. Only when different regions start to have similar career opportunities, public services and infrastructure, can the excessive migration to big cities be slowed down, the contradiction between supply and demand for house be relieved, and the stable development of the real estate market be accomplished.

9.5 Public participation should be promoted for the improvement of environmental quality

Without environmental protection, prosperity is only a disaster in disguise. Without saving resources, economy will surely reach its "limits to growth". Since the economic reform, China has created the "China Miracle" with an annual economic growth rate of 9.8%, but at the cost of our environment. According to the World Bank, China's GDP was about USD 4.9 trillion in 2010. However, for every USD 10000 of GDP, we consumed 20kg of oil equivalent - far more than the world average of 15kg of oil equivalent. China ranked No.16 worldwide, and was one of the countries of the highest energy consumption intensity. Besides, for every USD 10000 of GDP, China emitted 21.58 tons of CO_2 — far more than the world average of 7.43 tons. China ranked No.5 worldwide, and was one of the countries of the highest pollutant emission intensity. It is thus clear that the rapid economic growth over the decades was bought at the cost of high energy consumption and high pollution. Both the quality of such economic development and the resulting damage to the environment have become worrying issues.

With the progress of industrialization and urbanization, cities have turned

Conclusions and Enlightenments

and old-age care, and housing so that they will lead a better life". However, housing is the key to solving the above-mentioned livelihood problems and achieving a free and all-round development of individuals. With the progress of industrialization and urbanization, the housing demand of city dwellers will continue to increase, as well as that of many urbanized rural residents. Potential housing demand will keep rising in the cities. Therefore, as far as the future trend of the real estate industry is concerned, from the perspectives of the healthy development of real estates and the improvement of residents' QOL, purchases in the real estate market should turn from "investment-oriented" into "residence-oriented". For this reason, we would like to make the following suggestions: first, promote the legislation and implementation of real estate taxes. It will help to deflate real estate bubbles, reduce vacant rate, control property speculation and improve the ratio of small or medium-sized apartments. Therefore, it is an important supporting system for the healthy and sustainable development of the real estate industry in the long run. Second, expand the renovation of shanty towns and dilapidated buildings and promote the construction of low-income housing. Residents in shanty towns or dilapidated buildings are mostly employees of long-established enterprises. They have made great contributions to the development of the cities. Renovation of shanty towns can improve their living conditions, while bettering the environment of the cities as well as the QOL of city dwellers. Moreover, the construction of low-income housing should also be promoted to satisfy the needs of low-income residents and migrant workers. Third, further implement the regionalized development strategies, coordinate the development of different regions and narrow regional disparities. The unbalanced development of different regions and between cities and countryside is the main cause of soaring house prices in big cities, especially

6 and 7 cities more than that of last month respectively. Cities with a rise in the house price are: Beijing, Tianjin, Shijiazhuang, Taiyuan, Nanjing, Xiamen, Zhengzhou, Wuhan, Shenzhen, Nanning, Guiyang and Xuzhou. Cities with even house prices are: Shanghai, Fuzhou, Haikou, Baotou, Jinzhou, Anqing, Yueyang and Changde. Compared to that of the previous period, the comprehensive averages of new commodity house prices and second-hand house prices in first-tier cities have changed from dropping by 0.1% and staying even last month to rising by 0.2% and 0.3% this month respectively. The comprehensive averages of new commodity house prices and second-hand house prices in second- or third-tier cities have still dropped, but by smaller margins. Therefore, generally speaking, commercial house prices in first-tier cities will drop by smaller margins remain stable or rise slightly from the second half of 2015 on, owing to the marked differences in regional development. In first-tier cities, there are more opportunities of employment and career development, higher level of public services (especially education and medical care) and more convenient infrastructure. These are all key factors that attract migrant workers. In second-, third- or even fourth-tier cities, there exists a large amount of house inventory, and the house prices have risen by too big margins previously. In addition, there are less employment opportunities and lower level of public services. Therefore, the contradiction between supply and demand for houses will continue to exist there, and the house prices may drop significantly.

The report on the 18th CPC National Congress pointed out that "we should bring as much benefit as possible to the people, resolve as many difficulties as possible for them, and solve the most pressing and real problems of the greatest concern to them. We should keep making progress in ensuring that all the people enjoy their rights to education, employment, medical

Conclusions and Enlightenments

the decrease of consumption and had great impact on residents' QOL. That is exactly why we continued with the survey. According to the 2015 survey, however, the above-mentioned situation may change from now on. The 2015 weighted average of house price expectation indexes is 43.86 - below 50 (the critical point) and much lower than the 2014 average of 60.78. Since the first house price survey in 2012, it is the first time for house price expectation to change from appreciation to decline.

Viewed from actual economic data, changes in the house prices of 70 large or medium-sized cities have also proved residents' house price expectation. According to the house price indexes of the 70 large or medium-sized cities released by the National Bureau of Statistics (NBS), since June 2014, house prices have generally dropped compare to that of the previous period this year and slightly risen compare to that of the same period last year. After October 2014, house prices started to drop even when compared to that of the same period last year. Nevertheless, from our point of view, after about one year of price adjustment, with the relatively easy real estate policies released from the beginning of 2015, the house prices in different cities may change in different directions, although as a whole, the real estate industry will remain in the de-inventory stage, and house prices will still be hard to rise.

Latest statistics have revealed the trend. For example, according to the NBS data released in March 2015, the prices of new commodity houses in 50 out of the 70 large or medium-sized cities have dropped compare to that of the previous period - 16 cities less than that of last month. The prices have stayed even in 8 cities and risen in 12 cities - 6 and 10 cities more than that of last month respectively. And the prices of second-hand houses have declined in 48 cities compared to that of the previous period – 13 cities less than that of last month. The prices have stayed even in 10 cities and risen in 12 cities -

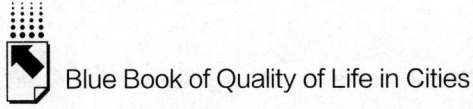

Such regional characteristics indicate that, as a whole, the quality of life in Chinese cities is not yet balanced, which is a reflection of the unbalanced economic development among east, central and western regions. Therefore, in the coming years, it is one of the most important tasks for all levels of government to figure out how to push forward system reforms, how to streamline administration and delegate power to the lower levels, and how to "free" the economic development of central and western regions and let the market mechanism play its decisive role in resource allocation. Meanwhile, central and western regions should seize the opportunity of the "One Belt and One Road" national project, develop regional economy and further improve residents' quality of life. Moreover, the Central Government also needs to work out practical strategies for the balanced development of different regions and between cities and countryside.

9.4 House price expectation continues to fall, and real estates are now bought more for residing purposes

On the eve of the 2015 "Two Sessions" (NPC & CPPCC), *Guangming Online* started an on-line survey "the 'foci' of the 2015 Two Sessions - key words of reform in common people's eyes". Results of the survey show that the "housing" problem has ranked among the top 5 for three consecutive years on the *Guangming Online* Two-Session Attention List. Housing has long become one of the most concerned livelihood issues. Since the start of the housing reform in 2003, house price has become a hot topic of the entire society, and the debate on house price has become increasingly fierce. Meanwhile, house prices in big cities have started to soar. In recent years, exorbitant house prices have become a major cause of high living costs which in turn led to

central and western regions. On the contrary, eastern cities have performed the worst and western cities the best in the objective index of living costs. It shows that the living costs of the eastern region are the highest, followed by those of central and then western regions. Viewed by dynamic changes, the living costs have dropped in all the three regions. As to the rest of the sub-indexes, eastern and central regions are of similar performance in the objective index of human capital, but western region is left far behind. The eastern region has also performed much better in the objective index of social security, but its score has fallen from above 60 to 55.47. And in the objective index of living experience, eastern region has still performed the best.

Table 9.4　The Five Objective Sub-indexes Viewed by Regions

Index	Region	2015	2014	2013	2012
Objective index of living standard	Eastern	62.31	71.53	69.00	62.99
	Central	56.12	62.77	59.39	52.03
	Western	54.74	61.96	58.54	49.60
Objective index of living costs	Eastern	50.85	50.37	54.96	52.12
	Central	56.98	56.42	61.47	57.41
	Western	61.72	61.18	65.46	60.94
Objective index of human capital	Eastern	57.25	57.32	57.18	58.72
	Central	57.57	57.02	58.39	56.18
	Western	55.62	55.30	55.19	57.22
Objective index of social security	Eastern	55.47	60.16	60.89	57.08
	Central	44.80	45.67	46.86	45.72
	Western	45.92	47.37	46.95	45.50
Objective index of living experience	Eastern	58.77	58.61	55.95	56.37
	Central	53.55	52.52	51.74	48.16
	Western	54.38	53.58	50.20	48.07

Human capital and social security satisfaction indexes are of the same characteristics, with eastern cities performing slightly better, and central and western cities performing similarly. As to the satisfaction index of living experience, no significant difference is observed, but western region has performed slightly better, followed by the central region and the eastern region.

Table 9.3 The Five Subjective Satisfaction Sub-indexes Viewed by Region

Index	Region	2015	2014	2013	2012
Satisfaction index of living standard	Eastern	60.56	54.55	53.28	51.91
	Central	60.49	53.21	51.44	51.00
	Western	59.37	53.38	52.87	50.57
Satisfaction index of living costs	Eastern	39.48	31.62	30.98	28.54
	Central	40.16	32.98	33.49	30.96
	Western	37.80	31.28	30.43	27.95
Satisfaction index of human capital	Eastern	62.33	59.60	59.58	60.42
	Central	61.15	58.08	58.28	58.51
	Western	60.81	58.51	58.53	58.62
Satisfaction index of social security	Eastern	60.65	58.83	57.86	60.12
	Central	60.09	56.87	55.54	57.80
	Western	60.13	56.70	55.60	58.84
Satisfaction index of living experience	Eastern	55.54	54.90	55.48	56.19
	Central	55.63	54.59	54.51	55.04
	Western	55.68	55.44	54.51	55.23

The five sub-indexes of the objective index are shown in Table 9.4. The 2015 survey results are similar to those of the previous surveys. Viewed by the objective index of living standard, eastern cities have performed obviously better than central cities, and central cities better than western cities. That is to say, the living standard of eastern region is the highest, followed by that of

Conclusions and Enlightenments

indexes obtained in the past four years by eastern, central and western regions (Table 9.2), we realize that not only the subjective and the objective indexes but also their sub-indexes are highly regional from 2012 to 2015. Viewed by subjective indexes, eastern cities have performed better than central cities, and central cities better than western cities. And the subjective indexes of all the three regions have remained stable with some improvement. Viewed by objective indexes, eastern cities have performed better than central and western cities, but there is no significant difference between the performance of central and western regions.

Table 9.2 Subjective Satisfaction Indexes and Objective Indexes

Index	Region	2015	2014	2013	2012
Subjective satisfaction index	Eastern	55.71	51.90	51.44	51.44
	Central	55.50	51.14	50.65	50.66
	Western	54.76	51.06	50.39	50.24
Objective index	Eastern	56.93	59.60	59.59	57.46
	Central	53.80	54.88	55.57	51.90
	Western	54.48	55.88	55.27	52.26

The five subjective satisfaction sub-indexes are highly regional as well (see Table 9.3). From 2012 to 2015, eastern cities have performed better in the satisfaction index of living standard than central and western cities, but no significant difference is observed between the performance of central and western regions. Central cities have performed the best in the living costs satisfaction index, followed by eastern cities and then western cities.[1]

---

[1] Please refer to the *Report on the Quality of Life in Chinese Cities (2014)*.

four surveys. Such an improvement indicates that living costs in the cities have dropped, and that residents are now more satisfied with their living costs, which is consistent with the rise of its objective index. The fact that the consumer price index (CPI) has remained below 2% (low inflation) for 8 months by the end of April 2015 may serve as another evidence. The improvement in the living costs satisfaction index is also reflected in the survey on primary concern: interviewees in the 35 cities now pay less attention to commodity prices than in 2014. Only 21.69% (2015) choose commodity prices to be their primary concern instead of 23.18% (2014). Despite all this, the residents are not yet satisfied with their living costs, since the index is still below 50.

Prime Minister Li Keqiang mentioned in 2014 that "reform is to fully mobilize people's initiative and creativity and to emancipate the productive forces. Streamlining administration and delegating power to the lower levels can increase people's business incomes and decrease their living costs. The government should see to it and give people a better life." It indicates that there are still lots to be done to lower the living costs in cities, which requires the continuous effort of all levels of government and the advancement of the reform of the economic system.

Among the five sub-indexes of the satisfaction indexes, the index of living costs is the lowest and the only one below 50 (the critical point). There is no getting around the fact that high living costs in big cities is a key factor that pulls down residents' quality of life.

9.3 The quality of life is better in eastern cities than in central or western cities

When we list up the weighted averages of the subjective and the objective

Conclusions and Enlightenments

Based on the data of Table 9.1, we find that it is the first time for the living standard subjective index to be higher than its objective index. During the "new normal" phase, the slowdown in economic growth has affected residents' living standard and led to the decline of its objective index, but its subjective index has improved. According to Table 5.2 (income status satisfaction sub-indexes) and 5.3 (income expectation satisfaction sub-indexes), the averages of the living standard indexes have gone up in all the 35 cities. Residents' satisfaction with their income status can be explained by the drop in living costs. And their satisfaction with income expectation may have resulted from different factors. Nevertheless, we can at least conclude that people's confidence in the future economic development of China is the main reason why the subjective indexes of income expectation have improved.

Table 9.1 also shows that, compared with results of the previous surveys, although the objective index of living costs has risen only slightly, its satisfaction index has improved significantly. Both the satisfaction and the objective indexes of human capital have remained stable with a slight improvement, with the former still higher than the latter. The satisfaction index of social security has somewhat risen, while its objective index has fallen. And the satisfaction index of living experience has started to improve after several years of decline and exceeded the scores of the previous years. Now it begins to change in line with its objective index.

9.2 Despite the drop, living costs remains the key factor that pulls down the quality of life

As is shown in Table 9.1, the weighted average of the living costs satisfaction indexes of the 35 cities is 38.94 - much higher than that of the previous

(60.07), living experience (55.66) and living costs (38.94). Compared to those of 2014, the weighted averages of all the five sub-indexes have improved, especially those of human capital, social security and living standard.

The objective index is 55.84 - lower than the 2014 index of 57.87. The objective index is also specified with five sub-indexes whose weighted averages are from the highest to the lowest: living standard (59.83), human capital (57.34), living experience (56.17), living costs (54.58) and social security (51.26). Compare with that of 2014, the weighted averages of living standard and social security objective indexes have dropped, especially that of the living standard. And the weighted averages of the rest three sub-indexes have somewhat improved.

Table 9.1 lists the five sub-indexes of the subjective and objective indexes from 2012 to 2015, and well illustrates the changes in these sub-indexes.

Table 9.1 The 2012–2015 Subjective and Objective Sub-indexes

		2015	2014	2013	2012
Subjective satisfaction indexes	Satisfaction index of living standard	60.07	54.32	52.51	51.28
	Satisfaction index of living costs	38.94	31.81	31.22	28.91
	Satisfaction index of human capital	61.73	58.98	58.89	59.42
	Satisfaction index of social security	60.47	57.87	56.64	59.19
	Satisfaction index of living experience	55.66	54.88	55.07	55.63
Objective indexes	Objective index of living standard	59.83	68.06	63.39	56.28
	Objective index of living costs	54.58	53.84	58.67	56.10
	Objective index of human capital	57.34	57.33	57.78	57.66
	Objective index of social security	51.26	54.66	55.26	50.85
	Objective index of living experience	56.17	55.57	53.67	51.89

Conclusions

B.9
Conclusions and Enlightenments

The 2015 survey was conducted in March and April this year. It involved about 200 staff members and took nearly two months to complete. The following conclusions and enlightenment can be drawn or obtained from the survey:

9.1 The subjective indexes continue to rise, while the objective indexes start to fall

As is shown in the 2015 survey, the subjective satisfaction index is 55.38 – above the satisfaction level and higher than the 2014 index of 51.57. The subjective index is still specified with five sub-indexes whose weighted averages are: human capital (61.73), social security (60.47), living standard

to wealth management, education does not seem to matter. The former group is only 0.02% higher than the latter, which can be omitted. Lower-educated interviewees think the Internet is of greater importance in providing convenient services. Employed residents tend to be affected by the Internet mainly in shopping and wealth management, while unemployed ones are affected mostly in communication and convenient services.

As is shown in Table 8.3, all the age groups believe that their lives are most influenced in communication. Shopping comes the second, in the eyes of the groups aged 20-30, 31-40, 41-50 and 51-60. To the group aged over 60, convenient services is the second most important, and shopping is the third. In wealth management, the group aged 41-50 has the highest percentage, followed by the groups aged 31-40, 51-60, 20-30 and above 60. And in convenient services, the group aged above 60 ranks the first, followed by the groups aged 51-60, 41-50, 20-30 and 31-40.

Table 8.3 Internet Usage of Different Age Groups

%

Most influenced factor	20-30	31-40	41-50	51-60	Above 60
Shopping	37.01	35.92	34.07	30.24	27.08
Communication	40.75	40.50	39.39	40.52	35.79
Wealth management	6.58	10.05	10.44	7.41	6.05
Convenient services	15.66	13.53	16.10	21.82	31.08
Total	100.00	100.00	100.00	100.00	100.00

the average data of the surveyed 35 cities, 40.27% of the residents choose communication; 35.52% choose shopping; 16.14% choose convenient services; and 8.07% choose wealth management. Generally speaking, the four factors reveal the influence of the Internet on residents' quality of life from the perspective of living convenience. With the development of the Internet, its influence will extend to all the aspects of our lives. By then, people will likely make different choices than the ones they made in this survey.

Further analysis shows people's choices may vary with their gender, education, employment and age conditions. Table 8.2 shows the choices made by groups of different background. See Table 8.2 and 8.3.

Table 8.2 Most Influenced Factors Chosen by Different Gender, Education or Employment Groups

%

Most Influenced Factor	Gender		Education		Employment	
	Male	Female	Junior college or above	Below junior college	Employed	Unemployed
Shopping	32.32	38.19	36.22	33.61	36.37	34.10
Communication	40.48	40.09	40.56	39.45	39.57	41.45
Wealth management	9.81	6.61	8.07	8.05	9.05	6.41
Convenient services	17.39	15.11	15.15	18.88	15.01	18.04
Total	100.00	100.00	100.00	100.00	100.00	100.00

As is shown in Table 8.2, more females use the Internet for shopping, while more males use it for wealth management and convenient services. No gender difference is detected in the use of the Internet on communication. The Internet is of greater influence on their ways of shopping and communication in the eyes of better-educated interviews than lower-educated ones. As

Continued table

City	Shopping	Communication	Wealth management	Convenient services
Fuzhou	34.36	40.73	8.55	16.36
Haikou	28.99	40.58	13.04	17.39
Jinan	34.59	40.27	8.11	17.03
Yinchuan	34.64	40.22	7.26	17.88
Beijing	35.22	40.02	8.46	16.30
Shanghai	34.74	39.70	9.33	16.22
Chongqing	37.29	39.57	6.65	16.49
Shenzhen	35.36	39.32	7.78	17.54
Zhengzhou	38.53	39.05	5.78	16.64
Hohhot	36.43	38.93	7.86	16.79
Urumqi	36.79	38.46	8.03	16.72
Tianjin	35.61	38.09	6.96	19.34
Wuhan	38.87	38.09	6.64	16.41
Shenyang	36.35	37.64	7.38	18.63
Nanchang	38.07	37.61	7.34	16.97
Xi'an	36.74	37.58	7.72	17.95
Dalian	37.47	37.22	9.87	15.44
Lanzhou	39.75	36.59	6.94	16.72
Qingdao	36.59	36.59	11.01	15.81
Taiyuan	40.68	34.92	7.12	17.29
Xining	42.86	33.14	8.57	15.43
Average*	35.52	40.27	8.07	16.14

* The average is obtained by dividing the number of interviews who choose the factor by the total number of interviews.

As is shown in Table 8.1, the residents of Wuhan, Nanchang, Dalian, Lanzhou, Taiyuan and Xining think the way of shopping is the most influenced factor. And the residents of Qingdao think shopping and communication are of equal importance. Interviewees in all the other 28 cities choose communication to be the most influenced factor. Viewed by

B.8
Survey of the Influence of Internet on the Quality of Urban Life

The Internet has now become an indispensable part of residents' daily life. Therefore, a survey of the influence of the Internet is added this year. The survey question was: "which part of your life is influenced most by the Internet?" And the answers given were: (1) shopping; (2) communication; (3) wealth management; and (4) convenient services. Table 8.1 lists the survey results of the 35 cities.

Table 8.1   Influence of Internet on QOL

%

City	Shopping	Communication	Wealth management	Convenient services
Changchun	30.54	46.88	7.53	15.05
Ningbo	30.72	45.38	9.44	14.46
Hefei	31.72	45.02	9.06	14.20
Harbin	31.61	44.82	10.20	13.38
Kunming	33.02	43.71	9.43	13.84
Nanjing	30.45	43.23	9.59	16.73
Shijiazhuang	35.22	42.61	6.96	15.22
Xiamen	34.87	42.53	8.43	14.18
Nanning	32.73	42.31	8.32	16.64
Guiyang	38.91	42.18	5.45	13.45
Guangzhou	35.24	42.00	7.41	15.34
Changsha	35.50	41.62	6.85	16.04
Chengdu	37.60	41.21	7.49	13.70
Hangzhou	37.42	40.96	8.11	13.51

while unemployed ones pay more attention to air quality. Employment seems to have no significant influence on the attention paid to transportation or commodity prices.

Table 7.3   Different Concerns of Different Age Groups over the Four Factors

%

Influential factor	20-30	31-40	41-50	51-60	Above 60
Food safety	26.45	29.09	31.96	33.87	37.03
Air quality	39.29	39.85	38.40	38.58	35.90
Commodity prices	22.20	20.48	20.28	19.55	18.26
Transportation	12.06	10.59	9.36	8.00	8.82
Total	100.00	100.00	100.00	100.00	100.00

Table 7.3 lists the different concerns of different age groups over the four factors. According to the survey results, the older the interviewees, the more attention is paid to food safety. Interviewees aged above 60 are the most concerns with food safety, while the youngest ones are the least concerned. Interviewees aged 20-40 are more concerned with air quality, followed by the age group of 41-60 and above 60. Among them, interviewees aged 31-40 is the age group that concerns with this factor most. Besides, the younger the interviews, the more attention is paid to commodity prices. As to transportation, the interviewees aged 20-30 are the most concerned, followed by the group of 31-40, 41-50, above 60 and 51-60.

transportation (10.94%). It should be noted that over 40% of the residents in Shijiazhuang, Beijing, Zhengzhou, Wuhan, Tianjin, Shenyang and Yinchuan think that air quality is the most influential factor of QOL. As a whole, residents of the 35 cities regard air quality as their primary concern (39.12%) followed by food safety (28.77%) and commodity prices (21.17%).

Further analysis shows the attention paid to air quality, food safety, commodity prices and transportation may vary with interviewees' gender, education, employment and age conditions. The survey results are shown in Table 7.2 and 7.3.

Table 7.2 Different Concerns of Different Gender / Education / Employment Conditions over the Four Factors

%

Influential factor	Gender		Education		Employment	
	Male	Female	Junior college or above	Below junior college	Employed	Unemployed
Food Safety	28.20	29.24	28.42	29.72	29.24	27.98
Air quality	37.48	40.50	40.08	36.48	38.48	40.21
Commodity Prices	22.14	20.36	20.55	22.88	21.20	21.13
Transportation	12.18	9.90	10.95	10.91	11.09	10.69
Total	100.00	100.00	100.00	100.00	100.00	100.00

As is shown in Table 7.2, similar to the result of 2014, air quality and food safety are the primary concerns of most interviewees, regardless of their gender, education and employment conditions. Comparatively speaking, males are more concerned with commodity prices and transportation than females, while females pay more attention to food safety and air quality than males. Better-educated interviewees are more concerned with air quality, but education seems have no effect on the attention paid to the other three factors. And employed interviewees are more concerned with food safety,

Continued table

City	Food safety	Air quality	Commodity prices	Transportation
Nanchang	32.34	38.07	21.10	8.49
Xiamen	29.12	37.93	21.07	11.88
Urumqi	30.43	37.46	21.74	10.37
Chongqing	30.22	37.35	20.86	11.57
Xi'an	28.52	37.08	21.81	12.58
Fuzhou	34.00	36.91	17.82	11.27
Xining	30.86	36.57	22.29	10.29
Hohhot	28.57	36.43	19.29	15.71
Hefei	30.51	36.25	20.85	12.39
Chengdu	29.84	35.92	23.26	10.98
Harbin	30.60	35.79	23.91	9.70
Shenzhen	29.00	35.79	22.35	12.87
Guangzhou	30.04	35.37	23.28	11.31
Qingdao	31.08	35.35	22.38	11.19
Guiyang	30.91	35.27	23.27	10.55
Nanning	30.74	34.18	22.60	12.48
Ningbo	33.94	33.13	25.10	7.83
Lanzhou	32.49	32.81	24.29	10.41
Kunming	33.02	32.08	23.27	11.64
Haikou	33.33	28.99	20.29	17.39
Average*	28.77	39.12	21.17	10.94

* The average is obtained by dividing the number of interviews who choose the factor by the total number of interviews.

As is shown in the 2015 survey, among the 35 cities, besides the residents of Ningbo, Kunming and Haikou who regard food safety as their primary concern, interviewees in the rest 32 cities think of air quality as the most important factor (15 cities more than that of 2014). In 2014, people in only 17 cities chose air quality to be their primary concern. It shows that people now pay much more attention to air quality. The most influential factors chosen are air quality (39.12%), food safety (28.77%), commodity prices (21.17%) and

B.7
Survey on Citizen's Primary Concern

In 2014, a new survey was added on residents' primary concern. According to the survey results, the most influential factors of QOL are air quality and food safety. In 2015, we continued with the telephone survey[①]. And the results are shown in Table 7.1.

Table 7.1   Results of the Survey on Primary Concern

Piece, %

City	Food safety	Air quality	Commodity prices	Transportation
Shijiazhuang	25.51	44.78	18.99	10.72
Beijing	25.66	43.19	19.27	11.88
Zhengzhou	25.74	42.56	20.67	11.03
Wuhan	27.34	42.38	19.73	10.55
Tianjin	29.25	41.63	19.93	9.20
Shenyang	27.49	40.96	21.59	9.96
Yinchuan	30.17	40.78	21.23	7.82
Nanjing	30.45	39.85	20.68	9.02
Shanghai	25.85	39.78	22.30	12.07
Hangzhou	29.73	39.71	20.79	9.77
Changsha	29.01	39.64	23.06	8.29
Changchun	30.54	38.49	22.58	8.39
Jinan	28.65	38.38	24.32	8.65
Taiyuan	29.15	38.31	23.73	8.81
Dalian	35.19	38.23	19.49	7.09

① The survey question was: "in your opinion, which factor is the most influential in your quality of life?" The answers given as: 1. food safety; 2. air quality; 3. commodity prices; and 4. transportation.

Expectations can be further divided into adaptive expectations and rational expectations. When people do not make systematic errors or deviations when predicting the future, and apply all information which can be obtained, their expectations are adaptive expectations. And when people form their expectations based on what has happened in the past, their expectations are adaptive expectations. Generally speaking, rational expectations only exist in economic theories. In real life, people's expectations of house prices are usually adaptive, because many unexpected factors, such as the administrative or policy intervention on the real estate market from the government, may affect their original expectations. Without such external factors, when most residents expect house prices to fall, the consumption of real estate will decrease, which will in turn lead to the decline of house prices, and vice versa. If the house prices generally decline in the coming one or two years as the residents of the 35 cities expected, it will greatly influence the living costs of city dwellers which plays a significant role in the improvement of their quality of life.

Survey on House Price Expectation

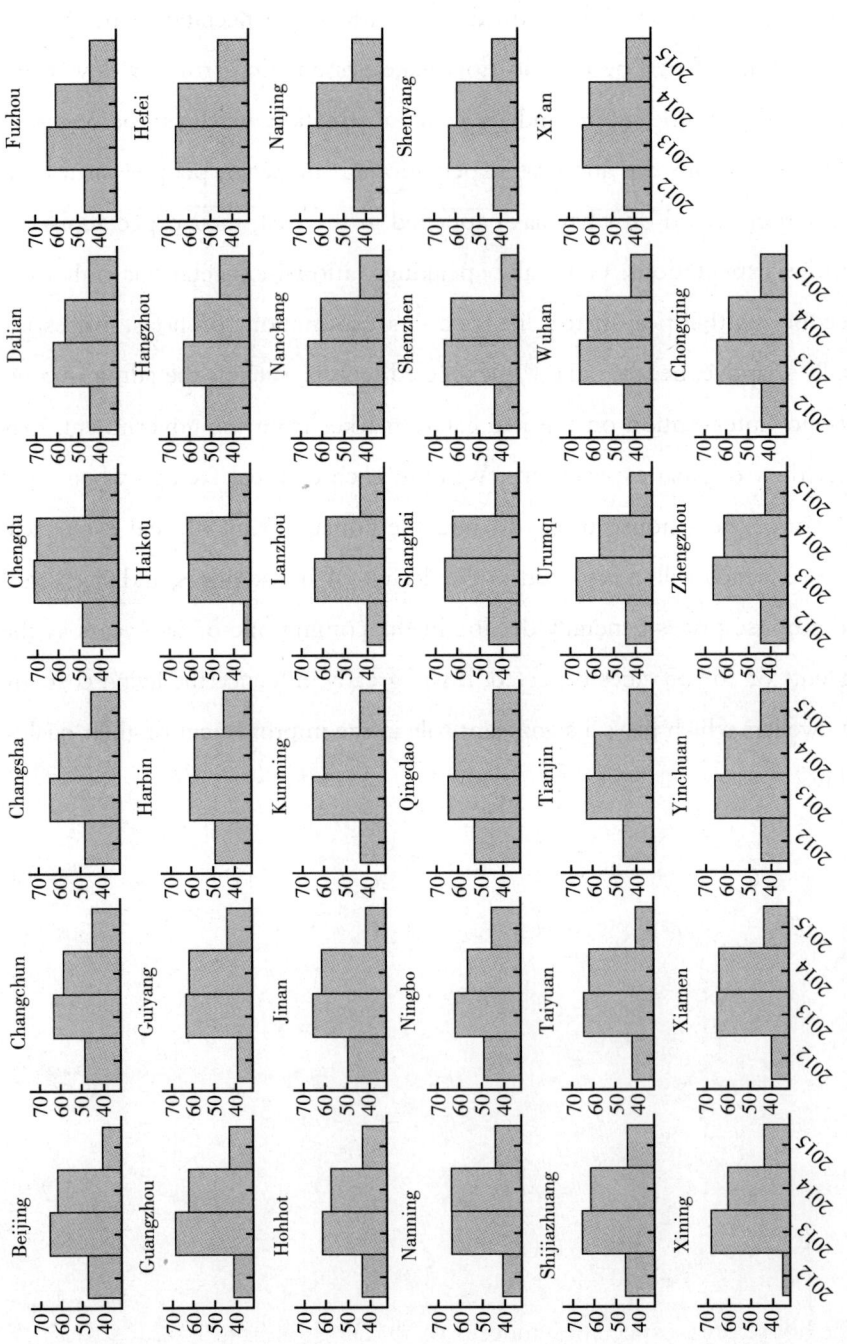

Table 6.2: The 2012–2015 House Price Expectation Indexes of the 35 Cities

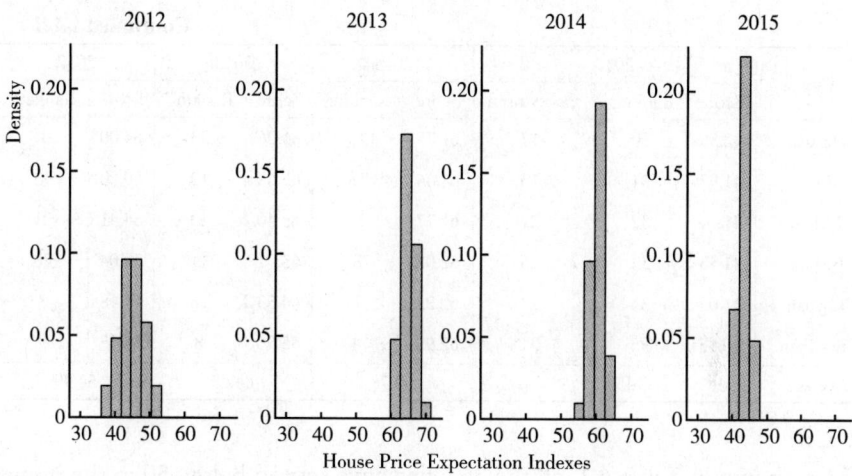

Graph 6.1: A Histogram of the 2012–2015 House Price Expectation Indexes

years, and that Hefei has ranked No.1 in the past two years. It indicates that residents in Hefei have the strongest expectation for house price appreciation in 2014 and the weakest expectation for house price decline in 2015. In Table 6.1, the bottom 10 cities on the list are: Tianjin (26), Guangzhou (27), Urumqi (28), Zhengzhou (29), Haikou (30), Jinan (31), Wuhan (32), Beijing (33), Taiyuan (34) and Shenzhen (35). That is to say, residents in the above 10 cities think the house prices will fall either greatly or very likely. It should also be pointed out that there is no big gap between the scores of different cities. The highest score is 46.70, while the lowest score is 40.15. It indicates that residents in different cities have similar expectations of house prices.

Viewed by dynamic changes, compared to that of 2014, cities with a dramatic rise in the ranking are: Ningbo (31), Hangzhou (29), Dalian (26), Harbin (24) and Changchun (23). And cities with a drastic drop in the ranking are: Shenzhen (-31), Taiyuan (-27), Beijing (-25), Guangzhou (-21), Wuhan (-21), Zhengzhou (-17) and Haikou (-17). Table 6.2 well illustrates the changes in the house price expectation indexes of the 35 cities from 2012 to 2015.

Continued table

City	2015			2014		2013		2012	
	Score	Ranking	Places risen	Score	Ranking	Score	Ranking	Score	Ranking
Haikou	42.55	30	-17	61.75	13	61.26	33	64.00	1
Jinan	41.97	31	-13	61.46	18	65.68	12	50.00	33
Wuhan	41.74	32	-21	61.77	11	65.40	13	54.41	21
Beijing	41.43	33	-25	62.08	8	65.71	11	52.04	28
Taiyuan	41.03	34	-27	62.22	7	64.53	18	57.18	8
Shenzhen	40.15	35	-31	62.92	4	65.96	8	56.55	9
Average	43.86			60.78		64.65		54.99	

As is shown in Table 6.1, all the 35 cities have scored below 50 in the house price expectation index. That is to say, unlike in previous years, residents in all the cities now expect the house prices to decline. In 2012, the average of the 35 cities was 54.99. Besides Hangzhou and Qingdao which scored below 50 (expecting the house prices to fall), residents in all the other 32 cities thought the house prices would rise. In 2013, the average was 64.65. All the 35 cities scored over 60 in the index, which indicated a widespread expectation of house price appreciation. In 2014, the average was 60.78. None of the cities scored below 50, and 24 cities scored over 60. Residents of all the cities still expected the house prices to rise. In 2015, the turning point appears. The average is only 43.86. Residents in none of the cities now expect the house prices to rise. Table 6.1 well illustrates the changes in the house price expectation indexes of the 35 cities from 2012 to 2015.

Among the surveyed 35 cities, top 10 on the list are: Hefei (1), Hangzhou (2), Nanjing (3), Ningbo (4), Changchun (5), Harbin (6), Yinchuan (7), Dalian (8), Changsha (9) and Shijiazhuang (10). Residents in all the above-mentioned 10 cities think the house prices will fall, but only slightly or unlikely. It should be noted that Hefei and Nanjing have been on the top 10 list for three successive

Table 6.1 House Price Expectation Indexes[①] of the 35 Cities

City	2015			2014		2013		2012	
	Score	Ranking	Places risen	Score	Ranking	Score	Ranking	Score	Ranking
Hefei	46.70	1	0	64.68	1	66.07	6	53.42	25
Hangzhou	46.40	2	29	58.05	31	62.85	29	47.17	34
Nanjing	45.83	3	6	61.98	9	65.92	10	54.36	22
Ningbo	45.76	4	31	56.74	35	62.15	31	50.68	31
Changchun	45.43	5	23	59.07	28	63.70	22	51.20	30
Harbin	45.33	6	24	58.63	30	60.99	35	50.39	32
Yinchuan	45.24	7	9	61.54	16	65.93	9	55.21	17
Dalian	45.18	8	26	56.83	34	62.13	32	54.91	19
Changsha	44.97	9	14	60.16	23	63.39	25	51.90	29
Shijiazhuang	44.62	10	7	61.49	17	65.19	15	54.13	23
Fuzhou	44.44	11	10	60.61	21	64.45	20	52.75	27
Chongqing	44.41	12	15	59.22	27	64.46	19	55.84	12
Qingdao	44.39	13	2	61.63	15	64.57	17	46.82	35
Xining	44.31	14	6	61.05	20	68.33	2	63.89	2
Nanning	44.24	15	-13	64.02	2	63.66	23	58.80	6
Chengdu	44.24	16	-6	61.80	10	63.06	27	54.53	20
Guiyang	44.05	17	-3	61.73	14	62.99	28	60.48	3
Xiamen	43.98	18	-15	64.02	3	65.14	16	59.59	5
Kunming	43.98	19	5	60.02	24	65.38	14	55.77	13
Shenyang	43.89	20	6	59.33	26	62.43	30	56.35	10
Shanghai	43.66	21	-16	62.53	5	65.97	7	53.35	26
Hohhot	43.64	22	10	57.81	32	61.26	34	56.07	11
Xi'an	43.61	23	-1	60.36	22	63.64	24	55.10	18
Nanchang	43.45	24	-5	61.13	19	66.73	4	55.28	14
Lanzhou	43.45	25	4	58.85	29	63.98	21	59.94	4
Tianjin	43.42	26	-1	59.49	25	63.18	26	53.65	24
Guangzhou	43.04	27	-21	62.28	6	68.64	1	58.55	7
Urumqi	42.71	28	5	57.04	33	67.37	3	55.26	15
Zhengzhou	42.67	29	-17	61.77	12	66.60	5	55.24	16

① The higher the index, the stronger the expectation of house price appreciation or the weaker the expectation of house price decline. And the lower the index, the weaker the expectation of house price appreciation or the stronger the expectation of house price decline. The critical point between appreciation and decline is 50 points.

Special Surveys

B.6
Survey on House Price Expectation

In 2015, we continued with the special survey on house price expectation.[1] Table 6.1 lists the house price expectation indexes of the 35 cities. According to the survey, the 2015 weighted average of house price expectation indexes is 43.86 which is in the range of "fall" and much lower than the 2014 average (60.78). In actuality, the index has kept dropping since 2013.

---

[1] The survey question was: in your opinion, will the house prices in your city of residence rise or fall in the future (1 or 2 years)? 1. Surge; 2. rise; 3. even; 4. fall; and 5. crash. And the values assigned were: 1. surge (100); 2. rise (75); 3. even (50); 4. fall (25); and 5. crash (0).

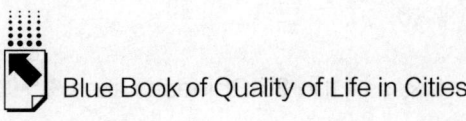

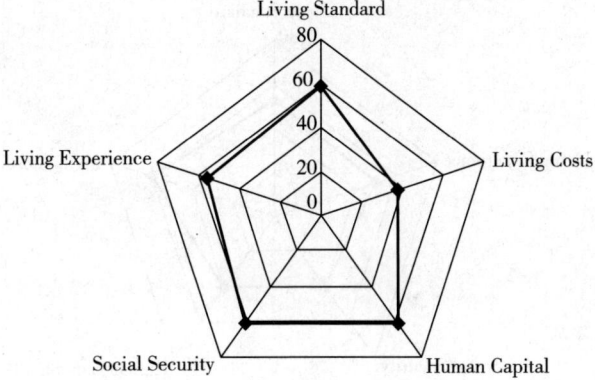

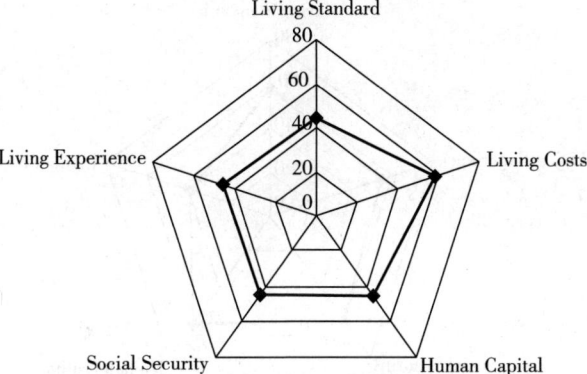

Graph 5.33: Radar Charts for the First Level Indicators of 35 Chinese Cities

Quality-of-life Sub-Indexes of the 35 Chinese Cities

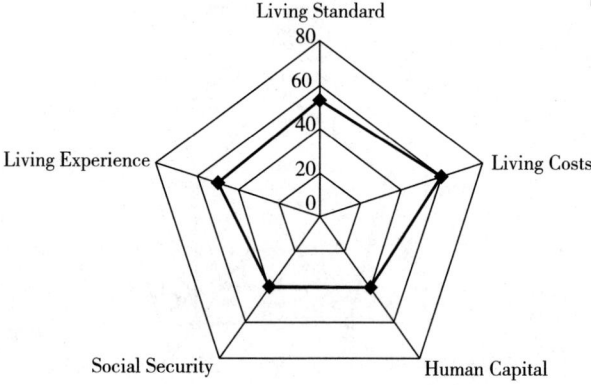

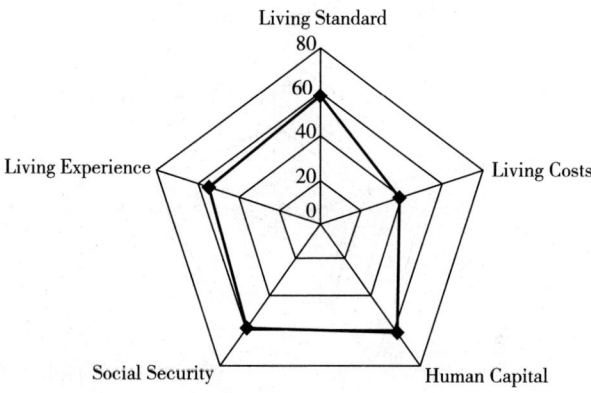

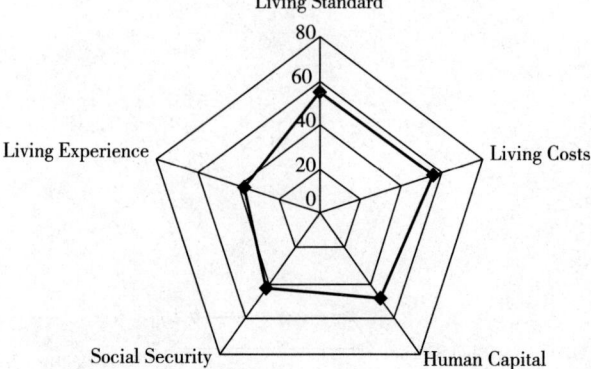

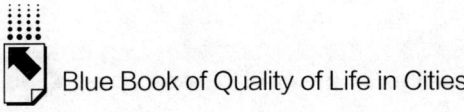

Blue Book of Quality of Life in Cities

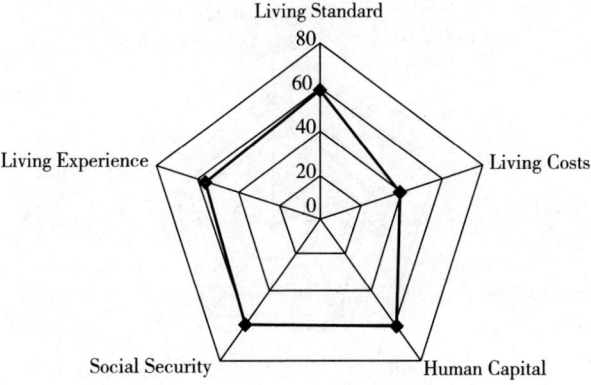

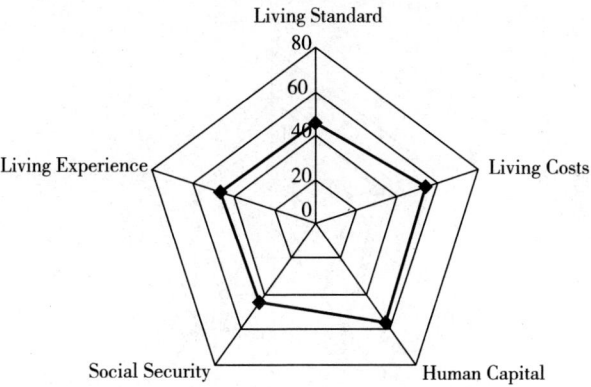

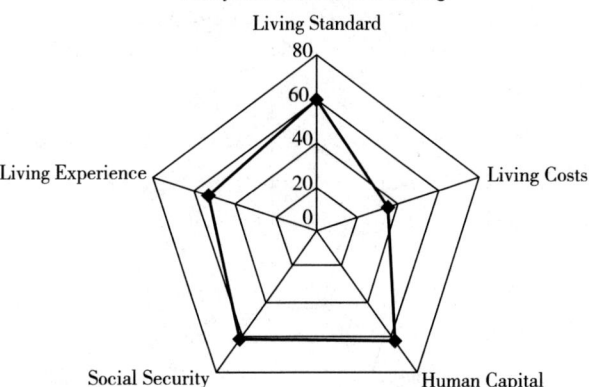

Quality-of-life Sub-Indexes of the 35 Chinese Cities

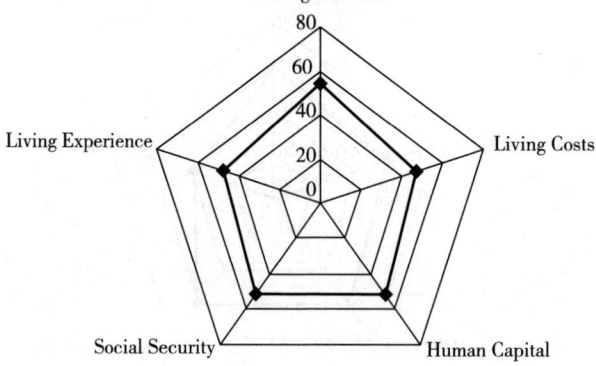

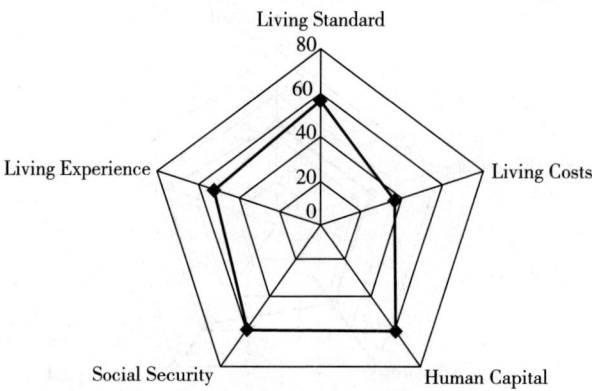

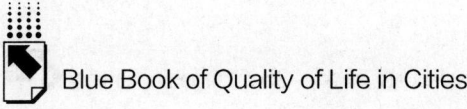

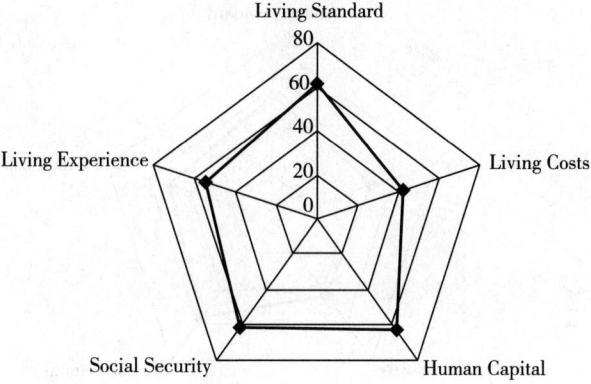

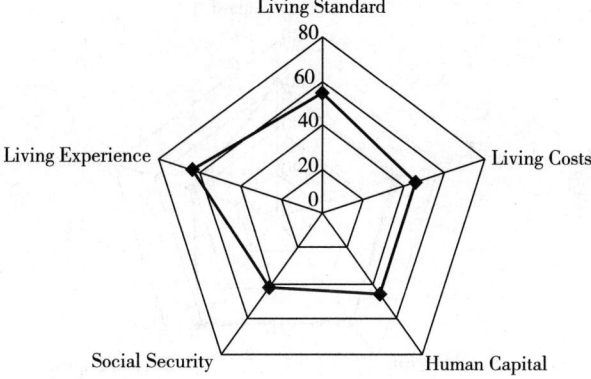

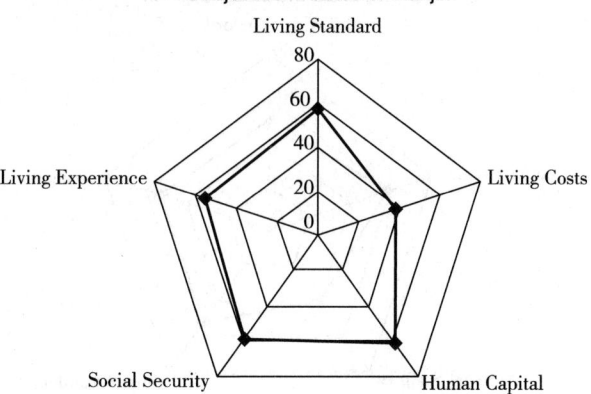

Quality-of-life Sub-Indexes of the 35 Chinese Cities

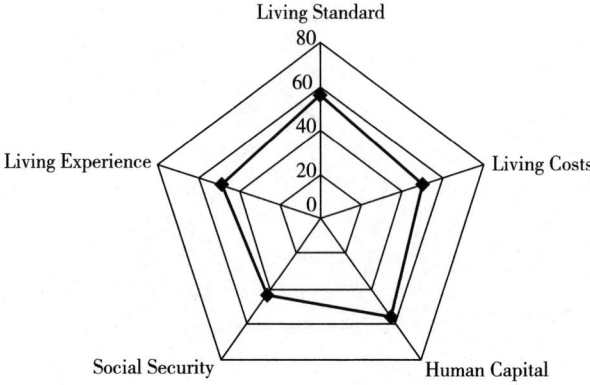

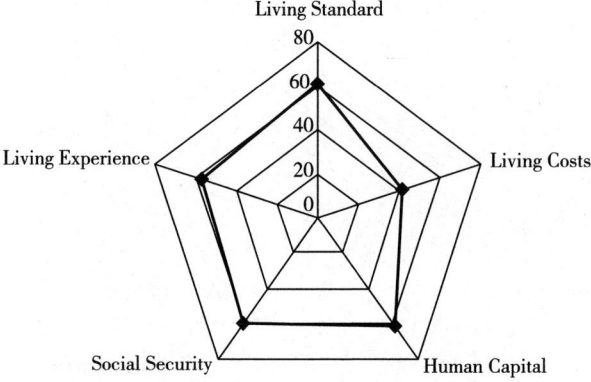

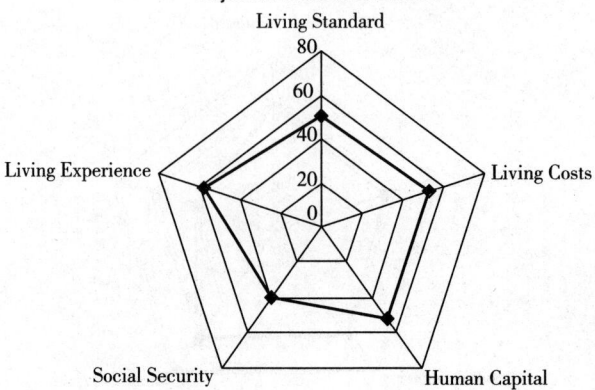

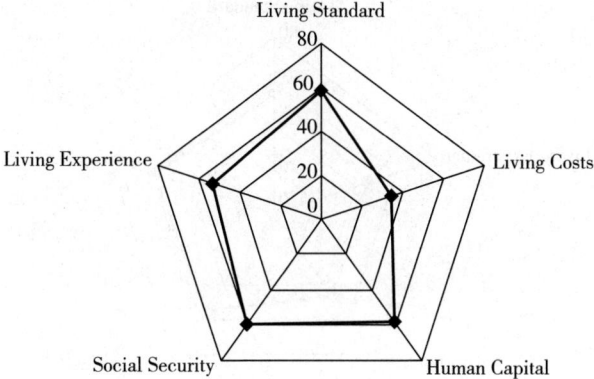

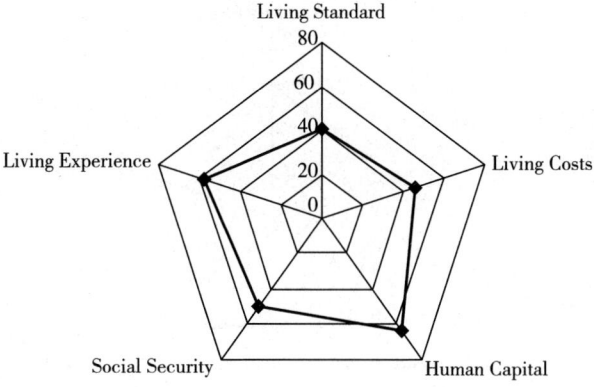

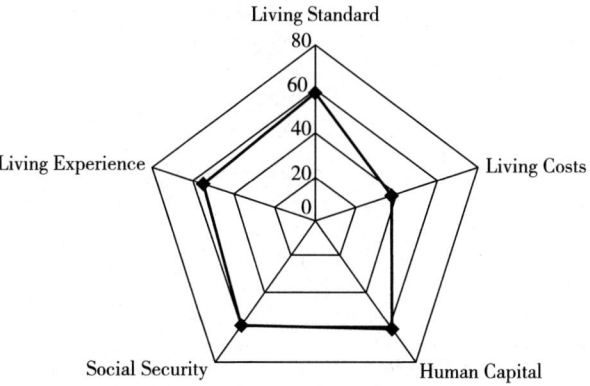

Quality-of-life Sub-Indexes of the 35 Chinese Cities

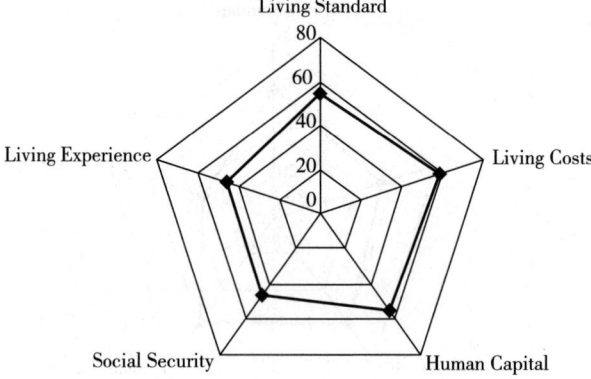

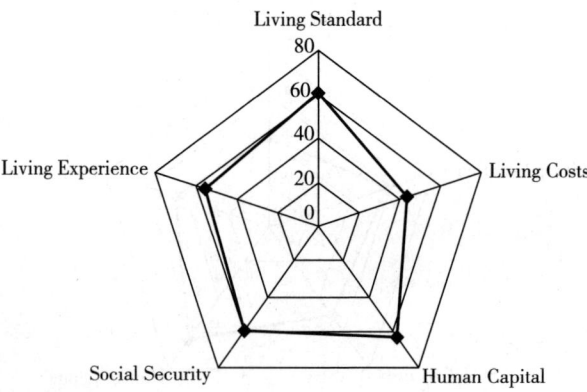

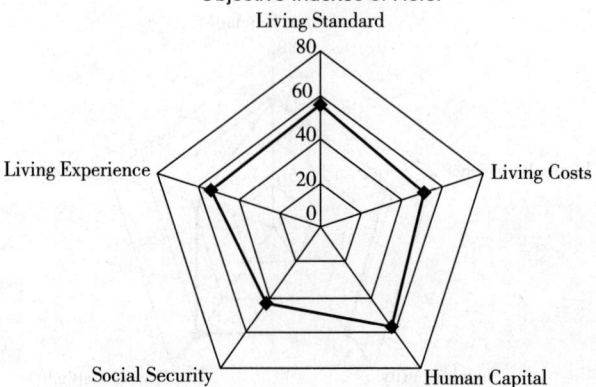

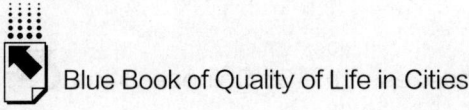

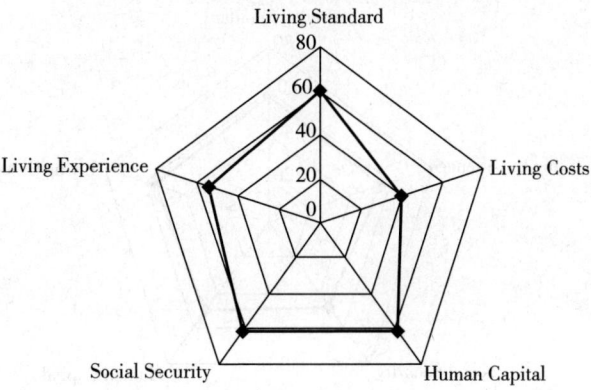

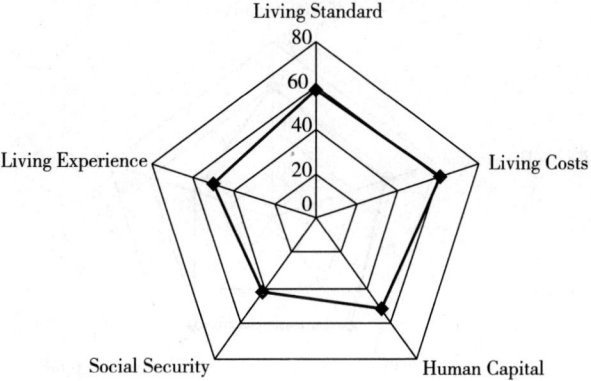

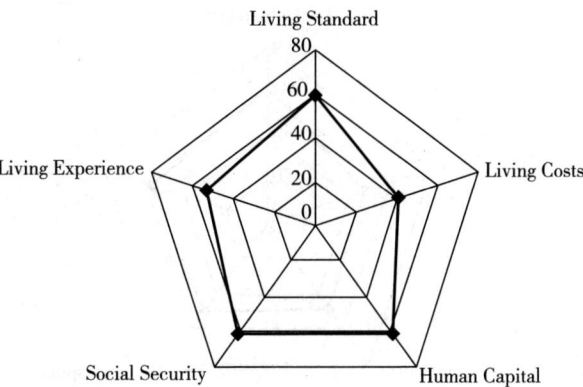

Quality-of-life Sub-Indexes of the 35 Chinese Cities

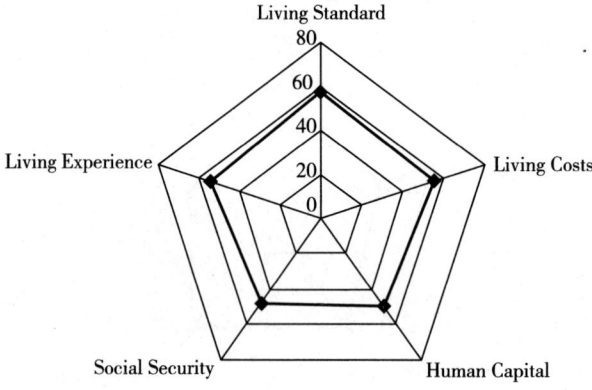

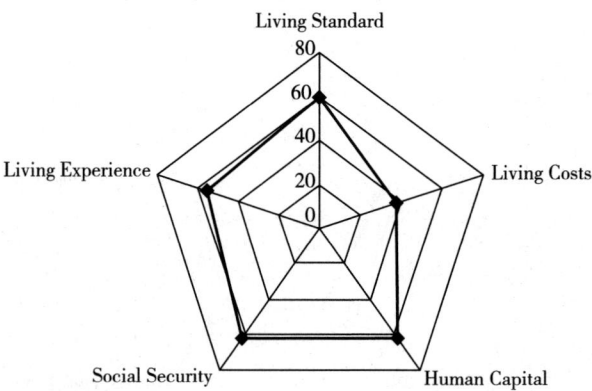

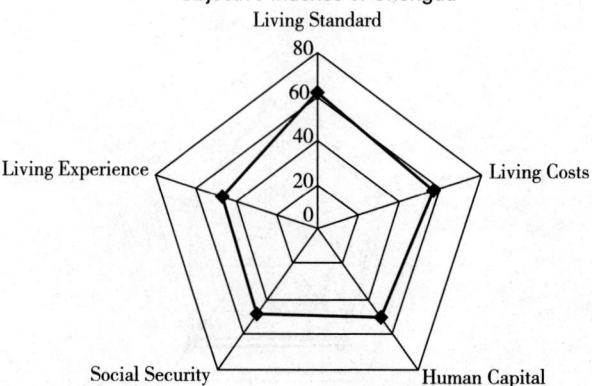

123

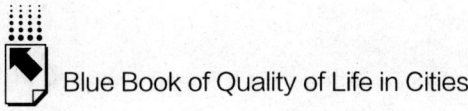

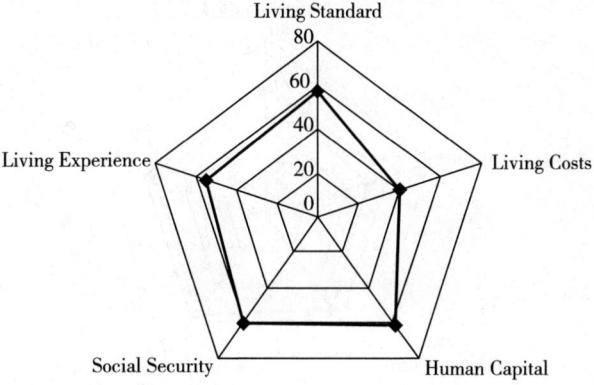

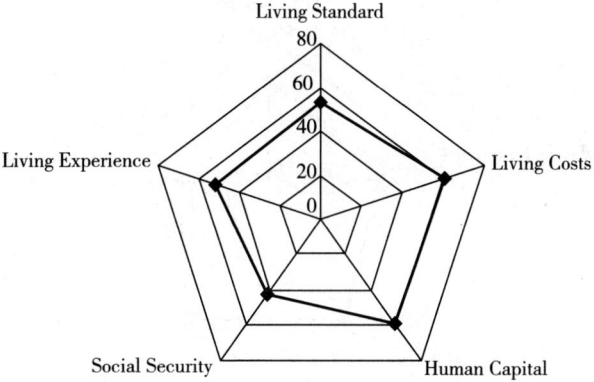

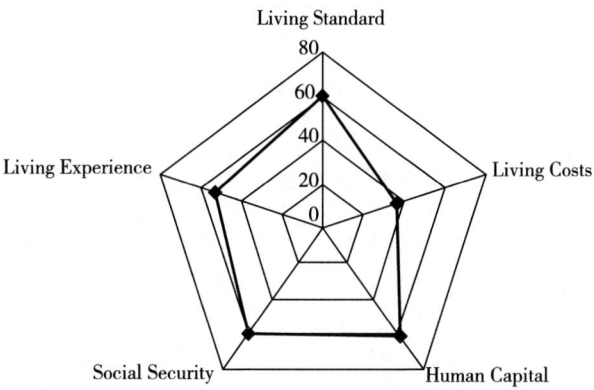

Quality-of-life Sub-Indexes of the 35 Chinese Cities

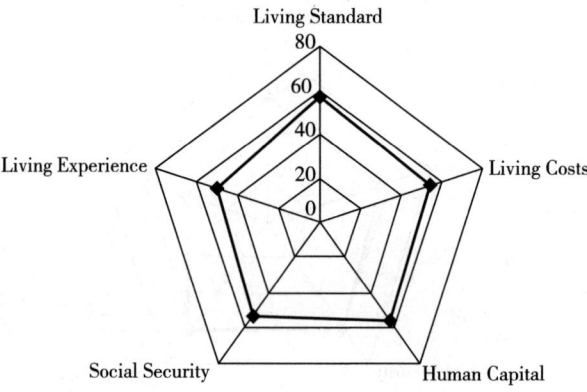

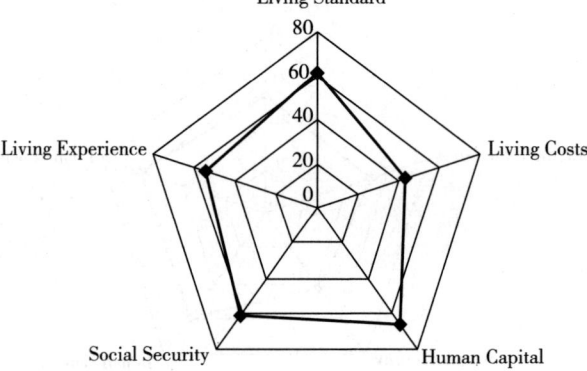

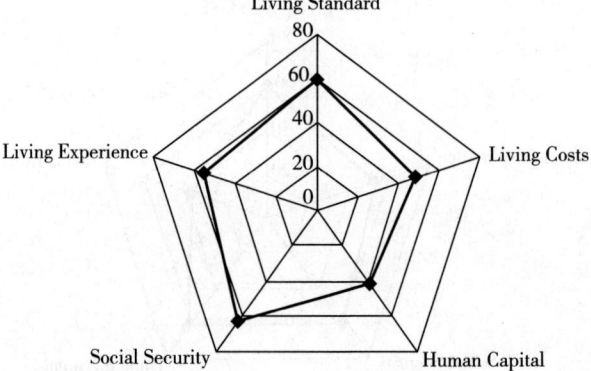

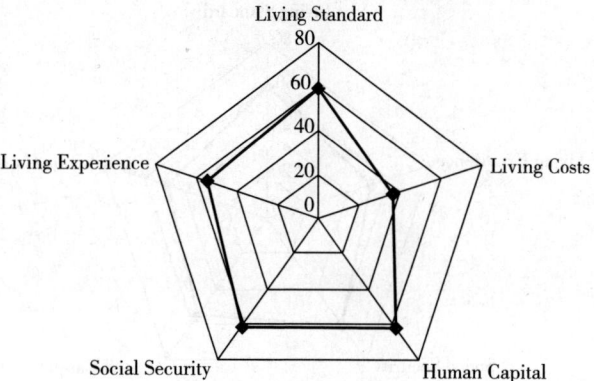

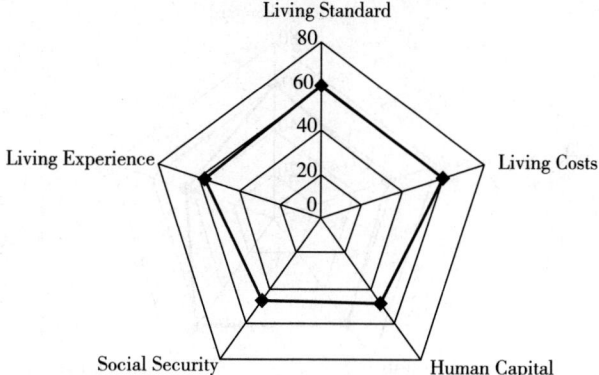

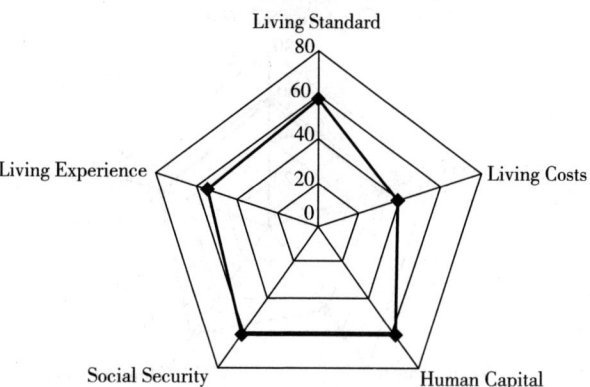

Quality-of-life Sub-Indexes of the 35 Chinese Cities

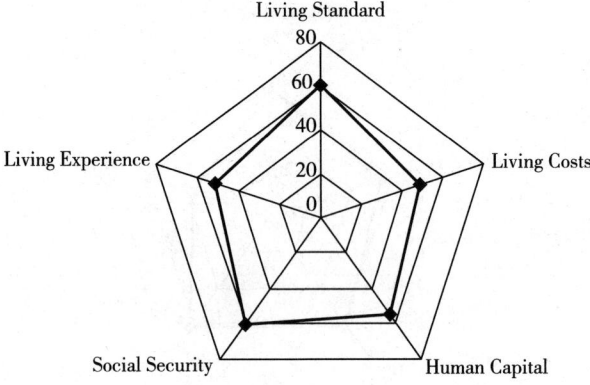

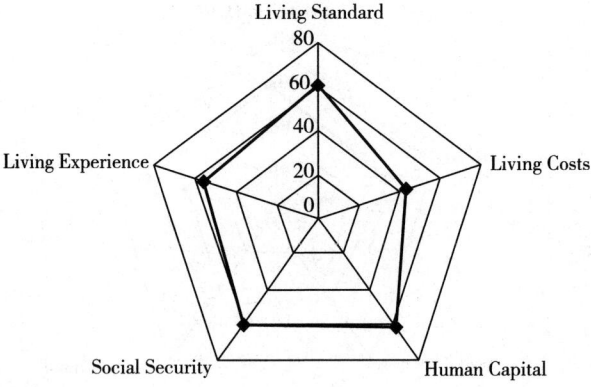

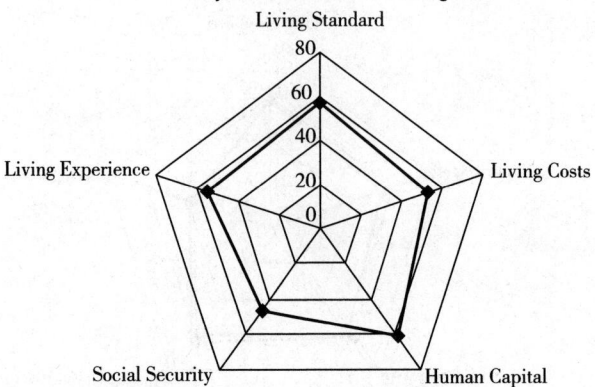

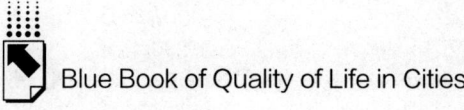
Blue Book of Quality of Life in Cities

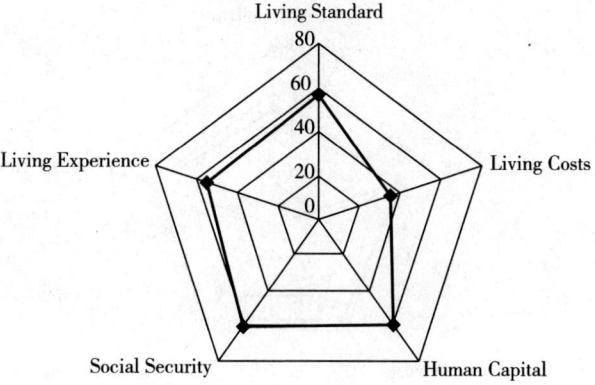

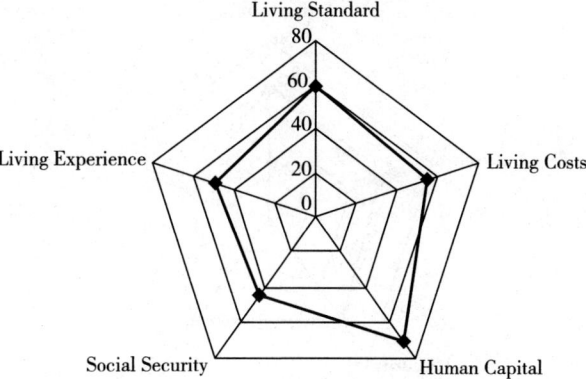

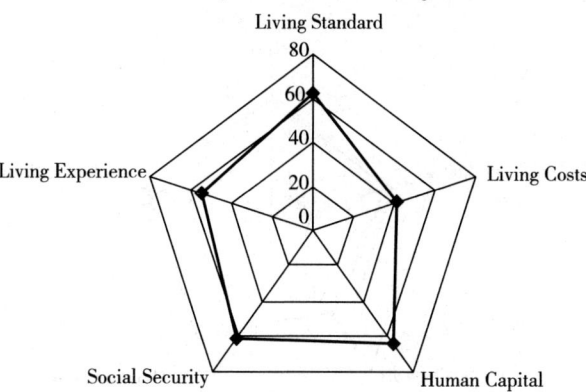

Quality-of-life Sub-Indexes of the 35 Chinese Cities

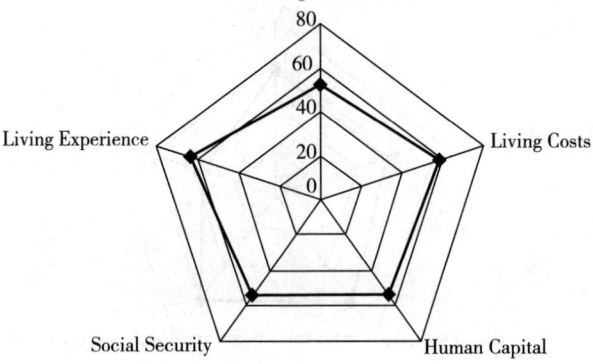

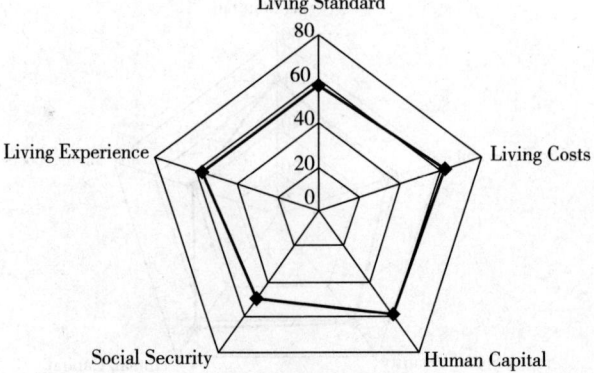

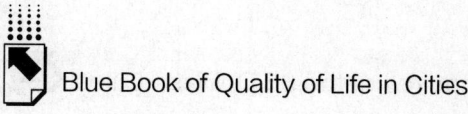

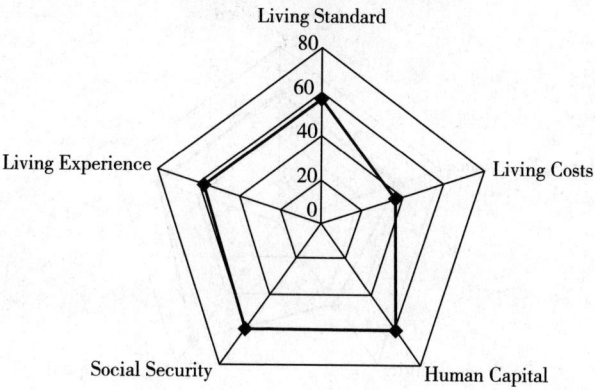

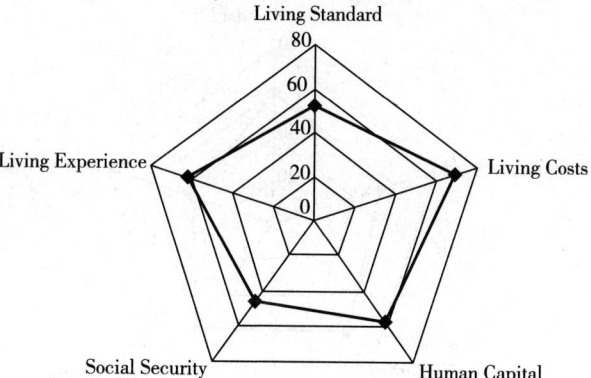

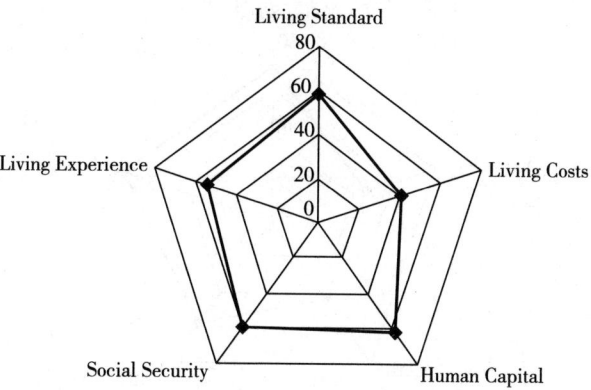

Quality-of-life Sub-Indexes of the 35 Chinese Cities

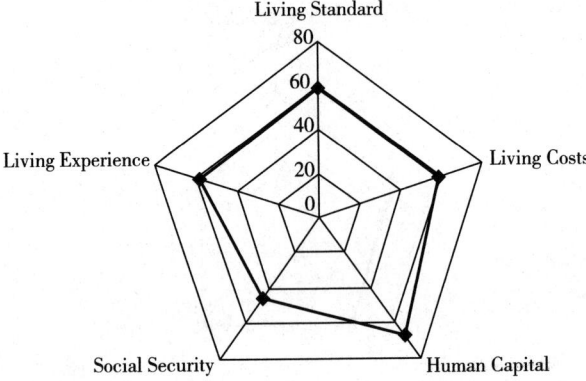

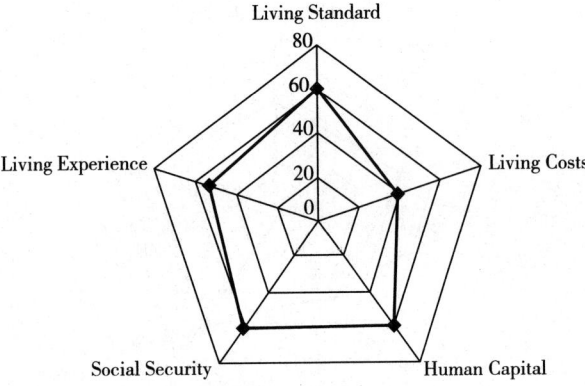

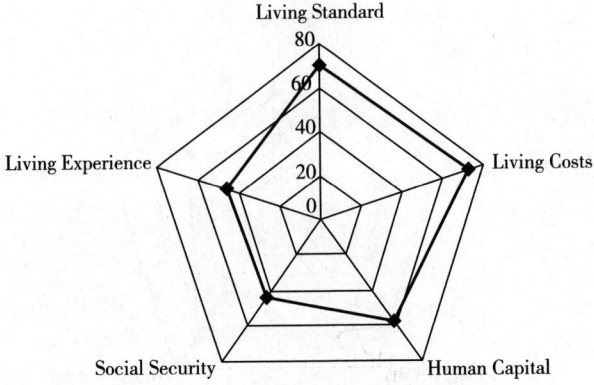

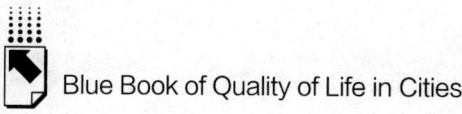

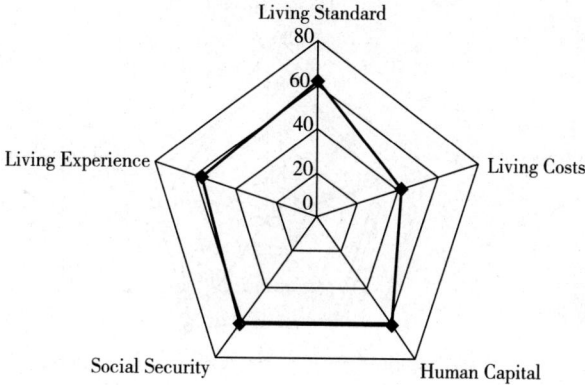

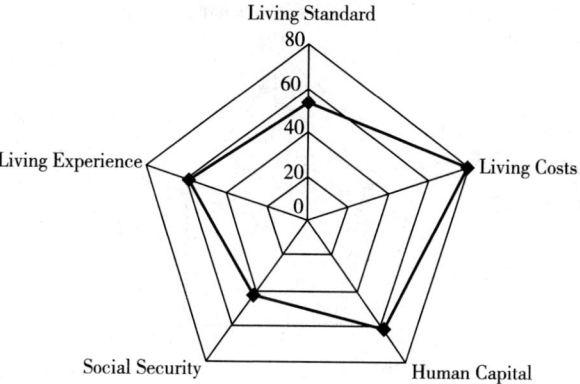

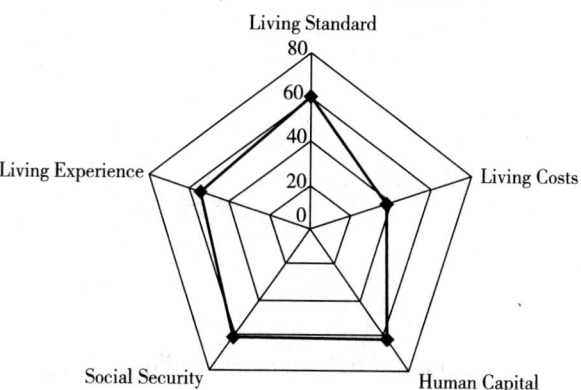

Quality-of-life Sub-Indexes of the 35 Chinese Cities

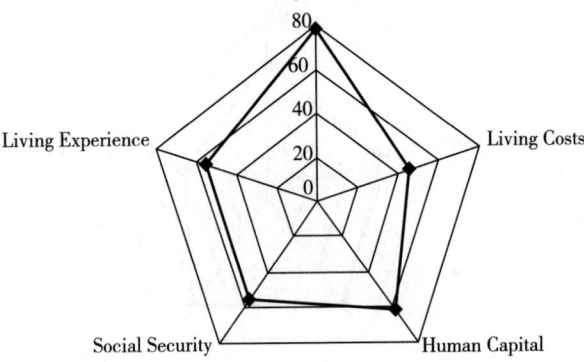

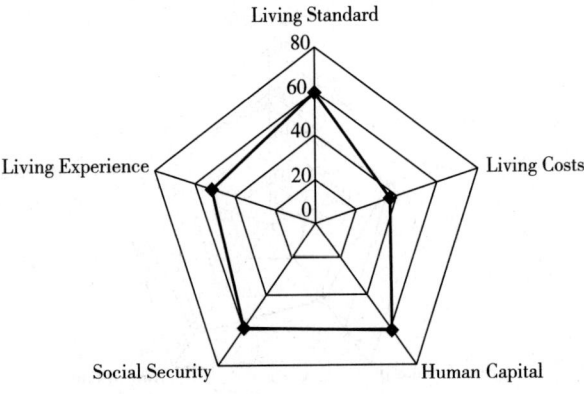

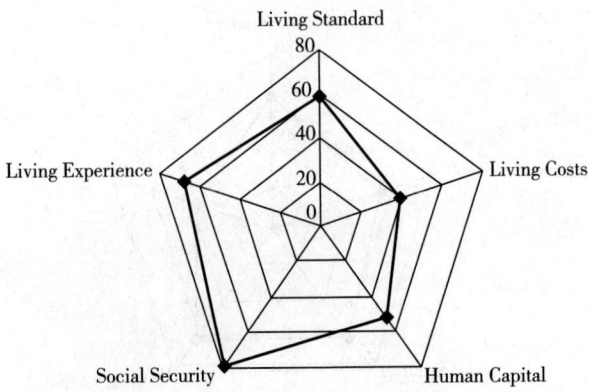

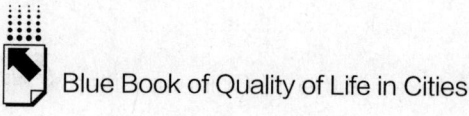

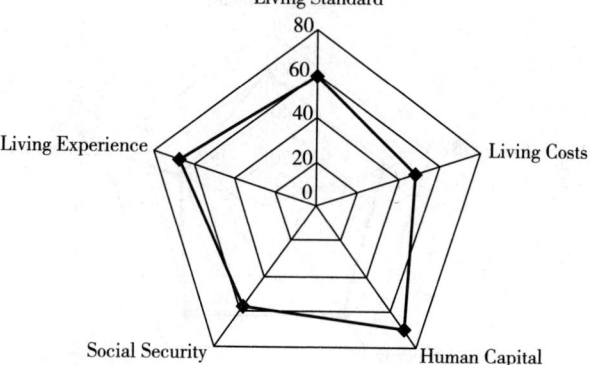

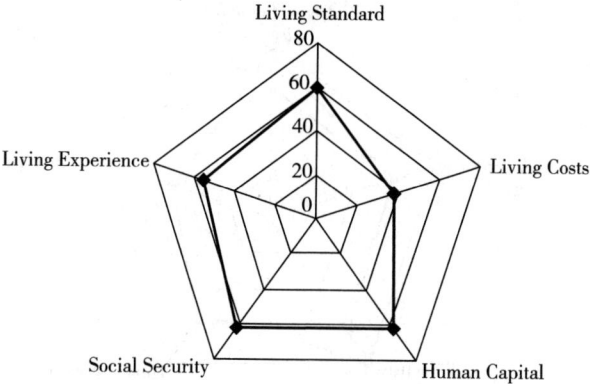

Quality-of-life Sub-Indexes of the 35 Chinese Cities

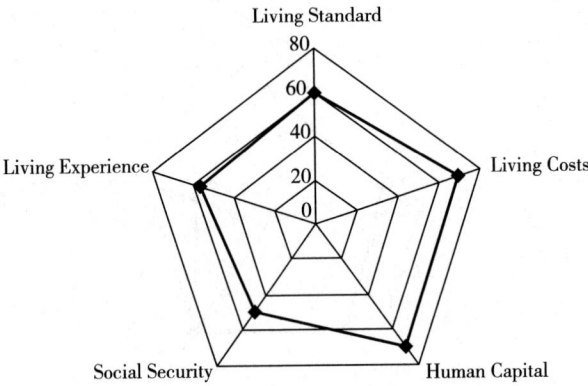

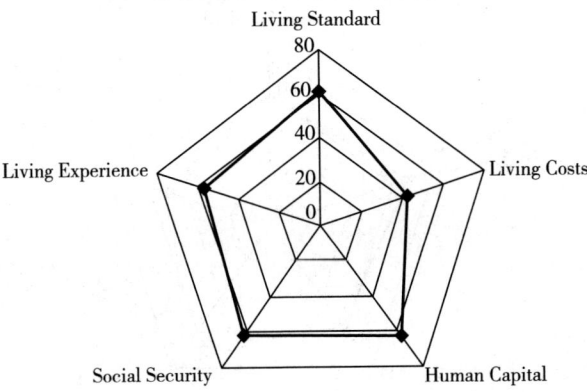

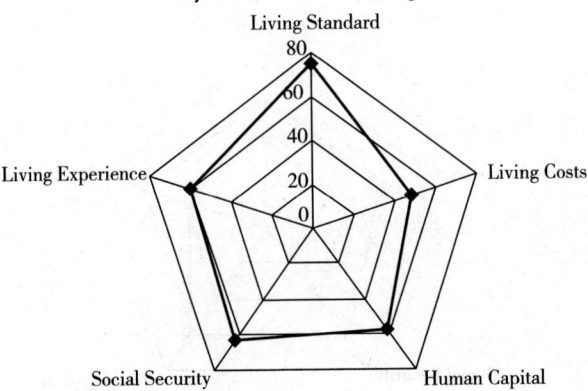

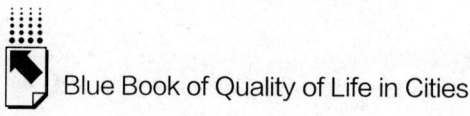
Blue Book of Quality of Life in Cities

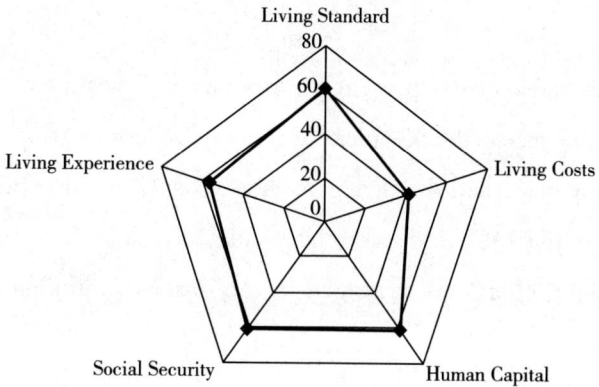

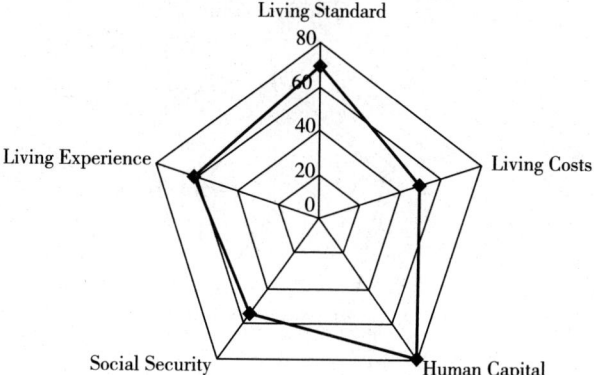

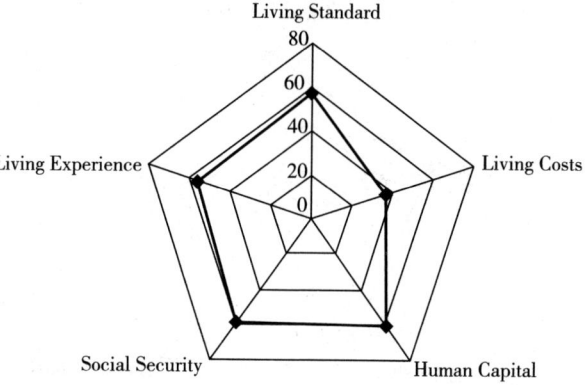

Quality-of-life Sub-Indexes of the 35 Chinese Cities

5.6 QLICC Primary Indicator Radar Charts

The following radar charts present the primary indicators of the subjective or objective indexes of the 35 cities for the sake of comparison and contrast. It can be easily discerned that living costs is a key factor that pulls down the subject or objective QOL indexes in large cities.

The following charts are arranged in the order of ranking of objective indexes.

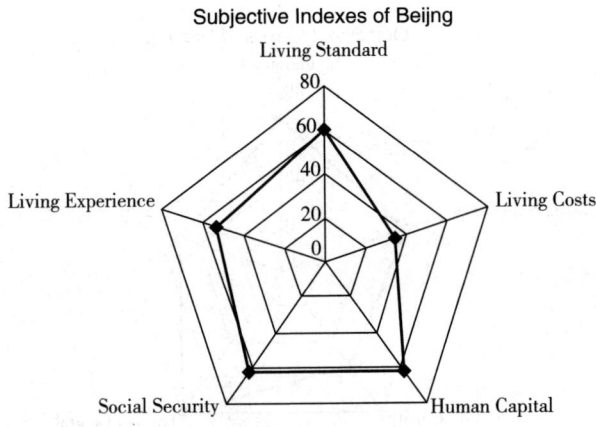

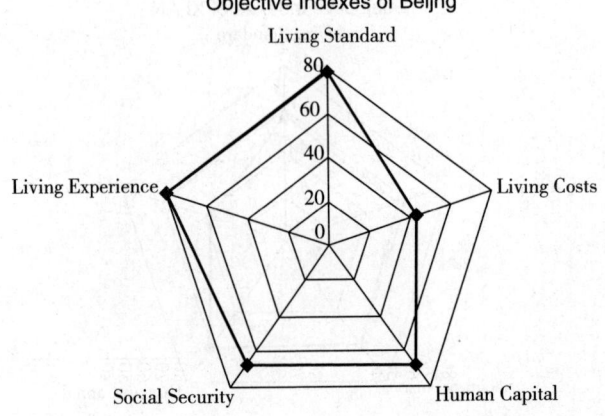

Blue Book of Quality of Life in Cities

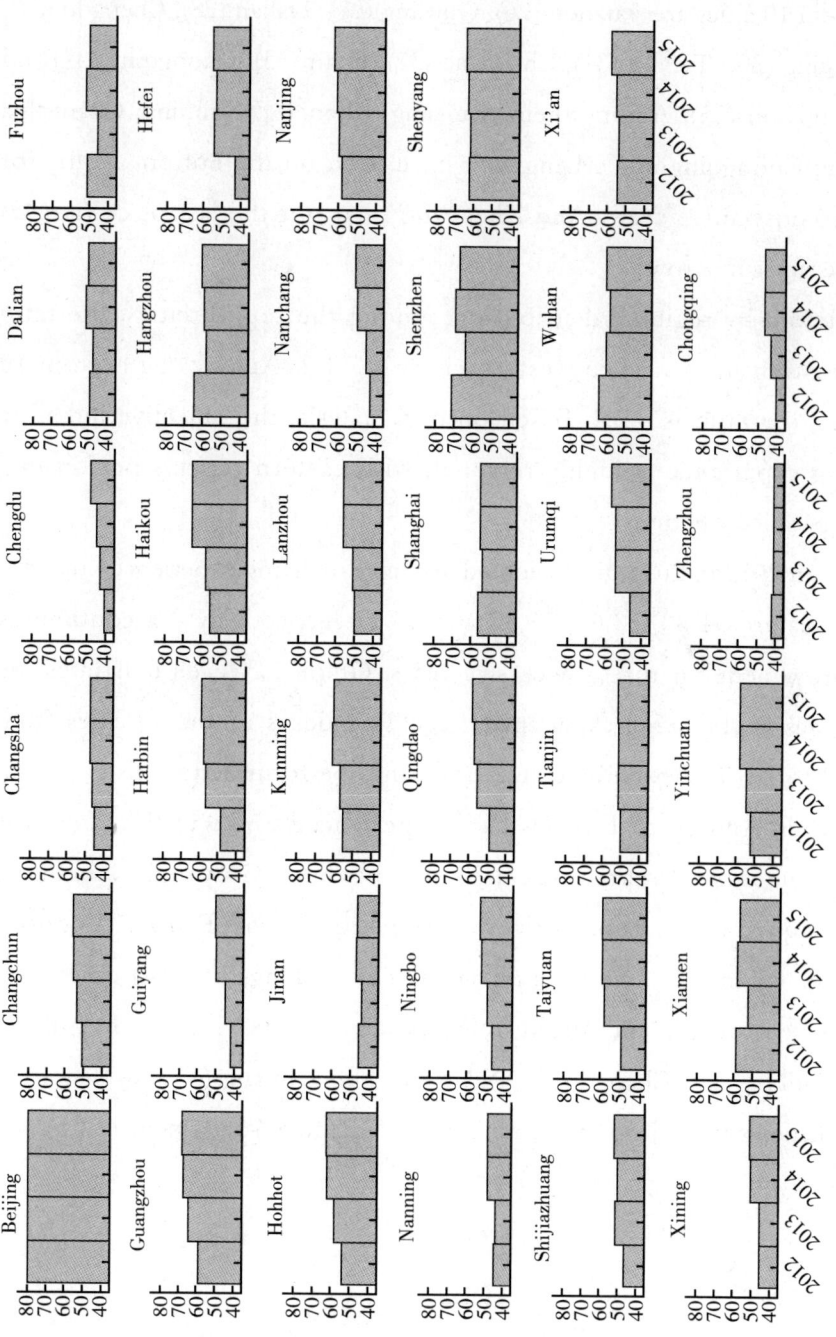

Graph 5.32: A Bar Chart of the 2012–2015 Living Experience Objective Indexes of the 35 Cities

bottom 10 cities are: Fuzhou (26), Guiyang (27), Dalian (28), Chengdu (29), Nanning (30), Tianjin (31), Changsha (32), Jinan (33), Chongqing (34) and Zhengzhou (35). Among them, Guiyang, Chengdu, Nanning, Changsha, Jinan, Chongqing and Zhengzhou have been on the bottom 10 list for four consecutive years. And Zhengzhou has got the last place (No.35) three times in a row.

Viewed by regional distribution, among the top 10 cities, the ratio of eastern to central to western cities is 7:1:2. Among the bottom 10 cities, the ratio is 4:2:4. Based on our analysis, the objective index of living experience is highly regional, with eastern regions performing comparatively better.

From 2012 to 2015, the weighted averages of living experience objective indexes are 51.89, 53.67, 55.57 and 56.17 respectively — a continuous improvement for three successive years. Graph 5.32 well illustrates the changes in the living experience objective indexes of the 35 cities from 2012 to 2015. Viewed by cities, most cities perform better this year than last year. And up to 18 cities have experienced a rise in the index for four successive years, especially Guangzhou, Guiyang, Nanchang, Urumqi and Ningbo. However, the indexes of Dalian, Fuzhou, Shenzhen and Xiamen have dropped. The rankings of most cities have remained roughly unchanged in the past two years. Cities with a rise in the ranking are: Chengdu (5), Xi'an (5), Shijiazhuang (3) and Nanchang (3). Cities with a drop in the ranking are: Xiamen (-5), Yinchuan (-5) and Dalian (-4).

secondary indicators, such differences are also manifested in transportation capacity, number of cinemas and theaters per 10,000 residents, medical care capacity, per capita green area, air quality and the Gini coefficient. Graph 5.31 well illustrates the changes in living experience objective indexes from 2012 to 2015.

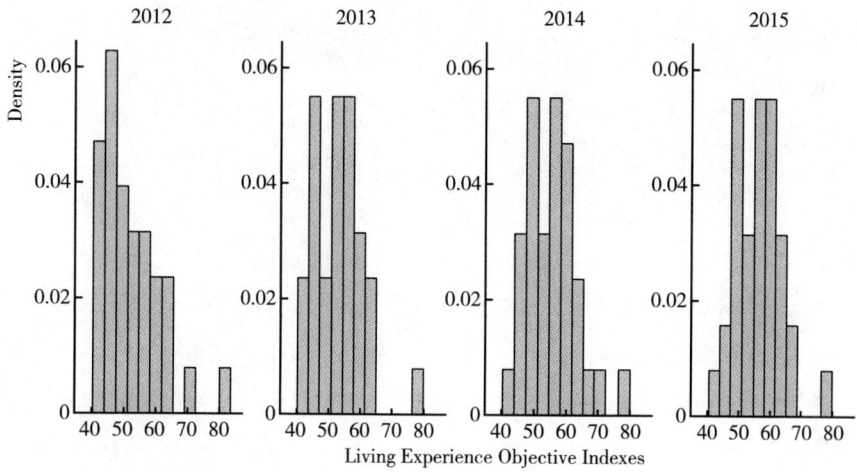

Graph 5.31: A Histogram of the 2012–2015 Living Experience Objective Indexes

According to the calculation, cities ranked top 10 on the list of living experience objective indexes are: Beijing (1), Shenzhen (2), Guangzhou (3), Haikou (4), Shenyang (5), Hohhot (6), Nanjing (7), Hangzhou (8), Kunming (9) and Wuhan (10). Rankings of the top 6 cities have remained the same as that of last year. Beijing, Shenzhen, Guangzhou, Shenyang, Nanjing, Hangzhou and Kunming have been ranked among the top 10 for four successive years, as well as Haikou and Hohhot for three consecutive years. Beijing have ranked No.1 for four years, scoring 80 or above. The

Quality-of-life Sub-Indexes of the 35 Chinese Cities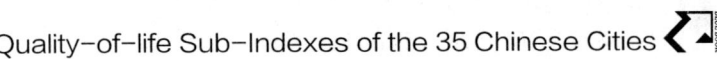

Continued table

City	2015			2014		2013		2012	
	Score	Ranking	Places risen	Score	Ranking	Score	Ranking	Score	Ranking
Xiamen	56.77	17	-5	58.20	12	52.07	20	58.95	6
Urumqi	56.39	18	2	54.22	20	54.20	18	46.58	23
Changchun	56.28	19	-2	55.92	17	53.70	19	51.25	16
Shanghai	55.67	20	-1	55.57	19	54.71	15	56.45	9
Hefei	54.81	21	0	53.30	21	54.46	16	42.91	31
Ningbo	53.10	22	0	52.51	22	48.24	23	46.35	24
Shijiazhuang	51.87	23	3	50.43	26	51.39	22	46.63	22
Xining	51.52	24	1	50.56	25	45.51	28	45.60	27
Nanchang	50.93	25	3	49.82	28	44.81	30	43.40	30
Fuzhou	50.76	26	-3	52.46	23	45.93	27	51.84	15
Guiyang	50.34	27	0	49.98	27	44.89	29	41.91	32
Dalian	50.29	28	-4	50.90	24	47.37	24	49.07	18
Chengdu	48.35	29	5	45.34	34	43.35	33	41.30	34
Nanning	48.05	30	-1	47.77	29	43.97	32	44.47	29
Tianjin	47.91	31	-1	47.34	30	47.28	25	46.20	25
Changsha	47.48	32	0	47.20	32	46.47	26	45.23	28
Jinan	47.07	33	-2	47.26	31	44.71	31	45.72	26
Chongqing	46.61	34	-1	46.34	33	43.18	34	40.02	35
Zhengzhou	40.00	35	0	40.00	35	40.00	35	41.65	33
Average	56.17			55.57		53.67		51.89	

As is shown in Table 5.16, the weighted average of living experience objective indexes is 56.17 – above the satisfaction level and slightly higher than that of 2014. The highest score is still 80.00 (Beijing). And the lowest score is still 40.00 (Zhengzhou). There is a big gap in between. Viewed by

5.5.2 Objective Indexes (Social and Economic Data Indexes) of Living Experience

In the QLICC system, the objective indexes of living experience are obtained by calculating three primary indicators (living convenience index, eco-environment index and perception of income disparities index) which are in turn made up of six secondary indicators. Table 5.16 lists the living experience objective indexes of the 35 cities.

Table 5.16 Living Experience Objective Indexes of the 35 Chinese Cities

City	2015			2014		2013		2012	
	Score	Ranking	Places risen	Score	Ranking	Score	Ranking	Score	Ranking
Beijing	80.00	1	0	80.00	1	80.00	1	80.01	1
Shenzhen	67.95	2	0	69.71	2	65.12	2	71.86	2
Guangzhou	67.86	3	0	66.66	3	64.16	3	58.88	7
Haikou	65.12	4	0	65.35	4	57.80	9	55.45	12
Shenyang	64.32	5	0	63.28	5	62.56	4	62.90	5
Hohhot	62.84	6	0	62.51	6	58.74	7	54.50	13
Nanjing	62.35	7	1	60.84	8	59.7	6	58.24	8
Hangzhou	60.82	8	1	59.56	9	58.41	8	64.43	4
Kunming	60.70	9	-2	61.54	7	57.57	10	55.61	10
Wuhan	60.39	10	3	57.93	13	60.15	5	64.52	3
Harbin	59.39	11	3	57.77	14	56.98	12	48.25	20
Taiyuan	59.08	12	-1	58.23	11	57.34	11	48.10	21
Xi'an	58.43	13	5	55.87	18	54.32	17	55.46	11
Qingdao	58.42	14	1	57.63	15	55.68	13	48.97	19
Yinchuan	58.14	15	-5	58.31	10	54.74	14	52.58	14
Lanzhou	56.78	16	0	56.98	16	51.76	21	50.77	17

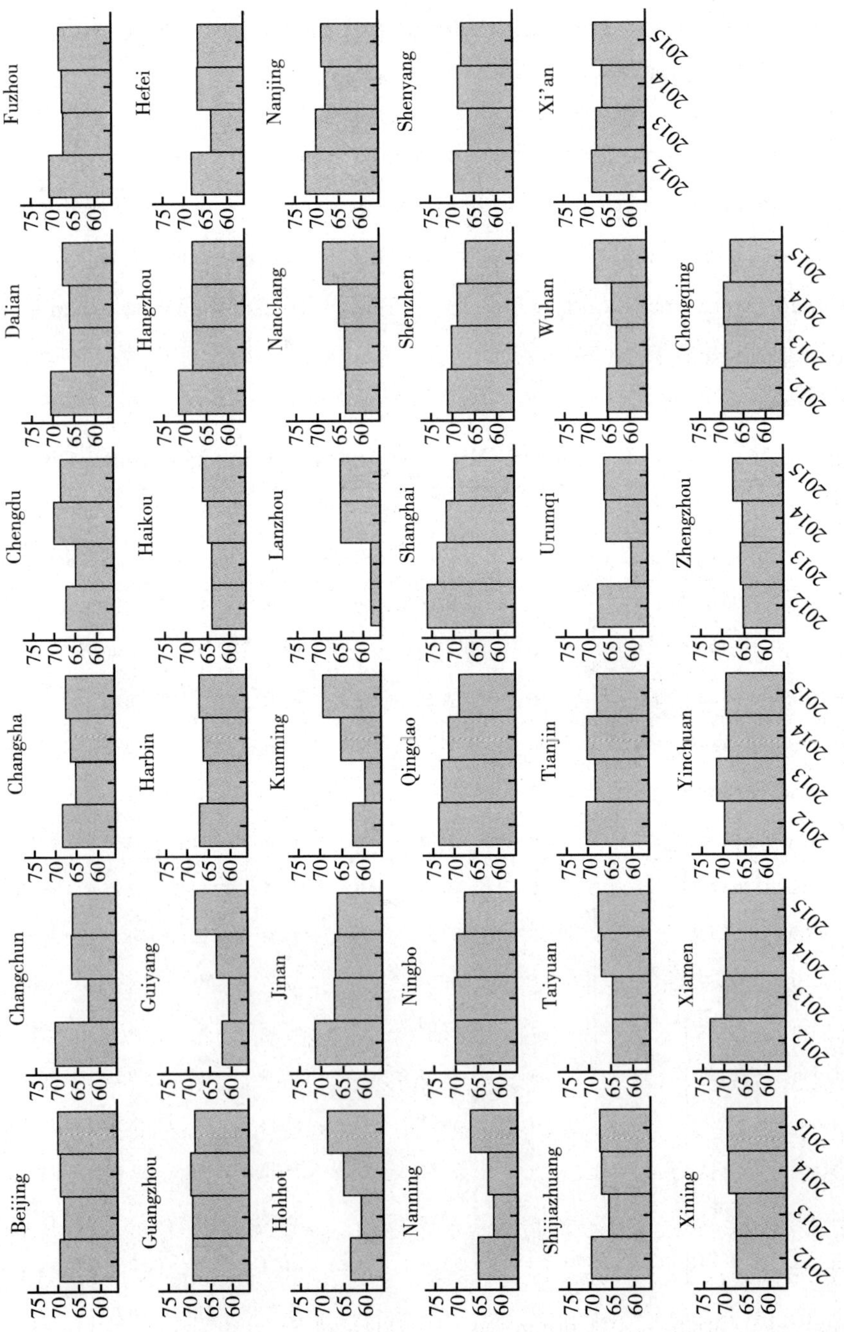

Quality-of-life Sub-Indexes of the 35 Chinese Cities

Graph 5.30: A Bar Chart of the 2012–2015 Living Convenience Satisfaction Indexes of the 35 cities

convenience satisfaction indexes are: Shanghai (1), Beijing (2), Xining (3), Kunming (4), Yinchuan (5), Nanjing (6), Qingdao (7), Xiamen (8), Hohhot (9) and Nanchang (10). Among them, Shanghai, Qingdao and Xiamen have been ranked among the top 10 for four successive years. It should also be noted that Shanghai has ranked No.1 for four years and scored 76.12 in 2012 which was in the "very satisfied" range (76-100 points). The bottom 10 cities are: Zhengzhou (26), Changsha (27), Harbin (28), Nanning (29), Hefei (30), Jinan (31), Haikou (32), Changchun (33), Urumqi (34) and Lanzhou (35). Among them, Nanning, Haikou and Lanzhou have been on the bottom 10 list for four consecutive years, as well as Urumqi for three successive years. And in the past four years, Lanzhou has got the last place (No.35) three times.

Viewed by regional distribution, among the top 10 cities, the ratio of eastern to central to western cities is 5:1:4. Among the bottom 10 cities, the ratio is 2:5:3. Based on our analysis, there is more advanced transportation infrastructure in the east, as well as more transportation facilities. Therefore, residents in eastern cities tend to be more satisfied with the convenience of their lives, while people in western cities are not so satisfied with it.

From 2012 to 2015, the weighted averages of living convenience satisfaction indexes are 68.39, 67.18, 67.66 and 68.20 respectively, generally of little change. Graph 5.30 well illustrates the changes in the living convenience satisfaction indexes of the 35 cities from 2012 to 2015. Viewed by cities, Haikou and Nanchang have experienced a rise in the indicator for three successive years. Viewed by rankings, Kunming has made the most obvious progress, rising 25 places to No.4 this year. Cities with a dramatic rise in the ranking also include: Hohhot (21), Guiyang (19), Nanchang (17) and Wuhan (15). And Shenzhen has experienced the most drastic drops, falling 20 places to No.25. Cities with a serious drop in the ranking also include: Ningbo (-14), Tianjin (-13), Jinan (-12), Chongqing (-10), Hefei (-10) and Changchun (-10).

Quality-of-life Sub-Indexes of the 35 Chinese Cities

Continued table

City	2015			2014		2013		2012	
	Score	Ranking	Places risen	Score	Ranking	Score	Ranking	Score	Ranking
Jinan	66.67	31	-12	67.07	19	67.25	16	71.54	7
Haikou	66.29	32	0	65.04	32	64.01	26	64.00	30
Changchun	66.16	33	-10	66.35	23	62.39	29	70.72	9
Urumqi	66.16	34	-8	65.74	26	59.89	34	67.76	22
Lanzhou	65.18	35	-4	65.09	31	58.48	35	58.52	35
Average		68.20		67.66		67.18		68.39	

According to the survey, the 2015 weighted average of living convenience satisfaction indexes is 68.20 – above the satisfaction level, slightly higher than that of 2013 and 2014, but lower than that of 2012. Compared with the results of the past three years, the highest score has kept falling. On the other hand, it should also be noted that the lowest score has improved by nearly 12% within three years. As a whole, residents of the 35 cities are generally satisfied with the convenience of their lives. Graph 5.29 well illustrates the changes in the living convenience satisfaction indexes from 2012 to 2015.

As is shown in Table 5.15, cities ranked top 10 on the list of living

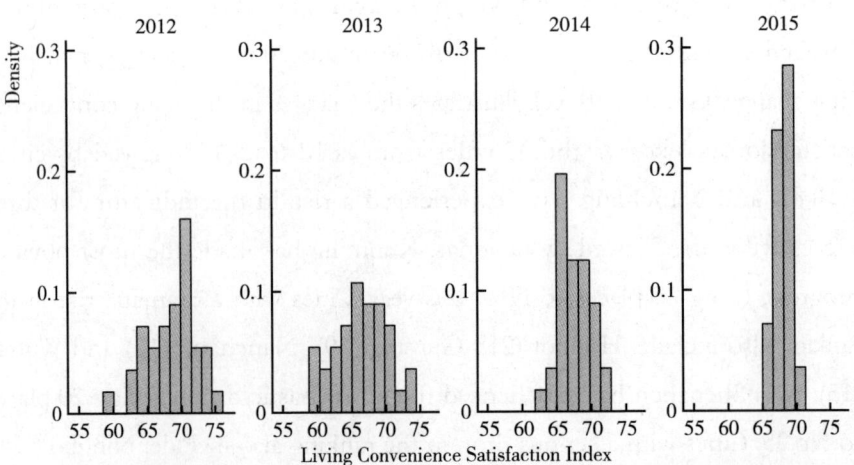

Graph 5.29: A Histogram of the 2012–2015 Living Convenience Satisfaction Indexes

Table 5.15   Living Convenience Satisfaction Indexes of the 35 Chinese Cities

City	2015			2014		2013		2012	
	Score	Ranking	Places risen	Score	Ranking	Score	Ranking	Score	Ranking
Shanghai	70.02	1	0	71.98	1	73.99	1	76.12	1
Beijing	69.98	2	8	69.38	10	68.42	11	69.50	17
Xining	69.56	3	8	69.20	11	67.57	14	67.59	23
Kunming	69.44	4	25	65.41	29	59.90	33	62.98	33
Yinchuan	69.42	5	7	68.99	12	71.43	3	69.79	16
Nanjing	69.13	6	8	68.39	14	70.46	5	72.95	4
Qingdao	69.09	7	-5	71.40	2	73.18	2	73.82	2
Xiamen	69.05	8	-1	69.79	7	70.28	6	73.26	3
Hohhot	68.99	9	21	65.19	30	61.40	31	63.93	31
Nanchang	68.69	10	17	65.57	27	64.06	25	63.82	32
Guangzhou	68.68	11	-3	69.65	8	69.31	9	69.23	18
Chengdu	68.46	12	-8	70.03	4	64.90	23	67.32	24
Fuzhou	68.44	13	3	67.74	16	67.49	15	70.95	8
Hangzhou	68.25	14	1	68.07	15	68.26	12	71.58	6
Guiyang	68.24	15	19	63.58	34	60.45	32	62.14	34
Tianjin	68.21	16	-13	70.33	3	68.55	10	70.56	10
Xi'an	68.18	17	7	66.18	24	67.59	13	68.69	19
Wuhan	68.14	18	15	64.17	33	62.89	28	65.13	28
Chongqing	68.06	19	-10	69.51	9	69.31	8	70.01	13
Ningbo	67.97	20	-14	69.81	6	70.14	7	70.14	12
Shenyang	67.87	21	-8	68.86	13	66.60	17	69.80	15
Taiyuan	67.83	22	-4	67.19	18	64.39	24	64.36	29
Dalian	67.83	23	2	66.13	25	65.83	19	70.55	11
Shijiazhuang	67.80	24	-7	67.37	17	65.75	20	69.86	14
Shenzhen	67.68	25	-20	69.89	5	71.21	4	72.22	5
Zhengzhou	67.54	26	2	65.54	28	65.91	18	65.36	26
Changsha	67.54	27	-6	66.64	21	65.07	22	68.42	20
Harbin	67.20	28	-6	66.37	22	65.36	21	67.28	25
Nanning	66.82	29	6	62.81	35	61.69	30	65.28	27
Hefei	66.68	30	-10	66.74	20	63.91	27	68.35	21

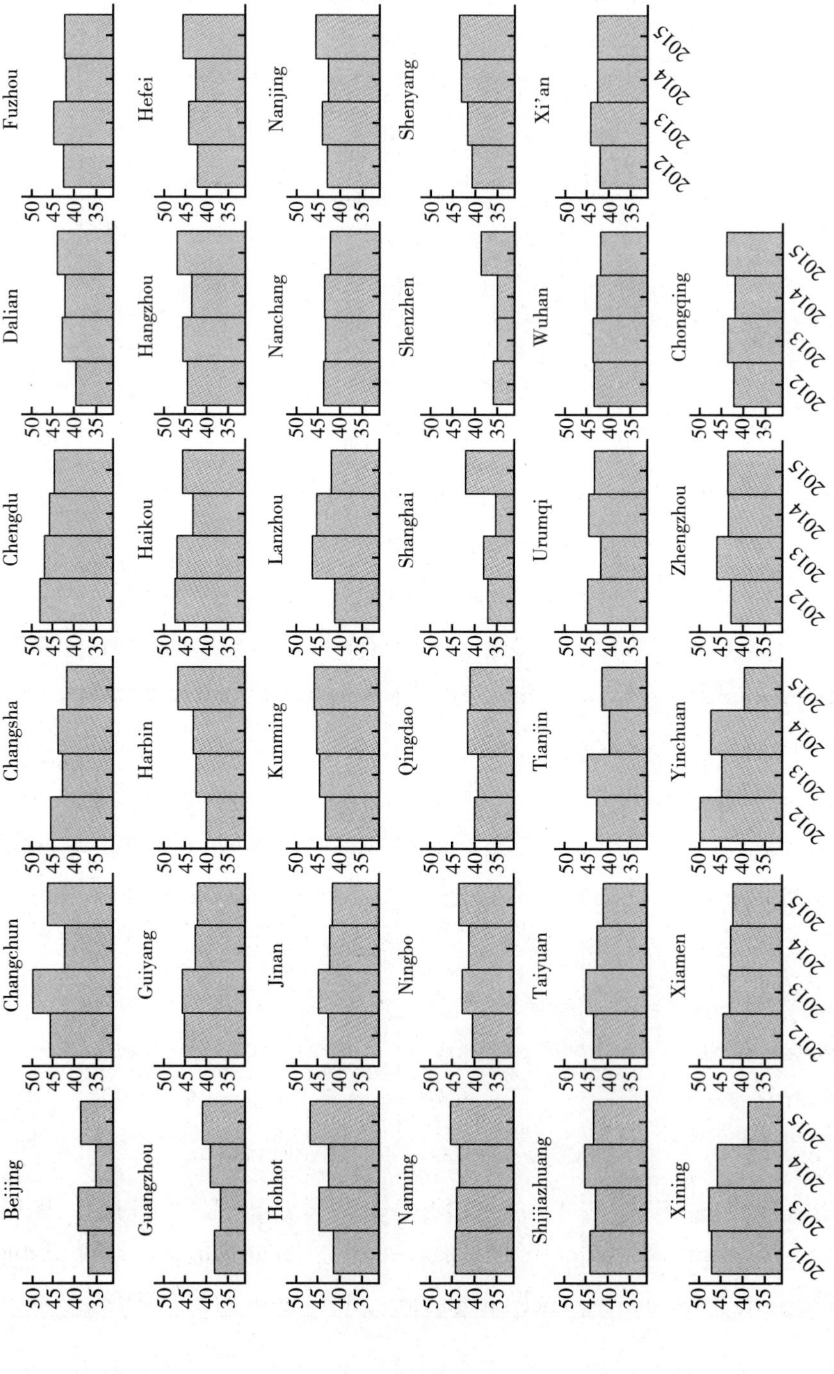

Quality-of-life Sub-Indexes of the 35 Chinese Cities

Graph 5.28: A Bar Chart of the 2012–2015 Pace of Life Satisfaction Indexes of the 35 Cities

Guangzhou and Qingdao have been on the bottom 10 list for four consecutive years. Yinchuan and Xining had ranked among top 10 for three years from 2012 to 2014, and falls onto the bottom 10 list for the first time in 2015.

Viewed by regional distribution, among the top 10 cities, the ratio of eastern to central to western cities is 4:2:4. Among the bottom 10 cities, the ratio is 6:2:2. Residents of central cities tend to be more satisfied with their pace of life. And the pace of life in some eastern cities seems too fast, especially in Beijing, Shanghai, Guangzhou and Shenzhen.

From 2012 to 2015, the weighted averages of pace of life satisfaction indexes are 42.87, 42.97, 41.90 and 43.12 respectively, generally of little change. Although there was a slight drop in 2014, it goes back up again in 2015. Graph 5.28 well illustrates the changes in the pace of life satisfaction indexes of the 35 cities from 2012 to 2015. Viewed by cities, Harbin, Kunming and Shenyang have experienced a rise in the indicator for three successive years, while Chengdu and Xiamen have seen a drop over the same period. The scores of Changchun and Hohhot have fluctuated over the four years, and the scores of Nanchang and Nanning have remained stable. Viewed by rankings, Changchun has made the most obvious progress, rising 23 places to No.4 in 2015. Cities with a dramatic rise in the ranking also include: Hohhot (22), Ningbo (16), Chongqing (15), Dalian (13), Shanghai (13), Hefei (12), Harbin (11), Nanjing (11), Hangzhou (9) and Haikou (9). And Yinchuan and Xining have experienced the most drastic drops, both falling 31 places. Cities with a serious drop in the ranking also include: Lanzhou (-20), Changsha (-19), Shijiazhuang (-12), Urumqi (-10) and Nanchang (-10).

Under the living experience index, there is another sub-index (living convenience satisfaction sub-index) besides the pace of life sub-index. Table 5.15 lists the living convenience satisfaction sub-indexes of the 35 cities.

Quality-of-life Sub-Indexes of the 35 Chinese Cities

As is shown in Table 5.14, the 2015 weighted average of pace of life satisfaction sub-indexes is 43.12, remaining on the low side (below the satisfaction level) and roughly unchanged compared with the results of the previous surveys. The highest score is 47.06 (Hangzhou), while the lowest score is 38.72 (Beijing). There exists quite a big gap in between. The highest score has remained comparatively stable with slight drops over the past four years. Generally speaking, residents of the 35 cities are not satisfied with their pace of life, maybe owing to the fact that the pace of life has quickened in most cities. Graph 5.27 well illustrates the changes in the pace of life satisfaction indexes from 2012 to 2015.

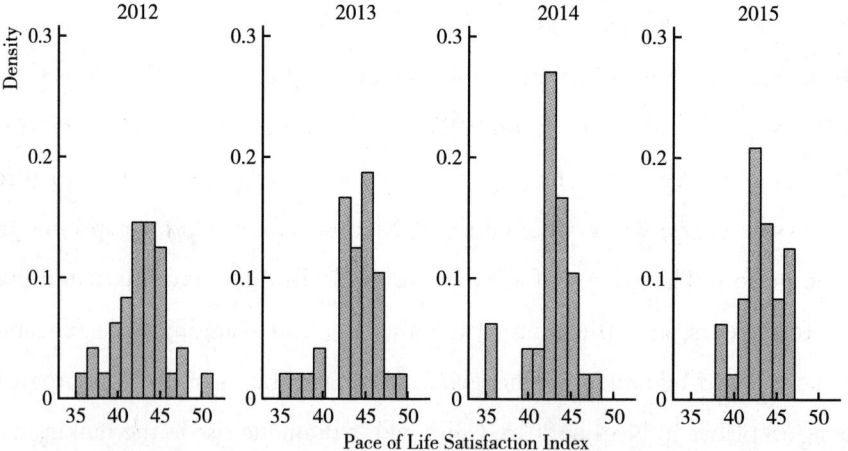

Graph 5.27: A Histogram of the 2012–2015 Pace of Life Satisfaction Indexes

As is shown in Table 5.14, cities ranked top 10 on the list of pace of life satisfaction indexes are: Hangzhou (1), Hohhot (2), Harbin (3), Changchun (4), Nanjing (5), Haikou (6), Kunming (7), Hefei (8), Nanning (9) and Chengdu (10). Among them, only Chengdu has been ranked among the top 10 for four successive years. The bottom 10 cities are: Jinan (26), Changsha (27), Tianjin (28), Qingdao (29), Taiyuan (30), Guangzhou (31), Yinchuan (32), Shenzhen (33), Xining (34) and Beijing (35). Among them, Beijing, Shenzhen,

Table 5.14 Pace of Life Satisfaction Indexes of the 35 Chinese Cities

City	2015			2014		2013		2012	
	Score	Ranking	Places risen	Score	Ranking	Score	Ranking	Score	Ranking
Hangzhou	47.06	1	9	43.63	10	45.83	8	44.93	8
Hohhot	46.96	2	22	42.45	24	44.74	15	41.43	26
Harbin	46.88	3	11	43.29	14	42.54	28	39.96	30
Changchun	46.35	4	23	42.17	27	49.88	1	45.72	5
Nanjing	46.07	5	11	43.11	16	44.62	16	43.21	17
Haikou	45.89	6	9	43.24	15	47.25	3	47.50	3
Kunming	45.83	7	-1	45.32	6	44.90	13	43.27	16
Hefei	45.67	8	12	42.66	20	44.27	18	42.27	23
Nanning	45.40	9	3	43.38	12	44.23	19	44.44	11
Chengdu	45.10	10	-8	45.98	2	47.22	4	48.39	2
Chongqing	44.15	11	15	42.19	26	44.01	20	42.34	22
Dalian	44.12	12	13	42.20	25	42.87	26	39.57	31
Zhengzhou	43.63	13	-2	43.57	11	46.27	6	42.98	18
Ningbo	43.61	14	16	41.17	30	42.99	25	40.54	28
Shenyang	43.56	15	-2	43.29	13	41.81	29	40.86	27
Shijiazhuang	43.52	16	-12	45.48	4	43.11	23	44.35	12
Urumqi	43.23	17	-10	44.54	7	41.81	30	44.74	10
Xi'an	42.79	18	-1	42.84	17	44.32	17	42.23	24
Nanchang	42.63	19	-10	43.66	9	43.62	22	43.90	13
Shanghai	42.43	20	13	35.69	33	38.20	33	37.05	34
Xiamen	42.42	21	-3	42.80	18	43.06	24	44.77	9
Guiyang	42.31	22	-1	42.65	21	45.90	7	45.48	7
Fuzhou	42.27	23	5	41.90	28	44.90	14	42.49	21
Wuhan	42.09	24	-5	42.80	19	43.69	21	43.49	14
Lanzhou	41.99	25	-20	45.44	5	46.47	5	41.48	25
Jinan	41.97	26	-3	42.45	23	45.02	11	42.92	19
Changsha	41.85	27	-19	44.02	8	42.81	27	45.61	6
Tianjin	41.70	28	3	39.93	31	44.95	12	42.70	20
Qingdao	41.25	29	0	41.69	29	39.22	32	40.09	29
Taiyuan	41.21	30	-8	42.63	22	45.11	9	43.32	15
Guangzhou	40.83	31	1	39.07	32	36.67	34	38.12	32
Yinchuan	39.88	32	-31	47.36	1	45.05	10	50.00	1
Shenzhen	38.84	33	2	34.90	35	34.93	35	35.81	35
Xining	38.83	34	-31	45.83	3	47.95	2	47.22	4
Beijing	38.72	35	-1	35.41	34	39.32	31	37.11	33
Average	43.12			41.90		42.97		42.87	

Quality-of-life Sub-Indexes of the 35 Chinese Cities

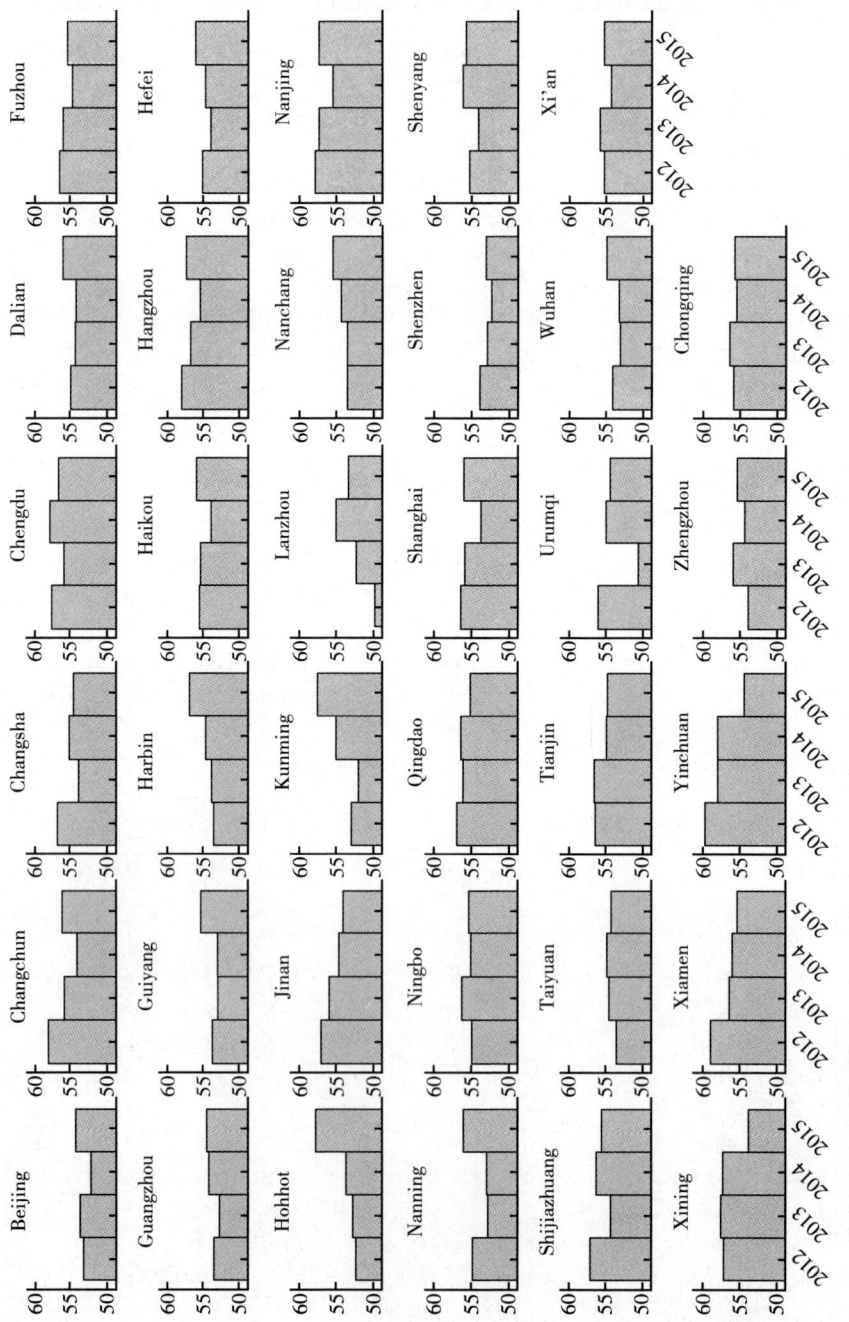

Graph 5.26: A Bar Chart of the 2012–2015 Living Experience Satisfaction Indexes of the 35 Cities

change. Although there was a slight drop in 2014, it goes back to 55 points again in 2015. Graph 5.26 well illustrates the changes in the living experience satisfaction indexes of the 35 cities from 2012 to 2015. Viewed by cities, Harbin, Hohhot and Nanchang have experienced a rise in the indicator for four successive years, while Jinan, Xiamen and Yinchuan have seen a drop over the same period. The scores of Changchun, Lanzhou and Urumqi have fluctuated. Viewed by rankings, Hohhot has made the most obvious progress, rising 29 places from No.30 in 2014 to No.1 in 2015. Cities with a dramatic rise in the ranking also include: Nanning (23), Shanghai (21), Changchun (19), Haikou (16), Dalian (14), Harbin (13), Hefei (12), Guiyang (10) and Kunming (9). And Xining has experienced the most drastic drop, falling 30 places from No.3 in 2014 to No.33 in 2015. Cities with a serious drop in the ranking also include: Yinchuan (-28), Lanzhou (-20), Qingdao (-19), Changsha (-14), Urumqi (-13), Taiyuan (-13), Shijiazhuang (-12), Jinan (-12), Xiamen (-9), Shenyang (-9) and Tianjin (-9). On the basis of the above-mentioned data, we may conclude that the living experience satisfaction indexes of many cities have fluctuated greatly from 2014 to 2015.

The satisfaction index of living experience consists of two sub-indexes (pace of life satisfaction index and living convenience satisfaction index) and is obtained by calculating their weighted average (50% each) in accordance with the design of the QLICC system. Therefore, fluctuations in the living experience satisfaction indexes can be explained by the changes in the two sub-indexes. In the following passage, the two sub-indexes will be introduced separately.

Table 5.14 lists the 2015 pace of life satisfaction sub-indexes of the 35 cities, along with the results of the previous surveys.

Quality-of-life Sub-Indexes of the 35 Chinese Cities

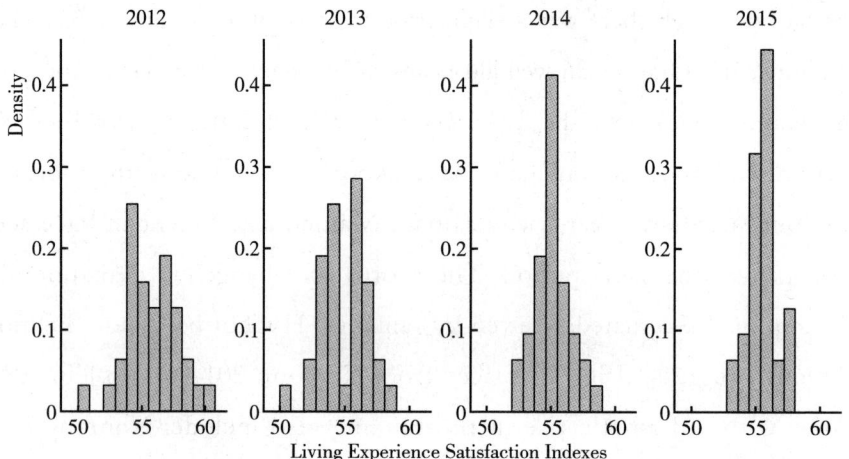

Graph 5.25: A Histogram of the 2012–2015 Living Experience Satisfaction Indexes

According to the 2015 survey, cities ranked top 10 on the list of living experience satisfaction indexes are: Hohhot (1), Hangzhou (2), Kunming (3), Nanjing (4), Harbin (5), Chengdu (6), Changchun (7), Shanghai (8), Hefei (9) and Nanning (10). Among them, Hangzhou and Nanjing have been ranked among the top 10 for four successive years. The bottom 10 cities are: Guangzhou (26), Changsha (27), Urumqi (28), Yinchuan (29), Taiyuan (30), Beijing (31), Jinan (32), Xining (33), Lanzhou (34) and Shenzhen (35). Among them, Shenzhen has been on the bottom 10 list for four consecutive years. From 2012 to 2015, Beijing and Guangzhou have ranked No.11 in one year and among the bottom 10 in the other three years.

Viewed by regional distribution, among the top 10 cities, the ratio of eastern to central to western cities is 3:3:4. And among the bottom 10 cities, the ratio is 4:2:4.

From 2012 to 2015, the weighted averages of living experience satisfaction indexes are 55.63, 55.07, 54.88 and 55.66 respectively, generally of little

Continued table

City	2015			2014		2013		2012	
	Score	Ranking	Places risen	Score	Ranking	Score	Ranking	Score	Ranking
Fuzhou	55.36	21	-2	54.82	19	56.20	10	56.72	12
Guiyang	55.28	22	10	53.12	32	53.18	28	53.81	29
Qingdao	55.17	23	-19	56.54	4	56.20	9	56.96	11
Wuhan	55.11	24	7	53.48	31	53.29	27	54.31	24
Tianjin	54.95	25	-9	55.13	16	56.75	5	56.63	13
Guangzhou	54.76	26	-1	54.36	25	52.99	31	53.67	30
Changsha	54.69	27	-14	55.33	13	53.94	24	57.02	10
Urumqi	54.69	28	-13	55.14	15	50.85	35	56.25	15
Yinchuan	54.65	29	-28	58.17	1	58.24	1	59.90	1
Taiyuan	54.52	30	-13	54.91	17	54.75	18	53.84	28
Beijing	54.35	31	4	52.39	35	53.87	25	53.30	32
Jinan	54.32	32	-12	54.76	20	56.13	12	57.23	8
Xining	54.20	33	-30	57.52	3	57.76	2	57.41	7
Lanzhou	53.59	34	-20	55.27	14	52.47	33	50.00	35
Shenzhen	53.26	35	-1	52.40	34	53.07	30	54.02	26
Average	55.66			54.88		55.07		55.63	

As is shown in Table 5.13, the 2015 weighted average of living experience satisfaction indexes is 55.66 — slightly higher than that of 2013 and 2014 and about the same as that of 2012. Generally speaking, the index has remained stable and above the satisfaction level in all the four years. And the performances of the cities are of no big difference. In 2015, the highest score is 57.98 (Hohhot), while the lowest score is 53.26 (Shenzhen). There is only a small gap in between. Compared with that of the previous three years, the highest score has slightly dropped, maybe owing to the fact that people now demand a higher living experience as the economy develops. On the other hand, the lowest score has greatly improved this year. Graph 5.25 well illustrates the changes in living experience satisfaction indexes from 2012 to 2015.

Quality-of-life Sub-Indexes of the 35 Chinese Cities

5.5 Living Experience Indexes

5.5.1 Satisfaction Indexes of Living Experience

In the QLICC system, the satisfaction indexes of living experience are obtained through a questionnaire survey and measured by the weighted averages of the pace of life satisfaction indexes and the living convenience satisfaction indexes. Table 5.13 lists the 2015 living experience satisfaction indexes of the 35 cities.

Table 5.13 Living Experience Satisfaction Indexes of the 35 Chinese Cities

City	2015			2014		2013		2012	
	Score	Ranking	Places risen	Score	Ranking	Score	Ranking	Score	Ranking
Hohhot	57.98	1	29	53.82	30	53.07	29	52.68	34
Hangzhou	57.65	2	7	55.85	9	57.05	4	58.25	3
Kunming	57.63	3	9	55.37	12	52.40	34	53.13	33
Nanjing	57.60	4	6	55.75	10	57.54	3	58.08	5
Harbin	57.04	5	13	54.83	18	53.95	23	53.62	31
Chengdu	56.78	6	-4	58.01	2	56.06	15	57.86	6
Changchun	56.25	7	19	54.26	26	56.14	11	58.22	4
Shanghai	56.22	8	21	53.84	29	56.10	13	56.58	14
Hefei	56.17	9	12	54.70	21	54.09	22	55.31	21
Nanning	56.11	10	23	53.09	33	52.96	32	54.86	23
Chongqing	56.10	11	-3	55.85	8	56.66	7	56.18	16
Haikou	56.09	12	16	54.14	28	55.63	17	55.75	17
Dalian	55.97	13	14	54.17	27	54.35	20	55.06	22
Ningbo	55.79	14	-3	55.49	11	56.56	8	55.34	19
Xiamen	55.74	15	-9	56.30	6	56.67	6	59.01	2
Shenyang	55.72	16	-9	56.08	7	54.21	21	55.33	20
Shijiazhuang	55.66	17	-12	56.43	5	54.43	19	57.11	9
Nanchang	55.66	18	4	54.61	22	53.84	26	53.86	27
Zhengzhou	55.59	19	4	54.55	23	56.09	14	54.17	25
Xi'an	55.48	20	4	54.51	24	55.96	16	55.46	18

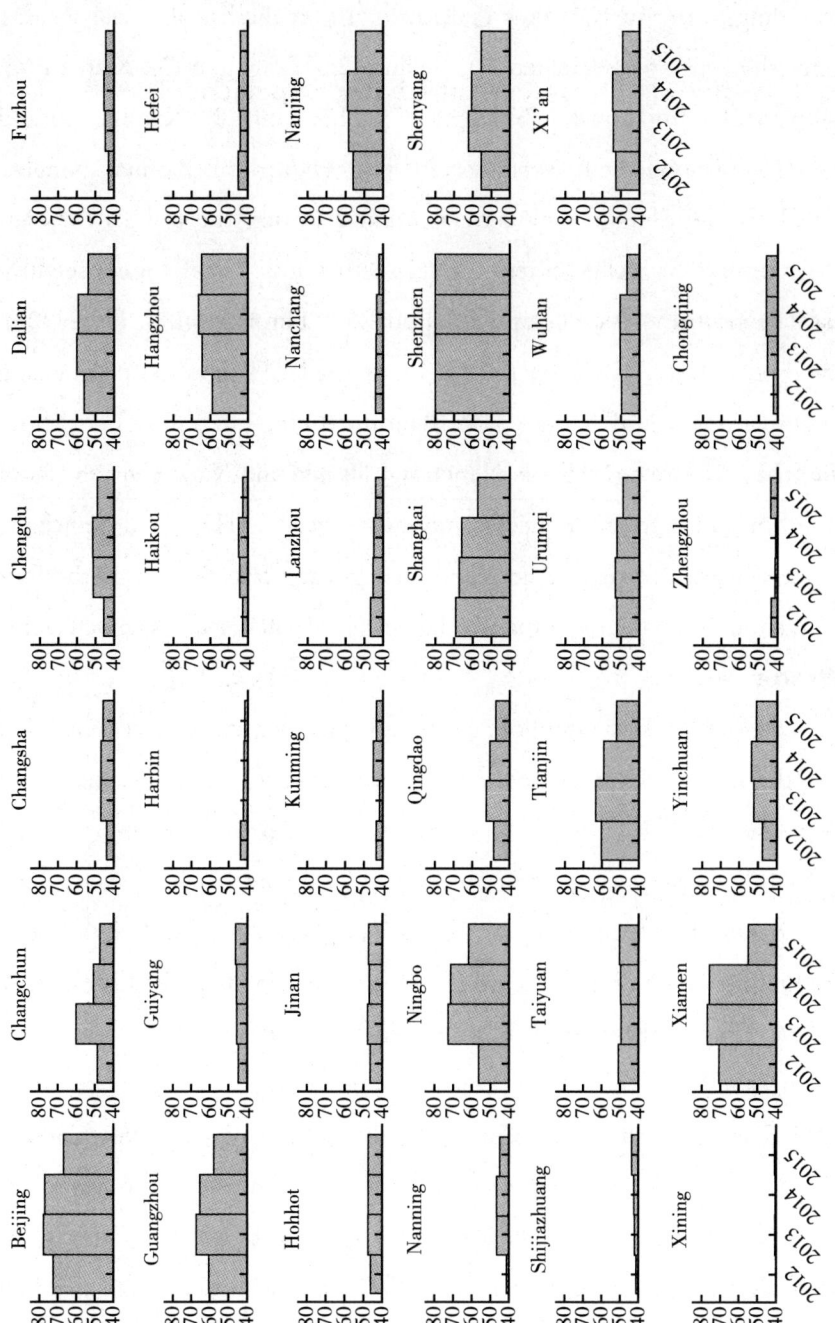

Graph 5.24: A Bar Chart of the 2012–2015 Social Security Objective Indexes of the 35 Cities

Quality-of-life Sub-Indexes of the 35 Chinese Cities

According to the survey, cities ranked top 10 on the list of social security objective indexes are: Shenzhen (1), Beijing (2), Hangzhou (3), Xiamen (4), Ningbo (5), Guangzhou (6), Shanghai (7), Shenyang (8), Nanjing (9) and Dalian (10). Among them, Shenzhen, Beijing, Hangzhou, Xiamen, Ningbo, Guangzhou and Shanghai have been ranked among the top 10 for four successive years, as well as Shenyang (No.8 this year) for three consecutive years. The bottom 10 cities are: Fuzhou (26), Lanzhou (27), Hefei (28), Zhengzhou (29), Shijiazhuang (30), Kunming (31), Haikou (32), Nanchang (33), Harbin (34) and Xining (35). Among them, Fuzhou, Zhengzhou, Shijiazhuang, Kunming, Haikou, Nanchang, Harbin and Xining have been on the bottom 10 list for four successive years, as well as Hefei and Nanchang for three consecutive years. And Xining has got the last place in all the four years. It should also be noted that the highest score 80 is twice as much as the lowest score 40.

Viewed by regional distribution, all the top 10 cities are eastern cities. And among the bottom 10 cities, there are 3 eastern cities, 3 central cities and 4 western cities.

Viewed by dynamic changes, from 2012 to 2015, the weighted averages of social security objective indexes are 50.85, 55.26, 54.66 and 51.26 respectively, which first rose then dropped during the four years. In 2012, the lowest score was 39.98. From 2013 to 2015, it has stayed at 40. Graph 5.24 well illustrates the changes in the social security objective indexes of the 35 cities from 2012 to 2015. Viewed by cities, only Guiyang and Shijiazhuang have experienced a rise in the index for three successive years. Cities with a dramatic rise in the ranking are: Taiyuan (6) and Zhengzhou (5). Cities with a drastic drop in the ranking are: Wuhan (-5) and Haikou (-4). Generally speaking, the rankings have remained roughly unchanged.

Continued table

City	2015			2014		2013		2012	
	Score	Ranking	Places risen	Score	Ranking	Score	Ranking	Score	Ranking
Hefei	43.49	28	2	44.14	30	43.72	29	44.71	23
Zhengzhou	43.19	29	5	40.61	34	40.98	34	42.99	28
Shijiazhuang	42.89	30	2	41.80	32	41.77	31	40.86	33
Kunming	42.77	31	-2	44.52	29	41.21	33	42.85	29
Haikou	42.55	32	-4	44.72	28	43.91	28	42.54	30
Nanchang	41.59	33	-2	42.87	31	43.05	30	43.46	25
Harbin	41.04	34	-1	41.58	33	41.73	32	43.21	26
Xining	40.00	35	0	40.00	35	40.00	35	39.98	35
Average	51.26			54.66		55.26		50.85	

According to the survey, the weighted average of social security objective indexes is 51.26 – much lower than the results of the previous surveys. 22 out of the 35 cities have scored below 50 in the index, while in 2014, there were only 17 cities. It should be noted that Shenzhen has ranked No.1 and scored over 80 in all the four years (2012-2015) which is in the "very satisfied" range (76-100 points). As a whole, the social security objective index has kept dropping despite a slight rise in 2013. Graph 5.23 well illustrates the changes in social security objective indexes from 2012 to 2015.

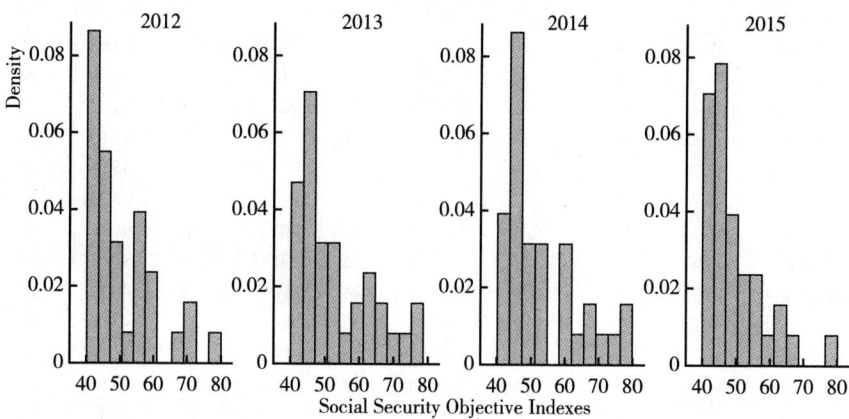

Graph 5.23: A Histogram of the 2012–2015 Social Security Objective Indexes

5.4.2 Objective Indexes (Social and Economic Data Indexes) of Social Security

In the QLICC system, the objective index of social security is measured by three secondary indicators (social security coverage, basic medical insurance coverage and unemployment insurance coverage). Table 5.12 lists the social security objective indexes of the 35 cities.

Table 5.12 Social Security Objective Indexes of the 35 Chinese Cities

City	2015			2014		2013		2012	
	Score	Ranking	Places risen	Score	Ranking	Score	Ranking	Score	Ranking
Shenzhen	80.00	1	0	80.00	1	80.00	1	80.01	1
Beijing	66.18	2	0	76.39	2	77.24	2	71.82	2
Hangzhou	64.23	3	2	65.70	5	63.84	7	58.36	7
Xiamen	63.40	4	-1	73.85	3	74.37	3	71.43	3
Ningbo	61.39	5	-1	71.22	4	72.36	4	56.19	8
Guangzhou	57.36	6	1	64.52	7	66.71	6	60.11	5
Shanghai	56.82	7	-1	65.66	6	67.23	5	68.68	4
Shenyang	55.30	8	0	60.46	8	62.01	9	55.20	12
Nanjing	54.14	9	2	58.56	11	58.11	12	55.65	10
Dalian	53.26	10	0	58.85	10	59.82	11	55.67	9
Tianjin	52.06	11	-2	58.90	9	63.13	8	59.89	6
Yinchuan	50.42	12	0	53.28	12	51.93	16	47.15	18
Taiyuan	50.23	13	6	49.40	19	49.08	19	50.61	14
Xi'an	49.57	14	-1	52.48	13	52.15	15	55.62	11
Chengdu	48.60	15	0	51.14	15	50.84	17	45.00	22
Urumqi	48.14	16	-2	51.79	14	52.63	13	51.44	13
Qingdao	47.16	17	0	50.50	17	52.34	14	48.63	16
Hohhot	47.01	18	2	46.75	20	46.91	21	45.68	21
Changchun	46.95	19	-1	50.17	18	59.84	10	48.23	17
Jinan	46.94	20	1	46.71	21	47.36	20	46.08	20
Wuhan	46.69	21	-5	50.71	16	50.48	18	49.51	15
Guiyang	45.70	22	2	45.22	24	44.95	25	44.14	24
Changsha	45.20	23	0	45.92	23	45.97	23	43.07	27
Chongqing	44.82	24	1	44.97	25	44.57	26	41.48	32
Nanning	44.61	25	-3	46.04	22	46.09	22	40.85	34
Fuzhou	43.76	26	1	44.79	27	44.06	27	42.17	31
Lanzhou	43.54	27	-1	44.91	26	45.14	24	46.35	19

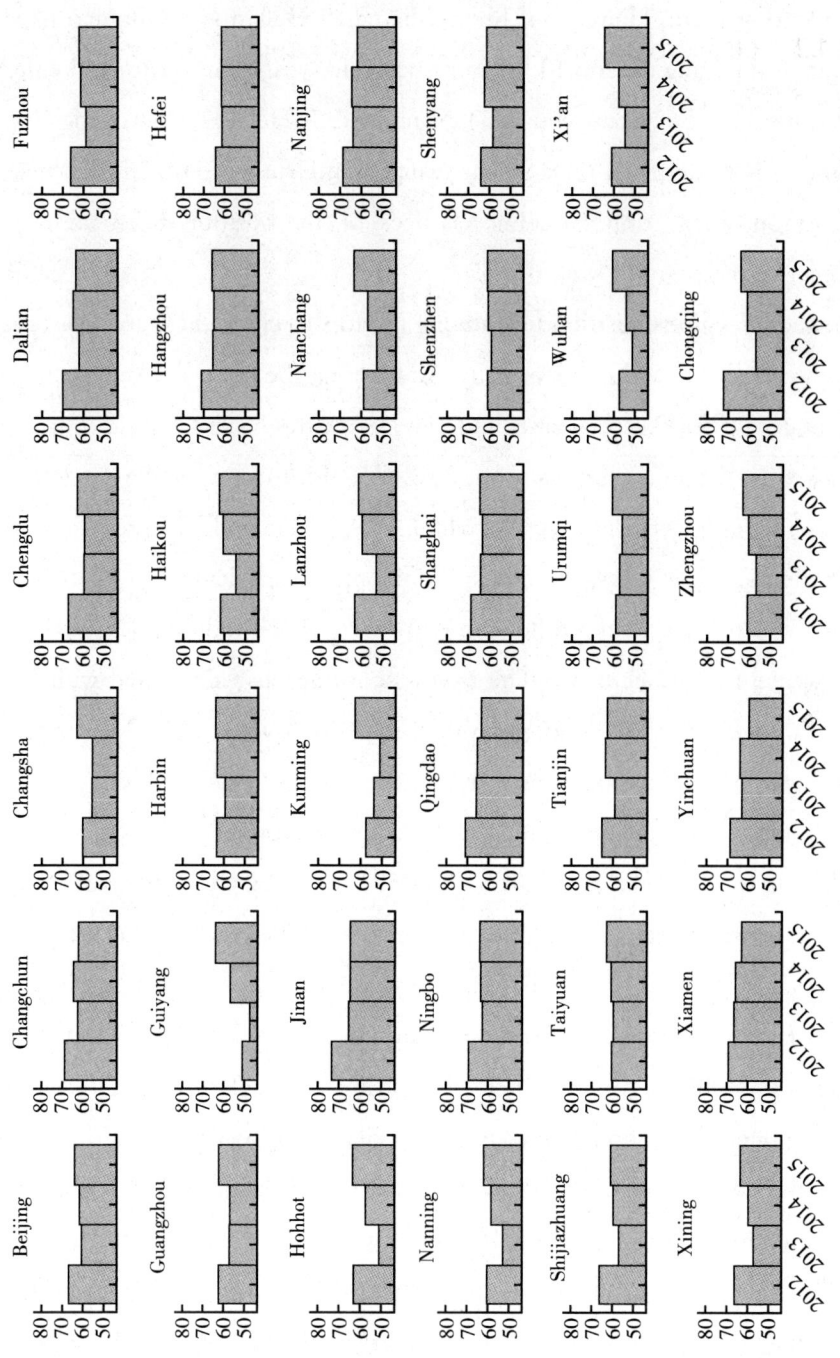

Graph 5.22: A Bar Chart of the 2012–2015 Urban Security (Public Order) Satisfaction Indexes of the 35 Cities

(10). Among them, Hangzhou, Jinan, Shanghai, Dalian and Qingdao have been ranked among the top 10 for four successive years. The bottom 10 cities are: Guangzhou (26), Changchun (27), Nanning (28), Hefei (29), Shenyang (30), Lanzhou (31), Shenzhen (32), Shijiazhuang (33), Urumqi (34) and Yinchuan (35). Among them, only Nanning has been on the bottom 10 list for four consecutive years.

Viewed by regional distribution, among the top 10 cities, there are 8 eastern cities, 1 central city and 1 western city. And among the bottom 10 cities, there are 4 eastern cities, 2 central cities and 4 western cities.

Viewed by dynamic changes, from 2012 to 2015, the weighted averages of public order satisfaction indexes are 64.58, 58.93, 60.45 and 62.90 respectively. Over the past four years, the index had dropped significantly in 2013, and went back up again in the following two years, which indicates an obvious improvement in public order. The lowest score has also fluctuated with the averages. In 2012, it was 50.95 (Guiyang). In 2013, it was 47.32 (Guiyang). In 2014, it was 51.15 (Kunming). And in 2015, it is 60.04 (Yinchuan). Graph 5.22 well illustrates the changes in the urban security or public order satisfaction indexes of the 35 cities from 2012 to 2015. Viewed by cities, none of them has experienced a rise in the index for three successive years, due to the poor performance in 2013. 19 cities have had a continuous improvement in the past two years, which are Wuhan, Beijing, Guiyang, Harbin, Chongqing, Ningbo, Nanchang, Hohhot, Xining, Zhengzhou, Taiyuan, Haikou, Xi'an, Fuzhou, Nanning, Hefei, Lanzhou, Shenzhen and Shijiazhuang. Cities with a dramatic rise in the ranking are: Guiyang (26), Wuhan (25), Changsha (19), Nanchang (18), Kunming (17) and Hohhot (16). Cities with a drastic drop in the ranking are: Yinchuan (-27), Changchun (-20), Nanjing (-19), Xiamen (-18), Shenyang (-17), Hefei (-14), Shenzhen (-13) and Tianjin (-12).

Continued table

City	2015			2014		2013		2012	
	Score	Ranking	Places risen	Score	Ranking	Score	Ranking	Score	Ranking
Shijiazhuang	60.97	33	-8	59.32	25	56.89	22	65.93	15
Urumqi	60.25	34	-1	55.63	33	56.78	23	58.55	33
Yinchuan	60.04	35	-27	63.94	8	63.46	7	68.75	8
Average	62.90			60.45		58.93		64.58	

According to the survey, the weighted average of urban security (public order) satisfaction indexes is 62.90 – above the satisfaction level, higher than that of 2013 and 2014, but slightly lower than that of 2012. All the 35 cities have scored over 60 in the index, while there were 21 cities in 2014 and only 12 cities in 2013. That is to say, public order has greatly improved since 2013. Despite all this, the index of 2015 is lower than that of 2012, and the average is still on the low side. It shows more need to be done to improve urban security. Graph 5.21 well illustrates such a trend.

According to the survey, cities ranked top 10 on the list of public order satisfaction indexes are: Hangzhou (1), Jinan (2), Wuhan (3), Shanghai (4), Beijing (5), Guiyang (6), Dalian (7), Harbin (8), Chongqing (9) and Qingdao

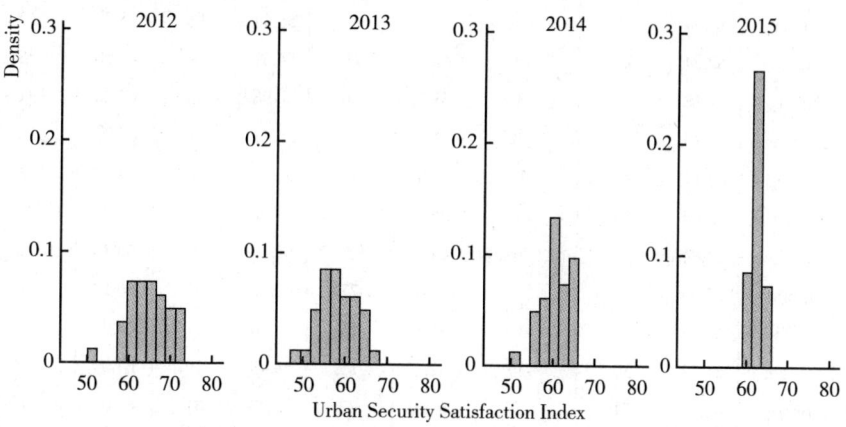

Graph 5.21: A Histogram of the 2012–2015 Urban Security Satisfaction Indexes

Quality-of-life Sub-Indexes of the 35 Chinese Cities

Table 5.11 Urban Security Satisfaction Indexes of the 35 Chinese Cities

City	2015			2014		2013		2012	
	Score	Ranking	Places risen	Score	Ranking	Score	Ranking	Score	Ranking
Hangzhou	65.98	1	2	65.20	3	65.42	3	70.99	4
Jinan	64.60	2	3	64.82	5	65.41	4	73.34	1
Wuhan	64.23	3	25	57.77	28	54.83	28	61.13	26
Shanghai	64.08	4	6	63.26	10	64.12	5	68.48	10
Beijing	63.97	5	9	61.56	14	60.58	12	66.82	13
Guiyang	63.92	6	26	56.73	32	47.32	35	50.95	35
Dalian	63.75	7	-3	65.07	4	62.22	9	70.09	5
Harbin	63.73	8	4	63.07	12	59.25	14	63.03	21
Chongqing	63.62	9	8	60.53	17	56.43	26	71.83	2
Qingdao	63.57	10	-8	65.51	2	65.55	2	71.11	3
Ningbo	63.57	11	0	63.21	11	62.08	10	69.05	7
Nanchang	63.28	12	18	56.80	30	52.55	33	58.74	32
Hohhot	63.21	13	16	57.38	29	50.73	34	62.86	22
Xining	63.16	14	9	59.60	23	56.94	21	66.20	14
Changsha	63.02	15	19	55.42	34	55.73	27	60.23	29
Zhengzhou	62.96	16	5	60.20	21	56.66	24	60.95	28
Chengdu	62.92	17	7	59.56	24	59.69	13	67.40	12
Kunming	62.92	18	17	51.15	35	53.75	30	57.53	34
Xiamen	62.85	19	-18	66.00	1	66.67	1	69.19	6
Taiyuan	62.60	20	0	60.32	20	59.22	15	60.15	31
Tianjin	62.54	21	-12	63.51	9	58.64	18	65.08	17
Haikou	62.24	22	-4	60.44	18	54.61	29	62.00	25
Xi'an	62.18	23	3	58.78	26	56.58	25	62.26	23
Fuzhou	62.13	24	-8	61.17	16	58.71	17	65.90	16
Nanjing	62.11	25	-19	64.41	6	63.83	6	68.59	9
Guangzhou	62.08	26	5	56.74	31	57.02	20	62.25	24
Changchun	61.84	27	-20	64.22	7	62.29	8	68.45	11
Nanning	61.83	28	-1	58.37	27	52.75	32	60.19	30
Hefei	61.33	29	-14	61.18	15	61.00	11	64.03	19
Shenyang	61.32	30	-17	62.37	13	58.43	19	64.09	18
Lanzhou	61.03	31	-9	59.63	22	52.97	31	63.07	20
Shenzhen	60.98	32	-13	60.39	19	58.98	16	61.11	27

Blue Book of Quality of Life in Cities

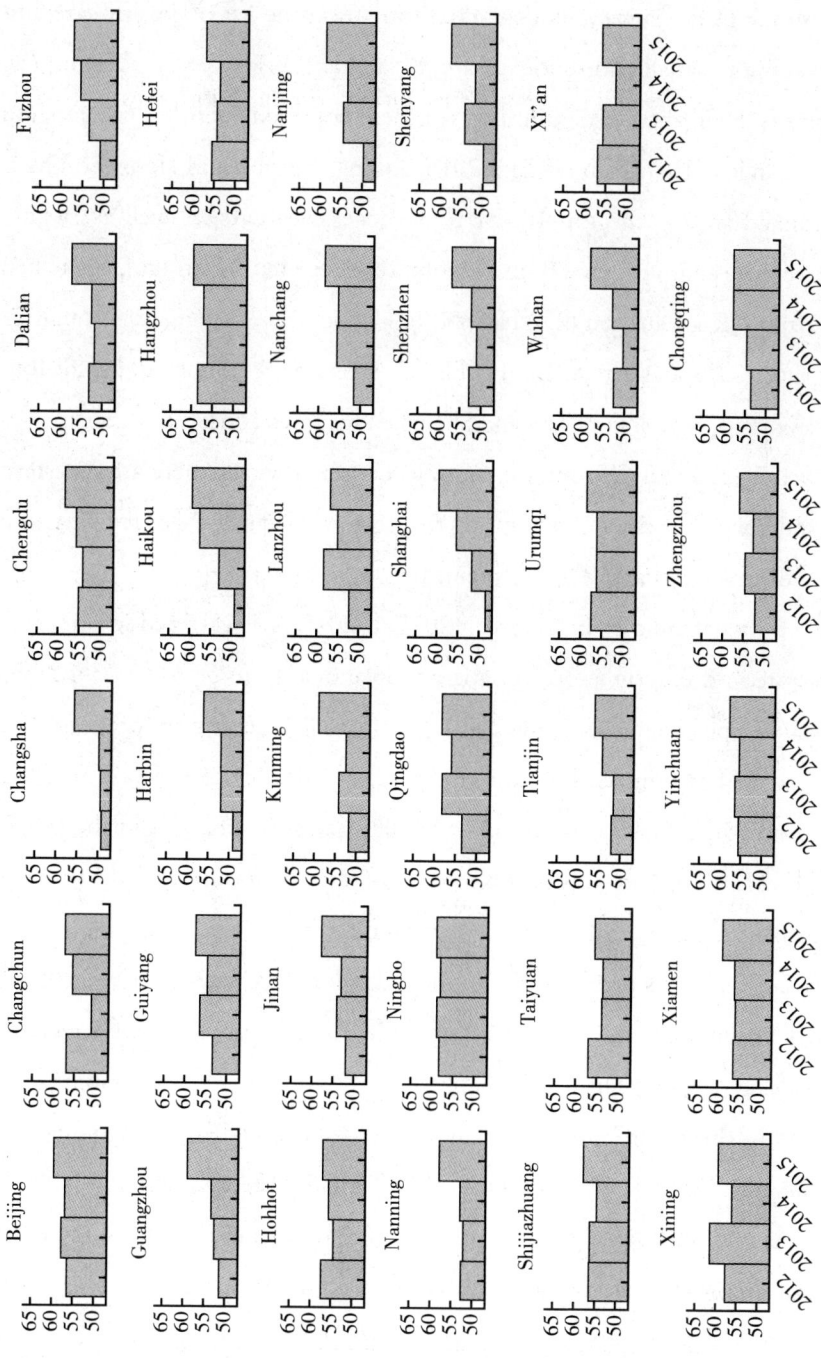

Graph 5.20: A Bar Chart of the 2012–2015 Health Care and Elderly Support Satisfaction Indexes of the 35 Cities

Quality-of-life Sub-Indexes of the 35 Chinese Cities

According to the survey, cities ranked top 10 on the list of health care and elderly support satisfaction indexes are: Shanghai (1), Haikou (2), Xining (3), Ningbo (4), Hangzhou (5), Kunming (6), Beijing (7), Xiamen (8), Guangzhou (9) and Nanjing (10). From 2012 to 2015, Xining, Ningbo and Hangzhou have been ranked among the top 10 for four successive years, as well as Beijing for three consecutive years. The bottom 10 cities are: Dalian (26), Shenzhen (27), Fuzhou (28), Lanzhou (29), Hefei (30), Harbin (31), Tianjin (32), Xi'an (33), Zhengzhou (34) and Taiyuan (35). Harbin has been on the bottom 10 list for four successive years, as well as Dalian and Shenzhen for three consecutive years.

Viewed by regional distribution, among the top 10 cities, there are 8 eastern cities and 2 western cities. And among the bottom 10 cities, there are 4 eastern cities, 4 central cities and 2 western cities.

Viewed by dynamic changes, from 2012 to 2015, the weighted averages of health care and elderly support satisfaction indexes are 53.61, 54.34, 54.80 and 58.04 respectively. Generally speaking, the index has kept improving. The lowest score has increased as well, from 48.93 (2012), to 50.45 (2013), 52.15 (2014) and 55.72 (2015). Graph 5.20 well illustrates the changes in the health care and elderly support satisfaction indexes of the 35 cities from 2012 to 2015. Viewed by cities, Shanghai, Haikou, Guangzhou, Changsha, Chongqing, Fuzhou and Harbin have experienced a rise in the index for three successive years. Cities with a dramatic rise in the ranking are: Kunming (26), Shenyang (17), Guangzhou (16), Nanjing (13), Shanghai (13), Changsha (12), Wuhan (11) and Nanning (10). Cities with a drastic drop in the ranking are: Changchun (-19), Chongqing (-18), Fuzhou (-15), Hohhot (-13), Taiyuan (-13), Tianjin (-12) and Lanzhou (-11).

The second sub-index of the social security satisfaction index is public order, or urban security. Table 5.11 lists the 2015 urban security (public order) satisfaction indexes of the 35 cities.

Continued table

City	2015			2014		2013		2012	
	Score	Ranking	Places risen	Score	Ranking	Score	Ranking	Score	Ranking
Fuzhou	57.07	28	-15	55.73	13	53.75	24	51.30	30
Lanzhou	56.98	29	-11	54.89	18	58.33	3	52.27	23
Hefei	56.89	30	-9	53.79	21	54.42	19	55.58	13
Harbin	56.85	31	2	52.58	33	52.47	27	49.52	33
Tianjin	56.19	32	-12	54.33	20	51.64	33	52.06	24
Xi'an	56.15	33	-5	52.90	28	55.96	11	57.04	8
Zhengzhou	56.13	34	-3	52.73	31	54.82	14	52.38	22
Taiyuan	55.72	35	-13	53.74	22	54.05	23	57.18	7
Average		58.04			54.80		54.34		53.61

As is shown in Table 5.10, the weighted average of health care and elderly support satisfaction indexes is 58.04 – above the satisfaction level and a significant improvement compared with the results of the previous surveys. In 2015, all the 35 cities have scored over 55 in the index, while in 2014, there were only 16 cities. That is to say, there are far more cities scoring over 55 this year. Generally speaking, the health care and elderly support satisfaction index has kept improving. Graph 5.19 well illustrates such a trend.

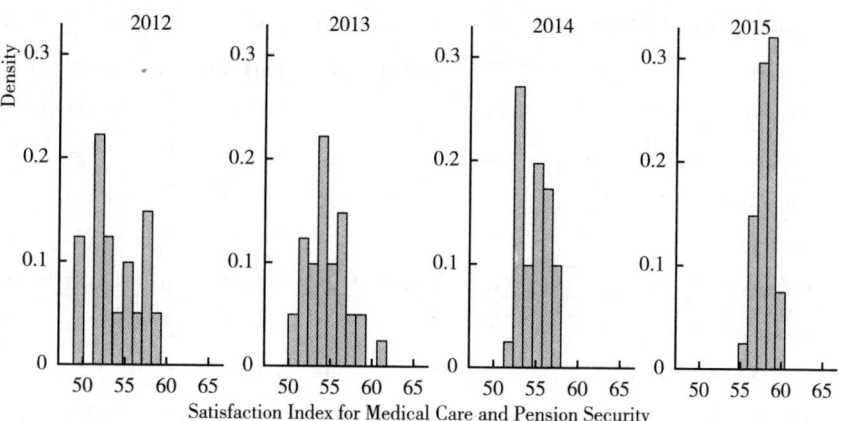

Graph 5.19: A Histogram of the 2012–2015 Health Care and Elderly Support Satisfaction Indexes

Quality-of-life Sub-Indexes of the 35 Chinese Cities

Table 5.10 Health Care and Elderly Support Satisfaction Indexes of the 35 Chinese Cities

City	2015			2014		2013		2012	
	Score	Ranking	Places risen	Score	Ranking	Score	Ranking	Score	Ranking
Shanghai	59.79	1	13	55.62	14	51.96	32	48.93	35
Haikou	59.65	2	1	57.68	3	53.11	25	49.50	34
Xining	59.60	3	4	56.34	7	61.67	1	57.87	3
Ningbo	59.31	4	-3	58.02	1	58.96	2	58.24	2
Hangzhou	59.23	5	-1	57.14	4	56.11	10	58.37	1
Kunming	59.21	6	26	52.62	32	54.42	18	51.76	27
Beijing	59.17	7	2	56.15	9	57.29	5	55.71	12
Xiamen	59.05	8	3	56.06	11	55.83	12	56.40	10
Guangzhou	59.01	9	16	53.32	25	52.37	29	51.38	29
Nanjing	58.83	10	13	53.73	23	54.61	16	49.74	32
Urumqi	58.76	11	-5	56.37	6	56.36	9	57.57	4
Chengdu	58.70	12	-4	56.23	8	54.40	20	55.26	14
Nanchang	58.61	13	3	55.36	16	55.64	13	51.63	28
Changsha	58.51	14	12	53.05	26	52.45	28	52.05	25
Qingdao	58.51	15	-5	56.09	10	58.19	4	53.42	17
Wuhan	58.33	16	11	53.01	27	50.45	35	52.52	20
Jinan	58.09	17	7	53.44	24	54.24	22	51.96	26
Shenyang	57.88	18	17	52.15	35	54.37	21	50.00	31
Nanning	57.85	19	10	52.85	29	52.11	31	52.47	21
Chongqing	57.84	20	-18	57.75	2	54.79	15	53.74	15
Shijiazhuang	57.78	21	-2	54.79	19	56.39	8	56.55	9
Yinchuan	57.75	22	-7	55.53	15	56.59	7	55.73	11
Guiyang	57.60	23	-6	54.94	17	56.64	6	53.57	16
Changchun	57.44	24	-19	56.73	5	52.90	26	57.22	6
Hohhot	57.34	25	-13	55.73	12	54.53	17	57.50	5
Dalian	57.22	26	4	52.75	30	52.13	30	53.37	18
Shenzhen	57.13	27	7	52.58	34	51.23	34	52.98	19

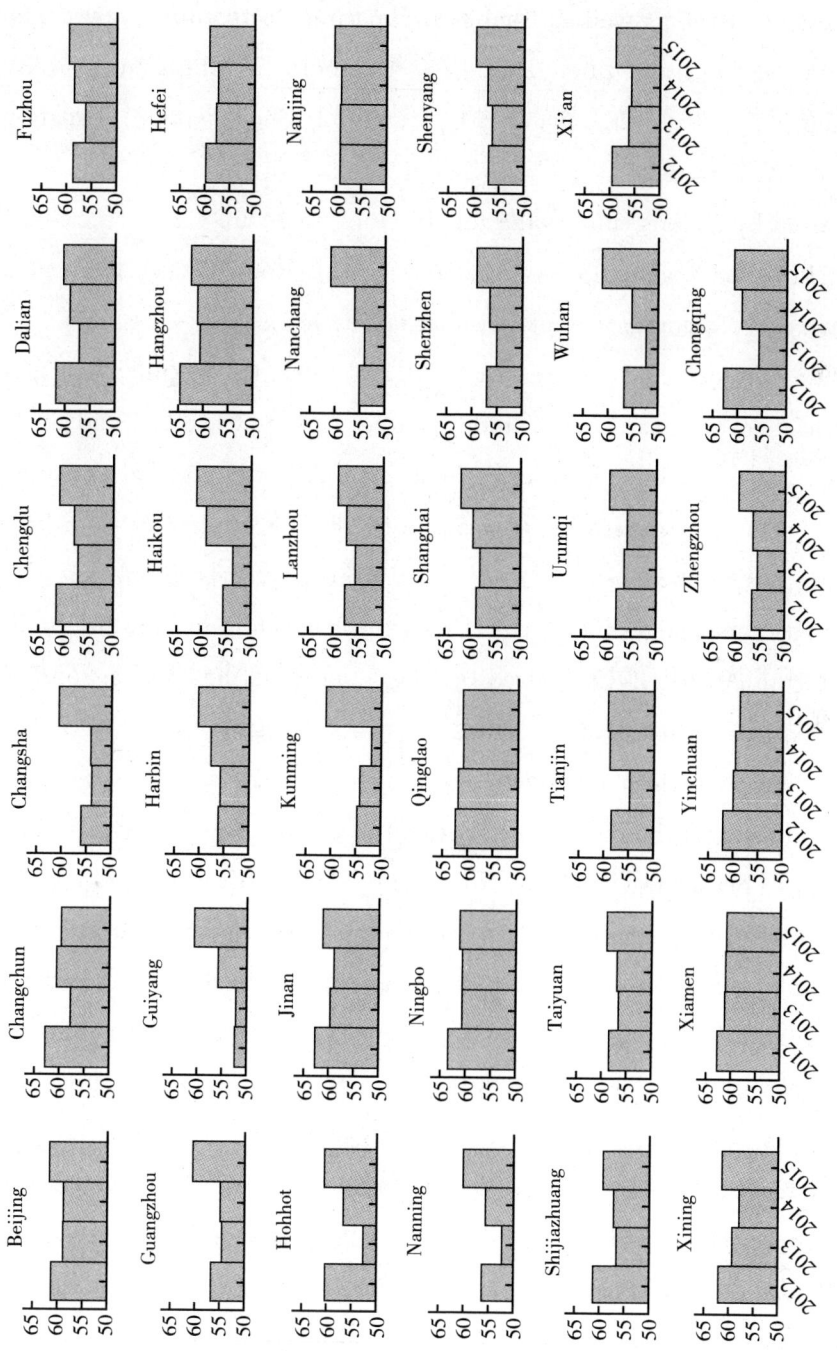

Graph 5.18: A Bar Chart of the 2012–2015 Social Security Subjective Satisfaction Indexes of the 35 Cities

successive years, as well as Shanghai for three consecutive years. The bottom 10 cities are: Zhengzhou (26), Urumqi (27), Shijiazhuang (28), Tianjin (29), Xi'an (30), Taiyuan (31), Hefei (32), Shenzhen (33), Lanzhou (34) and Yinchuan (35).

Viewed by regions, among the top 10 cities, there are 7 eastern cities, 1 central city and 2 western cities. And among the bottom 10 cities, there are 3 eastern cities, 3 central cities and 4 western cities.

Viewed by dynamic changes, from 2012 to 2015, the weighted averages of social security satisfaction indexes are 59.19, 56.64, 57.87 and 60.47 respectively. Despite the drop in 2013 and 2014, the index goes back up again in 2015. And the lowest scores are 52.26, 51.98, 51.88 and 58.89 from 2012 to 2015, which fluctuated along with the weighted averages. Graph 5.18 well illustrates the changes in the social security satisfaction indexes of the 35 cities from 2012 to 2015. Viewed by cities, 23 out of the 35 cities (65.7%) have experienced a rise in the index for two successive years (2013-2015), which are: Hangzhou, Shanghai, Ningbo, Wuhan, Haikou, Nanchang, Chengdu, Changsha, Guiyang, Chongqing, Guangzhou, Dalian, Harbin, Hohhot, Nanning, Fuzhou, Shenyang, Zhengzhou, Shijiazhuang, Tianjin, Taiyuan, Shenzhen and Lanzhou. Cities with a dramatic rise in the ranking are: Kunming (27), Wuhan (25), Changsha (20), Nanchang (15), Guiyang (15), Beijing (11) and Xining (11). Cities with a drastic drop in the ranking are: Yinchuan (-29), Changchun (-18), Tianjin (-17), Lanzhou (-14) and Hefei (-13).

The satisfaction index of social security consists of a health care and elderly support satisfaction index and a public order satisfaction index. Survey results of the two sub-indexes are shown in Table 5.10 and 5.11.

Hangzhou has ranked No. 1 in 2012, 2014 and 2015 and No. 3 in 2013. It shows that both the health care and elderly support satisfaction index and the public order satisfaction index of Hangzhou have been quite stable. Although its health care and elderly support satisfaction index is not among the top, its public order satisfaction index has ranked No. 1, resulting in the excellent performance of its social security satisfaction index (No.1). Generally speaking, improvements in the health care and elderly support satisfaction index and the public order satisfaction index will lead to the rise of the social security satisfaction index. Graph 5.17 well illustrates such a trend.

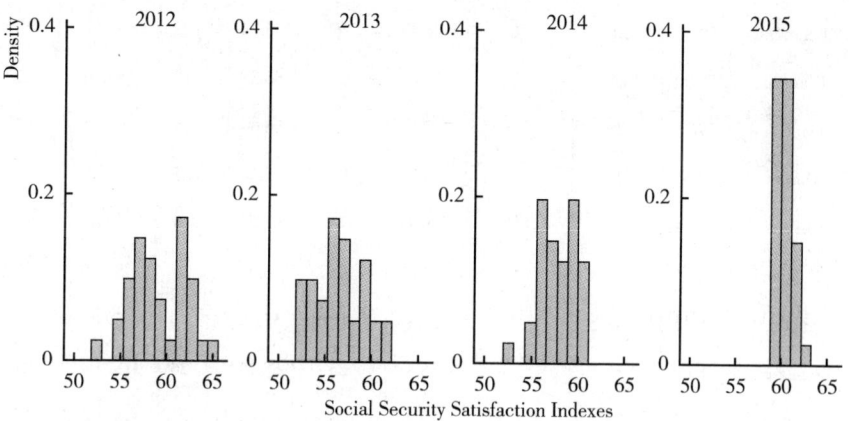

Graph 5.17: A Histogram of the 2012–2015 Social Security Satisfaction Indexes

According to the survey, cities ranked top 10 on the list of social security satisfaction (subjective) indexes are: Hangzhou (1), Shanghai (2), Beijing (3), Ningbo (4), Xining (5), Jinan (6), Wuhan (7), Kunming (8), Qingdao (9) and Xiamen (10). It should be noted that Hangzhou, Ningbo, Jinan, Qingdao and Xiamen have been ranked among the top 10 for four

Quality-of-life Sub-Indexes of the 35 Chinese Cities

Continued table

City	2015			2014		2013		2012	
	Score	Ranking	Places risen	Score	Ranking	Score	Ranking	Score	Ranking
Guangzhou	60.54	17	16	55.03	33	54.70	27	56.81	27
Dalian	60.49	18	-5	58.91	13	57.18	13	61.73	10
Nanjing	60.47	19	-9	59.07	10	59.22	8	59.17	17
Harbin	60.29	20	-2	57.83	18	55.86	21	56.27	30
Hohhot	60.28	21	3	56.55	24	52.63	33	60.18	14
Nanning	59.84	22	9	55.61	31	52.43	34	56.33	29
Changchun	59.64	23	-18	60.47	5	57.59	12	62.83	3
Fuzhou	59.60	24	-9	58.45	15	56.23	20	58.60	20
Shenyang	59.60	25	-4	57.26	21	56.40	18	57.04	25
Zhengzhou	59.55	26	0	56.47	26	55.74	22	56.67	28
Urumqi	59.50	27	1	56.00	28	56.57	17	58.06	22
Shijiazhuang	59.38	28	-6	57.05	22	56.64	15	61.24	13
Tianjin	59.36	29	-17	58.92	12	55.14	25	58.57	21
Xi'an	59.16	30	-1	55.84	29	56.27	19	59.65	16
Taiyuan	59.16	31	-8	57.03	23	56.63	16	58.66	19
Hefei	59.11	32	-13	57.48	19	57.71	11	59.80	15
Shenzhen	59.06	33	-8	56.48	25	55.11	26	57.04	24
Lanzhou	59.01	34	-14	57.26	20	55.65	23	57.67	23
Yinchuan	58.89	35	-29	59.74	6	60.03	5	62.24	8
Average	60.47			57.87		56.64		59.19	

As is shown in Table 5.9, the weighted average of social security satisfaction indexes is 60.47 – above the satisfaction level and a significant improvement compared with the results of the previous surveys. This year, 21 out of the 35 cities have scored over 60, while last year, there were only 5 cities. It should be noted that

5.4 Social Security Indexes

5.4.1 Satisfaction Indexes of Social Security Indexes

In the QLICC system, the satisfaction index of social security comes from the weighted average of health care and elderly support satisfaction index and urban security satisfaction index. Same as before, the indexes are obtained through a questionnaire survey by assigning values to survey answers. Table 5.9 lists the social security satisfaction indexes of the 35 cities, along with their respective rankings.

Table 5.9 Social Security Satisfaction Indexes of the 35 Chinese Cities

City	2015			2014		2013		2012	
	Score	Ranking	Places risen	Score	Ranking	Score	Ranking	Score	Ranking
Hangzhou	62.60	1	0	61.17	1	60.76	3	64.68	1
Shanghai	61.94	2	5	59.44	7	58.04	10	58.71	18
Beijing	61.57	3	11	58.85	14	58.94	9	61.27	12
Ningbo	61.44	4	0	60.61	4	60.52	4	63.65	2
Xining	61.38	5	11	57.97	16	59.31	7	62.04	9
Jinan	61.34	6	3	59.13	9	59.82	6	62.65	6
Wuhan	61.28	7	25	55.39	32	52.64	32	56.83	26
Kunming	61.06	8	27	51.88	35	54.09	30	54.65	34
Qingdao	61.04	9	-6	60.80	3	61.87	1	62.26	7
Xiamen	60.95	10	-8	61.03	2	61.25	2	62.79	4
Haikou	60.95	11	0	59.06	11	53.86	31	55.75	32
Nanchang	60.94	12	15	56.08	27	54.09	28	55.18	33
Chengdu	60.81	13	4	57.90	17	57.05	14	61.33	11
Changsha	60.77	14	20	54.23	34	54.09	29	56.14	31
Guiyang	60.76	15	15	55.83	30	51.98	35	52.26	35
Chongqing	60.73	16	-8	59.14	8	55.61	24	62.78	5

Quality-of-life Sub-Indexes of the 35 Chinese Cities

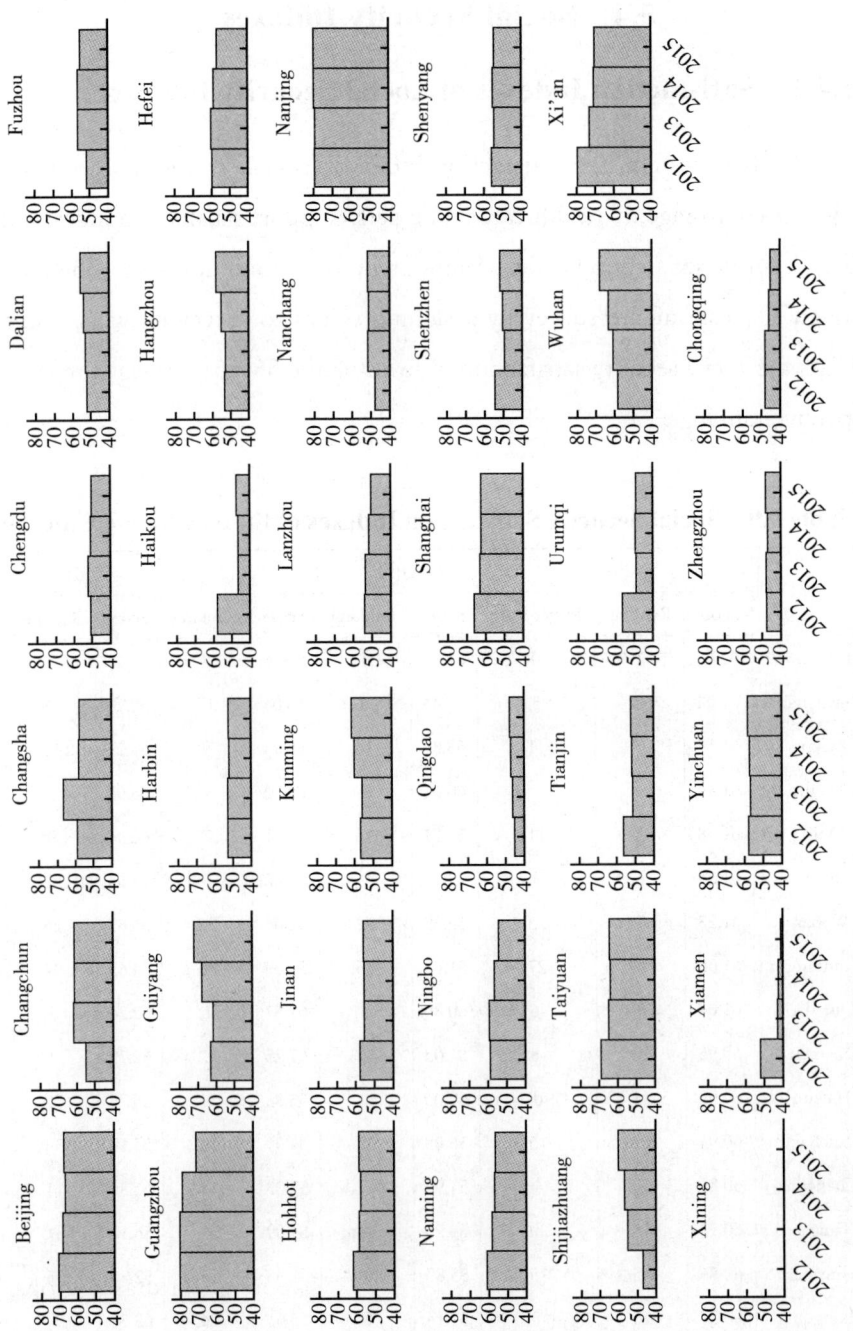

Graph 5.16: A Bar Chart of the 2012–2015 Human Capital Objective Indexes of the 35 Cities

As is shown by the calculation result, cities ranked top 10 on the list of human capital objective indexes are: Nanjing (1), Guiyang (2), Guangzhou (3), Xi'an (4), Beijing (5), Wuhan (6), Taiyuan (7), Shanghai (8), Kunming (9) and Changchun (10). Among the top 10 cities, Nanjing, Guiyang, Guangzhou, Xi'an, Beijing, Taiyuan and Shanghai have been on the top 10 list for four successive years, as well as Wuhan and Changchun for three consecutive years. And the bottom 10 cities are: Nanchang (26), Lanzhou (27), Chengdu (28), Urumqi (29), Qingdao (30), Zhengzhou (31), Haikou (32), Chongqing (33), Xiamen (34) and Xining (35). Xining, Xiamen, Chongqing, Zhengzhou and Qingdao have ranked among the bottom 10 in the past four years, as well as Haikou and Urumqi in the past three years.

Viewed by regional distribution, among the top 10 cities, the ratio of eastern to central to western cities is 4:3:3. And among the bottom 10 cities, the ratio is 3:2:5. Among the top 10 cities, the regional difference is insignificant for the human capital objective index, while among the bottom 10 cities, the difference is quite obvious, since 50% of them are western cities.

From 2012 to 2015, the weighted averages of human capital objective indexes are 57.66, 57.78, 57.33 and 57.34 respectively, with no significant difference among them. As is shown in Graph 5.16, Dalian, Qingdao, Shijiazhuang and Wuhan have experienced a growth for three successive years, while Nanning, Lanzhou, Xiamen, Xi'an and Changqing have seen a drop in the indicator over the same period. Scores of the rest of the cities have fluctuated over the past four years. Viewed by rankings, Hangzhou has the most significant improvement, rising 7 places from No. 21 in 2014 to No. 14 in 2015. Cities with an obvious rise in the ranking also include: Shijiazhuang (4), Dalian (4) and Shenzhen (3). Hefei and Ningbo have the most drastic drops, both falling 5 places only. The ranking of Changsha (-3) has dropped as well.

Quality-of-life Sub-Indexes of the 35 Chinese Cities

Continued table

City	2015			2014		2013		2012	
	Score	Ranking	Places risen	Score	Ranking	Score	Ranking	Score	Ranking
Chengdu	49.95	28	-1	50.77	27	51.79	26	50.62	29
Urumqi	49.26	29	0	49.40	29	49.17	29	56.49	19
Qingdao	48.10	30	1	47.37	31	46.32	33	45.56	34
Zhengzhou	48.03	31	-1	47.47	30	48.02	31	47.50	32
Haikou	47.14	32	0	46.59	32	46.39	32	58.08	14
Chongqing	45.26	33	0	46.15	33	48.03	30	48.28	31
Xiamen	41.32	34	0	42.54	34	43.09	34	52.32	26
Xining	40.00	35	0	40.00	35	40.00	35	39.99	35
Average	57.34			57.33		57.78		57.66	

According to the calculation result, the 2015 weighted average of human capital objective indexes is 57.34, which is above the satisfaction level and about the same as the results of the previous three surveys. Among the 35 cities, 27 have scored over 50 (above the satisfaction level), while 8 have scored below 50 (below the satisfaction level). Nanjing has ranked No. 1 and scored 80 which is in the "very satisfied" range (76-100 points). Generally speaking, the objective indexes of human capital have remained roughly unchanged. Graph 5.15 well illustrates such a trend.

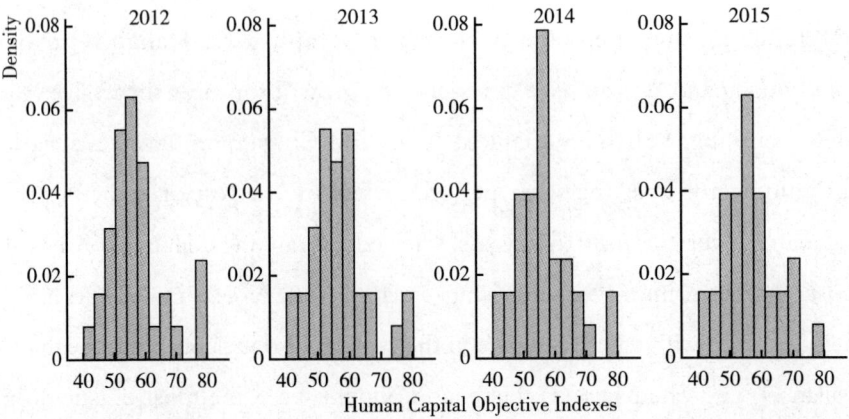

Graph 5.15: A Histogram of the 2012–2015 Human Capital Objective Indexes

5.3.2 Objective Indexes (Social and Economic Data Indexes) of Human Capital

In the QLICC system, the human capital objective index of each city is obtained by calculating two secondary indicators (educational provision index and ratio of education, culture and entertainment expenditures). Table 5.8 lists the result of the human capital objective indexes of the 35 cities.

Table 5.8 Human Capital Objective Indexes of the 35 Chinese Cities

City	2015			2014		2013		2012	
	Score	Ranking	Places risen	Score	Ranking	Score	Ranking	Score	Ranking
Nanjing	80.00	1	0	80.00	1	79.73	2	79.52	2
Guiyang	71.66	2	2	67.62	4	61.65	9	62.79	7
Guangzhou	71.29	3	-1	78.68	2	80.00	1	80.01	1
Xi'an	70.29	4	-1	70.94	3	72.94	3	79.42	3
Beijing	67.89	5	0	67.51	5	68.76	4	70.96	4
Wuhan	67.81	6	1	63.45	7	60.89	10	58.52	13
Taiyuan	64.28	7	-1	63.84	6	64.68	6	69.05	5
Shanghai	62.68	8	0	62.25	8	63.03	7	66.15	6
Kunming	61.64	9	1	59.92	10	56.19	17	57.20	17
Changchun	61.19	10	-1	61.22	9	61.79	8	54.72	21
Shijiazhuang	59.99	11	4	57.15	15	55.22	19	47.11	33
Hohhot	58.65	12	1	57.59	13	58.83	13	61.75	8
Yinchuan	58.23	13	1	57.17	14	56.57	15	57.57	16
Hangzhou	58.16	14	7	55.18	21	52.89	23	53.38	24
Changsha	57.50	15	-3	57.92	12	66.65	5	58.80	11
Hefei	57.15	16	-5	58.70	11	60.28	11	59.72	10
Nanning	56.49	17	-1	56.98	16	58.27	14	60.93	9
Dalian	55.84	18	4	53.98	22	52.62	24	52.09	27
Jinan	55.51	19	0	55.33	19	55.28	18	57.66	15
Fuzhou	55.01	20	-2	56.40	18	56.38	16	51.09	28
Shenyang	54.56	21	-1	55.32	20	54.67	20	55.90	20
Ningbo	54.15	22	-5	56.55	17	59.09	12	58.62	12
Harbin	52.53	23	0	52.17	23	52.90	22	52.83	25
Tianjin	52.24	24	0	51.76	24	51.63	27	56.58	18
Shenzhen	52.08	25	3	50.48	28	49.79	28	54.43	22
Nanchang	52.06	26	0	51.40	26	51.88	25	48.30	30
Lanzhou	50.44	27	-2	51.73	25	53.68	21	54.33	23

Quality-of-life Sub-Indexes of the 35 Chinese Cities

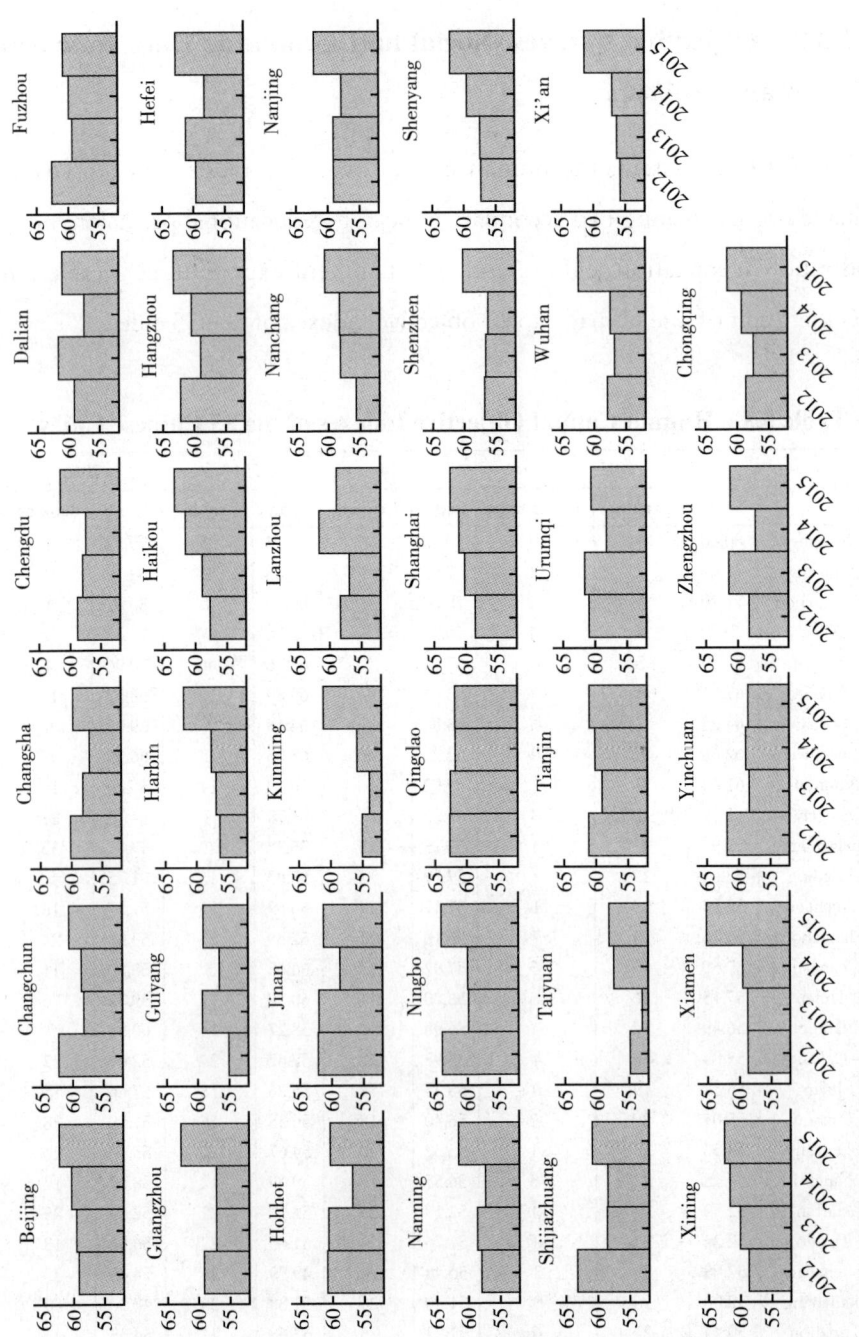

Graph 5.14: A Bar Chart of the 2012–2015 Human Capital Satisfaction Indexes of the 35 cities

According to the survey, cities ranked top 10 on the list of human capital satisfaction indexes are: Xiamen (1), Ningbo (2), Hangzhou (3), Haikou (4), Guangzhou (5), Hefei (6), Xining (7), Shanghai (8), Wuhan (9) and Beijing (10). Ningbo has been on the top 10 list for four successive years, as well as Xining and Shanghai for three consecutive years. And the bottom 10 cities are: Shijiazhuang (26), Urumqi (27), Nanchang (28), Hohhot (29), Shenzhen (30), Changsha (31), Guiyang (32), Lanzhou (33), Yinchuan (34) and Taiyuan (35). Shenzhen has ranked among the bottom 10 in the past four years.

Viewed by regional distribution, among the top 10 cities, the ratio of eastern to central to western cities is 7:2:1. And among the bottom 10 cities, the ratio is 2:3:5. Accordingly, we may conclude that residents' satisfaction with human capital is highly regional.

Viewed by dynamic changes, from 2012 to 2015, the weighted averages of human capital satisfaction indexes are 59.42, 58.89, 58.98 and 61.73 respectively. Graph 5.14 well illustrates the changes in the human capital satisfaction indexes of the 35 cities from 2012 to 2015. Viewed by cities, Beijing, Harbin, Haikou, Nanchang, Shanghai, Xining, Xiamen, Shenyang and Xi'an have experienced a growth for three successive years, while Qingdao has seen a drop in the indicator for three consecutive years. Scores of the rest have fluctuated over the past four years. Viewed by rankings, Guangzhou has the most significant improvement, rising 18 places from No. 23 in 2014 to No. 5 in 2015. Cities with an obvious rise in the ranking also include: Wuhan (17), Hefei (14), Chengdu (12), Xi'an (12), Kunming (12) and Xiamen (11). Lanzhou has the most drastic drop – falling 31 places from No. 2 in 2014 to No. 33 in 2015. Cities with an evident drop in the ranking also include: Yinchuan (-19), Tianjin (-15), Fuzhou (-15), Qingdao (-13) and Taiyuan (-11).

Quality-of-life Sub-Indexes of the 35 Chinese Cities

Continued table

City	2015			2014		2013		2012	
	Score	Ranking	Places risen	Score	Ranking	Score	Ranking	Score	Ranking
Urumqi	60.80	27	-9	58.54	18	61.86	3	61.18	10
Nanchang	60.78	28	-9	58.51	19	58.45	23	56.10	32
Hohhot	60.63	29	1	57.29	30	60.96	7	61.07	11
Shenzhen	60.54	30	4	56.75	34	57.03	32	57.34	29
Changsha	59.76	31	1	57.26	32	58.20	24	60.38	12
Guiyang	59.50	32	1	56.98	33	59.60	12	55.48	33
Lanzhou	59.09	33	-31	61.74	2	57.20	30	58.52	23
Yinchuan	58.63	34	-19	59.13	15	58.52	22	61.98	8
Taiyuan	58.34	35	-11	57.70	24	53.49	35	55.20	35
Average	61.73			58.98		58.89		59.42	

According to the survey, the 2015 weighted average of human capital satisfaction indexes is 61.73, which is an improvement compared with the previous three surveys, for the score of this index is over 60 for the first time, although it never goes beyond the "satisfaction" range. Among the 35 cities, 30 have scored over 60. No city has scored over 70, but the best score is higher than that of last year. Xiamen ranks No. 1, scoring 65.60. Generally speaking, the satisfaction indexes of human capital have improved steadily since 2013. Graph 5.13 well illustrates such a trend.

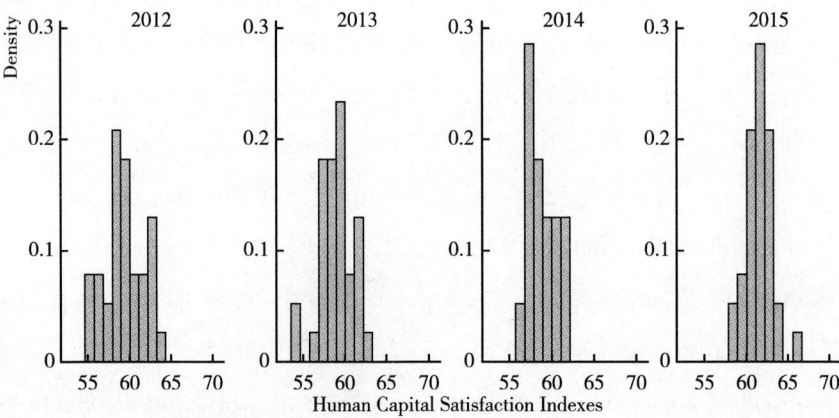

Graph 5.13: A Histogram of the 2012-2015 Human Capital Satisfaction Indexes

5.3 Human Capital Indexes

5.3.1 Satisfaction Indexes of Human Capital

The satisfaction indexes of human capital are obtained through a questionnaire survey by assigning values to survey answers. Table 5.7 lists the 2015 survey results of human capital satisfaction indexes of the 35 cities.

Table 5.7 Human Capital Satisfaction Indexes of the 35 Chinese Cities

City	2015			2014		2013		2012	
	Score	Ranking	Places risen	Score	Ranking	Score	Ranking	Score	Ranking
Xiamen	65.60	1	11	59.75	12	59.03	18	59.01	19
Ningbo	64.32	2	6	60.24	8	60.14	9	64.19	1
Hangzhou	63.43	3	3	60.57	6	59.24	16	62.38	6
Haikou	63.37	4	-1	61.69	3	59.11	17	58.00	27
Guangzhou	63.03	5	18	57.71	23	57.59	28	59.43	14
Hefei	62.90	6	14	58.50	20	61.37	6	59.71	13
Xining	62.48	7	-3	61.59	4	60.09	10	58.80	21
Shanghai	62.44	8	-3	61.26	5	60.35	8	58.79	22
Wuhan	62.43	9	17	57.67	26	57.09	31	58.09	26
Beijing	62.36	10	-3	60.47	7	59.68	11	59.33	16
Shenyang	62.36	11	0	59.78	11	57.79	26	57.61	28
Nanjing	62.27	12	9	58.10	21	59.29	15	59.36	15
Harbin	62.10	13	9	58.01	22	57.23	29	56.76	30
Qingdao	61.91	14	-13	61.84	1	62.61	1	62.62	5
Chengdu	61.86	15	12	57.66	27	58.17	25	59.14	18
Chongqing	61.70	16	-3	59.56	13	57.74	27	58.83	20
Changchun	61.58	17	-3	59.48	14	58.90	19	63.37	2
Nanning	61.52	18	7	57.69	25	58.73	21	58.18	25
Xi'an	61.46	19	12	57.29	31	56.65	33	56.19	31
Jinan	61.39	20	-4	58.98	16	61.99	2	62.20	7
Zhengzhou	61.29	21	7	57.51	28	61.54	5	58.45	24
Dalian	61.20	22	7	57.45	29	61.67	4	59.20	17
Kunming	61.19	23	12	56.15	35	54.33	34	55.45	34
Tianjin	61.10	24	-15	60.20	9	59.30	14	61.27	9
Fuzhou	61.02	25	-15	60.13	10	59.60	13	62.72	4
Shijiazhuang	60.99	26	-9	58.67	17	58.86	20	63.31	3

Quality-of-life Sub-Indexes of the 35 Chinese Cities

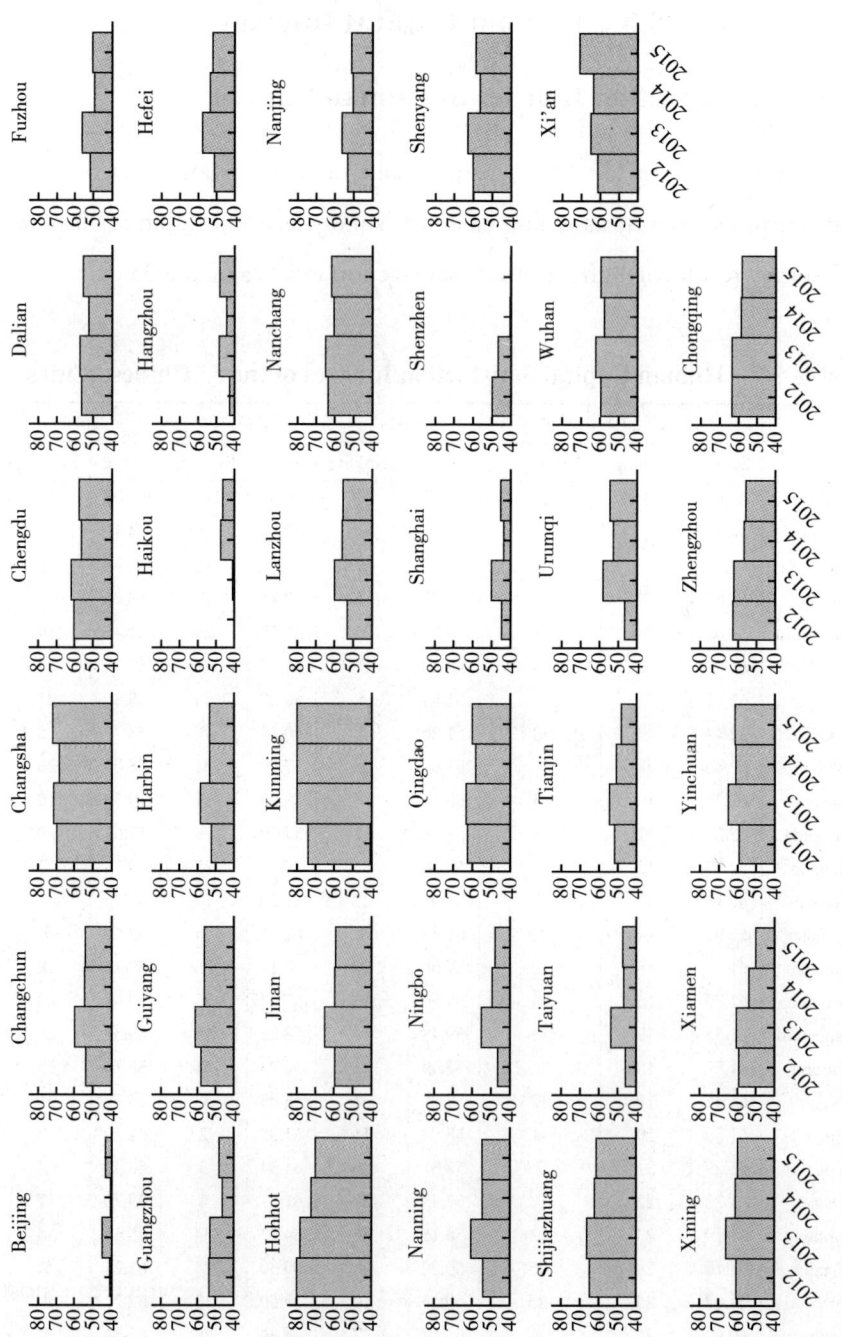

Graph 5.12: A Bar Chart of the 2012–2015 Living Costs Objective Indexes of the 35 Cities

the rest 8 cities have ranked among the bottom 10 in the past four years. That is to say, the living costs in these cities have remained the highest among all the 35 cities. In 2015, Xiamen is on the bottom 10 list for the first time. Tianjin has ranked No.25 for two years and among the bottom 10 for the other two years. Fuzhou had been on the bottom 10 list from 2012 to 2014, while in 2015, it is out of the list for the first time and ranks No. 25.

Viewed by regional distribution, among the top 10 cities, there are 2 eastern cities, 3 central cities and 5 western cities. And among the bottom 10 cities, there are 9 eastern cities and 1 central city. It shows the living costs are absolutely higher in eastern cities than in western cities.

Viewed by dynamic changes, from 2012 to 2015, the weighted averages of living costs objective indexes are 56.10, 58.67, 53.84 and 54.58 respectively. There was a significant drop in 2014 and a slight rise in 2015. The lowest score has remained roughly unchanged. In 2012, the lowest score was 39.97. And in 2013, 2014 and 2015, it has stayed at 40.

Graph 5.12 well illustrates the changes in the living costs objective indexes of the 35 cities from 2012 to 2015. Viewed by cities, Hohhot, Zhengzhou and Shenzhen have experienced a drop in the index and a rise in the living costs for three successive years. And 16 cities have had the same experience for two consecutive years, which are: Hohhot, Shijiazhuang, Xining, Jinan, Chongqing, Guiyang, Zhengzhou, Lanzhou, Nanning, Changchun, Harbin, Hefei, Xiamen, Tianjin, Ningbo and Shenzhen. Viewed by rankings, there is seldom any change. Cities with an obvious rise in the ranking are: Dalian (7), Hangzhou (5) and Kunming. The ranking of Shanghai remains the same. Some cities have experienced a slight drop in the ranking, of which the most significant one is that of Xiamen, falling 4 places only.

Quality-of-life Sub-Indexes of the 35 Chinese Cities

As is shown in Table 5.6, the 2015 weighted average of living costs objective indexes is 54.58, which is above the satisfaction level and an improvement compared with that of 2014. All the 35 cities have scored over 40. And the highest score is 80, same as in the previous two surveys. Generally speaking, the objective indexes of living costs have remained stable with slight drops. Graph 5.11 well illustrates such a trend.

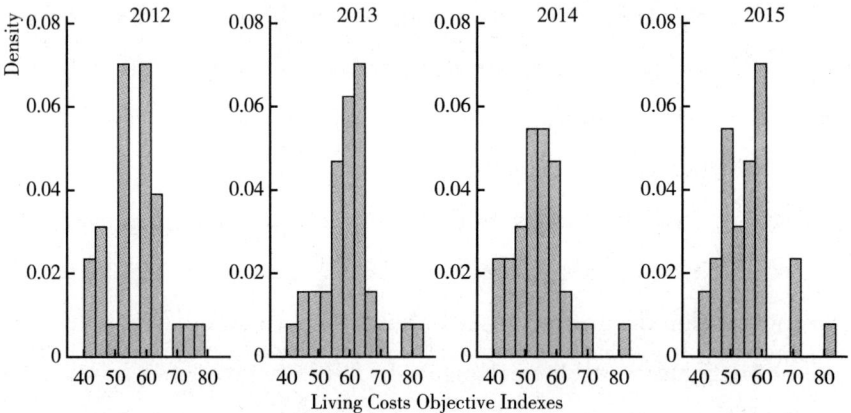

Graph 5.11: A Histogram of the 2012–2015 Living Costs Objective Indexes

According to the survey, cities ranked top 10 on the list of living costs objective indexes are: Kunming (1), Changsha (2), Xi'an (3), Hohhot (4), Yinchuan (5), Shijiazhuang (6), Nanchang (7), Xining (8), Qingdao (9) and Wuhan (10). Kunming has scored 80 and ranked No. 1 for three successive years. And Kunming, Changsha, Xi'an, Hohhot, Shijiazhuang, Nanchang and Xining have been on the top 10 list for four consecutive years. And the bottom 10 cities are: Xiamen (26), Hangzhou (27), Tianjin (28), Guangzhou (29), Ningbo (30), Taiyuan (31), Haikou (32), Shanghai (33), Beijing (34) and Shenzhen (35). Among the bottom 10 cities, except for Tianjin and Xiamen,

Table 5.6 Living Costs Objective Indexes of the 35 Chinese Cities

City	2015			2014		2013		2012	
	Score	Ranking	Places risen	Score	Ranking	Score	Ranking	Score	Ranking
Kunming	80.00	1	0	80.00	1	80.00	1	74.00	2
Changsha	72.10	2	1	68.58	3	71.79	3	69.57	3
Xi'an	71.13	3	1	63.89	4	65.27	6	61.38	9
Hohhot	69.49	4	-2	72.25	2	77.96	2	79.97	1
Yinchuan	61.74	5	2	60.96	7	65.18	7	59.38	14
Shijiazhuang	61.45	6	-1	62.30	5	66.75	4	64.74	4
Nanchang	61.35	7	1	59.61	8	64.81	8	63.36	5
Xining	60.30	8	-2	61.08	6	66.05	5	60.51	10
Qingdao	60.11	9	2	58.38	11	63.40	10	62.34	8
Wuhan	59.73	10	2	57.75	12	62.61	13	59.68	13
Shenyang	59.19	11	4	56.66	15	62.89	12	60.11	11
Jinan	58.94	12	-3	59.29	9	64.59	9	59.19	16
Chongqing	58.35	13	-3	58.89	10	63.36	11	63.34	6
Chengdu	57.21	14	2	55.97	16	61.68	15	60.06	12
Guiyang	56.32	15	-1	56.67	14	61.67	16	58.21	17
Zhengzhou	55.75	16	-3	56.88	13	62.30	14	63.02	7
Dalian	55.35	17	7	52.44	24	57.15	24	56.00	18
Lanzhou	55.20	18	-1	55.50	17	59.93	19	52.63	22
Urumqi	54.76	19	4	52.94	23	58.33	22	46.58	29
Nanning	54.44	20	-2	54.83	18	60.61	18	54.24	19
Changchun	53.84	21	-2	54.10	19	59.57	20	53.58	20
Harbin	53.71	22	-1	53.87	21	58.67	21	52.46	23
Hefei	52.21	23	-3	53.89	20	58.17	23	51.49	26
Nanjing	50.60	24	2	50.28	26	55.70	25	52.18	24
Fuzhou	50.26	25	3	49.00	28	55.43	26	51.01	27
Xiamen	49.57	26	-4	53.86	22	60.70	17	59.22	15
Hangzhou	48.89	27	5	44.41	32	48.73	32	42.50	33
Tianjin	48.50	28	-3	51.02	25	54.63	28	51.83	25
Guangzhou	48.16	29	2	46.32	31	53.15	30	53.24	21
Ningbo	47.78	30	-3	49.75	27	55.19	27	46.16	30
Taiyuan	47.17	31	-1	46.66	30	53.84	29	46.09	31
Haikou	46.31	32	-3	47.74	29	40.00	35	39.97	35
Shanghai	45.57	33	0	43.59	33	50.00	31	44.50	32
Beijing	42.99	34	1	40.00	35	45.17	34	40.80	34
Shenzhen	40.00	35	-1	40.87	34	45.82	33	50.14	28
Average	54.58			53.84		58.67		56.10	

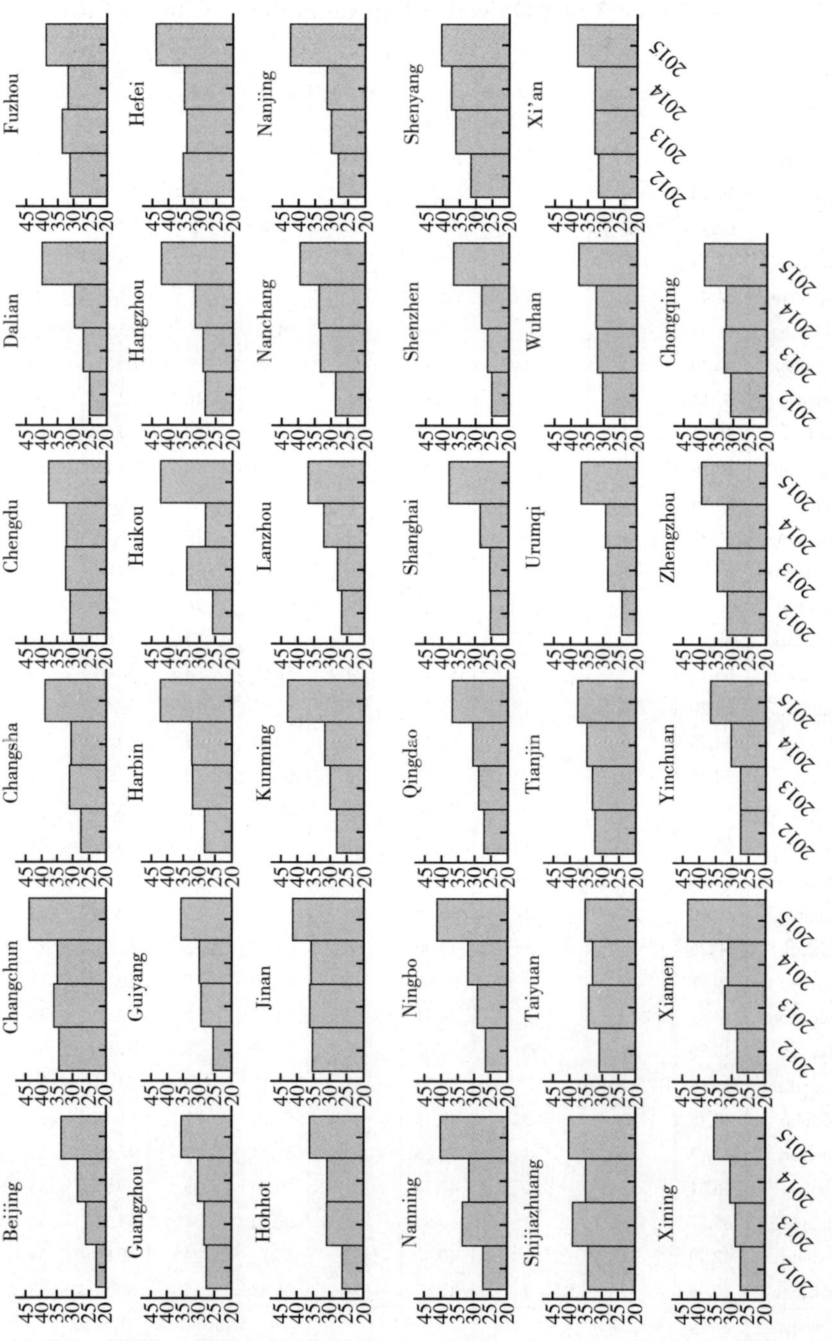

Quality-of-life Sub-Indexes of the 35 Chinese Cities

Graph 5.10: A Bar Chart of the 2012–2015 Living Costs Satisfaction Indexes of the 35 Cities

Viewed by dynamic changes, from 2012 to 2015, the weighted averages of living costs satisfaction indexes are 28.91, 31.22, 31.81 and 38.94 respectively. That is to say, residents' satisfaction toward their living costs has kept improving over the past three years, especially in 2015. The lowest score has gone up as well from 2012 to 2015. In 2012, the lowest score was 23.06. In 2013, it was 25.59. In 2014, it was 28.25. And in 2015, it is 33.76.

Graph 5.10 well illustrates the changes in the living costs satisfaction indexes of the 35 cities from 2012 to 2015. Viewed by cities, 20 out of the 35 cities have experienced a rise in the index for 3 successive years, which are: Kunming, Nanjing, Harbin, Hangzhou, Ningbo, Shenyang, Dalian, Nanchang, Shanghai, Wuhan, Tianjin, Urumqi, Shenzhen, Qingdao, Lanzhou, Hohhot, Guiyang, Guangzhou, Xining and Beijing.

Cities with a dramatic rise in the ranking are: Haikou (29), Xiamen (19), Nanjing (16), Dalian (16), Kunming (12), Hangzhou (12) and Shanghai (11). Cities with a drastic drop in the ranking are: Taiyuan (-26), Tianjin (-18), Wuhan (-13), Lanzhou (-13), Xi'an (-11) and Shenyang (-10).

5.2.2 Objective Indexes (Social and Economic Data Indexes) of Living Costs

In the QLICC system, the living costs objective index of each city is obtained by calculating three secondary indicators (house price index, inflation rate and house-price-to-income ratio). Table 5.6 lists the living costs objective indexes of the 35 cities, along with their respective rankings.

Quality-of-life Sub-Indexes of the 35 Chinese Cities

higher than the best scores of the past three years. Generally speaking, the satisfaction index of living costs has greatly improved this year in all the ranges. Graph 5.9 well illustrates such a trend.

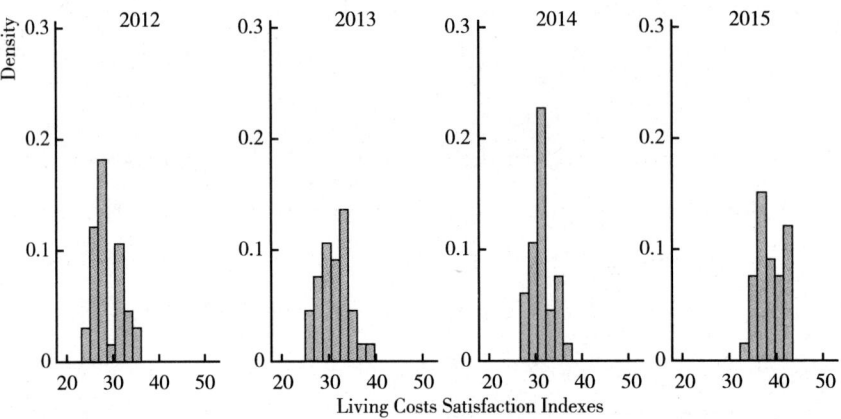

Graph 5.9: A Histogram of the 2012–2015 Living Costs Satisfaction Indexes

According to the survey, cities ranked top 10 on the list of living costs satisfaction indexes are: Changchun (1), Hefei (2), Xiamen (3), Kunming (4), Nanjing (5), Haikou (6), Harbin (7), Hangzhou (8), Ningbo (9) and Jinan (10). Changchun, Hefei and Jinan have been on the top 10 list in the past four years. And the bottom 10 cities are: Shenzhen (26), Qingdao (27), Lanzhou (28), Yinchuan (29), Hohhot (30), Guiyang (31), Guangzhou (32), Xining (33), Taiyuan (34) and Beijing (35). Shenzhen and Beijing have ranked among the bottom 10 for four successive years, as well as Guangzhou and Yinchuan for three consecutive years.

Viewed by regional distribution, among the top 10 cities, there are 6 eastern cities, 3 central cities and 1 western city. And among the bottom 10 cities, there are 4 eastern cities, 1 central city and 5 western cities.

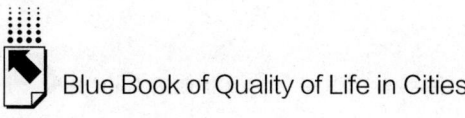
Blue Book of Quality of Life in Cities

Continued table

City	2015			2014		2013		2012	
	Score	Ranking	Places risen	Score	Ranking	Score	Ranking	Score	Ranking
Changsha	38.93	17	9	30.49	26	31.08	19	27.63	21
Fuzhou	38.87	18	1	31.70	19	33.65	9	31.21	9
Chongqing	38.76	19	-7	32.27	12	32.94	14	30.98	10
Xi'an	38.19	20	-11	32.98	9	33.03	13	31.92	6
Shanghai	37.96	21	11	28.58	32	25.59	35	25.45	31
Chengdu	37.93	22	-8	32.12	14	32.41	15	30.92	12
Wuhan	37.81	23	-13	32.44	10	31.96	18	30.57	13
Tianjin	37.77	24	-18	34.82	6	33.32	11	32.62	5
Urumqi	37.10	25	6	29.23	31	28.53	28	24.67	34
Shenzhen	37.03	26	8	28.42	34	26.56	33	25.30	32
Qingdao	36.80	27	-3	30.75	24	28.78	27	27.12	25
Lanzhou	36.79	28	-13	31.84	15	27.82	30	26.70	26
Yinchuan	36.56	29	-1	30.29	28	27.47	31	27.60	22
Hohhot	36.15	30	-7	30.99	23	30.85	20	26.43	28
Guiyang	35.71	31	-2	30.19	29	29.38	23	25.71	30
Guangzhou	35.58	32	-5	30.39	27	28.46	29	27.79	20
Xining	35.48	33	-8	30.62	25	28.89	26	27.31	23
Taiyuan	35.32	34	-26	33.04	8	34.22	7	30.94	11
Beijing	33.76	35	-2	28.53	33	26.13	34	23.06	35
Average	38.94			31.81		31.22		28.91	

As is shown in Table 5.5, the 2015 weighted average of living costs satisfaction indexes is 38.94, which is a significant improvement compared with the results of the previous surveys. That is to say, residents of the 35 cities are more satisfied with their living costs now, but the score still remains below the satisfaction level (below 50). All the 35 cities have scored over 30 in the satisfaction index of living costs. And 14 cities have scored over 40 –

Quality-of-life Sub-Indexes of the 35 Chinese Cities

5.2 Living Costs Indexes

5.2.1 Subjective Satisfaction Indexes of Living Costs

Just like before, the satisfaction indexes of living costs are obtained through a questionnaire survey by assigning values to survey answers. Table 5.5 lists the living costs subjective satisfaction indexes of the 35 cities, along with their respective rankings. Same as the previous three surveys, the higher the living costs index, the lower the living costs in the city, and the higher the satisfaction among the residents, and vice versa.

Table 5.5 Living Costs Satisfaction Indexes of the 35 Chinese Cities

City	2015			2014		2013		2012	
	Score	Ranking	Places risen	Score	Ranking	Score	Ranking	Score	Ranking
Changchun	43.86	1	4	34.89	5	36.02	4	34.36	3
Hefei	43.82	2	1	35.02	3	34.40	6	35.43	1
Xiamen	43.34	3	19	31.25	22	32.36	16	28.49	15
Kunming	42.97	4	12	31.82	16	30.00	22	28.04	18
Nanjing	42.50	5	16	31.55	21	30.10	21	27.95	19
Haikou	42.28	6	29	28.25	35	33.96	8	26.00	29
Harbin	42.21	7	4	32.33	11	32.06	17	28.38	17
Hangzhou	42.19	8	12	31.58	20	29.10	24	28.42	16
Ningbo	41.49	9	4	32.21	13	29.03	25	26.62	27
Jinan	41.33	10	-8	35.72	2	36.16	3	35.39	2
Shenyang	40.45	11	-10	37.48	1	36.31	2	31.73	7
Shijiazhuang	40.26	12	-8	34.92	4	39.13	1	34.27	4
Nanning	40.15	13	5	31.72	18	33.45	10	27.16	24
Dalian	40.06	14	16	29.70	30	27.04	32	25.15	33
Nanchang	39.68	15	-8	33.87	7	33.18	12	28.66	14
Zhengzhou	39.66	16	1	31.75	17	35.03	5	31.67	8

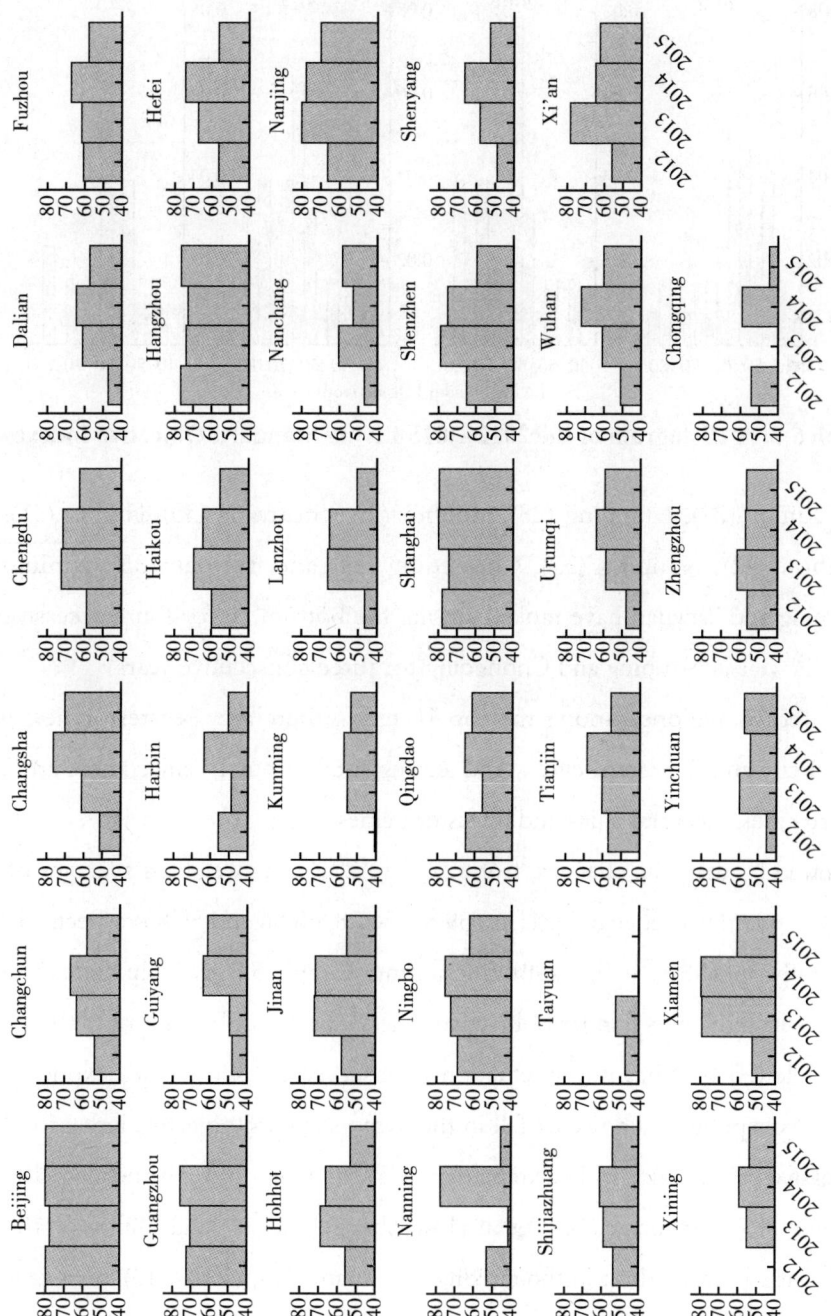

Graph 5.8: A Bar Chart of the 2012–2015 Living Standard Objective Indexes of the 35 Cities

Quality-of-life Sub-Indexes of the 35 Chinese Cities

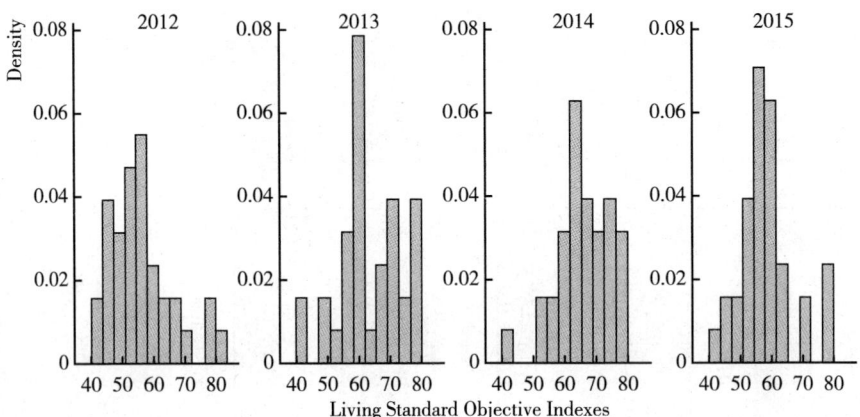

Graph 5.7: A Histogram of the 2012–2015 Living Standard Objective Indexes

(26), Xining (27), Kunming (28), Hohhot (29), Shenyang (30), Harbin (31), Lanzhou (32), Nanning (33), Chongqing (34) and Taiyuan (35). Xining, Kunming and Taiyuan have ranked among the bottom 10 for four successive years, as well as Nanning and Chongqing for three consecutive years.

Viewed by regions, among the top 10 cities, there are 7 eastern cities, 1 central city and 2 western cities. And among the bottom 10 cities, there are 2 eastern cities, 2 central cities and 6 western cities.

Viewed by dynamic changes, from 2012 to 2015, the weighted averages of living standard objective indexes are 59.83, 56.28, 68.06 and 59.83 respectively. Generally speaking, it has kept fluctuating. Graph 5.8 well illustrates the changes in the living standard objective indexes of the 35 cities from 2012 to 2015. Viewed by cities, the fluctuation is observed in all the cities. None of them has experienced a rise or fall in the living standard objective index for 3 successive years. Cities with a dramatic rise in the ranking are: Nanchang (18), Guiyang (15), Yinchuan (14), Xi'an (13), Zhengzhou (11) and Qingdao (10). Cities with a drastic drop in the ranking are: Jinan (-14), Hefei (-13), Shenyang (-13), Hohhot (-11) and Lanzhou (-11).

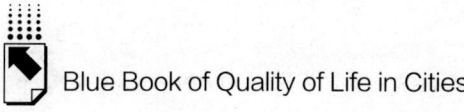

Continued table

City	2015			2014		2013		2012	
	Score	Ranking	Places risen	Score	Ranking	Score	Ranking	Score	Ranking
Yinchuan	57.45	19	14	54.12	33	60.00	24	45.55	33
Dalian	57.17	20	2	64.56	22	61.23	19	47.14	29
Zhengzhou	56.44	21	11	57.00	32	61.40	18	56.11	14
Hefei	55.80	22	-13	74.09	9	67.04	14	55.75	17
Tianjin	55.56	23	-9	68.39	14	60.42	23	57.02	13
Haikou	55.30	24	-1	64.21	23	69.40	12	59.80	10
Jinan	55.16	25	-14	71.92	11	72.27	9	57.43	12
Shijiazhuang	53.79	26	1	60.53	27	58.80	25	53.09	21
Xining	53.61	27	1	59.10	28	54.92	30	40.00	35
Kunming	53.32	28	3	57.07	31	55.27	29	40.76	34
Hohhot	52.83	29	-11	65.87	18	68.67	13	55.87	16
Shenyang	52.73	30	-13	66.32	17	57.82	27	48.84	26
Harbin	50.58	31	-6	63.60	25	49.04	33	55.47	18
Lanzhou	50.15	32	-11	64.84	21	65.59	15	46.30	32
Nanning	45.35	33	-4	59.04	29	41.04	34	52.98	22
Chongqing	44.60	34	-4	58.86	30	40.00	35	53.90	19
Taiyuan	40.00	35	0	40.00	35	52.32	31	46.87	30
Average	59.83			68.06		56.28		59.83	

As is clearly shown in Table 5.4, the 2015 weighted average of living standard objective indexes is 59.83 — same as the score of 2012, higher than that of 2013 and lower than that of 2014. The lowest score is 40, and the highest is 80. Same as last year, 32 cities have scored over 50. Beijing still ranks No. 1 among all the cities. Generally speaking, the income level index has kept fluctuating over the past few years. Graph 5.7 well illustrates such a trend.

According to Table 5.4, cities ranked top 10 on the list of living standard objective indexes are: Beijing (1), Shanghai (2), Hangzhou (3), Changsha (4), Nanjing (5), Chengdu (6), Xi'an (7), Ningbo (8), Qingdao (9) and Guangzhou (10). Beijing, Shanghai, Hangzhou, Nanjing and Ningbo have been on the top 10 list in the past four years. And the bottom 10 cities are: Shijiazhuang

5.1.2 Objective Indexes (Social and Economic Data Indexes) of Living Standard

In the QLICC system, the objective index of living standard consists of 2 primary indicators (income level and life improvements indexes) which are in turn made up of 6 secondary indicators (consumption rate, per capita wealth, per capita disposable income, per capita consumption growth, per capita wealth growth and per capita disposable income growth). The living standard objective indexes of the 35 cities are obtained by calculating these primary indicators and secondary indicators. Results of the calculation are shown in Table 5.4.

Table 5.4 Living Standard Objective Indexes of the 35 Chinese Cities

City	2015			2014		2013		2012	
	Score	Ranking	Places risen	Score	Ranking	Score	Ranking	Score	Ranking
Beijing	80.00	1	0	80.00	1	77.84	5	80.03	1
Shanghai	79.02	2	0	79.45	2	73.93	6	77.84	2
Hangzhou	76.42	3	7	72.60	10	73.83	7	76.79	3
Changsha	70.09	4	1	76.15	5	60.91	20	50.97	24
Nanjing	69.77	5	-1	77.90	4	80.00	1	66.33	6
Chengdu	62.62	6	7	71.21	13	72.13	10	58.80	11
Xi'an	62.55	7	13	64.90	20	78.59	4	56.07	15
Ningbo	62.08	8	-1	75.54	7	72.47	8	68.70	5
Qingdao	61.36	9	10	65.47	19	56.06	28	64.76	8
Guangzhou	60.71	10	-4	75.76	6	70.24	11	72.14	4
Guiyang	60.58	11	15	62.79	26	49.09	32	47.86	27
Xiamen	60.56	12	-9	79.43	3	79.22	2	52.40	23
Wuhan	59.72	13	-1	71.82	12	60.51	22	50.81	25
Shenzhen	59.30	14	-6	75.18	8	78.91	3	64.78	7
Urumqi	59.11	15	9	63.78	24	58.61	26	47.54	28
Nanchang	58.46	16	18	52.77	34	60.59	21	46.60	31
Fuzhou	57.98	17	-2	67.16	15	61.51	17	60.75	9
Changchun	57.86	18	-2	66.77	16	63.27	16	53.67	20

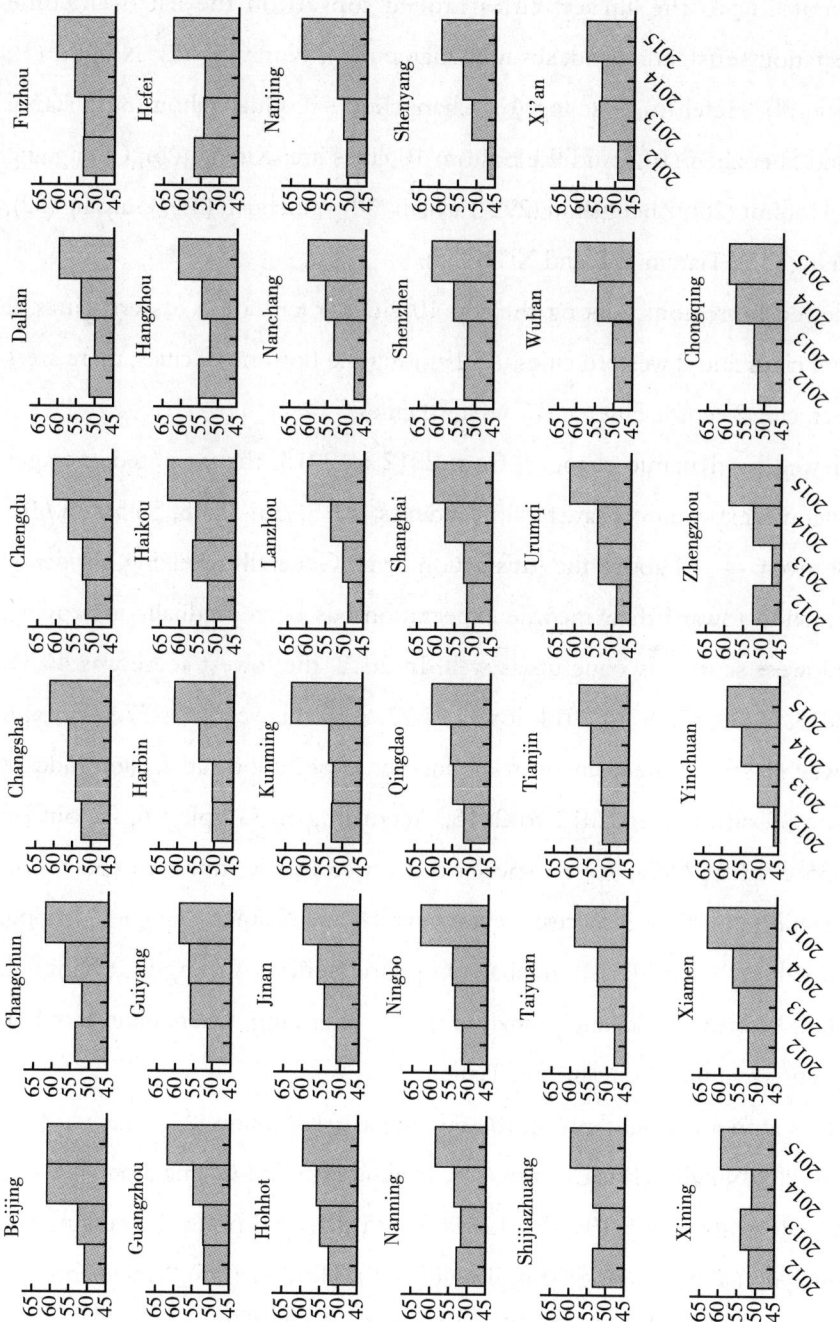

Graph 5.6: A Bar Chart of the 2012–2015 Income Expectation Satisfaction Indexes of the 35 Cities

Quality-of-life Sub-Indexes of the 35 Chinese Cities

According to the survey, cities ranked top 10 on the list of income expectation satisfaction indexes are: Xiamen (1), Kunming (2), Ningbo (3), Haikou (4), Hefei (5), Nanjing (6), Changchun (7), Guangzhou (8), Urumqi (9) and Shenzhen (10). And the bottom 10 cities are: Xining (26), Chongqing (27), Hohhot (28), Zhengzhou (29), Taiyuan (30), Yinchuan (31), Guiyang (32), Nanning (33), Tianjin (34) and Xi'an (35).

Viewed by regions, among the top 10 cities, there are 6 eastern cities, 2 central cities and 2 western cities. And among the bottom 10 cities, there are 1 eastern city, 2 central cities and 7 western cities.

Viewed by dynamic changes, from 2012 to 2015, the weighted averages of income expectation satisfaction indexes are 51.36, 52.48, 55.5 and 60.5 respectively — all above the satisfaction level. Generally speaking, residents' satisfaction toward their income expectation has been gradually improving. The lowest score has gone up as well. In 2012, the lowest score was 46.35. In 2013, it was 47.58. In 2014, it was 51.27. And this year, it is 57.81. Graph 5.6 well illustrates the changes in the income expectation satisfaction indexes of the 35 cities from 2012 to 2015. According to Graph 5.6, 22 out of the 35 cities (62.9%) have experienced a rise in the income expectation satisfaction index for 3 successive years, which are: Xiamen, Ningbo, Nanjing, Guangzhou, Urumqi, Changsha, Qingdao, Beijing, Chengdu, Shanghai, Harbin, Wuhan, Nanchang, Lanzhou, Jinan, Shenyang, Chongqing, Hohhot, Taiyuan, Yinchuan, Guiyang and Tianjin.

Cities with a dramatic rise in the ranking are: Kunming (27), Nanjing (26), Hefei (20), Ningbo (15), Urumqi (15), Haikou (12) and Guangzhou (11) – all ranked among the top 10 cities. Cities with a drastic drop in the ranking are: Chongqing (-24), Guiyang (-24), Tianjin (-19), Hohhot (-15), Yinchuan (-14), Shanghai (-13), Jinan (-13), Beijing (-12) and Chengdu (-10).

Continued table

City	2015			2014		2013		2012	
	Score	Ranking	Places risen	Score	Ranking	Score	Ranking	Score	Ranking
Yinchuan	58.93	31	-14	55.05	17	50.82	30	46.35	35
Guiyang	58.83	32	-24	56.05	8	55.51	3	50.95	23
Nanning	58.70	33	-3	53.72	30	51.76	24	52.93	6
Tianjin	58.45	34	-19	55.29	15	52.34	21	51.75	20
Xi'an	57.81	35	-7	53.79	28	54.50	7	49.27	29
Average	60.50			55.50		52.48		51.36	

As is shown in Table 5.3, the 2015 weighted average of income expectation satisfaction indexes is 60.50, which is above the satisfaction level and a continuous improvement compared with the results of the previous surveys. All the 35 cities have scored over 50 in the satisfaction index of income expectation, and 20 cities over 60. The scores of all the cities have seen a significant rise compared to those of last year. Xiamen has ranked No. 1 and scored 63.69 – higher than that of Beijing the highest scorer of 2014. Generally speaking, the satisfaction index of income expectation has kept improving. Graph 5.5 well illustrates such a trend.

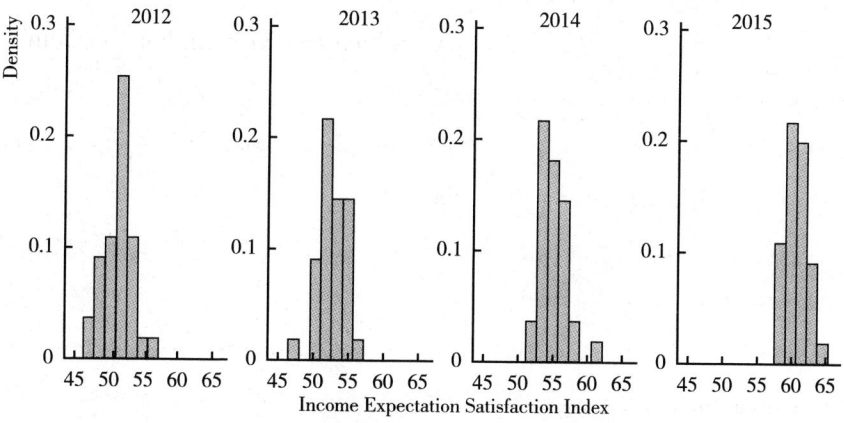

Graph 5.5: A Histogram of the 2012–2015 Income Expectation Satisfaction Indexes

Quality-of-life Sub-Indexes of the 35 Chinese Cities

Table 5.3 Income Expectation Satisfaction Indexes of the 35 Chinese Cities

City	2015			2014		2013		2012	
	Score	Ranking	Places risen	Score	Ranking	Score	Ranking	Score	Ranking
Xiamen	63.69	1	4	56.63	5	55.00	5	52.33	12
Kunming	63.52	2	27	53.77	29	52.50	20	52.88	7
Ningbo	63.03	3	15	54.58	18	54.03	10	51.89	16
Haikou	62.70	4	12	55.22	16	56.04	1	52.00	14
Hefei	62.45	5	20	53.83	25	53.85	11	56.47	1
Nanjing	62.28	6	26	52.91	32	51.26	29	50.38	26
Changchun	61.80	7	-1	56.52	6	51.62	27	53.48	3
Guangzhou	61.53	8	11	54.34	19	51.71	26	51.38	22
Urumqi	61.51	9	15	53.87	24	53.81	12	48.68	31
Shenzhen	61.46	10	0	55.99	10	52.18	22	52.78	8
Changsha	61.25	11	-4	56.23	7	54.26	9	52.49	11
Qingdao	61.17	12	-1	55.89	11	55.04	4	52.00	13
Beijing	61.05	13	-12	60.79	1	52.74	17	50.63	25
Chengdu	60.84	14	-10	56.65	4	52.78	16	51.90	15
Shanghai	60.79	15	-13	57.87	2	52.57	18	51.88	17
Hangzhou	60.69	16	5	54.27	21	51.94	23	54.72	2
Fuzhou	60.61	17	-5	55.80	12	52.90	14	53.32	5
Harbin	60.53	18	4	54.03	22	50.39	32	50.00	28
Wuhan	60.34	19	1	54.33	20	50.39	33	50.21	27
Nanchang	60.31	20	-6	55.46	14	53.18	13	47.97	33
Lanzhou	59.97	21	6	53.80	27	50.56	31	49.15	30
Jinan	59.82	22	-13	56.04	9	54.43	8	50.75	24
Dalian	59.80	23	3	53.81	26	50.09	34	51.69	21
Shijiazhuang	59.70	24	7	53.43	31	51.74	25	53.33	4
Shenyang	59.67	25	-2	53.90	23	51.33	28	47.34	34
Xining	59.51	26	9	51.27	35	55.56	2	51.85	18
Chongqing	59.43	27	-24	57.67	3	52.84	15	51.82	19
Hohhot	59.40	28	-15	55.73	13	54.82	6	52.50	10
Zhengzhou	59.08	29	5	52.51	34	47.58	35	52.62	9
Taiyuan	58.95	30	3	52.90	33	52.51	19	48.02	32

049

Blue Book of Quality of Life in Cities

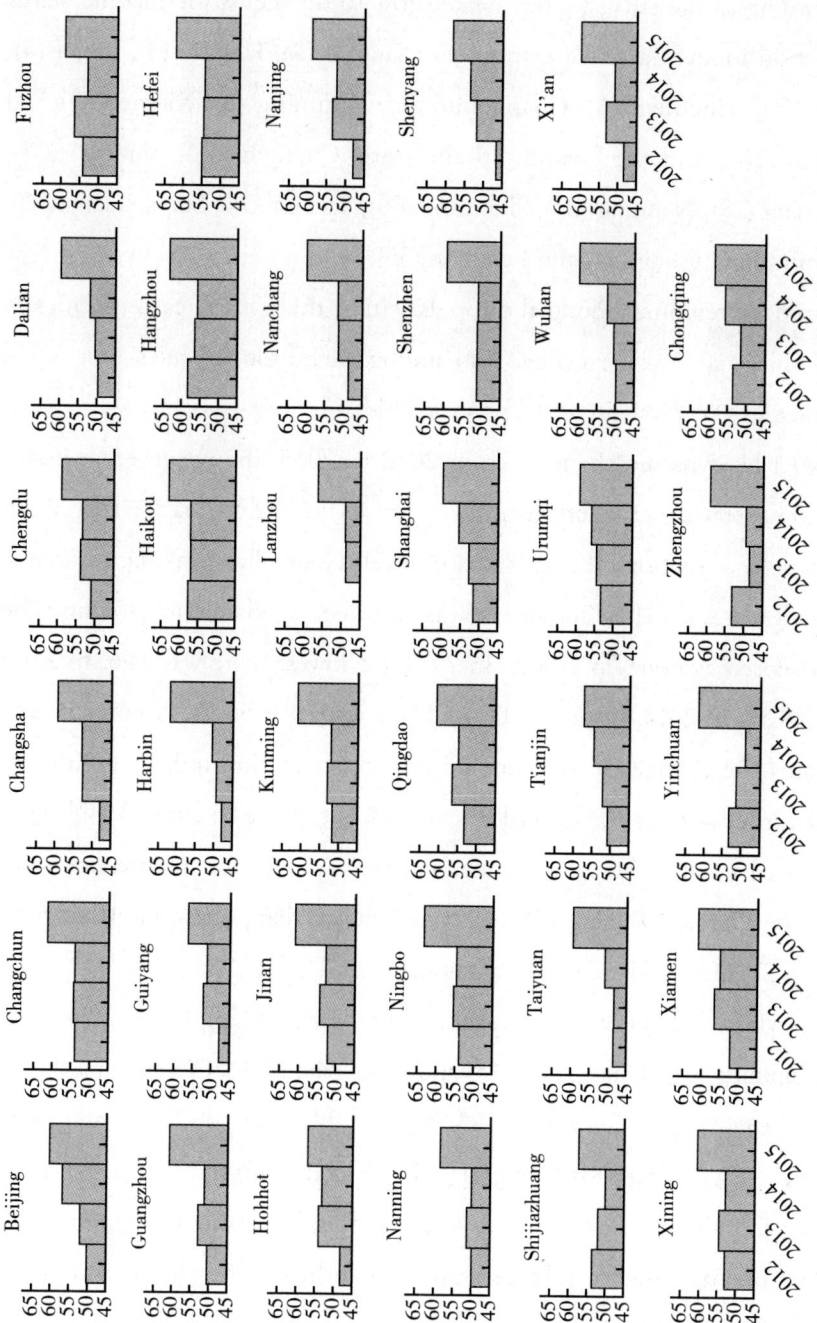

Graph 5.4: A Bar Chart of the 2012–2015 Income Status Satisfaction Indexes of the 35 Cities

Quality-of-life Sub-Indexes of the 35 Chinese Cities

According to the survey, cities ranked top 10 on the list of income status satisfaction indexes are: Hangzhou (1), Ningbo (2), Haikou (3), Hefei (4), Harbin (5), Yinchuan (6), Changchun (7), Kunming (8), Xiamen (9) and Qingdao (10). And the bottom 10 cities are: Chengdu (26), Fuzhou (27), Chongqing (28), Nanning (29), Shenyang (30), Tianjin (31), Shijiazhuang (32), Hohhot (33), Guiyang (34) and Lanzhou (35).

Viewed by regions, among the top 10 cities, there are 5 eastern cities, 3 central cities and 2 western cities. And among the bottom 10 cities, there are 4 eastern cities, 0 central city and 6 western cities.

Viewed by dynamic changes, from 2012 to 2015, the weighted averages of income status satisfaction indexes are 51.52, 52.54, 52.92 and 59.65 respectively – all above the satisfaction level. Generally speaking, residents' satisfaction toward their income status has been gradually improving. The lowest score has gone up as well. In 2012, the lowest score was 44.6. In 2013, it was 48.32. In 2014, it was 49.03. And this year, it is 56.12. Graph 5.4 well illustrates the changes in the income status satisfaction indexes of the 35 cities from 2012 to 2015. Viewed by cities, 11 out of the 35 cities (31.4%) have experienced a rise in the income status satisfaction index for 3 successive years, which are: Harbin, Wuhan, Beijing, Nanchang, Dalian, Shanghai, Changsha, Urumqi, Shenyang, Tianjin and Lanzhou.

Cities with a dramatic rise in the ranking are: Yinchuan (28), Harbin (25), Xi'an (15), Kunming (14), Guangzhou (13) and Zhengzhou (10). Cities with a drastic drop in the ranking are: Chongqing (-23), Tianjin (-22), Urumqi (-21), Hohhot (-18), Shenyang (-17), Beijing (-14), Shanghai (-14), Chengdu (-12) and Fuzhou (-11).

Table 5.3 shows the scores and rankings of the income expectation satisfaction (optimism) indexes - another indicator of the income level satisfaction sub-index.

Continued table

City	2015			2014		2013		2012	
	Score	Ranking	Places risen	Score	Ranking	Score	Ranking	Score	Ranking
Tianjin	57.34	31	-22	54.67	9	52.15	20	50.79	20
Shijiazhuang	57.22	32	0	49.95	32	51.85	22	53.43	8
Hohhot	56.89	33	-18	53.13	15	53.80	13	48.21	29
Guiyang	56.33	34	-8	51.17	26	51.98	21	47.86	32
Lanzhou	56.12	35	0	49.03	35	48.87	33	44.60	35
Average	59.65			52.92		52.54		51.52	

As is shown in Table 5.2, the 2015 weighted average of income status satisfaction indexes is 59.65, which is above the satisfaction level and a continuous improvement compared with the results of the previous surveys. All the 35 cities have scored over 50 in the satisfaction index of income status, and 14 cities over 60. The scores of all the cities have seen a significant rise compared to those of last year. Hangzhou has ranked No. 1 and scored 63.38 — higher than that of Haikou the highest scorer of 2014. Generally speaking, the satisfaction index of income status has kept improving. Graph 5.3 well illustrates such a trend.

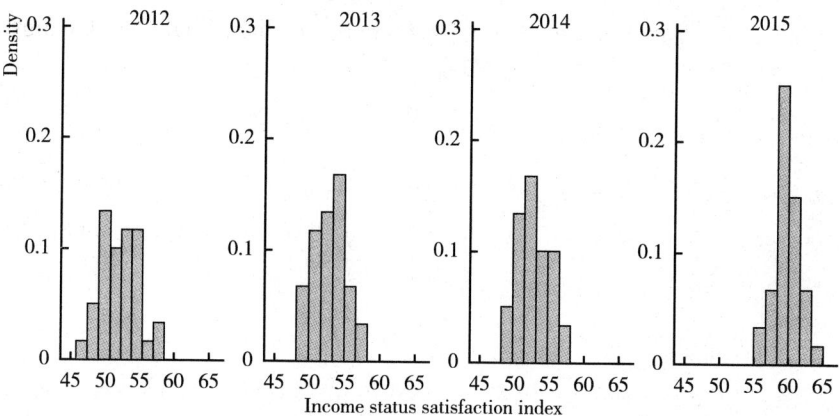

Graph 5.3: A Histogram of the 2012–2015 Income Status Satisfaction Indexes

Quality-of-life Sub-Indexes of the 35 Chinese Cities

Table 5.2 Income Status Satisfaction Indexes of the 35 Chinese Cities

City	2015			2014		2013		2012	
	Score	Ranking	Places risen	Score	Ranking	Score	Ranking	Score	Ranking
Hangzhou	63.38	1	3	55.67	4	56.25	5	58.25	1
Ningbo	63.28	2	8	54.58	10	55.21	6	53.65	6
Haikou	62.86	3	-2	56.83	1	56.87	1	57.50	2
Hefei	62.09	4	7	54.15	11	54.42	9	55.04	3
Harbin	62.09	5	25	50.52	30	49.33	32	47.78	33
Yinchuan	61.65	6	28	49.28	34	51.37	26	53.13	11
Changchun	61.49	7	5	54.12	12	54.52	7	54.01	5
Kunming	61.05	8	14	52.05	22	53.17	16	51.76	16
Xiamen	60.83	9	-2	54.92	7	56.39	3	52.03	15
Qingdao	60.77	10	-2	54.85	8	56.58	2	53.18	10
Jinan	60.72	11	8	52.52	19	54.15	11	52.11	14
Guangzhou	60.65	12	13	51.20	25	52.94	17	50.57	21
Xining	60.57	13	5	52.72	18	54.44	8	52.78	13
Xi'an	60.07	14	15	50.73	29	53.25	15	48.30	28
Wuhan	59.80	15	6	52.17	21	50.39	31	49.68	25
Beijing	59.80	16	-14	56.56	2	51.65	24	50.10	22
Nanchang	59.68	17	7	51.49	24	51.18	28	48.58	26
Dalian	59.68	18	5	51.86	23	50.46	30	49.69	24
Taiyuan	59.55	19	9	50.78	28	48.32	35	48.51	27
Shanghai	59.54	20	-14	55.33	6	52.60	19	51.43	17
Shenzhen	59.37	21	6	50.98	27	51.12	29	51.39	18
Changsha	59.37	22	-5	52.83	17	52.62	18	48.10	30
Zhengzhou	59.08	23	10	49.44	33	48.42	34	53.10	12
Urumqi	59.08	24	-21	55.92	3	54.38	10	53.29	9
Nanjing	59.01	25	-5	52.46	20	53.42	14	48.08	31
Chengdu	58.99	26	-12	53.39	14	53.82	12	50.88	19
Fuzhou	58.90	27	-11	53.00	16	56.39	4	54.19	4
Chongqing	58.57	28	-23	55.58	5	51.38	25	53.45	7
Nanning	58.45	29	2	50.05	31	51.20	27	50.00	23
Shenyang	58.12	30	-17	53.40	13	51.75	23	46.57	34

Blue Book of Quality of Life in Cities

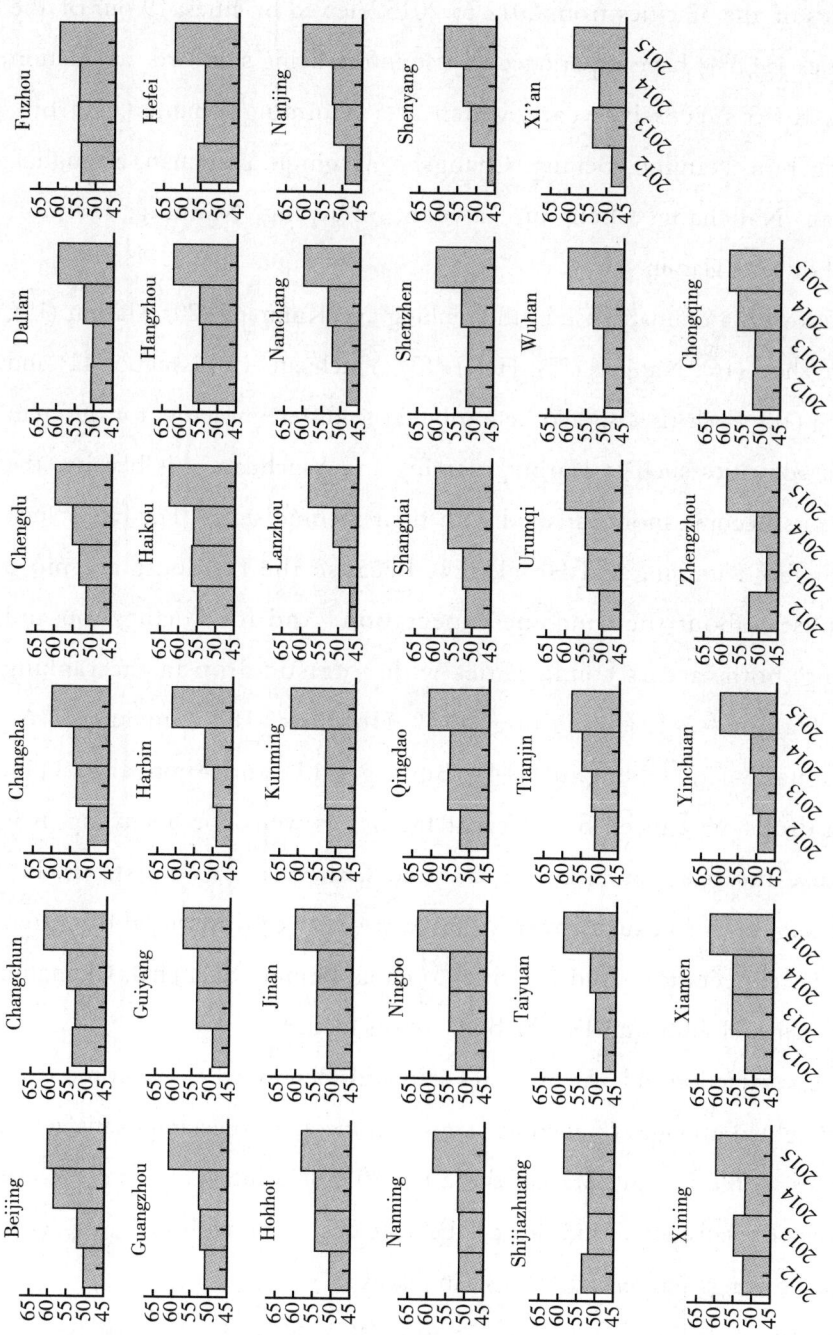

Graph 5.2: A Bar Chart of the 2012–2015 Living Standard Satisfaction Indexes of the 35 Cities

Quality-of-life Sub-Indexes of the 35 Chinese Cities

indexes of the 35 cities from 2012 to 2015.Viewed by cities, 19 out of the 35 cities (54.3%) have experienced a rise in the living standard satisfaction index for 3 successive years, which are: Kunming, Xiamen, Harbin, Guangzhou, Nanjing, Beijing, Changsha, Urumqi, Yinchuan, Shanghai, Wuhan, Nanchang, Chengdu, Taiyuan, Shenyang, Nanning, Hohhot, Lanzhou and Tianjin.

Cities with a dramatic rise in the ranking are: Kunming (20), Harbin (19), Guangzhou (16), Nanjing (15), Hefei (13), Yinchuan (13), Ningbo (11) and Xining (10). Such rises should be attributed to different factors for different cities. For cities such as Harbin, Nanjing and Yinchuan, it is because the residents become more satisfied with their income status. For cities such as Ningbo, Kunming and Hefei, it is because the residents are more optimistic about their income expectation. And for Guangzhou and Xining, both factors count. Cities with a drastic drop in the ranking are: Tianjin (-25), Chongqing (-25), Hohhot (-18), Guiyang (-16), Shanghai (-15), Chengdu (-14), Beijing (-11) and Shenyang (-11). Such drops are caused by different factors as well. For Shenyang, it is because the residents are less satisfied with their income status. For Guiyang, it is because the residents are less optimistic about their income expectation. And for cities such as Beijing, Shanghai, Chengdu, Chongqing, Hohhot and Tianjin, both factors matter.

The satisfaction indexes of living standard mentioned above come from the weighted averages of income status and income expectation satisfaction indexes. Table 5.2 and 5.3 list the 2012-2015 income status and income expectation satisfaction indexes of the 35 cities, along with their respective scores, rankings and relative changes in places.

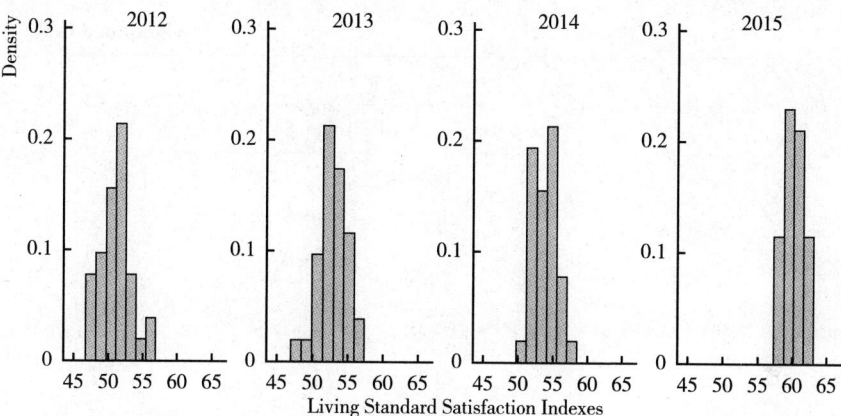

Graph 5.1: A Histogram of the 2012–2015 Living Standard Satisfaction Indexes

According to the survey, cities ranked top 10 on the list of living standard satisfaction indexes are: Ningbo (1), Haikou (2), Kunming (3), Hefei (4), Xiamen (5), Hangzhou (6), Changchun (7), Harbin (8), Guangzhou (9) and Qingdao (10). And the bottom 10 cities are: Zhengzhou (26), Chongqing (27), Xi'an (28), Shenyang (29), Nanning (30), Shijiazhuang (31), Hohhot (32), Lanzhou (33), Tianjin (34) and Guiyang (35).

Viewed by regions, among the top 10 cities, there are 6 eastern cities, 3 central cities and 1 western city. And among the bottom 10 cities, there are 3 eastern cities, 1 central city and 6 western cities.

From 2012 to 2015, the weighted averages of living standard satisfaction indexes are 51.28, 52.51, 54.32 and 60.07 respectively – all above the satisfaction level. Generally speaking, residents' satisfaction toward their living standard has been gradually improving. The lowest score has gone up as well. In 2012, the lowest score was 46.88 (Lanzhou). In 2013, it was 48 (Zhengzhou). In 2014, it was 50.98 (still Zhengzhou). In 2015, it is 57.58 (Guiyang). Graph 5.2 well illustrates the changes in the satisfaction

Quality-of-life Sub-Indexes of the 35 Chinese Cities

Continued table

City	2015			2014		2013		2012	
	Score	Ranking	Places risen	Score	Ranking	Score	Ranking	Score	Ranking
Zhengzhou	59.08	26	9	50.98	35	48.00	35	52.86	7
Chongqing	59.00	27	-25	56.63	2	52.11	24	52.64	9
Xi'an	58.94	28	0	52.26	28	53.88	12	48.79	31
Shenyang	58.89	29	-11	53.65	18	51.54	27	46.95	34
Nanning	58.58	30	1	51.89	31	51.48	28	51.47	16
Shijiazhuang	58.46	31	2	51.69	33	51.79	25	53.38	6
Hohhot	58.14	32	-18	54.43	14	54.31	7	50.36	24
Lanzhou	58.04	33	1	51.42	34	49.72	34	46.88	35
Tianjin	57.89	34	-25	54.98	9	52.24	21	51.27	19
Guiyang	57.58	35	-16	53.61	19	53.74	13	49.40	28
Average		60.07		54.32		52.51		51.28	

As is shown in Table 5.1, the 2015 weighted average of living standard satisfaction indexes is 60.07 – a continuous improvement compared with the results of the previous surveys. Although the score is over 60 and above the satisfaction level, there is still a long way to go before it reaches the "very satisfied" range of income status or the "very optimistic" range of income expectation (76-100 points). All the 35 cities have scored over 50 (the critical point between satisfaction and dissatisfaction) in the satisfaction index of living standard, and 21 cities over 60. The scores of all the cities have seen a significant rise compared to those of last year. Ningbo has ranked No. 1 and scored 63.16 – higher than that of Beijing the highest scorer of 2014. Generally speaking, the satisfaction index of living standard has kept improving. Graph 5.1 well illustrates such a trend.

Table 5.1 Living Standard Satisfaction Indexes of the 35 Chinese Cities

City	2015			2014		2013		2012	
	Score	Ranking	Places risen	Score	Ranking	Score	Ranking	Score	Ranking
Ningbo	63.16	1	11	54.58	12	54.62	6	52.77	8
Haikou	62.78	2	2	56.03	4	56.46	1	54.75	3
Kunming	62.28	3	20	52.91	23	52.84	17	52.32	11
Hefei	62.27	4	13	53.99	17	54.14	9	55.76	2
Xiamen	62.26	5	0	55.78	5	55.69	3	52.18	13
Hangzhou	62.04	6	4	54.97	10	54.10	10	56.49	1
Changchun	61.64	7	0	55.32	7	53.07	16	53.74	5
Harbin	61.31	8	19	52.27	27	49.86	33	48.89	30
Guangzhou	61.09	9	16	52.77	25	52.32	20	50.97	21
Qingdao	60.97	10	-4	55.37	6	55.81	2	52.59	10
Nanjing	60.65	11	15	52.69	26	52.34	19	49.23	29
Beijing	60.43	12	-11	58.68	1	52.19	22	50.37	23
Shenzhen	60.41	13	7	53.49	20	51.65	26	52.08	14
Changsha	60.31	14	-1	54.53	13	53.44	14	50.29	25
Urumqi	60.29	15	-4	54.90	11	54.10	11	50.99	20
Yinchuan	60.29	16	13	52.16	29	51.10	29	49.74	27
Jinan	60.27	17	-1	54.28	16	54.29	8	51.43	17
Shanghai	60.16	18	-15	56.60	3	52.59	18	51.65	15
Wuhan	60.07	19	3	53.25	22	50.39	31	49.95	26
Xining	60.04	20	10	51.99	30	55.00	4	52.31	12
Nanchang	60.00	21	0	53.48	21	52.18	23	48.27	32
Chengdu	59.91	22	-14	55.02	8	53.30	15	51.39	18
Fuzhou	59.76	23	-8	54.40	15	54.64	5	53.76	4
Dalian	59.74	24	0	52.84	24	50.28	32	50.69	22
Taiyuan	59.25	25	7	51.84	32	50.42	30	48.27	33

B.5
Quality-of-life Sub-Indexes of the 35 Chinese Cities

Scores and rankings of the subjective satisfaction and the objective (social and economic data) indexes can be explained by their respective sub-indexes [1] which will be compared and analyzed separately in this part.

5.1 Living Standard Indexes

The living standard index consists of a subjective satisfaction index and an objective index (social and economic data index). The former was obtained through a telephone survey by assigning values to survey answers, including the survey results of income status and income expectation. And the latter was acquired objectively by calculating the social and economic indicators of the 35 cities, including 2 primary indicators (income level and life improvements) and their 6 secondary indicators.

5.1.1 Subjective Satisfaction Indexes of Living Standard

Table 5.1 lists the 2012-2015 living standard subjective indexes of the 35 cities, along with their respective rankings.

---

[1] Same as in the previous surveys, the sub-indexes supporting the general indexes of the 35 cities are: living standard, living costs, human capital, social security and living experience sub-indexes. And each sub-index consists of a subjective satisfaction index and an objective index (social and economic data index).

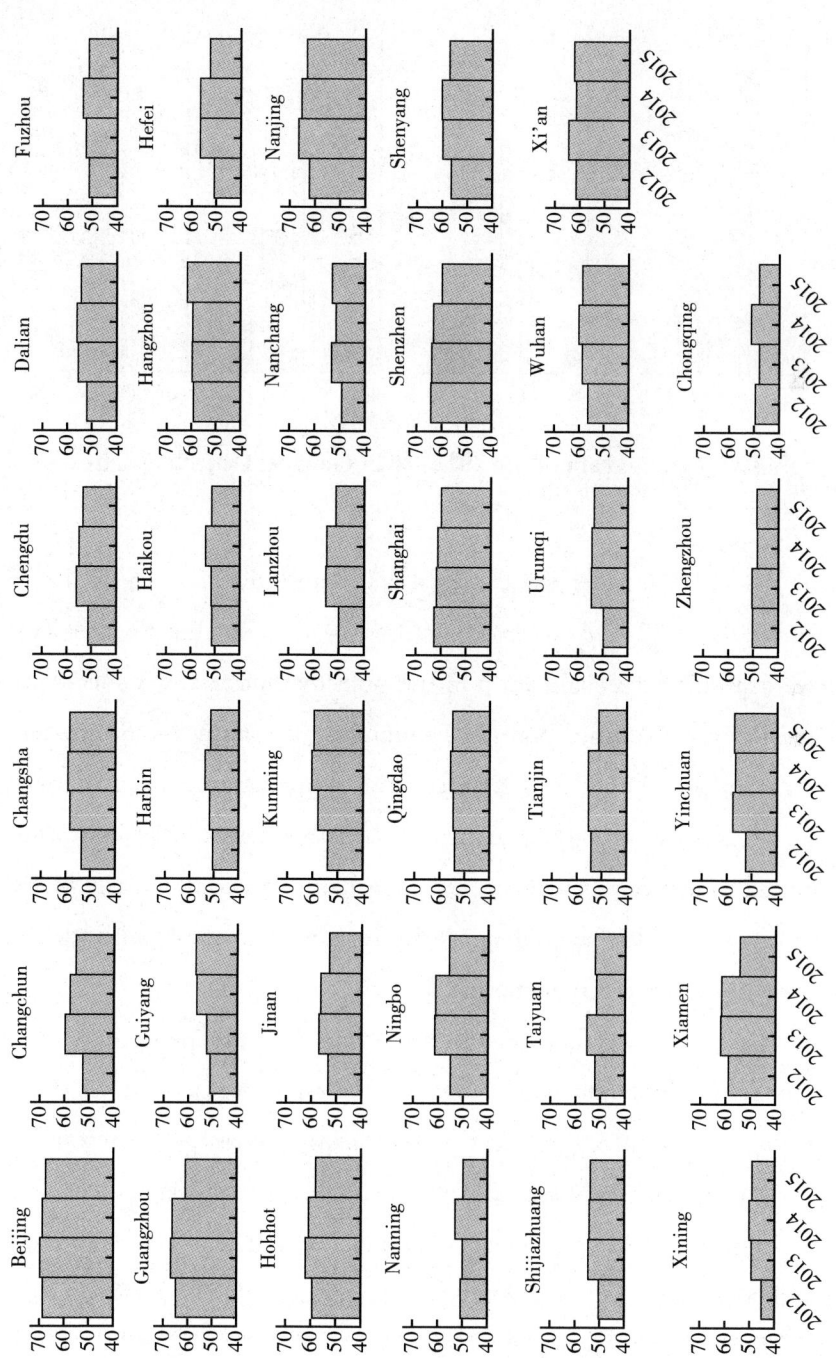

Graph 4.4: A Bar Chart of the 2012–2015 Objective Indexes of the 35 Cities

Quality-of-life Indexes of the 35 Chinese Cities

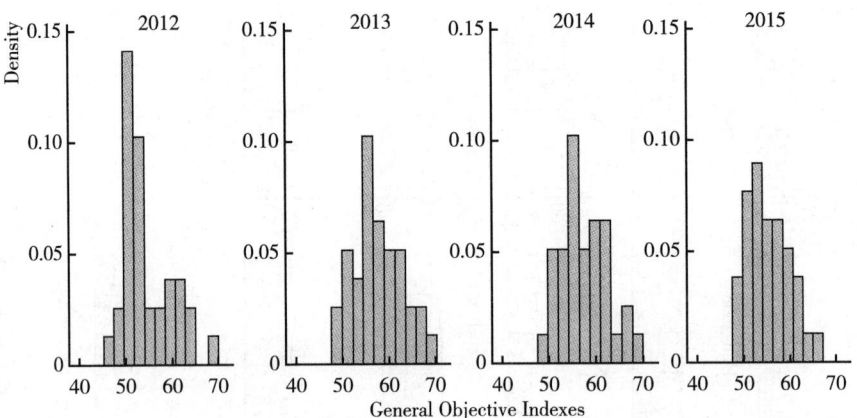

Graph 4.3: A Histogram of the 2012–2015 General Objective Indexes

Graph 4.4 well illustrates the changes in the objective indexes of the 35 cities from 2012 to 2015. As is shown in Graph 4.4, among the 35 cities, over 1/3 have experienced a slight drop in the objective index for 3 successive years, which are: Beijing, Nanjing, Guangzhou, Shanghai, Shenzhen, Hohhot, Ningbo, Changchun, Xiamen, Shijiazhuang, Urumqi, Chengdu, Jinan and Lanzhou. It should also be noted that despite the economic downturn, the objective index of Guiyang has risen continuously in the past three years, while that of Hangzhou has remained stable with a slight improvement during the same period.

Viewed by rankings, Hangzhou and Nanchang have experienced the most significant rises. The ranking of Hangzhou has raised 9 places from No. 13 in 2014 to No. 4 in 2015, while that of Nanchang has also gone up 9 places from No. 32 last year to No. 23 this year. The ranking of Xiamen has seen the most drastic drop, falling 13 places from No. 6 in 2014 to No. 19 in 2015. Cities with a dramatic drop in the ranking also include: Hefei (-9), Tianjin (-8), Ningbo (-7) and Lanzhou (-7).

satisfaction level.

According to the calculation result, cities ranked top 10 on the list of objective indexes are: Beijing (1), Nanjing (2), Xi'an (3), Hangzhou (4), Guangzhou (5), Shanghai (6), Shenzhen (7), Kunming (8), Wuhan (9) and Changsha (10). The highest score (Beijing, 67.41) is still below 70. Changsha is on the list for the first time in the past 4 years. And Hohhot is out of the list for the first time, ranking No. 11 which is not a big change.

The bottom 10 cities on the list are: Taiyuan (26), Fuzhou (27), Harbin (28), Haikou (29), Tianjin (30), Lanzhou (31), Nanning (32), Xining (33), Zhengzhou (34) and Chongqing (35). It is the first time for Tianjin to be in the bottom 10 since 2012, and for Lanzhou as well since 2013. Last year, there was only one city (Zhengzhou) which scored below 50 in the objective index, while in 2015, there are four cities (Zhengzhou, Nanning, Xining and Chongqing). The lowest scorer is Chongqing (47.93) which has stayed among the bottom 3 since 2012. According to the standards of the QLICC system, if the score of the objective index is below 50 (the critical point between satisfaction and dissatisfaction), then it is within the dissatisfaction range. That is to say, as far as the calculation of the objective indicators is concerned, the QOL in these 4 cities is dissatisfactory.

Viewed by regional distribution, among the top 10 cities, the ratio of eastern to central to western cities is 6:2:2. And among the bottom 10 cities, the ratio is 3:3:4. There is a significant regional difference in the QOL of these cities. The objective statistics of eastern cities are generally higher than those of central or western cities. Graph 4.3 well illustrates the changes in the objective indexes from 2012 to 2015.

Quality-of-life Indexes of the 35 Chinese Cities

Continued table

City	2015			2014		2013		2012	
	Score	Ranking	Places risen	Score	Ranking	Score	Ranking	Score	Ranking
Changchun	55.22	16	-1	57.63	15	59.64	11	52.29	19
Qingdao	55.03	17	4	55.87	21	54.76	25	54.05	15
Dalian	54.38	18	1	56.15	19	55.64	20	52.00	21
Xiamen	54.32	19	-13	61.58	6	61.89	7	58.86	9
Shijiazhuang	54.00	20	5	54.44	25	54.78	24	50.49	28
Urumqi	53.53	21	5	54.42	26	54.59	26	49.73	32
Chengdu	53.35	22	1	54.89	23	55.96	19	51.15	24
Nanchang	52.88	23	9	51.29	32	53.03	27	49.03	34
Jinan	52.72	24	-4	56.10	20	56.84	17	53.22	17
Hefei	52.69	25	-9	56.83	16	56.73	18	50.92	26
Taiyuan	52.15	26	5	51.62	31	55.45	21	52.15	20
Fuzhou	51.55	27	0	53.96	27	52.66	28	51.37	22
Harbin	51.45	28	0	53.80	28	51.86	30	50.44	29
Haikou	51.28	29	0	53.72	29	51.50	31	51.17	23
Tianjin	51.25	30	-8	55.48	22	55.42	22	54.30	13
Lanzhou	51.22	31	-7	54.79	24	55.22	23	50.08	31
Nanning	49.79	32	-2	52.93	30	50.00	33	50.69	27
Xining	49.08	33	1	50.15	34	49.29	34	45.21	35
Zhengzhou	48.68	34	1	48.39	35	50.54	32	50.26	30
Chongqing	47.93	35	-2	51.04	33	47.83	35	49.40	33
Average		55.84			57.87		57.75		54.56

As is shown in Table 4.2, the weighted average of the general objective indexes is 55.84 this year. Viewed by dynamic changes, the average of the 35 cities had improved dramatically in 2013 compared to that of 2012, remained stable in 2014, and fell slightly for the first time in 2015. The objective index has decreased by 2.03 points this year, although still remaining above the

4.2 The 2015 Objective Indexes (Social and Economic Data Indexes)

The objective indexes were obtained in the same way as previously. First, we calculated the 20 objective economic secondary indicators of the 35 cities. Then, we got the 8 primary indicators of QOL with the weighted average normalization method. At last, we averaged the primary indicators to generate the 5 objective sub-indexes, which in turn were averaged to obtain the general objective index (social and economic data index) of each city. The 2015 results of general objective indexes are shown in Table 4.2.

Table 4.2 Objective Indexes of the 35 Chinese Cities

City	2015			2014		2013		2012	
	Score	Ranking	Places risen	Score	Ranking	Score	Ranking	Score	Ranking
Beijing	67.41	1	0	68.78	1	69.80	1	68.72	1
Nanjing	63.37	2	1	65.52	3	66.65	3	62.38	5
Xi'an	62.39	3	2	61.61	5	64.65	4	61.59	6
Hangzhou	61.70	4	9	59.49	13	59.54	12	59.09	8
Guangzhou	61.08	5	-3	66.39	2	66.85	2	64.87	2
Shanghai	59.95	6	1	61.30	7	61.78	8	62.72	4
Shenzhen	59.87	7	-3	63.25	4	63.93	5	64.24	3
Kunming	59.69	8	2	60.61	10	58.05	15	54.08	14
Wuhan	58.87	9	3	60.33	12	58.93	13	56.61	10
Changsha	58.48	10	4	59.15	14	58.36	14	53.53	16
Hohhot	58.16	11	-2	60.99	9	62.22	6	59.55	7
Shenyang	57.22	12	-1	60.41	11	59.99	10	56.59	11
Yinchuan	57.19	13	4	56.77	17	57.68	16	52.45	18
Guiyang	56.92	14	4	56.46	18	52.45	29	50.98	25
Ningbo	55.70	15	-7	61.11	8	61.47	9	55.21	12

Quality-of-life Indexes of the 35 Chinese Cities

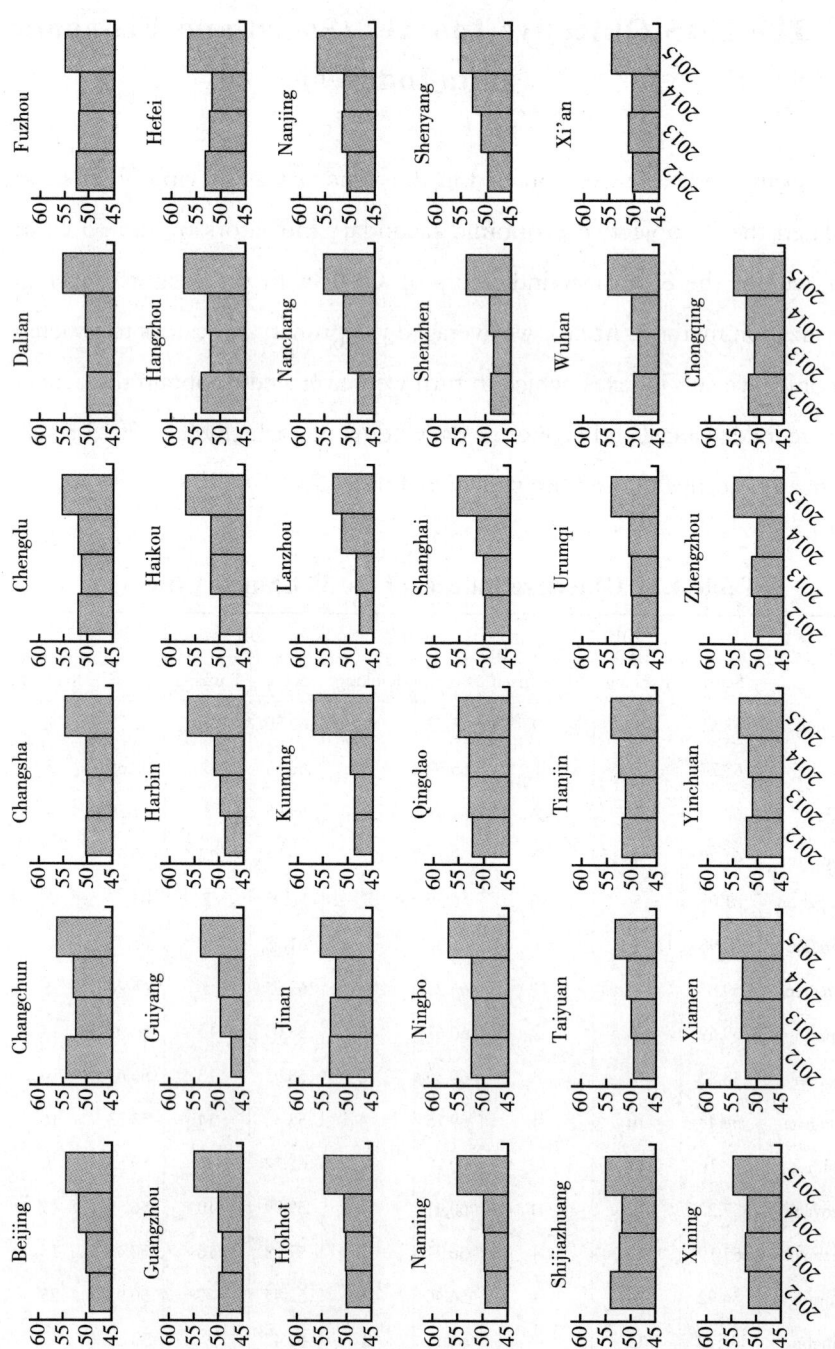

Graph 4.2: A Bar Chart of the 2012–2015 Subjective Satisfaction Indexes of the 35 Cities

and Lanzhou (35). Shenzhen and Guiyang have ranked bottom 10 in the past 4 years. Urumchi, Tianjin and Yinchuan are on the bottom 10 list for the first time. From 2012 to 2015, Beijing has ranked No. 28, 24, 17 and 28 respectively. Kunming was among the bottom 10 last year and jumps to top 10 this year. Dalian, Wuhan, Nanning, Zhengzhou, Guangzhou and Changsha have ranked between 12 and 24.

Viewed by regional distribution, among the top 10 cities, there are 6 eastern cities, 3 central cities and 1 western city. And among the bottom 10 cities, there are 3 eastern cities, 1 central city and 6 western cities.

From 2012 to 2015, the weighted averages of satisfaction indexes are 50.88, 50.87, 51.57 and 55.38 respectively. Generally speaking, after entering the satisfaction range in 2013, it has been improving over the past four years. The lowest score has increased as well, from 47.33 (2012), to 48.57 (2013), 49.51 (2014) and over 50 (2015). Graph 4.2 well illustrates the changes of satisfaction indexes from 2012 to 2015. As is shown in Graph 4.2, over 1/3 of the cities (14 out of the 35 cities) have progressed in the satisfaction index for at least three successive years from 2012 to 2015, which are Haikou, Harbin, Shanghai, Nanchang, Shenyang, Nanning, Qingdao, Hohhot, Beijing, Urumqi, Guiyang, Taiyuan, Lanzhou and Kunming.

Compare to the results of 2014, cities with a dramatic rise in the ranking are: Kunming (29), Dalian (14), Nanning (14), Nanjing (13), Harbin (13), Haikou (12), Wuhan (12), Zhengzhou (10) and Guangzhou (10). And cities with a dramatic drop in the ranking are: Tianjin (-24), Qingdao (-18), Yinchuan (-17), Lanzhou (-16), Shenyang (-12), Xining (-12), Beijing (-11), Taiyuan (-11) and Chongqing (-10).[1]

---

[1] Numbers in brackets stand for the places risen or fallen.

residents are still barely satisfied with their lives. All the 35 cities have scored over 50 on the subjective index. Although none of them is over 60, the highest scorer (Hangzhou, 57.58) has still performed slightly better than that of 2014 (Qingdao). Generally speaking, the satisfaction indexes have been improving steadily since 2012. Graph 4.1 well illustrates the above-mentioned changes.

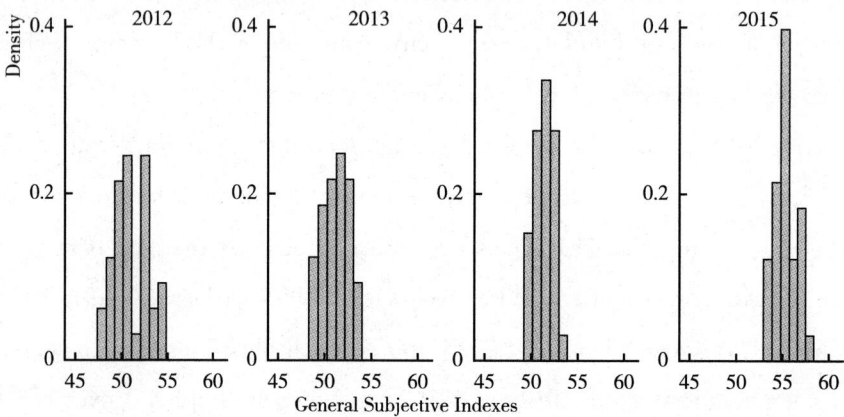

Graph 4.1: A Histogram of the 2012–2015 Subjective Satisfaction Indexes

According to the survey, cities ranked top 10 on the list of subjective satisfaction indexes are: Hangzhou (1), Xiamen (2), Ningbo (3), Haikou (4), Kunming (5), Hefei (6), Nanjing (7), Changchun (8), Harbin (9) and Shanghai (10). Since 2012, 4 of them have ranked top 10 for 4 consecutive years, which are Hangzhou, Xiamen, Ningbo and Changchun; and 4 of them are on the list for the first time, which are Haikou, Kunming, Nanjing and Harbin. Jinan, Chengdu, Shenyang, Chongqing and Qingdao are out of the top ten list in 2015.

The bottom 10 cities are: Xi'an (26), Hohhot (27), Beijing (28), Urumqi (29), Tianjin (30), Shenzhen (31), Yinchuan (32), Guiyang (33), Taiyuan (34)

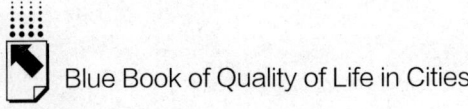

Continued table

City	2015			2014		2013		2012	
	Score	Ranking	Places risen	Score	Ranking	Score	Ranking	Score	Ranking
Shenyang	55.40	15	-12	52.85	3	51.25	16	49.73	26
Wuhan	55.34	16	12	50.45	28	49.07	32	49.95	24
Chongqing	55.26	17	-10	52.69	7	51.01	19	52.28	11
Nanning	55.24	18	14	50.00	32	49.81	28	49.60	27
Qingdao	55.18	19	-18	53.06	1	53.05	2	52.31	8
Zhengzhou	55.03	20	10	50.25	30	51.28	15	50.76	15
Guangzhou	55.00	21	10	50.05	31	49.21	31	49.74	25
Shijiazhuang	54.95	22	-4	51.75	18	52.17	8	53.86	3
Fuzhou	54.92	23	-9	51.90	14	52.06	9	52.60	6
Changsha	54.89	24	5	50.37	29	50.15	25	50.29	19
Xining	54.72	25	-12	51.94	13	52.21	6	51.57	14
Xi'an	54.65	26	1	50.58	27	51.16	17	50.40	17
Hohhot	54.64	27	-2	50.62	25	50.37	22	50.14	22
Beijing	54.49	28	-11	51.78	17	50.16	24	49.47	28
Urumqi	54.48	29	-5	50.76	24	50.38	21	50.23	21
Tianjin	54.22	30	-24	52.81	6	51.35	14	52.07	13
Shenzhen	54.06	31	4	49.51	35	48.68	34	49.16	30
Yinchuan	53.81	32	-17	51.90	15	51.07	18	52.29	10
Guiyang	53.77	33	0	49.94	33	49.58	30	47.33	35
Taiyuan	53.32	34	-11	50.90	23	49.90	27	49.38	29
Lanzhou	53.30	35	-16	51.50	19	48.57	35	47.95	34
Average	55.38			51.57		50.87		50.88	

As is shown in Table 4.1, the 2015 weighted average of subjective satisfaction indexes is 55.38, which remains above the satisfaction level and is higher than the weighted averages of the previous surveys. However, since the satisfaction range of values is between 50 and 75, such a score means the

B.4
Quality-of-life Indexes of the 35 Chinese Cities

4.1 The 2015 Subjective Satisfaction Indexes

The 2015 survey results and rankings of subjective satisfaction indexes are shown in Table 4.1.

Table 4.1 Subjective Satisfaction Indexes of the 35 Chinese Cities

City	2015			2014		2013		2012	
	Score	Ranking	Places risen	Score	Ranking	Score	Ranking	Score	Ranking
Hangzhou	57.58	1	3	52.83	4	52.05	10	54.04	2
Xiamen	57.58	2	3	52.82	5	53.00	3	52.30	9
Ningbo	57.24	3	5	52.63	8	52.17	7	52.51	7
Haikou	57.09	4	12	51.83	16	51.80	11	50.05	23
Kunming	57.03	5	29	49.63	34	48.73	33	48.72	32
Hefei	56.85	6	6	51.94	12	52.34	5	53.20	5
Nanjing	56.70	7	13	51.43	20	51.70	12	50.75	16
Changchun	56.60	8	-6	52.88	2	52.34	4	54.51	1
Harbin	56.59	9	13	51.05	22	49.79	29	48.78	31
Shanghai	55.74	10	1	51.94	11	50.53	20	50.24	20
Jinan	55.73	11	-2	52.57	9	53.68	1	53.78	4
Dalian	55.49	12	14	50.61	26	50.10	26	50.37	18
Chengdu	55.46	13	-3	52.14	10	51.40	13	52.13	12
Nanchang	55.41	14	7	51.31	21	50.35	23	48.41	33

Continued table

Social and economic data index (objective index)	Primary indicator	Secondary indicator	Impact on the Quality of Urban Life
Objective index of living experience	Living convenience	Transportation capacity (including per capita road area, number of public transportation vehicles per 10000 residents, number of taxies per 10000 residents)	+
		Number of cinemas and theaters per 10000 residents	+
		Medical care capacity (including number of hospital beds per 10000 residents, number of hospitals per 10000 residents, number of doctors per 10000 residents)	+
	Eco-environment	Per capita green area	+
		Air quality	+
	Perception of income disparities	Gini coefficient	–

Note: In the column, "+" = positive impact; "–" = negative impact.

Besides the surveys on house price expectation and primary concerns, a new special survey on on-line shopping was added to the telephone survey this year, in order to find out the influence it has on residents' QOL. Results of the three special surveys were not calculated in the QLICC system, but they may serve as references in understanding residents' satisfaction with living costs and living experience.

Introduction to the 2015 Survey

Continued table

Satisfaction index (subjective index)	Subjective questions	Answers and Values				
		100	75	50	25	0
Satisfaction index of human capital	Human capital	Very satisfied	Satisfied	Average	Dissatisfied	Very dissatisfied
Satisfaction index of social security	Health care and elderly support (50%)	Very satisfied	Satisfied	Average	Dissatisfied	Very dissatisfied
	Public order (50%)	Very satisfied	Satisfied	Average	Dissatisfied	Very dissatisfied
Satisfaction index of living experience	Pace of life (50%)	Very slow	Slow	Average	Quick	Very quick
	Living convenience (50%)	Very convenient	Convenient	Average	Inconvenient	Very inconvenient

Table 3.2 The QLICC Objective Indicator System

Social and economic data index (objective index)	Primary indicator	Secondary indicator	Impact on the Quality of Urban Life
Objective index of living standard	Income level	Consumption rate (consumption/income)	+
		Per capita wealth (including per capita savings and per capita housing wealth)	+
		Per capita disposable income	+
	Life improvements	Per capita consumption growth	+
		Per capita wealth growth	+
		Per capita disposable income growth	+
Objective index of living costs	Living costs	House price index	−
		Inflation rate	−
		House-price-to-income ratio	−
Objective index of human capital	Human capital	Educational provision index (including number of schools per 10000 residents and number of teachers per 10000 residents)	+
		Ratio of education, culture and entertainment expenditures	+
Objective index of social security	Social security	Social security coverage	+
		Basic medical insurance coverage	+
		Unemployment insurance coverage	+

both the expansiveness of spatial distribution and the randomness of sample choosing. Mobile phone users were interviewed as well with the same sampling method. The 2015 survey took more than two months. 395,537 calls were made. 22,939 effective random samples were obtained, including 12,669 fixed telephone calls and 10,270 mobile phone calls. The standard error of the overall subjective indexes was reduced to 0.139, which further enhanced the creditability of the survey. As for objective indicators, the 2014 method was adopted. Please refer to the *Report on the Quality of Life in Chinese Cities (2014)* for specifics.

3.2 Set-up of the Subjective/Objective Indicator System and the Special Surveys

The QLICC (Quality-of-life Index of Chinese Cities) system was established in 2011 by NIEE on the basis of our perceptions and the reality of China. It was made up of two parts: the subjective satisfaction index system and the objective index (social and economic data index) system. The indicator systems of the 2015 survey are in the same structure as the previous three surveys (see Table 3.1 and Table 3.2).

Table 3.1 The QLICC Subjective Satisfaction Indicator System

Satisfaction index (subjective index)	Subjective questions	Answers and Values				
		100	75	50	25	0
Satisfaction index of living standard	Income status (50%)	Very satisfied	Satisfied	Average	Dissatisfied	Very dissatisfied
	Income expectation (50%)	Very optimistic	Optimistic	Average	Pessimistic	Very pessimistic
Satisfaction index of living costs	Living costs	Very low	Low	Average	High	Very high

Analysis Reports

B.3 Introduction to the 2015 Survey

To ensure the continuity and comparability of survey results, the 2015 survey retained the whole set of adopted techniques, indicator system set-up and sample choosing method used in the last three years, while making small adjustments and improvements.

3.1 Introduction to the Survey

For the sake of continuity, 35 city samples were still chosen in the 2015 survey, including 30 provincial capitals and 5 municipalities separately listed on the State plan. Just like before, the subjective satisfaction indexes were obtained through the standard Computer Assisted Telephone Interview (CATI) method, and the drawing of fixed telephone numbers was proceeded through the stratified two-stage random sampling method, which ensured

Continued table

Natural and living environment	① Subjective (personal feelings) ② Objective (air pollution index)	In Europe of the past decades, environmental protection has already become a highly-valued subject in the agenda. Most European citizens find it a very important matter. Air, water and noise pollution will directly influence not only people's health but also social economic prosperity. The environment indicator plays a major role in the comprehensive evaluation of QOL, which includes both subjective (personal views) and objective (air pollution index) indicators
Overall experience of life	① Satisfaction with life ② Impacts ③ Ways of gaining happiness	Impacts involve the state of personal emotions or moods. It can be measured on the basis of a certain point of time and from both positive and negative aspects

Continued table

Health	① Life expectancy ② Infant mortality ③ Healthy years ④ Right to health care ⑤ Self-assessment of health	Health is an important part of QOL. Bad health conditions will impede the progress of the entire society. Psychological problems will also have negative impacts on subjective happiness. Health state is measured mainly with objective health result indicators, but there are subjective indicators as well
Education	① Education level of the population ② Number of early graduates ③ Ability of self-evaluation or assessment ④ Lifelong learning	In a knowledge-oriented economic entity, education plays a crucial part in the life of its citizens, and is a decisive factor of their progress. Education can determine what job a citizen can get. Personal skill and ability limits will usually shut the door to most jobs, or sometimes even to the opportunity of realizing one's value or achieving one's goal in the society
Leisure and social interactions	① Frequency of participating in sports or cultural activities ② Frequency of participating in volunteer works for different organizations	When measuring personal welfare, the power of network and social relations should never be underestimated, because they have direct influences on the satisfaction with life. Besides, an indicator of the frequency of social support and communication available was added under this dimension
Economic and physical safety	Number of people killed in each country	Safety of life is an important aspect. It can help to plan in advance and overcome the impacts of sudden economic recession or extensive environmental degeneration on QOL. For the latter, wealth indicator should be used. But currently, there is no reference data in any European country for this item. Therefore, whether there are resulted debts when facing unexpected expenses is used instead
Governance and basic rights	① Residents' participation in public and political affairs ② Citizens' degree of trust in the mechanism ③ Citizens' degree of satisfaction with public service ④ Income gap	Rights of debating with the public and influencing public-policy-making is an important aspect of QOL. Moreover, the foundation of a democratic society is built on proper legislation guarantee

Some studies measured QOL with only one indicator - GDP, which was not really proper. GDP is the most common indicator in the measurement of the economic activities in a given period for a country or region, and often serves as the standard criterion to many decision- or policy-makers. It includes all the final goods and services produced by an economic entity, and provides a snapshot of all this. GDP is of great use in the measurement of market production. Although it cannot be used as an indicator of social progress, it is still considered closely related to residents' welfare.

To compensate for the shortages of the GDP indicator, the Statistics Bureau of the European Union released the "quality of life indicators" in the first half of 2014. There are "8+1" indicators, constituting a multi-dimensional system. The "8" refers to: material living conditions, productive or main activity, health, education, leisure and social interactions, economic and physical safety, governance and basic rights, natural and living environment; and the "1" refers to overall experience of life. The "8+1" QOL Indicator framework is shown in Table 2.2.

Table 2.2 The "8+1" Quality-of-life Indicator Framework of the European Union

Material living conditions	① Income ② Consumption ③ Material conditions (housing)	Income is an important indicator, since it can affect most of the other indicators in the framework. Indicators of consumption include per capita family consumption, total per capita consumption as well as other indicators of the family budget survey. Material conditions (housing) provides important supplementary information for these currency-oriented methods
Productive or main activity	① Number of jobs available ② Quality of jobs available	The daily lives of citizens involve many activities, especially their jobs. The number and quality of jobs available are mainly evaluated from the aspect of working hours, balance of working and non-working life, safety and ethics of work, which are the indicators used in Europe for the evaluation of QOL in this aspect

subjective quality of life. On the other hand however, higher-educated people are usually more talented, have more chances of employment and promotion, and are more likely to acquire social recognition as well as attention and respect, which results in a higher quality of life. And lower-educated people are generally not so capable, and tend to lack self-confidence or feel inferior, resulting in negative or even antisocial emotions that will lower the quality of life.

And the last one is the state of health. As Edwards and Mark (1973) pointed out, health is a better indicator of happiness (quality of life), especially when other variables such as age and social status remain unchanged.

2.4 "Quality-of-life Indicators" of the European Union

Quality of life is a broad concept which has multiple dimensions (in our opinion, various elements or factors constitute an entity which can be measured with a set of sub-dimensions and many related indicators). Among them, there are objective factors (such as material resources, health, working conditions and living conditions) as well as corresponding subjective factors which are decided by residents' needs and preferences. It is a complicated task to measure the QOL of different peoples and countries with a comparable method. For the sake of research, it is necessary to have a system which includes many related dimensions.

A primary goal of the European Integration is sustainable economic and social progress. The *Treaty of Maastricht* summarized it as the improvement of the QOL and living conditions of the Member States. The "European QOL indicator system" is an important achievement of the European Union. Its continuous perfection has provided important reference data for the monitoring and analyzing of the welfare and QOL development of EU members.

are content with their present lives, they will be happier than males. However, according to the study of Zheng Xue et al. (2001), females in China are faced with similar pressures in life and work with that of males, owing to the economic development. As a result, the gender difference of QOL becomes insignificant.

The second one is the age difference. As people grow older, their social cognition, life experiences, thinking modes, emotional control and personal hobbies will change as well, which leads to differences in their feelings toward the quality of life. According to Diener and Eunkook's study (1997), emotions and happiness peak at 20, and then drop as people grow older. Yan Biaobing et al. (2003) discovered that the young is usually more passionate about life and full of dreams, while the old generally has a deeper understanding of the society and is more mature in thinking. Therefore, they tend to have different quality of life.

The third one is the difference in the state of employment. In a society, the more job opportunities there are, and the easier it is to climb up the ladder, the higher personal quality of life will be. Employment is the major source for a person to acquire his/her means of subsistence. If one has an ideal job, with one's value fully realized, one will have a stronger sense of social identity and happiness, and one's quality of life will be higher as well. On the other hand, if one is unwillingly unemployed, one will not be able to realize one's personal value, and will lose the sense of social identity and the confidence in life. Sometimes, even one's basic needs cannot be met. In such cases, negative feelings will likely appear, and one's quality of life will thus be affected.

The fourth one is education. Education is an important indicator of national or regional population quality. Different educational backgrounds will lead to differences in the quality of life. When material and income levels remain the same, lower-educated people tend to have lower expectations of their lives compared to that of higher-educated people, and thus have higher

Williams (1990) furthered Moon and Dixon's study (1985) by analyzing the data of different countries from 1965 to 1970, and concluded that political democracy has a positive correlation with QOL and can improve QOL significantly. Wickrama and Mulford (1996) reached a similar conclusion based on the data of underdeveloped countries. Frey and Roumi (1999) made use of more extensive data samples, including those of both developed and underdeveloped countries in 1970, 1980 and 1990. After ruling out factors such as national development, government interference and demographic pressure, the study concluded that in 1970, 1980 and 1990, political democracy had a positive correlation with the quality of life. The higher the political democracy level, the higher the residents' quality of life.

All the above-mentioned literature came to the same conclusion - political democracy has a positive correlation with the quality of life. While other factors remain the same, the better the democracy system of a country is, the higher residents' quality of life will be. The question is, how does political democracy influence the quality of life? And through what? In this aspect, there exist many different theories among western scholars. However, four mechanisms are the most widely accepted, namely political participation, election, free media and opposition party (Frey and Roumi, 1999).

2.4.4 Demographic Factors

There are many demographic factors that can influence personal quality of life, such as gender, age, employment and education, which will in turn affect the QOL of the entire society.

The first one is gender difference. Owing to the differences in social roles and status, the QOL of males and females in different societies vary significantly. Compared to males, females tend to be more sensitive and emotionally active (Wood et al., 1996). Fujita (1991) discovered that if females cannot become a part of this new sociocultural environment, do not accept or even reject new values, lack the sense of sociocultural identity and keep a distance with the new culture, then he/she will likely have a lower level of happiness and QOL.

Finally, personal quality of life may vary in different cultures. Kennon and Tim (2001) discovered that people of different sociocultural backgrounds have different values, outlooks, social orientations and different ideas of happiness. When one's personal behaviors consist with the normal sociocultural patterns, one tends to be more satisfied with and happier about one's personal life (Marks et al., 1998). According to Oishi, Diener and Lucas (2003), as long as one's personal behaviors agree with one's goal, one will feel happy. Nevertheless, Marks et al. (1996) propounded that it is one's views of and identification with one's culture rather than the culture itself that is the primary factor which determines one's happiness. There exist differences in the cultures, the values and the ways of life, as well as in objective conditions. No wonder people have different quality of life.

2.3.3 Political Factors

According to existing literature, political democracy can also influence people's quality of life. Through studies of their relations, western scholars have drawn the conclusion that democracy has a positive correlation with QOL. That is to say, democratic and developed countries generally have higher quality of life, while non-democratic and underdeveloped countries usually perform inferior in all the indicators of QOL. Moon and Dixon (1985) collected the cross-section data of 116 countries, and analyzed the relations between democracy and QOL accordingly. Their research showed that democracy did improve the objective quality of life. Moon (1991) drew a similar conclusion on the basis of more precise data. London and

and happiness are quite different in China and in the west. Nevertheless, as society changes and integrates, sociocultural environment is also changing, along with people's perceptions of happiness.

Firstly, social changes will affect people's subjective quality of life. Since the initiation of China's reform and open-up, great changes have taken place in the sociocultural environment of China. People's minds have changed entirely. Social problems and family problems have become increasingly acute. Social transformation has accelerated. Besides all this, there are also problems such as materialism, corruption, unemployment and maldistribution of educational and other resources. These sociocultural changes have led to the improvement of people's objective quality of life, while having great impacts on people's values and how they view the world and their lives. Their subjective quality of life has been thus affected. Some of them took the initiative, adjusted to these social changes and remained optimistic about their lives. Their subjective QOL has kept rising as the society changes. Others, on the other hand, were unwilling to make adjustments and stuck to the traditional psychological and behavioral patterns. When faced with external pressures that came with these social changes, they tended to panic, feeling uneasy or anxious. As a result, their subjective QOL would be hard to improve.

Secondly, sociocultural integration will influence the quality of life. Cultural integration is a process during which different cultures interact with and adapt to each other. As a member of the society, one's ability of adapting his/her own thoughts and behaviors to a different cultural environment determines how good his/her subjective quality of life will be. If he/she can integrate into this different sociocultural environment, accept and adapt to different values, find his/her position and a sense of cultural identity in the new environment, then his/her QOL will be better. On the contrary, if he/she

not only absolute income, but also relative income or reference income. $U=U(y, y', h, i, j)$. In the equation, y' refers to relative income or reference income. If the absolute income of a person increases, while his/her relative income decreases or remains the same, then the overall utility level should also go up. Nevertheless, if the absolute income increases along with his/her relative income or reference income, then they will counteract each other, and the overall utility level may not change.

According to the relative welfare theory, people's quality of life and happiness are influenced by both income level and income gaps. As Wilkinson and Picot mentioned in their book *The Spirit Level: Why Equality is Better for Everyone*, material living standard has diminishing marginal utility in deciding people's happiness. Reducing social inequality helps to improve the general QOL level of the society. Wang Tong and Su Zhengshe (2002) also pointed out that under the circumstance of severe social inequality and huge income gaps, people with lower incomes would not be able to enjoy the benefits of economic growth, which often led to resentment, anger, anti-social feelings and hatred of the rich. "Venting one's anger on the society" is often caused by inequality and income gaps. In such cases, not only individuals' quality of life, but also that of the entire society is significantly affected.

2.3.2 Sociocultural Factors

Quality of life can be of some differences in different sociocultural environments. In traditional Chinese culture, social value is stressed. Personal will should coincide with collective will or state will, and individual behaviors should always consist with group behaviors, while personal opinions and feelings are not encouraged. In western culture however, individual behaviors and personal value are encouraged and emphasized (Eunkook, 2000). Owing to the differences in our sociocultural backgrounds, the perceptions of QOL

2.3.1 Economic Factors

Income level is the most influential economic factor of QOL. Diener and Biswas (2002) researched on the relations between wealth and happiness. Their study shows: people in rich countries are happier than those in poor countries; and within the same country, the happiness indexes of rich people are higher than those of the poor ones. In microeconomics, utility is regarded as the function of income, leisure time, individual factor and job parameter. $U=U(y, h, i, j)$. U stands for individual utility level. The higher the utility value, the higher the quality of life, and the happier people are. y stands for residents' absolute income level which has a positive correlation with utility. h stands for leisure time, and i, j stand for individual factors and job parameter respectively. If h, i, j remain the same, then the bigger y (absolute income) is, the higher U (overall utility level) is.

However, people later find that changes of absolute income level are not always consistent with those of QOL. Economic growth and absolute income increase may improve QOL objectively, but not always subjectively. According to Easterlin (1974), if people's incomes all increase at the same rate, their happiness may remain unchanged. Kubiszewski et al. (2013) found that although the economic aggregate at the time was three times more than that of 1950, the actual welfare level was in an inverted U shape. That is to say, it went up gradually from 1950 to 1978, peaked in 1978, and started to drop in 1978. Their research also came to a surprising conclusion: after per capita Gross Domestic Product (GDP) > USD 7000, there is no much room left for welfare improvement. Obviously, compared to absolute income level, relative income level has greater impact on the quality of life. In 1960, the relative welfare theory put forward an argument that relative income is of greater significance to personal happiness. Utility should be the function of

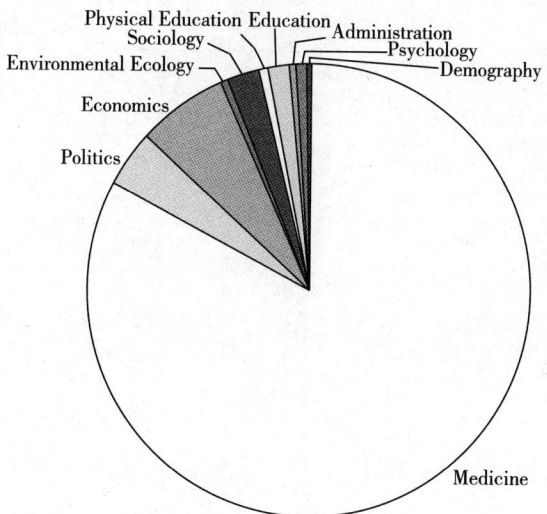

Graph 2.1   Disciplinary Statistics of QOL Literature

satisfied, and living conditions start to improve. People will naturally begin to pay more attention to the negative effects caused by economic growth, such as resource exhaustion, environmental pollution and the widening of income gaps. These problems affect both people's objective quality of life and their inner feelings. Under such circumstances, academic study of QOL developed rapidly, and different theoretical systems came into being. These systems are the results of our exploration and transformation of Nature, and a common treasure of human beings.

2.3   Influential Factors

Quality of life can be influenced by not only objective but also subjective factors. Based on this understanding, we may conclude that the influential factors of QOL can be either economic, social, political or cultural.

Continued table

Year	QOL	Happiness	Sub-Total	Percentage
1993	32	1	33	0.12
1994	51	0	51	0.19
1995	72	1	73	0.28
1996	86	3	89	0.34
1997	91	5	96	0.36
1998	121	6	127	0.48
1999	146	5	151	0.57
2000	192	9	201	0.76
2001	246	6	252	0.95
2002	322	26	348	1.31
2003	488	56	544	2.05
2004	128	66	194	0.73
2005	868	150	1018	3.84
2006	1112	250	1362	5.13
2007	1052	530	1582	5.96
2008	1151	526	1677	6.32
2009	1271	727	1998	7.53
2010	1512	825	2337	8.81
2011	1678	1550	3228	12.16
2012	1901	1514	3415	12.87
2013	2169	1507	3676	13.85
2014	2549	1448	3997	15.06
Total	17324	9213	26537	100.00

Viewed by disciplines, most QOL literature is medical related (15405 treatises). Some are economic (1220) or political (751). Only a few of them are demographic. Graph 2.1 shows the disciplinary statistics of QOL literature.

In a word, the study of QOL is an inevitable outcome of economic development. When economy grows to a certain stage, physiological needs are

treatises were published in this field — 26 treatises in 10 years, averaging 2.6 treatises per year. The second stage is take-off (1990~1997), during which the study of QOL had experienced a rapid development. Within 8 years, 404 treatises were published, averaging 50.5 per year. The third stage is development (1998~2004), during which over 100 treatises were published each year. There were in total 1817 treatises in 7 years, averaging about 260 per year, 4 times more than that of the previous stage. The last stage is rapid development (2005 till now). As people pay more and more attention to the quality of life, a large number of treatises have been published in the past ten years, totaling 24290 treatises, averaging 2429 per year. Moreover, the literature has covered many different fields, such as economics, sociology, medicine and psychology.

Table 2.1 Statistics of Domestic Literature on the "Quality of Life"

Piece, %

Year	QOL	Happiness	Sub-Total	Percentage
1980	1	0	1	0.00
1981	1	0	1	0.00
1982	0	0	0	0.00
1983	2	0	2	0.01
1984	1	0	1	0.00
1985	3	0	3	0.01
1986	2	0	2	0.01
1987	1	0	1	0.00
1988	6	0	6	0.02
1989	9	0	9	0.03
1990	18	0	18	0.07
1991	18	1	19	0.07
1992	24	1	25	0.09

high mass consumption → pursuit of QOL. He believed that the ultimate goal of social development should be an extremely high quality of life, and that economic growth and social progress should be measured by the improvement in QOL rather than the quantity of tangible products. Another scholar Goulet (1971) thought the quality of life had three levels: life-sustenance, self-esteem and freedom. Freedom was deemed the highest form of QOL.

As the study of QOL progressed, scholars of different disciplines started to research on QOL from different angles. Sociologist Campbell (1976) defined QOL as "the overall perception toward well-being" and the subjective feelings people had of their lives. Milbrath believed that QOL depended on the natural environment and that without a good natural environment, QOL could not be guaranteed.

In China, the study of QOL did not start until 1980s after the beginning of the reform and open-up. The concept of QOL was introduced from abroad and attracted the attention of Chinese scholars. Earlier studies focused mainly on the evaluation and research of residents' QOL. In 1985 and 1987, respectively, the Sociology Institute of Tianjin Academy of Social Sciences and the Sociology Institute of Shanghai Academy of Social Sciences made investigations into the quality of life in the two cities, and evaluated both residents' quality and satisfaction of their lives. In 1986, Professor Li Yining a famous economist proposed his own theory of QOL.

In recent years, the research in this field has developed rapidly. We searched for related literature in the cnki database using "quality of life" or "happiness" as the key words. The statistical result is shown in table 2.1. Viewed by quantity of the literature, the study of QOL in China can be divided into four stages. The first stage is infancy (1980~1989), during which only a few

QOL and social indicators.[①] When the economy developed, basic material needs were satisfied, and living conditions were further improved. Meanwhile, numerous social and ecological problems arose in America and other western countries, such as income gaps, overexploitation of resources, environmental pollution and deterioration of the eco-environment. When their lives were thus affected, people gradually realized that improvements of material life were only a part of their pursuit, and that spiritual life was of equal importance. All of a sudden, they were conscious of the urgent need for a quality life. Under such circumstances, the study of QOL began to prosper and soon drew the attention of the entire society. Related works were thus published. Veroff and Field (1957) made a sampling survey on the mental health and sense of happiness among Americans. Economist Galbaith (1958) first brought up the concept of QOL and defined it as the spiritual satisfaction and enjoyment people receive from comfort and convenience. In his opinion, the overall value of a society concerned the realization of not only economic values but also cultural values. A society should aim to improve the quality of life which is a combination of both economic values and cultural values. In addition to the QOL concept, he further propounded that economic growth and social welfare should be reevaluated with the criterion of QOL. Samuelson (1970) thought that modern economics should not focus merely on quantity and ignore the quality of life, a viewpoint shared by economists Tobin and Nordhaus.

Rostow contributed greatly to the theoretical research of QOL with his book *Politics and the Stages of Growth* (1971). He divided economic development into 6 stages: traditional society → preconditions → take-off → maturity →

[①] Yi Songguo, "A Summary of the Quality of Urban Life in Other Countries", *Shenzhen University Journal* (1)1998.

religious aspects. A high quality of life should include: ① a beautiful natural environment and a comfortable living environment; ② higher material living standards and disposable income level, reasonable income distribution, less poverty, lower unemployment rate, and better living convenience; ③ a rich spiritual life, ample leisure time and popularized cultural consumption; ④ a stable political and social environment, good social order and widespread sense of security; ⑤ a sound social security system; ⑥ improved health care and education systems, and a better quality of service; ⑦ an easy pace of life; ⑧ confidence in the future development of the economy, the society and individuals, etc. Of course, people's perception of QOL never remains static. It changes constantly as human society develops.

2.2 Current Progresses at Home and Abroad

The west has first started studying the quality of life. It was an inevitable outcome of economic growth and social progress, and evolved as people's perceptions of QOL changed. The concept of welfare was brought up by the welfare economists such as Pigou in the beginning of the 20th century, and gradually became a theoretical system based on the theories of utility, producer surplus and consumer surplus, with the Pareto Efficiency theory as its criterion. At that time, the focus of study was economic welfare. QOL was not yet mentioned. In other words, Pigou and other welfare economists paid more attention to the study of material production, and did not realize the importance of subjective factors such as people's spiritual life and happiness.

In 1927, Professor W. Ogburn started to study the social trends of America, which resulted in the publication of *American Statistical Association* as well as his other works. Such study later evolved into two mainstreams: the study of

aspect is related to the beautification, optimization and purification of the environment, while the social aspect involves culture, education, health care, social customs and order. Rostow's definition (1971) was similar. Feng Litian (1992) thought that "the quality of life is a comprehensive reflection of living conditions, and refers to people's overall living conditions at a certain stage of economic development". Feng Xiaotian and Yi Songguo (2000) regarded the quality of life as "a comprehensive description of the overall living standard of people in a society, and a major indicator in the evaluation of social development".

In our opinion, the quality of life is a concept of comprehensive connotations, which involves both subjective and objective, macro and micro factors. In the subjective aspect, the quality of life refers to people's subjective satisfaction toward their lives. Such perceptions can be either micro (such as personal feelings toward income level, living costs or educational opportunities), or macro (such as opinions on income distribution, public order or social security). These subjective perceptions always come from objective existence. Therefore, the influences of objective factors (both micro and macro) should also be taken into consideration in order for a more thorough evaluation of people's quality of life. For example, factors such as disposable income level, per capita disposable income growth rate, inflation rate, social security level, medical insurance coverage, employment or unemployment rate, living convenience, eco-environment, can all affect people's quality of life objectively.

Considering all this, we came to the conclusion that the quality of life should refer to the overall status of people's living standards in a country or a region, and reflect the comprehensive situation of social development. It involves not only economic, social, cultural but also natural, political and

disciplines tend to understand and emphasize its connotations differently. Medicine and psychology usually take an individual or micro approach. In medical or psychological literature, quality of life is generally referred to as "health-related quality of life", namely the quality of health. And the study mainly focuses on the assessment of health care service through analyzing patients' psychological, physiological and social functions. Other disciplines pay more attention to residents' quality of life which can reflect the living and development conditions of individuals in a country or region. According to the World Health Organization (WHO), quality of life concerns four aspects: residents' material living condition, and the status of their physiological function, social function and psychological health.

As the economy develops and society progresses, residents' material and spiritual living standards have both reached a new level. People now have a deeper understanding and a greater need for quality life. Nevertheless, different persons may have quite different pictures of what it is.

Many American scholars often prefer to understand the quality of life from a subjective and micro perspective. Campbell et al. (1976) defined QOL as "the overall perception toward well-being". Galbraith propounded in his book *The Affluent Society* that the quality of life is the spiritual satisfaction and enjoyment people receive from comfort and convenience or in spirit. And Lin Nan (1985) proposed that QOL is "people's overall experience of their lives". In a sense, the concepts of subjective QOL and "happiness" are of similar connotations. When people get a better quality of life, they tend to be happier, and vice versa.

Other economists, such as Li Yining and W.W. Rostow, tend to define the concept of QOL more objectively. Li stressed that the quality of life should consist of two aspects - the natural aspect and the social aspect. The natural

B.2
Latest Research Progresses

Ever since the industrial revolution, with the development of science and technology, human beings have acquired much greater power in the conquest and transformation of Nature. Huge material wealth has been created, which laid the foundation for modern civilization. Especially since the beginning of the 20th century, rapid development of science and technology has expanded the scope of human activities and further enhanced our ability to create wealth. Both material and spiritual civilization has thus prospered. Despite all the achievements however, the world is still faced with many challenges, such as global warming, environmental crisis, resource exhaustion and the widening of income gaps. In some countries, although the economy has developed rapidly, people's quality of life and happiness remain roughly unchanged. As Karl Marx once wrote, the ultimate goal of social development is to realize the free and comprehensive development of individuals. And the appearance of such problems is obviously against this goal. Therefore, the big question for many countries now is how to help people live a better and happier life as economy and material living conditions improve. Finding the answers to this question is of great significance.

2.1 Concept

Quality of life is a multi-dimensional concept which has broad connotations. So far, there is no consensus on its definition among scholars. Different

1.3 Report Outline

The second part of this book is about latest research progresses on the quality of urban life. In this part, the concept of QOL is first explained, followed by a review of related researches worldwide, an analysis of the influential factors (economic, sociocultural, political and demographic) and an introduction to the "8+1" QOL indicator system released lately by the European Union.

The third part is an introduction to the 2015 survey, which explains the survey techniques of the subjective data, the design of the objective data indicators and the sources of the objective data.

The fourth part presents the QOL indexes of the 35 cities, including the rankings and related explanations of both subjective and objective indexes. For the convenience of analyzing the QOL changes of each city dynamically, the score and ranking of each city's general index is listed out in this part and compared with the figures in the previous four surveys. Meanwhile, histograms of the 2012-2014 subjective and objective indexes and bar charts of the 2015 subjective and objective indexes of the 35 cities are also provided here.

The fifth part is about the QOL sub-indexes of the 35 Chinese cities. The sub-indexes and their respective rankings are listed one by one, along with their primary indicator radar charts. Histograms and bar charts of the sub-indexes are also provided for the sake of dynamic comparison.

The sixth, seventh and eighth parts are introductions to the three special surveys on house price expectation, residents' primary concern and on-line shopping.

The ninth part is about the main findings and enlightenments of the survey, along with suggestions on policies.

capital, living experience and living costs have improved. Cities ranked top 10 on the list of general objective indexes are: Beijing (1), Nanjing (2), Xi'an (3), Hangzhou (4), Guangzhou (5), Shanghai (6), Shenzhen (7), Kunming (8), Wuhan (9) and Changsha (10). And the bottom 10 cities are: Taiyuan (26), Fuzhou (27), Harbin (28), Haikou (29), Tianjin (30), Lanzhou (31), Nanning (32), Xining (33), Zhengzhou (34) and Chongqing (35).

The special survey on primary concern shows: among the 35 cities, interviewees in 32 cities ranked air quality the most influential factor, while people in the rest 3 cities chose food safety to be their primary concern. In 2014, people in only 17 cities regarded air quality as the most influential factor, which is 15 cities less than that of 2015. That is to say, people now pay much more attention to air quality. According to the survey, the top influential factors of QOL are: air quality (39.12%), food safety (28.77%), commodity prices (21.17%) and transportation (10.94%). Generally speaking, air quality is the most influential factor of QOL. As for the special survey on house price expectation, the house price expectation indexes average 43.86, lower than the 2014 average of 60.78. All the 35 cities have scored below 50 (the critical point between house price appreciation and decline) in the index. It means residents' expectation of house prices has changed from appreciation to decline.

During the "new normal" phase, economic growth has slow down. Although the objective indexes of the 35 cities have somewhat dropped, the corresponding subjective indexes have improved. It means that our citizens are confident about the future development of China, and that the series of growth-stabilizing and life-improving policies of the Central Government have become more specific and effective this year. At the same time, however, we still face challenges, such as the problems of living costs, air quality, food safety and pace of life, which are hindering the further improvement of urban life quality.

The 2015 Survey on the Quality of Urban Life

1.2 Main Findings

As is shown in the survey, the subjective satisfaction index of the 35 cities has risen from 51.57 in 2014 to 55.38 in 2015 which is above the satisfaction level. However, considering the values we obtained in the subjective satisfaction survey, the scores of most cities are still on the low side. In 2015, all the 35 cities have scored over 50 in subjective indexes - 4 cities more than in 2014. The 5 subjective satisfaction sub-indexes average respectively: human capital (61.73), social security (60.47), living standard (60.07), living experience (55.66) and living costs (38.94). Compare to those of last year, the weighted averages of all the 5 sub-indexes have gone up, especially in human capital, social security and living standard.

The satisfaction (subjective) indexes are highly regional, with eastern cities performing better than central or western cities. Cities ranked top 10 on the list are: Hangzhou (1), Xiamen (2), Ningbo (3), Haikou (4), Kunming (5), Hefei (6), Nanjing (7), Changchun (8), Harbin (9) and Shanghai (10). And the bottom 10 cities are: Xi'an (26), Hohhot (27), Beijing (28), Urumqi (29), Tianjin (30), Shenzhen (31), Yinchuan (32), Guiyang (33), Taiyuan (34) and Lanzhou (35).

Eastern cities have performed still better than central or western cities in the objective indexes (social and economic data indexes) this year. However, there is a discrepancy between the subjective and the objective indexes of some cities. In 2015, the objective indexes of the 35 cities average 55.84, lower than the 2014 average of 57.87. 31 cities have scored over 50 – 3 cities less than in 2014. The 5 objective sub-index averages respectively: living standard (59.83), human capital (57.34), living experience (56.17), social security (51.26) and living costs (54.58). Compared to those of 2014, the objective sub-indexes of living standard and social security have dropped, while those of human

this period, paying continued attention to people's quality of life is of great practical significance. On one hand, improving resident's QOL can contribute to the stability of the society which lays the foundations for economic growth, economic transition and the reform of the economic system. On the other hand, improving people's lives is exactly what such economic changes are for. In other words, residents' quality of life will be better as the economy develops. In actuality, it is the same process.

The subjective indexes came from random telephone interviews. The last several digits of telephone numbers were chosen randomly, which produced 22,939 effective random samples. The overall standard error of subjective indexes was reduced from 0.15 in 2014 to 0.139 in 2015, and the creditability of the entire survey was thus further improved. Based on the data of telephone interviews, the 5 subjective satisfaction sub-indexes of QOL (living standard, living costs, human capital, social security and living experience) were obtained through statistical analysis. And besides the surveys on house price expectation and on residents' primary concern, the internet was added as a new topic to reveal the influence of internet on residents' QOL.

The objective indexes (social and economic data indexes) were calculated on the basis of social and economic data of the 35 cities released by the authorities, which ensured the objectivity and authority of the indexes. The objective and the subjective indexes are consistent. That is to say, they both have 5 sub-indexes (living standard, human capital, living experience, social security and living costs). The 5 objective (social and economic data) sub-indexes are in turn made up of 20 social and economic data indicators, and can therefore reflect most aspects of residents' QOL in Chinese cities at the present stage.

General Reports

B.1
The 2015 Survey on the Quality of Urban Life

1.1 Introduction

The Quality of Urban Life Research Centre under NIEE started its QOL tracking survey in 35 cities around China in 2011. Related subjective satisfaction indexes were obtained through a questionnaire survey, while the objective indexes (social and economic data indexes) were acquired through analysis and calculation of objective statistics. By April 2015, the survey has been conducted for 5 successive years. At present, China is going through a complicated period of gear-shifting of economic growth, birth pangs of economic readjustment and assimilation of pervious stimulus package. And our economy is at a crucial stage - the "new normal" phase. During

B III Special Surveys

B.6　Survey on House Price Expectation　／ 133
B.7　Survey on Citizen's Primary Concern　／ 139
B.8　Survey of the Influence of Internet on the Quality of Urban Life
　　　　　　　　　　　　　　　　　　　　／ 143

B IV Conclusions

B.9　Conclusions and Enlightenments　／ 147

CONTENTS

B I General Reports

B.1 The 2015 Survey on the Quality of Urban Life / 001
   1.1 Introduction / 001
   1.2 Main Findings / 003
   1.3 Report Outline / 005

B.2 Latest Research Progresses / 006
   2.1 Concept / 006
   2.2 Current Progresses at Home and Abroad / 009
   2.3 Influential Factors / 014
   2.4 "Quality-of-life Indicators" of the European Union / 021

B II Analysis Reports

B.3 Introduction to the 2015 Survey / 025
B.4 Quality-of-life Indexes of the 35 Chinese Cities / 029
B.5 Quality-of-life Sub-Indexes of the 35 Chinese Cities / 039

are confident about the future development of China, and that the series of growth-stabilizing and life-improving policies of the Central Government have become more specific and effective this year. At the same time, however, we still face challenges, such as the problems of living costs, air quality, food safety and pace of life, which are hindering the further improvement of urban life quality.

Keywords: Quality of Urban Life (QOUL), Subjective Satisfaction Index, Objective Index, House Price Expectation, Internet +

Abstract

Abstract: In 2015, the Quality of Urban Life Research Centre under National Institute for Economic Experimentation (NIEE) continued with its telephone survey of residents' subjective satisfaction toward the Quality of Life (QOL) in 35 cities around China, besides the calculation of their respective objective QOL indexes. It is the fifth annual tracking survey which involved more than 200 staff members and took over 2 months to complete. Related subjective satisfaction indexes and objective indexes were obtained through investigation and calculation. As is shown in the survey, the subjective satisfaction indexes have again improved slightly, while the objective indexes have somewhat dropped due to the economic downturn. Results of the special surveys indicate that the expectation of house price appreciation (HPA) has fallen dramatically in all the cities. Air quality has remained the most influential factor of QOL, followed by food safety, commodity prices and transportation. Besides, the Era of "Internet+" has come. From the residents' point of view, the Internet has influenced not only their ways of communication, but also their ways of shopping, obtaining services and managing money. It can therefore be concluded that during the "new normal" phase, the economic growth of China has slowed down. Although the objective indexes of the 35 cities have somewhat dropped, the corresponding subjective indexes have improved. It means that our citizens

from the capital cities to medium-sized cities, from domestic to international cities, while normalizing the release of the indexe. In addition, life quality is only part of economic growth quality, so after the Institute was founded, the quality of the whole economic growth will gradually be incorporated into the institute's research horizon and strive for a group of high-quality scientific research.

Thirdly, the institute will continue to expand the scope of research on economic experiments, carry out experiments for economic reform, policies effect and economic growth pressure, and provide quantitative decision support for China's reform, government agencies and relevant departments, as well as the whole society.

Fourthly, we will establish a graduates guidance team with international features, closely cooperate with foreign universities, co-direct master and doctoral students, and enroll post doctors for the benefits of talent construction for Capital University of Economics and Business.

Finally, NIEE have a close working relationship with more than 20 universities abroad, after the Institute was founded, it will carry out extensive international cooperation and academic exchanges, joint research, collaborative innovation, which further international character of the institute.

The purpose of National Institute for Economic Experimentation (NIEE) is: Promote economic experimentation research, prosper science and economic, push forward China's economic system reform, improve the quality of economic growth, and promote economic development. The objective of NIEE is: Through our unremitting efforts, NIEE will become an internationally first class research institute in this field in the future.

academic exchanges for well-known economists whose research field focus on macroeconomics. In 2010, CUEB established "Research Center of China City Life Quality" together with Institute of Economics of CASS. After months of research on the city's life quality index, the center firstly released life quality index of 30 capital cities in China in the fifth session of the "Forum on China Economic Growth and Business Cycle" in 2011, which caused a great response, and attracted the attention of international counterparts including the World Bank and other international bodies. NIEE is based on the above research institute.

Currently, the Institute has set up "Research Center of China Economic Growth and Business Cycle " "Research Center of China City Life Quality ""Research Center of Quantitative Economics " and "WTO Research Center", and the Economic Operation and International Trade Laboratory, Economic Warning Laboratories, Economic Data Processing and Computer Simulation Lab and Digital Investigations Center.

After integration of the original institutions and laboratories, NIEE proposed the following institutions:

1. Experts Committee of National Institute for Economic Experimentation;
2. Research Center of China Economic Growth and Business Cycle;
3. Research Center of China City Life Quality;
4. Research Center of Quantitative Economics;
5. Post-doctoral Stations;
6. Forum on China Economic Growth and Business Cycle;
7. Research Center for Beijing Economic Transition and Development;
8. Economic Operation and Warning Laboratories, Computer Simulation Laboratories.

The recent tasks of NIEE are as follows.

Firstly, we will continue the research on the economic growth and business cycle of China, and we will try our best to make the forum better and better, and to make it an international forum.

Secondly, we will expand research on life quality index, gradually extended

National Institute for Economic Experimentation (NIEE)

Since the reform and opening up, especially after the establishment of socialist market economic system, China's economic development has entered a new stage. China has become the world's second largest economy; its per capita income has reached the level of middle-income countries. Meanwhile, China's reform is changing from the "shallow water area" into "deep water area", the reform will face more difficult and complex situation, the "practice trial and error" of China reform must change from "feeling the stones" policy toward the "experimental trial and error" by the use of modern means of simulation and evaluation. On the other hand, from the perspective of academic development, current scientific research is directing to cooperative study and cross-disciplinary collaborative research. This situation requires China's universities, research institutions to break the disciplinary boundaries and sectoral boundaries, integrating all available resources, cooperate and innovate together, so as to face new challenges in China's society. In this context, after a long term investigation, demonstration and carefully prepared, Capital University of Economics and Business (CUEB) and Institute of Economics of Chinese Academy of Social Sciences (CASS) decide to set up the "National Institute for Economic Experimentation" jointly.

Early in the year of 2006, CUEB has set up "Research Center of China Economic Growth and Business Cycle" together with Institute of Economics of CASS. Since 2007, this Center has successfully held six sessions of "Forum on China Economic Growth and Business Cycle" with Hong Kong Economic Herald. This Forum has become an important platform for

National Institute for Economic Experimentation

Editor-in-chief: Zhang Liancheng, Zhang Ping, Yang Chunxue, Lang Lihua

Deputy Editor-in-chief: Zhao Jiazhang, Zhang Ziran

Authors of the report: Zhang Liancheng, Zhao Jiazhang, Zhang Ziran, Wang Yin, He Yubiao, Chen Jianxian, Du Wencui

Researchers attended in this study: Zhang Ping, Zhang Liancheng, Yang Chunxue, Ji Hong, Liu Xiahui, Lang Lihua, Xu Xue, Wang Cheng, Zhang Xiaojing, Tian Xinmin, Yuan Fuhua, Zhang Ziran, Zhao Jiazhang, Wang Yin, Cai Bin

REPORT ON THE QUALITY OF LIFE IN CHINESE CITIES (2015)

Economy Facing Challenges, People with Confidence

Editor-in-chief / Zhang Liancheng   Zhang Ping
Yang Chunxue   Lang Lihua
Deputy Editor-in-chief / Zhao Jiazhang
Zhang Ziran

权威报告・热点资讯・特色资源

皮书数据库
ANNUAL REPORT(YEARBOOK) DATABASE

当代中国与世界发展高端智库平台

皮书俱乐部会员服务指南

1. 谁能成为皮书俱乐部成员？
- 皮书作者自动成为俱乐部会员
- 购买了皮书产品（纸质书/电子书）的个人用户

2. 会员可以享受的增值服务
- 免费获赠皮书数据库100元充值卡
- 加入皮书俱乐部，免费获赠该纸质图书的电子书
- 免费定期获赠皮书电子期刊
- 优先参与各类皮书学术活动
- 优先享受皮书产品的最新优惠

3. 如何享受增值服务？

（1）免费获赠100元皮书数据库体验卡

第1步 刮开附赠充值的涂层（右下）；
第2步 登录皮书数据库网站（www.pishu.com.cn），注册账号；
第3步 登录并进入"会员中心"—"在线充值"—"充值卡充值"，充值成功后即可使用。

（2）加入皮书俱乐部，凭数据库体验卡获赠该书的电子书

第1步 登录社会科学文献出版社官网（www.ssap.com.cn），注册账号；
第2步 登录并进入"会员中心"—"皮书俱乐部"，提交加入皮书俱乐部申请；
第3步 审核通过后，再次进入皮书俱乐部，填写页面所需图书、体验卡信息即可自动兑换相应电子书。

4. 声明

解释权归社会科学文献出版社所有

皮书俱乐部会员可享受社会科学文献出版社其他相关免费增值服务，有任何疑问，均可与我们联系。

图书销售热线：010-59367070/7028
图书服务QQ：800045692
图书服务邮箱：duzhe@ssap.cn

数据库服务热线：400-008-6695
数据库服务QQ：2475522410
数据库服务邮箱：database@ssap.com

欢迎登录社会科学文献出版社官网
（www.ssap.com.cn）
和中国皮书网（www.pishu.cn）
了解更多信息

社会科学文献出版社 皮书系列
SOCIAL SCIENCES ACADEMIC PRESS (CHINA)

卡号：910808547666
密码：

子库介绍
Sub-Database Introduction

中国经济发展数据库

涵盖宏观经济、农业经济、工业经济、产业经济、财政金融、交通旅游、商业贸易、劳动经济、企业经济、房地产经济、城市经济、区域经济等领域，为用户实时了解经济运行态势、把握经济发展规律、洞察经济形势、做出经济决策提供参考和依据。

中国社会发展数据库

全面整合国内外有关中国社会发展的统计数据、深度分析报告、专家解读和热点资讯构建而成的专业学术数据库。涉及宗教、社会、人口、政治、外交、法律、文化、教育、体育、文学艺术、医药卫生、资源环境等多个领域。

中国行业发展数据库

以中国国民经济行业分类为依据，跟踪分析国民经济各行业市场运行状况和政策导向，提供行业发展最前沿的资讯，为用户投资、从业及各种经济决策提供理论基础和实践指导。内容涵盖农业，能源与矿产业，交通运输业，制造业，金融业，房地产业，租赁和商务服务业，科学研究，环境和公共设施管理，居民服务业，教育，卫生和社会保障，文化、体育和娱乐业等 100 余个行业。

中国区域发展数据库

以特定区域内的经济、社会、文化、法治、资源环境等领域的现状与发展情况进行分析和预测。涵盖中部、西部、东北、西北等地区，长三角、珠三角、黄三角、京津冀、环渤海、合肥经济圈、长株潭城市群、关中天水经济区、海峡经济区等区域经济体和城市圈，北京、上海、浙江、河南、陕西等 34 个省份及中国台湾地区。

中国文化传媒数据库

包括文化事业、文化产业、宗教、群众文化、图书馆事业、博物馆事业、档案事业、语言文字、文学、历史地理、新闻传播、广播电视、出版业、艺术、电影、娱乐等多个子库。

世界经济与国际政治数据库

以皮书系列中涉及世界经济与国际政治的研究成果为基础，全面整合国内外有关世界经济与国际政治的统计数据、深度分析报告、专家解读和热点资讯构建而成的专业学术数据库。包括世界经济、世界政治、世界文化、国际社会、国际关系、国际组织、区域发展、国别发展等多个子库。

权威・前沿・原创

皮书系列为
"十二五"国家重点图书出版规划项目